"Martyn Lloyd-Jones was one of God's special gifts to the church in the twentieth century."

**Mark Dever,** Senior Pastor, Capitol Hill Baptist Church, Washington, DC; President, 9Marks

"Lloyd-Jones's preaching was based on deep reading and scholarship, yet it was accessible to everyone—it stirred the affections and changed the heart."

**Timothy Keller,** Pastor, Redeemer Presbyterian Church, New York City; best-selling author, *The Reason for God*

"I regarded Martyn Lloyd-Jones with admiration and affection during the years that we were both preaching in London, so I am delighted that his unique ministry is to be more widely available in the United States."

**John Stott,** The Late Rector Emeritus, All Souls Church, London

"Lloyd-Jones was a titan of Christian ministry, and it thrills me to see his influence accelerating today for the benefit of the church around the world."

**R. C. Sproul,** Chairman, Ligonier Ministries; Copastor, St. Andrew's Chapel, Sanford, Florida

"Without question the finest biblical expositor of the twentieth century. In fact, when the final chapter of church history is written, I believe he will stand as one of the greatest preachers of all time."

**John MacArthur,** Pastor, Grace Community Church, Sun Valley, California

"The preaching and subsequent writing of Lloyd-Jones have been and continue to be a huge source of inspiration in my own life and ministry."

**Alistair Begg,** Senior Pastor, Parkside Church, Cleveland, Ohio

"I loved to hear Lloyd-Jones for the sheer quality of his biblical expositions and his stance for evangelical Christianity."

**I. Howard Marshall,** Professor Emeritus, University of Aberdeen, Scotland

*Experiencing the New Birth*

## Other Crossway Books by Martyn Lloyd-Jones

# Experiencing *the* New Birth

## STUDIES IN JOHN 3

Martyn Lloyd-Jones

WHEATON, ILLINOIS

*Experiencing the New Birth*

Copyright © 2015 by Elizabeth Catherwood and Ann Beatt

Published by Crossway
        1300 Crescent Street
        Wheaton, Illinois 60187

Cover design: Studio Gearbox

First printing 2015

Printed in the United States of America

Scripture quotations are from the *King James Version* of the Bible.

All emphases in Scripture quotations have been added by the author.

Trade paperback: 978-1-4335-3960-2
PDF ISBN: 978-1-4335-3961-9
Mobipocket ISBN: 978-1-4335-3962-6
ePub ISBN: 978-1-4335-3963-3

---

**Library of Congress Cataloging-in-Publication Data**
Lloyd-Jones, David Martyn.
Experiencing the new birth : studies in John 3 / Martyn
Lloyd-Jones.
    pages cm
  Includes bibliographical references.
  ISBN 978-1-4335-3960-2 (hc)
1. Bible. John, III--Sermons. 2.Sermons, English. I. Title.
BS2615.54.L56      2015
226.5'06—dc23                  2014014345

---

Crossway is a publishing ministry of Good News Publishers.

| SH | | 25 | 24 | 23 | 22 | 21 | 20 | 19 | 18 | 17 | 16 | 15 |
|----|----|----|----|----|----|----|----|----|----|----|----|----|
| 15 | 14 | 13 | 12 | 11 | 10 | 9 | 8 | 7 | 6 | 5 | 4 | 3 | 2 | 1 |

# Contents

# 1

# Nicodemus

## JOHN 3:1-30

Sunday morning sermon preached in
Westminster Chapel, January 9, 1966.

I should like to call your attention to the incident that is recorded in the
first part of the third chapter of the Gospel according to St. John, the
incident concerning the man Nicodemus. We are continuing our studies
in this Gospel, but let me make it quite clear that we are not working
systematically through the Gospel as such and dealing with every part
and portion, but rather selecting the great theme that I would suggest is
the main object and purpose of this Gospel. And I have suggested that
the real key to the understanding of John is in the sixteenth verse of the
first chapter where he says, "And of his fullness have all we received, and
grace for grace" (John 1:16).

Now we are concentrating on that particular theme because, after all,
that is what is meant by being Christian. This, it seems to me more and
more, is the greatest need of the hour, that we should all realize what a
Christian really is and is meant to be, and there is no better definition
than this one. It involves, of course, believing certain things. There is the
creedal element; that is vital. But Christianity is primarily life receiving
of his fullness, and if we forget that, we miss the greatness and the glory
and the splendor of it all. Our danger always, even as Christian people,

is to be reducing this life—eternal life—to something that is merely a point of view, a teaching, a philosophy, a theology, or whatever. We must never do that. Its essence is that it is a *life*, and that means receiving of his fullness. This is the greatest thing in the world, the greatest thing that any of us can ever realize.

So I make no apology for asking at the beginning of a new year and as we resume these studies, do you know that you have received of this fullness? Are you receiving of it, "grace for [upon] grace"? Is it going on; is it increasing? Are you living on a past experience or a past decision? Or are you in the position that you *know* that you are linked to the Head and that life from the great Head is coming down to you and permeating the whole of your being? This, I emphasize, is Christianity, and it is only as the church is manifesting this life and this "fullness" that she really functions as the church and counts at all in the world.

Now I need not take time to remind you that the church counts so little today, it counts less and less, alas, and ultimately it is all due to this. The church cannot live on activities, on her own efforts and organizations. She has been trying to do so, but it does not work. It is an astonishing thing, it is the paradox of the faith in many ways, that the world outside, in its ignorance and darkness and death, recognizes one thing only, and that is *life*. That is the whole story of the book of Acts, indeed of the whole of the New Testament. So I say again that the great question that all of us should be concerned about is this: Do I know that I have received of his fullness? Is it my greatest desire, my highest ambition, to receive more and more of him?

So I suggest that the great purpose of this Gospel of John is to instruct us in this one great matter. Of course, it gives us historical details, and we thank God for that. But they are surely meant to help us and to act as illustrations. There are difficulties about this question, but it is we who make the difficulties. It is because we are not sufficiently childlike, not sufficiently simple. We are all so sophisticated, so clever, so philosophical. That is always the greatest hindrance of all. Our Lord said, "Except ye be converted, and become as little children, ye shall not enter into the kingdom of heaven" (Matt. 18:3). We create and make these difficulties. And so we are given these records and accounts of people like ourselves—how they blundered, how they went astray, how they had their false notions and ideas. And we must thank God for this because, through looking at and seeing the pitfalls and the errors into which others have fallen, we are warned and we are instructed, and so we are able to look again more positively at the whole subject.

Now after laying down the great doctrines, particularly in the first eighteen verses of the first chapter, John has then gone on to give us the testimony of John the Baptist. Then, at the end of the first chapter, he has given us a series of men who came to our Lord and who were brought to him. And in these men who subsequently became apostles we have learned great lessons. Then in the second chapter, in various ways our Lord gave further instruction. He did so even at the marriage feast of Cana in Galilee, in connection with the miracle of turning the water into wine. He also did it when he went up to Jerusalem and saw what was happening in the temple. And then he did it again when certain people came to him when he was in Jerusalem—people who "believed in his name, when they saw the miracles which he did. But Jesus did not commit himself unto them" (John 2:23–24). And in all these ways John shows the particular error, the particular fault in those various approaches, and how they all have messages to convey to us. And what is so interesting is that we see the variety and the number of mistakes that we can make in connection with this matter. Each one of them has a particular point to emphasize, a particular aspect of the truth to bring out and to put before us, and so we continue with this study of John's Gospel.

I am anxious to emphasize this point, but I am not doing so merely out of a theoretical or academic interest. I did not just decide to expound the Gospel according to St. John. The thing that came to me and gripped me was this great question of *life*, the life of God in the soul, this supreme need, this supreme glory of the Christian life. And all these passages are given to us just to help us to arrive at that. There is nothing so fatal as to approach the Bible as just a textbook that you get to know; that is not its business. Its whole object is to bring you to him in whom is all this fullness of which we stand in need.

So now we come to this third chapter and to this particular interest, and we shall see that there are very fundamental and basic questions raised and put before us that will show us some of the difficulties with regard to this matter. It is often the case that people have regarded the story of Nicodemus as evangelistic, and in a sense, of course, it is that, as we shall see. But at the same time it has a great deal to say to many of us who are Christians, and I trust we shall see, as we analyze this case, further difficulties that lie in the way of people experiencing this fullness of his and receiving it more and more.

Let us look then at Nicodemus. The first thing that strikes you here is that he is a different case and a different problem. Back in the second chapter we see the Jewish leaders and how they had abused the temple and so on, and other Jews came and said to our Lord, "What sign shewest thou unto us, seeing that thou doest these things?" (John 2:18). The people who had not seen the significance of his miracles were asking for some startling, outstanding phenomenon. And then we see the people at the end of the chapter, the credulous people who came rushing to him, carried away for the time being by the spectacular nature of his work.

But here in the case of Nicodemus we are looking at a man who does not fit into any of those categories. He is quite a separate and a distinct type. And I am concerned to hold him before you because he does seem to me to represent a very definite type at the present time. So the important thing for us is to discover the characteristics of this man, because the whole object of the record is to show us that he was entirely wrong. That is the astounding thing. Not in the same way as the others, but in his own particular way.

What, then, are the characteristics of Nicodemus? The first, obviously, is that he was a very religious man. In addition to that, he was a very able man, a master, a teacher in Israel; he was a man whose whole lifework and occupation was to be religious and to study the Scriptures and to teach and instruct others. It is very important that we should remember all this about him. I take it that the people described at the end of the second chapter were heedless, thoughtless people, part of the crowd in Jerusalem who, when something startling happened, crowded together and were ready to believe anything that was said and to join any new movement.

Now Nicodemus is completely removed from all that. Here is a man who is a great man in many ways, a highly religious intellectual teacher. And another thing that one must add about him is that he is a man who is obviously free from prejudices. We have evidence of the prejudice against our Lord in these religious leaders. That is why they demanded a sign of him. "This man who suddenly appears and who takes this action in the temple is not a Pharisee. What right has he to do and to say these things?" Nothing is so obvious about the Pharisees, as you read the Gospels, as their prejudice against our Lord, a kind of instinctive prejudice. They were intolerant, always waiting for opportunities to trip him in his words and in his teaching and to prove that he was wrong.

Now Nicodemus seems to be entirely free from all that, and this is a wonderful thing. The harm that is done by prejudice is incalculable. It is always based on ignorance, of course, and the lack of clear thinking. But it is a terrible thing because it is deep and it is emotional and it can do great damage. But here is a man who is obviously entirely free from all that. His whole attitude toward the Lord is unlike that of the majority of the Pharisees, and as you read about him later on in this same Gospel, you find that this same trait in him continues to manifest itself. So all honor to him for these things.

There then is Nicodemus as it were by nature, there he is in general. But there are certain special, peculiar virtues in him that I must emphasize because the thing that he illustrates so perfectly is that a man can be so right and yet be all wrong. And there are many such people. I have known many who are genuinely and honestly seeking God's blessing, but they never get it because they belong to this particular type, and I suggest there are many like this at the present time.

So what are these special virtues? The first one we must emphasize is the one that is put before us in the words of Nicodemus himself. We are told that this man "came to Jesus by night, and said unto him, 'Rabbi, we know that thou art a teacher come from God: for no man can do these miracles that thou doest, except God be with him,'" (John 3:2). In other words, here is a man who sees the real meaning of the miracles. Now you see the contrast with the previous people in chapter 2 who did not. There were some who did not see it at all, and others saw it in a credulous, superficial manner. Not so here. Nicodemus is not just interested in the spectacular; he sees that there is something deeper here. He has watched these miracles, and he has said to himself: *These miracles show quite plainly that this is no ordinary person; here is a man who has been sinless in a unique manner and is used of God and blessed by God. There is something special about this man.*

In other words, he makes a true appraisal of the miracles and does not merely look at our Lord as a miracle worker, a wonder, a phenomenon; he says, "You must be a teacher come from God." We know that; it is indisputable. "For no man can do these miracles that thou doest, except God be with him." In other words, he is a thinker, he thinks beneath the surface, and he is sufficiently enlightened spiritually to see the real meaning of these miracles worked by our Lord.

But then beyond that, obviously Nicodemus detects something in the person and character of our Lord himself. He comes to him and says, "Rabbi . . ." Though Jesus is just a carpenter he calls him teacher, master, and in using the term he is revealing the fact that he has sensed—I do not know how deeply—that there is something here quite unusual and exceptional.

Now this is a most important characteristic. The rest of the chapter emphasizes it and goes on to deal with it, and it is basic to our whole position. People who do not recognize something of the uniqueness of our Lord are not Christians. Those who just put him into the same category as other great religious teachers have not started and have no hope of ever receiving this fullness. But here is a man who addresses him as "Rabbi"—"Master." He is aware of this strange something that he had never encountered before.

And beyond that, and this is what brings us to the very heart of this matter, Nicodemus is clearly aware that our Lord has something that he does not have. Now that to me is the great thing about Nicodemus. He watches Jesus though he is a great man and is in a high position. And though all the rest in the same position are prejudiced, this man looks on in a wistful manner. And he is struck by this and convicted, I think, by this—our Lord is not merely one who actually is able to work these miracles: he is able to do so because of some relationship to God that is special, unique, quite above the ordinary.

Now I emphasize this because this is one of the great keys to the spiritual life. It is one of the great keys to receiving this fullness and to growing in grace and in knowledge of him and receiving his fullness, which puts us into the category of men and women who know something about heaven on earth and who have foretastes of the glory everlasting.

In other words, to put it negatively, Nicodemus is not self-satisfied or complacent. This is a great and fundamental principle. He desires something greater. The trouble with so many is that they are self-satisfied, they feel they have arrived, they have it all! They have been converted—haven't they made a decision? And once they do that, well, they just go on freewheeling, as it were, and they spend the rest of their lives like that. Not so a man like Nicodemus. He has every reason to feel like that. He has arrived at a great position; he is one of the authorities; he is one of the masters of Israel. But this man is sensitive to the spiritual realm, and when he sees this strange new Person who is able to work these extraordinary miracles, what strikes him at once is, "That man has something that I don't have." There is a knowledge of God here, there is an intimacy with God—"We know that thou art a teacher come from God." Nicodemus is not only interested, he is not only intrigued by this new teacher—he is convicted in a sense, and he has a desire within him to get hold of this something extra, this further something that this new teacher so obviously possesses.

Now here is an important question that I must hold before you: Are you satisfied? Self-satisfied? Or are you dissatisfied, lacking in satisfaction? Is there a hunger and thirst within you for righteousness? Is there a longing for something bigger and greater and deeper? There is nothing better about Nicodemus than this: coming into contact with our Lord he is aware of and recognizes and acknowledges this need in himself, this lack of something, this longing for a greater fullness and a receiving of a greater fullness from God.

There is no hope in the Christian life unless we are aware of that. There is nothing that is more important to any one of us than this. Do we have a hunger and a thirst after righteousness? Do we, "as the hart panteth after the water brooks" (Ps. 42:1), long for the living God and a knowledge of him? Oh, we may have attained up to a certain point, we may look back across the years and be satisfied with our record, but do we stop there, are we content, do we feel that this is excellent? Are we always comparing ourselves with people who are obviously worse? There are many heretics these days, people who deny the truth—do we spend all our time denouncing heretics or showing what is obviously and plainly wrong, looking at the world as it is in its raucous laughter and its blasphemous godlessness at the present time?

That is all right, but that is not the way to measure ourselves. The way to measure ourselves is this: as we read our New Testament, as we look at our Lord, is there a profound hunger within us, a profound thirst, a feeling that we are lacking, that we need a fullness that we do not possess and that we have not known hitherto and that we feel we must have? Do we feel this way when we read the lives of saints who have lived in this world before us and who have adorned the life of the church? There is nothing, I repeat, greater about Nicodemus than that. That is why he went to our Lord; he was conscious of a need.

The next thing we notice about him is that he was not only sufficiently conscious of his need, but he was also sufficiently humbled to go and seek an interview with our Lord and to seek instruction. It is very difficult for us to realize what this meant to a man like Nicodemus, but here it is. He is a "a ruler of the Jews," remember. Our Lord is an unknown person, but Nicodemus is sufficiently humble to go and seek an interview with him. And the key to this humility is the fact I have been emphasizing—his awareness of need. He has been given the feeling by our Lord that there is a quality of life, a depth of experience, an association with God that he knows transcends everything that he or any of his fellow masters in Israel has ever attained. We cannot make ourselves humble. There is only one thing that will ever make us really humble, and that is when we see perfection and then see what we are by contrast. That is what always makes people humble. They are "the poor in spirit" because they "hunger and thirst after righteousness" (Matt. 5:3, 6). Each one of the Beatitudes helps the other, and in a sense each describes the other.

But somebody may say, "You are over-praising this man Nicodemus. He went to our Lord by night. Why didn't he go like a man in the daytime? Why does he slink under the cover of darkness to seek this interview with our Lord?" I do not accept that criticism of him for a moment. I think that even this is a virtue in him. He is a very wise man, he is conscious of all that I am describing, but our Lord is an unknown teacher, and there is nothing wrong in being cautious. Indeed there is everything right in being cautious. The teaching of the New Testament teaches us to be discriminating. We have to "prove" and to "test" and to "examine." The previous people at the end of the second chapter of John are those who rush after the latest phenomenon, but they are not accepted. Going at night is a virtue; this is in Nicodemus's favor. He is a man in a responsible position, and a man in such a position cannot afford to plunge into things unwarily and without considering. But these factors are balanced here. In spite of his upbringing and his background and the prejudices of his fellows, he is made aware of his need, and then he says, "I must find out more about this." But he must think of his whole position. This is excellent, it is a mark of his true greatness—this wonderful combination of awareness of his responsibility and yet his desire for this greater fullness that he feels the Lord has to give him. So he seeks his interview by night. I put the two things together.

But the truth that we gather, therefore, from all this and the first great lesson that comes to us I would put like this: Nicodemus acts on what he feels. Why do I emphasize that? It is because I know from personal experience, and I know that you are all exactly the same, that one of our greatest dangers is this: something influences and affects us, we are suddenly disturbed, perhaps in a meeting or in reading a book or in some event that happens, and we are made to feel something of this longing of which I have been speaking. Something disturbs us, we feel we cannot go on as we are, we see that there is something better and higher, and we are anxious to get it. But nothing ever comes of it. Why? Because we do not do anything about it. It comes, and it goes. There is a ripple on the surface of the soul, but it ceases. The gale has come, and we are moved, but soon it is gone. We forget all about it, and back we go to where we were before.

Here is one of the great lessons that is taught to us by this great man Nicodemus. He does not allow the feeling to pass. He does not say, "Well, that's very interesting, but, of course, this sort of thing comes and goes. New teacher? Well, I have seen many new teachers before, and nothing has come of them." You will find all that put in detail later on. That was the kind of way in which these people argued. But Nicodemus is aware that something is here that he has never seen before, and he says, "I cannot leave it. I must, I am bound to find out about this." So he decides that whatever the risk, whatever the cost, he is bound to have an interview with this new teacher who has suddenly appeared. He is so concerned about it that he acts upon his feelings.

That sounds very simple and elemental, does it not? But it is the key to the whole of the Christian life and Christian living—the absolute necessity of application and of action and of following our impulses, following our feelings, listening to these deep convictions that come to us, and not giving ourselves rest or peace until we have discovered the secret.

I could illustrate this to you endlessly in the lives of God's saints throughout the centuries. That has been the quality that has characterized them. They did not just sit down and allow the feeling to go away; they got up and said, "I must know; I cannot rest." There is a determination here. This is taught in the New Testament. "Ask, and it shall be given you; seek, and ye shall find; knock, and it shall be opened unto you" (Matt. 7:7). Our Lord himself was constantly teaching such importunity, and it is exemplified constantly throughout the whole history of the Christian church and her greatest people. Nicodemus gets up and says, "This is something that, surely, I ought to have. I don't have it, but he does. What is it? I must find out! I'll go and see him." So he did.

I trust that I have been able to rouse you all to follow on beyond any dissatisfaction that is in you. Do not allow yourself just to have the feeling and to be content with the fact that you have had it and say, "At any rate I am aware of a need." Do not stop at that. The question is, have you received of the fullness? So what should you do? Do what Nicodemus did. Go to the Lord himself. It is the one thing to do.

So far, then, everything that Nicodemus does is right, and all that we have had to say about him is commendation. And yet the whole point of the story is to show us that Nicodemus was wrong at a very fundamental point. Are you this type of person? I have known many people like this. Perhaps you really do desire this "something" that you feel you do not possess or that at any rate you do not possess in sufficient measure; you are not content just to keep going through the motions. You have been converted, you have been given tasks to do, and you just go on and on from the beginning of the year to the end, and you are the same at the end of fifty years as you were at the beginning. But you are not content with that; you know this is not full Christianity. It is Christianity, but it is not what is described in the New Testament; it is not this profound, this thrilling quality of life. So what I say to you is, emulate this man's example. Act! Go to Christ! Why? Because he will deal with you.

And so I come to the second great matter, which is the picture that is given here of our blessed Lord and Savior. This is what is so wonderful in all these varied pictures at which we have been looking. There is only one constant, and Christ is the constant. People vary. We are different in temperament, psychology, outlook; we are different in our makeup or our abilities or our particular experiences, and we come from all sorts of different directions. But when we come to him, he is always the same. He stands out. The moment you meet him in the Bible, he always towers over everything; he commands the situation always. He may merely be a guest at a marriage feast in Cana of Galilee, but he is still in control, he cannot be hidden. He walks up to Jerusalem at the time of the Passover feast and takes charge of the temple. He does so with ease, with grace. He does it in the most natural manner. He is the Lord of the temple. The leaders of the Jews come to him and question him and put a wrong suggestion to him, and he deals with them in the same magisterial manner. Other people come rushing to him, wanting to join him, carried away by the phenomena that he works, but he does not commit himself to them.

19

And here he is approached by a great teacher, a master of Israel, one of the great authorities. "He is nothing but a carpenter," you say, "He has had no training; he's a nobody and comes from nowhere." Oh, but he is always the same, he is always in command, he is in charge of the situation. And this is the first great thing we must realize about him always. He is the Lord.

As we are reminded at the end of the previous chapter, which gives the setting and the context for this one, "Jesus did not commit himself unto them, because he knew all men, and needed not that any should testify of man: for he knew what was in man." He does not need to be surrounded by secretaries and undersecretaries who have put a note in front of him or whispered in his ear, "Ah, the man who is coming now is a master of Israel; he is a great man." He knows all men; he knows what is in man. He knows all about Nicodemus before he ever comes. We can see this in the case of Nathaniel. "Jesus saw Nathaniel coming to him, and saith of him, Behold an Israelite indeed, in whom is no guile!" (John 1:47).

This is the first thing we must realize—he knows all about us. In one sense that is terrifying, but in another sense it is the most comforting fact in the world, because in your need and as you are at this moment, when you go to him you can be certain he knows exactly what you need. We think we know, but we do not. Nicodemus thought he knew, but he was wrong. With all his excellencies he was wrong, he did not know himself. None of us know ourselves. We are ever ready to balance the good with the bad, to draw up our balance sheets; we are always ready to rationalize our sins; we think we know what we want. But if you know anything about the spiritual life you will agree with the man who says, "I cannot trust my best feelings."

> I dare not trust the sweetest frame,
> But wholly lean on Jesus' name.[1]

Here is a most wonderful and glorious fact: when you go to him, you go to One who knows all about you. He knows your real fundamental need. He will put his finger immediately on the essence of your trouble.

He does not need any help or assistance, and this, I repeat, is to me a most comforting and encouraging thought. He will cut through all that we have put up and erected around ourselves, he will expose the ill—there it is staring us in the face. He will do that, he always does it, and he did it here with Nicodemus. At once he cuts through the conversation and brings him to the point.

And then we must emphasize this: he did so on this occasion in a rather sharp, almost a brusque manner. Here it is: "The same came to Jesus by night, and said unto him, Rabbi, we know that thou art a teacher come from God: for no man can do these miracles that thou doest, except God be with him" (John 3:2). Cannot you hear the tone of voice, cannot you sense the feeling that is in it? But listen: "Jesus answered and said unto him, Verily, verily, I say unto thee"—master of Israel as you are—"Except a man be born again, [except *you* be born again], he cannot see the kingdom of God" (John 3:3). He interrupts him, breaks across what he was about to say, and he does so in a manner that can only be described as sharp.

Why does our Lord behave like this? The answer is, because he knew Nicodemus, because he knew this was the only way to bring Nicodemus to the point at which he could get the blessing he was seeking. The seeking was right. The thing that had brought Nicodemus to our Lord was absolutely right. But what was wrong was Nicodemus's attitude to this and the way in which he thought the problem was to be solved. Now our Lord, because of his love and because of his knowledge, brings Nicodemus face-to-face with the central condition, the central need. And, my dear friends, he will do that to us.

I must point out here that we must all be ready for this. We tend to come to our Lord, do we not, with our own ideas and, like his mother, Mary, we want to dictate to him; we think the blessing will come in this way or that. Now you must get rid of that at the very beginning, because if you do not, he will do it for you. You may well find, as many have found, once you begin to feel this need and begin to act upon it and to seek him, at first you may feel that he is all against you. You may feel that you are rebuffed, that things are worse even than they were before, and you wish

21

you had not gone to see him. You must be ready for this, but above all you must realize why this happens.

In other words, once more here is our great principle: you must submit utterly and absolutely to him. If you do not do so voluntarily he will make you do it. He will insist upon it; he is always in charge. You cannot go to him with any kind of reservations because he knows everything. He knows all about you, and he will always make it plain. He will bring you to face the one big obstacle that stands between you and receiving his fullness and grace upon grace.

What was it in the case of Nicodemus? There are quite a number of things here. We cannot deal with them all now, but they are all revealed in the way in which our Lord handled Nicodemus and in the dialogue that took place between them. The first one is this: Nicodemus was still in charge of himself. "What do you mean?" asks someone. "Shouldn't people be in charge of themselves?" Well, yes, they should, until they come face-to-face with the Lord. Then you become as a little child. You are a master of Israel! All right. You also have the humility that takes you to seek an interview with Jesus. All excellent. But the moment you meet him you are no longer the master; you are very much the pupil, you are very much the pauper, you are no longer in charge of yourself.

Now this is extraordinary. You say, "You have emphasized the humility of Nicodemus, and yet you are now saying that his main trouble was that he was still in charge of himself. Is that not a contradiction in terms?" In a remarkable manner it is not because you often find those two things present in the same person. Truly great scholars are always humble, and yet they know they have great knowledge. They have a kind of confidence because they know what they know, and they know that they do know; they have the confidence of a scholar. And yet because of what they do know they realize so much of what they do *not* know. So you can find these two things together in the same person. And thus is the extraordinary thing about a person of this type. In humility Nicodemus goes to our Lord, and yet his trouble is that he is not sufficiently humbled. He is big enough and great enough to be humbled, he is not like the man with little knowledge, and yet he has not become as a little child. That is the difference, and this is what has stood between thousands, even millions, of men and women of this type and really knowing the Lord. Have you not met such people? They are great, and they are truly humble people; there is no arrogance about them at all. But they have never become Christians. Why? Because they have never become as little children, they have never seen the need of being born again; in fact they object to that. There is something, therefore, about the pride of knowledge that can follow a person through all his or her humility even into the presence of Christ and ultimately become the greatest stumbling block of all.

Let me put it like this. Nicodemus goes to our Lord because of his consciousness of this lack, this need, this awareness that there is something in this Other that he does not have, and yet in a sense he is going to him as an equal. It is the recognition of another scholar, if you like, another teacher who is yet greater than himself, but he still sees himself as one of the teachers, he is in the same category, in the same class. Nicodemus is a humble man, but he has not become as a little child.

Or to put it another way, he still goes to Christ as a teacher; he says, "Rabbi." But he does not go to him as the Savior. He goes to him, in a sense, as one who is ready to learn from him, but he does not go as a penitent. Nicodemus has felt the need of help, he feels the need of a little further instruction, and he is prepared to humble himself and go to the unknown teacher in order to get it. Oh, yes, he has felt the need of help, but he has never felt helpless.

Is this a vital distinction to you? The people who eventually receive this fullness are those who know they are completely helpless and absolutely hopeless. There is no more subtle point, I sometimes think, in the whole of spiritual life than just that. You may feel the need of help, but you must feel helpless, you must feel completely hopeless. As long as you feel you only need further help, you are still standing on your own feet; you are still in charge of yourself. You say, "He is one stop further. I have to go from here to there." That is a fatal problem in the whole matter. That is why our Lord handles Nicodemus as he does. Nicodemus feels that this "something" that our Lord has is something he can add to what he already has. He feels that what he needs is a supplement, an appendix to the book. But this is not what he needs. The whole book is wrong; it needs to be rewritten from the beginning. That is the trouble. And, of course, he feels that it is something he can add on himself, and he goes therefore and says, "Now then, I have been watching you, and I can see your uniqueness. I am a master in Israel. What is the extra? Can I get this? Tell me what must I do." Fatal thinking!

And the last thing we notice is this—he is so anxious to understand; he keeps on saying that. "How can a man be born when he is old? . . . How can these things be?" (John 3:4, 9). We will continue with this, but there it is—those are the main troubles in the whole attitude of Nicodemus. These are the things that vitiate all his excellent qualities. He has not realized it is a *life*. He thinks of it only as a teaching a man can take up, add on, and so put into practice. Oh no, it is not! It is a life; it is becoming part of this great Head, this great Person. It is becoming parts and members of the body of Christ. It is receiving the life of God in the soul. It is becoming "partakers of the divine nature." And because it is that, anything we may have, whether it be religion or morality or philosophy or anything else, is of no value, and our Lord says to such a person, "Stop! 'Ye must be born again. Ye must be born of water and of the Spirit.' Your whole outlook upon this thing is wrong, and you can never receive anything of it until you have been born again."

# 2

# The Essential Foundation

## John 3:1-8

Sunday morning sermon preached in
Westminster Chapel, January 16, 1966.

There was a man of the Pharisees, named Nicodemus, a ruler of the Jews:

The same came to Jesus by night, and said until him, Rabbi, we
know that thou art a teacher come from God: for no man can do
these miracles that thou doest, except God be with him.

Jesus answered and said unto him, Verily, verily, I say unto thee,
Except a man be born again, he cannot see the kingdom of God.

Nicodemus saith unto him, How can a man be born when he
is old? can he enter the second time into his mother's womb, and
be born?

Jesus answered, Verily, verily, I say unto thee, Except a man be
born of water and of the Spirit, he cannot enter into the kingdom
of God.

That which is born of the flesh is flesh; and that which is born
of the Spirit is spirit.

Marvel not that I said unto thee, Ye must be born again.

The wind bloweth where it listeth, and thou hearest the sound
thereof, but canst not tell whence it cometh, and whither it goeth:
so is every one that is born of the Spirit. (John 3:1–8)

We have begun to consider this story, this particular case of Nicodemus, and I would remind you that we are approaching it from a particular angle. We are concerned about the condition of all those who are seeking the fullness that is to be found in our blessed Lord and Savior, and we are discovering how this fullness is to be received. In order to do that, we must consider some of the mistakes and errors that others before us (and we ourselves in our time) have made in this endeavor. So that is the way in which we are approaching the case of Nicodemus. He, obviously, is an example of this very matter, and we have seen where he was wrong in his approach. Now we have considered these various points in a general way, but we must go on to work them out a little more in detail and apply them, because this really is a most important matter. There are lessons to be learned from Nicodemus that apply in a special way to a certain kind of person who is religious, as he was, and who really is concerned for something bigger, something deeper, something more vital.

Let me, then, try to put the lessons in a more spiritual form. First I would lay down as a principle that one of the things we are taught here is to beware of the danger, if I may so put it, of trying to go on before we have started. I do not put it like that in order to be paradoxical. I literally mean what I say. Nicodemus was a man who was trying to go on before he had started.

Now here is the point at which the Devil very frequently misleads this particular type of person, the one who has been brought up in a religious atmosphere. The extraordinary thing, as we have all discovered from personal experience and in dealing with others and discussing these things with them, is that though we all eventually come to the same place, we come there in very different ways. People have varying difficulties and problems. For instance, there is the case of the man who has perhaps never been to a place of worship in his life. He was not brought up in a Christian home, never went to a Christian church, never went to Sunday school, and so on; he lived a purely worldly, materialistic life, but suddenly, in some mysterious manner, he is apprehended and arrested and becomes a Christian.

But there is another case of a man who has been brought up in a

Christian home, who has been hearing about these things, knows the Bible, has gone to services, has gone to Sunday school, and so on, one who has this whole religious background. Well, by the nature of things these two men are going to face different kinds of problems and difficulties, and they are confronted by different pitfalls. And the Devil in his subtlety, knowing all about us and all about our background, knows exactly the kind of trap to set for each and every one of us.

Now here with Nicodemus we are looking at a man who is typical of the religious kind of person, one who has been brought up in all this. These are people who, perhaps meeting someone else or reading a biography or reading something of the history of the church throughout the centuries, come across a type and an order of Christian living that they recognize at once is quite beyond anything they have ever known and experienced. And being religious people with this background, they are anxious to be like that and to discover how that fullness is to be obtained, and immediately they set out to seek it.

There are large numbers of such people, and very often they can spend a whole lifetime in seeking and inquiring and following various leads, taking up certain interests, reading in a certain direction or attending certain types of meetings. Their motive is exactly the same as that of Nicodemus, and it is an excellent motive. They recognize something different, something higher, something better, and they are very anxious to attain this, but they never seem to obtain it. They say you can spend a lifetime in that condition, always seeking, never finding.

What is the trouble with these people? Well, the first problem is something that, surely, is taught plainly in this record concerning Nicodemus. It is the danger of assuming the vital thing instead of making quite certain that we have it. That is obviously the main trouble with Nicodemus; he acts on an assumption. His whole approach suggests that. If I may put it quite simply and plainly, this is really the danger of assuming that we are Christians when we are not. Now if we do not recognize that such a thing is possible, then obviously we are in this condition, and many of us have known this in our own experience. Perhaps you assume that you are a Christian. You assume it for the reasons that I have given.

You say, "I have always been a Christian, never was anything else. I was brought up to be a Christian." So the assumption is that we are Christians, and then all we need, of course, is some addition or modification of that which we already have. But that is one of the most fatal errors of which one can ever be guilty.

Let me put it a little more theologically. It is the danger of seeking sanctification before we have justification. There is no greater danger, it seems to me, to the religious kind of person than just this. And oh, how often one can illustrate this in the long history and story of the Christian church. You go for sanctification without ever having been justified.

Or let me put it in another way that is still more relevant to this case. It is the danger of seeking sanctification before we know anything at all about regeneration, or to put it still more simply, it is the mistake of trying to grow before you have been born. It sounds ridiculous, and yet that is the very thing that so many are trying to do. They are trying to develop, they are trying to grow and increase, but they do not have any life. That is the obvious trouble with Nicodemus. He comes and says, "Now, master, we know that thou art a teacher come from God: for no man can do these miracles that thou doest, except God be with him." And obviously he was going on to say, "Well now, what is this something extra? I want it. Tell me what to do." But he is interrupted: "I say unto thee, Except a man be born again, he cannot see the kingdom of God," let alone enter into it. You cannot begin to grow and to discover what is necessary to stimulate growth and development and increase unless you have the seed of life in you. This is a common error, and it is obviously a basic and fundamental one. It is the danger of having a concern about the application of Christian truth before there is any definite evidence of Christian life.

Now there are many tendencies that tend to encourage us to fall into this particular error, and I suppose that if we were to single out one more than any other as being particularly dangerous, it is the whole teaching that goes under the heading of *mysticism*. That is to many people, and especially to this religious type, a very attractive kind of teaching. You read of people—monks, hermits, anchorites, those in the past who were anxious to get to a knowledge of God—who had become very dissatisfied with their lives and discontented with things as they were in themselves and in the church. They felt that they must go all out for this knowledge of God, and they felt that the way to do that was to separate themselves from the world. They must undergo a very rigorous kind of life and existence—fasting, praying, sometimes wearing camel-hair shirts, and so on, all with the object of mortifying the flesh and encouraging the development of the spiritual life and understanding. And as the centuries passed, the teaching of these people became very systematized. They drew up their manuals of the devout life and books of instruction as to what one is to do. There are many such books always available on the market—*The Practice of the Presence of God* and various other books by mystics and about mystics—all designed to deal with the culture and the nurture of the spiritual life.

Such books have a great fascination for the religious type of person. They seem to show us what we must do in order that we may ultimately come to full knowledge of God, this *summum bonum* vision of God. You must go through various processes, "the dark night of the soul," negation, and so on, and at last you come to the point of illumination.

There have probably been thousands (if not more) of Christian people—at least people brought up in the bosom of the Christian church—conscientious, intellectual people generally who, because they take these things seriously, have this feeling of dissatisfaction. Then they confront this teaching of mysticism, and they begin to take it up and to study it and to try to put it into practice. So they try to press on and on in this, but they never seem to find any satisfaction at all. And their whole trouble is the very thing that comes out in this story of Nicodemus: they are seeking sanctification, but they know nothing about justification. They are assuming that they are in the right relationship to God. They are trying to develop their Christian life. But the question is, do they have any Christian life at all?

Here is obviously something that demands our closest attention.

Let me give you some examples to illustrate what I mean. Was not this the whole trouble with Martin Luther before that great crisis took place in his life? He was assuming that he was in a relationship to God that was a right one, but he was dissatisfied. So he became a monk and did all that he did. But he came to the critical understanding that his whole process was wrong and that the teaching that he had been given was also all wrong. Suddenly his eyes were opened to this great preliminary truth, "The just shall live by faith," and he saw that there is no starting in the Christian life until and unless you come to that point. His great problem was that of justification; he thought it was sanctification. He was concentrating on the road to sanctification, but it was all wrong. He was only put right and could only begin to grow and develop and become sanctified as he understood this great teaching concerning justification.

Now the particular reason for this in Luther's case was that, brought up as he had been as a Roman Catholic, he believed that his baptism had given him new life, that it had regenerated him and so on. So it was inevitable that he should assume that he had the fundamental thing. But he came to see that he did not. He was a bit muddled even after that about the relationship of these two, but this is the trouble with that whole kind of teaching. It does tend to place our justification upon our sanctification instead of putting them the other way around.

Now that is one notable example, but there are others also. People like George Whitefield and the brothers Wesley and all the members of the Holy Club in Oxford were doing exactly the same thing. Here were men, particularly the Wesley brothers, brought up in an unusually religious atmosphere where Christianity was taken very seriously, and they were dissatisfied. So they met together as a body of students and graduates at Oxford, and their concern was to develop the holy life. And they went in for holy practices—fasting, visiting prisoners, self-mortification, going to preach to the pagans in Georgia, and all the rest of it. What were they trying to do? They were trying to promote their sanctification, trying to get this extra "something." They were like Nicodemus. They said, "We are religious people, but there is something more, something better," and they were searching and seeking after that.

But there again, as in the case of Luther, they came to the sudden realization that they did not have a foundation and that their whole endeavor had been wrong. Whitefield undoubtedly was so religious in his practice of these things that he ruined his health through too much fasting and so on. But the difficulty was that they were assuming that they were already in this life, and they were brought to see that they were not. And from the moment they saw that, and the centrality and the primary position of the doctrine of justification, they were put right, but not until then. They might have gone on spending the rest of their lives like that, as thousands are doing today, the so-called "religious" as distinct from the "laity." And that whole body of teaching encourages one to go astray, because it assumes the vital factor even as Nicodemus did.

I could give you many other examples. I remember one personal one, if you will forgive it. I remember preaching in Toronto in Canada in 1932, and the first Sunday, having been welcomed by the minister, I felt I should inform the congregation, which was strange to me and I strange to them, that it was my custom to divide my ministry roughly into two halves. I said that on Sunday mornings I preached, as it were, to the saints, acting on the assumption that I was preaching to Christian people who needed to be built up and established in the faith. Then on Sunday evening I preached with the general assumption that I was preaching to unbelievers, preaching evangelistically and for conversion. Then at the end of the service I was standing at the door with the minister, meeting people as they were going out, when a very prominent old lady, a member of that church, astounded the minister, who knew her so well and regarded her as one of the pillars of the cause, by saying to me, "I am going to come again this evening." She never went to the evening service, only to the morning one, as such people so often do. But she told the minister that she was coming in the evening, and he was amazed. "Oh no," she said, "having listened to what was said this morning, I have come to the conclusion that I need the evening service." There was evidently something in the morning service that made her query as to whether she was one of these people who needed to be built up or whether she was really somebody who needed to be born again.

I have often been told the same thing. People have come to me and said, "You know, when I first came here, I came assuming that I was a Christian. I had always thought of myself as a Christian. But the first thing I discovered here was that I had never been a Christian at all." Some of them admit that at first they disliked this very much. They came under a kind of condemnation, and they resented it. But then they came to the point when they saw it was true, and they thanked God for it, and later they had their experience of regeneration and truly became Christians. This, then, is a very real danger. You assume you are a Christian and that all you need is to be built up, but there is nothing there. You cannot go on until you have started; you cannot grow unless you are born. What a fatal error that is!

But let us put it in other ways. It is this whole danger of thinking of Christianity in terms of ideas—ideas that we are to apply—rather than in terms of *life*. That is really the cardinal error. And how common this is. Christianity is thought of in terms of ideas, points of view, notions, and it is our business to get hold of these, to understand them and grasp them and then to proceed to put them into operation. I do not want to be misunderstood in what I am about to say, but I feel constrained to put it like this. There are far too many of us who are prone to think that way.

This was brought home very forcibly to me only last week by a man who has just become interested in these matters. He had come from a purely nonreligious background. He had never been taken to a place of worship as a child, but now as a student he has met others and is becoming interested in these things, and he made a most interesting and significant remark. He told me that while he was away recently on vacation, he had not been attending a place of worship too regularly. "Why not?" I asked. "Well," he said, "you know there is a limit to the amount that one can take in," and thereby he betrayed his whole position.

The attitude is this: here is a subject, here are a number of teachings and ideas; so you listen, and you make your notes, and you are exactly like a student taking up any other subject. At first, of course, students find it very difficult. They are entering upon the study of a new subject that they never touched before; they do not know anything about it, and there is a limit to what one can take in. That is quite all right. You get tired; you get brain fatigue and so on. So you can only take in a certain amount, and you have to try to ration this in order that you may go on and develop.

But I maintain that is not true when you come to this particular realm, and that is where the fallacy comes in. It is the fallacy of assuming that *we* must do this, it is *our* grasping ideas, then masticating them, as it were, and they become a part of us, and then we proceed to put them into practice. Of course, Christianity does involve a teaching, but not in that way. There is something else here, something extra, something that the world knows nothing about—the Holy Spirit and his action and his operation. So as I have often said to such people, "Attend church as regularly as you can." "But," they say, "I find I cannot take it in." I say, "Don't you worry about that." Experience has taught me—and it is one of the most wonderful things about preaching and about the whole pastoral office—that some side-glancing remark has often been the very thing that the Spirit has used to bring a person to a knowledge of the truth. The minister rightly prepares his sermon, he has order, he has logic, he has development, and the danger, of course, is to think that is what is going to do the work. No, it is not; that is merely the scaffolding. The Spirit does the work. And one is therefore often humbled and corrected by finding that something that one merely said as an aside is the very thing that was used by God.

In other words, we are not left to ourselves; this is not a subject, this is not a matter of ideas. This other element, this spiritual element, matters above everything else. Sometimes I am almost tempted to criticize those of you who takes notes in the service. I mean just this: it is right, I know, in a sense to take notes; it helps you think these things over and work them out. But let me give you a warning—be careful lest while you are taking notes you are missing out on the Spirit himself, and he is altogether unheard. I am simply emphasizing that the Spirit is more important than the knowledge the preacher gives, and that is where this realm is altogether different from every other realm.

Let us put it like this: the danger for the religious person is to go in for a study and a knowledge of the Bible, and it is possible to have a knowledge of the Bible that is really expert, and yet you have never known its meaning, you have never seen its teaching. There are people who have an almost perfect knowledge of the letter of the Scripture but have never known the message of the Scripture. You can attend Bible schools and classes, you can attend colleges, and you can get knowledge and information that is purely intellectual, and in the meantime you may know nothing about the message at all; you may have missed the spirit and the meaning completely. This is a very terrible danger, this notion that obviously Nicodemus had of some extra idea, some additional knowledge. It is the danger of this purely intellectual approach that forgets the heart, the whole man, the emotional, feeling element.

Or let me put it like this, and this is equally true and has been true of large numbers of people: it is the danger of putting a *decision* in the place of *regeneration*. I mean that you can decide to go in for religion, you can decide to go in for what you regard as Christianity. You listen to a sermon, you read a book or something like that, or you talk to people. They put the truth before you, and you are convinced about this thing intellectually, so you decide to go in for it. So you change your way of life; you join this society of people who are interested in this matter, and you become one of them. And that is something that not only can be done but that many people do. They not only do it in evangelistic campaigns, they do it in ordinary church services, they do it in private conversations. They take up religion, and they think they are taking up Christianity.

Now I am mentioning this because I am asserting that it is possible for us to do that while remaining unregenerate. It is entirely our action. There has been no vital operation in the soul; there is no seed of new life placed in such a person.

I make that statement on the grounds that throughout the years one observes what happens, and I have been in meetings that have been very deeply concerned about this matter. I have been interested in organizations that have had to inquire into a phenomenon like this, organizations working among a certain class of person and getting large numbers of decisions. Here are people who appear to be converted and to have become truly Christians, and they are active and zealous in the cause. But then these people have to go into a different kind of life; they go out of the atmosphere where they have been and go out into the world and work with various kinds of people, and they not only cease to practice what they have been doing before, they deny everything that they believed and pour scorn and ridicule upon it. They not only drop it, they become antagonistic to it.

This is a fact, a phenomenon; it is called leakage that takes place in Christian unions in universities. And the statistics with regard to evangelistic campaigns show exactly the same thing. There are a given number of professions, but if you examine the position in a year, in five years, you will find an amazing story. There are evangelists who say that they do not expect more than 10 percent of their converts to stand. What about all that? Our eyes are made to concentrate upon a very great and a very real possibility. You can have a temporary persuasion, a kind of intellectual conviction; if a number of people are going in for this, then you do the same thing.

People take up cults in exactly the same way. Many of the cults that are round and about us today can give the same sort of statistics of converts, people who have joined them. You are familiar with many of them; they come to your houses selling their books and so on, and they can give you facts and figures. They can tell you of the additions that are taking place, people who say that they have suddenly been taken hold of by this; they have seen it, and they go in for it and are most zealous and active.

But you can even do something like that in the realm of the Christian church. You can say that you believe these things, and you can become a great church worker, but that does not of necessity prove that you really are truly a Christian. You can be in the position of a man like Nicodemus who thinks that he can decide to take this up and add it on to what he already has and so on. Many, it seems to me, are relying simply upon a decision that they once made. They made that decision, and they think that it has somehow put them right. All I am concerned to say is that you can make a decision without being regenerate, and if you are not regenerate, you are not a Christian.

And we see this, it seems to me, on the very surface of this story of Nicodemus. It is a very real thing, and it is very dangerous. It is a point about which the Protestant Reformers, and the Puritans after them, were very concerned. They talked about "false professors." They were very fond of preaching on the Parable of the Ten Virgins, for we must never forget that the five foolish virgins were as satisfied that they were right as were the five wise ones. They were astonished and amazed to be shut out, and our Lord himself teaches us that there are people who at the final day of judgment are going to have a great shock. They are the people who will say, "Lord, Lord, have we not done this-that-and-the-other?" And he will say, "I never knew you; depart from me." There is nothing more dangerous than to attempt to proceed in the Christian life without being absolutely certain that you have the life within you.

That, then, brings me to my last point, which can be summed up by citing the failure to realize that this is a gift of a new and a divine kind of life; it is altogether different. It is the failure to see this that accounts for so much of the trouble. Our Lord puts that here in this great statement in verse 6: "That which is born of the flesh is flesh; and that which is born of the Spirit is spirit." They are as different as that. We must get rid of all the natural ideas with which we have started. It is not something you go in for, it is not something that you understand and get hold of its principles and then proceed to apply them. That is one of the great troubles, is it not?

That was the trouble with an ancient heresy that goes by the name of Pelagianism. It is to expect Christian conduct from people who are not Christians, and that is very common today. People regard Christianity as a body of teaching that others can apply. They say that people become Christians by recognizing the truth of these principles and then trying to proceed to put them into practice and to persuade others to join them in doing so. So you try to get the state to apply Christian principles. But the state is not Christian. You try to get members of the state to act in a Christian way, but they cannot do so unless they are first and foremost Christians. No men or women can live the Sermon on the Mount as they are; it is impossible. It was surely preached in order to show that. Before you can live the Christian life you must be a Christian. And not to recognize that is to fall into that ancient heresy of Pelagianism.

So what is this Christian life? Well, as our Lord makes plain and clear here to Nicodemus, the glory of this is that it is something that happens to us. It is not something we do; it is something that is done to us. "The wind bloweth where it listeth, and thou hearest the sound thereof, but canst not tell whence it cometh, and whither it goeth: so is every one that is born of the Spirit." You cannot give birth to yourself. Becoming a Christian is something that happens to you. The new birth is a new creation. It is comparable to the original creation, something being made out of nothing, something being produced. Not by man but by God! "Born again"; born from above; "born of the Spirit." "Except a man be born of water and of the Spirit, he cannot enter into the kingdom of God." So it is taken right out of our hands.

You cannot *decide* to be born again. There are people who give that impression. They say, "You decide for Christ, and you will be born again." That is putting it the wrong way round. It is impossible. If you could decide for Christ you would not need to be born again. We are told, "The natural man receiveth not the things of the Spirit of God: for they are foolishness unto him: neither can he know them, because they are spiritually discerned" (1 Cor. 2:14). The princes of this world did not recognize him. The only person who can believe in Christ is the one to whom these things have been revealed by the Spirit, the Spirit who "searcheth all things, yea, the deep things of God" (1 Cor. 2:10). You must be "born again." You cannot even decide that, because if you could, as I say, it would indicate spiritual understanding. But here is a man who does not have any understanding of this at all. The fact that he is told that he must be born again means he must be made from the very beginning, from the foundation; there is nothing to build on. It is an entirely new creation.

There, then, is the fundamental thing, and of course, because of that, it is something very mysterious. "Marvel not that I said unto thee, Ye must be born again." "Don't marvel at this; don't be surprised at it. I am not talking about the flesh." Nicodemus thinks he is and makes his clever debating point: "How can a man be born when he is old?" He is thinking in fleshly terms. That is the mistake. This is not flesh, this is Spirit; it is a different realm. "Don't marvel at this."

And then our Lord goes on to use that extraordinary comparison: "The wind bloweth where it listeth, and thou hearest the sound thereof, but canst not tell whence it cometh, and whither it goeth" (John 3:8). There is a mystery about it. You see the effects and results, but you do not understand. And the one who is "born of the Spirit" is like that. My dear friends, you are outside the realm of understanding; you are above it, beyond it. It is not irrational; it is suprarational. This is divine. This is a realm, as Pascal came to see, that is "beyond the limits of reason." "The supreme achievement of reason," he said, "is to bring us to see that there is a limit to reason," and here we have reached the limit and are beyond it. This is the realm of the mysterious, the supernatural, the divine, God acting. And we do not try to understand here; we just stand in amazement and astonishment. We realize that it would be utter folly for us to try to understand at all; that would be an assertion of something still in us. We cannot and we do not attempt to understand. We are outside the realm of intellect, and thank God we are.

Can you not see that if this were not true, Christianity would be the prerogative of certain special people; it would be the special prerogative of intellectuals, able people. If it is all a matter of ideas and understanding and being able to take in philosophic concepts and then trying to persuade others, those who have ability have a great advantage over everybody else. But that is not Christianity. There is as much hope here for the unintelligent as for the intelligent. There is an equal hope for all. That is the glory of the Christian faith. It includes all classes, all types, and all kinds. Why? Because it is the action of God, not the action of man. It does not presuppose anything in us, except that we are lost and helpless and hopeless. It is all his action. The Spirit operates like the wind. So you are not just taking ideas and making notes and then grasping them and putting them into practice. Not at all! Something possesses you, and you are aware of the fact that God has been dealing with your soul and that you are a new man.

All you and I can realize is this: there is something that we do not have if we are not truly Christians. We realize our need of something, and there is only one thing we can do, and that is, as Nicodemus did, to go to him and just wait and listen. You must go to him, as I said earlier, but you cannot do any more than that. You will even find that your motive for going was wrong and that your whole approach was wrong. Do not worry about that, he will put it right—he does that. All we can do at that point is to have the feeling within us that there is something there. We do not understand it, we do not know what it is, but we do not want to argue any longer, we do not want to be clever; we are just aware of bankruptcy and of need, and we listen, we wait.

The next thing is that you know it has happened to you. How do we know this? I hope to go on with that later, but when it happens, you know it has happened, and when it has happened you can begin to grow. "Being justified by faith" you can begin to consider development, sanctification, advance, growth in grace and in the knowledge of the Lord (Rom. 5:1). But if you try—as I vary my picture—to build your building without a foundation, it will collapse, it will be nothing. You cannot grow until you are born. You cannot proceed on the journey until you have started.

So this great word comes to us, and it comes in the form of a question: Have we been born again? Have we received the life of God in our souls? It is no use proceeding a step further until you are certain and sure of the answer to that great preliminary question. Otherwise if you try to grow he will stop you, and he will say to you, "Verily, verily, I say unto thee, Except a man be born again, he cannot see [let alone enter] the kingdom of God."

# 3

# Characteristics of the New Birth

JOHN 3:8

Sunday morning sermon preached in
Westminster Chapel, January 23, 1966.

We have been considering together the error of trying to go on in the Christian life without ever having first been *in* the Christian life. You can waste years doing that, and that is why this story of Nicodemus is such an important and such a crucial case. What our Lord says to all such people is, "Ye must be born again." It is no use considering the higher reaches, if we may so term them, of the Christian life or the depths of the Christian experience unless we are absolutely certain that we have Christian life, that we have been born again. Rebirth is an absolute necessity. No one can be a Christian without it. You are not born a Christian. The fact that you belong to a certain country does not make you a Christian, nor does church membership. That means this new birth, birth from above, birth of the Spirit, this mysterious, miraculous operation of God the Holy Ghost upon the soul, as mysterious as the wind itself, is something we cannot understand. Poor Nicodemus keeps trying to. "How can these things be?" he keeps saying. "How can a man be born when he is old?" That is the utter folly that is displayed by this kind of person who will try to understand everything, whereas by definition this is something beyond understanding because it is the miraculous, mysterious, supernatural action of God in the soul.

This is clearly, therefore, a doctrine, a truth, that is given very great prominence in the New Testament, and nothing shows its importance more than the variety of terms that are used in order to bring it forth. It is called here being *born again*; it is described as *regeneration*. Now there is nothing more radical than that—yes, *generation*, that which gives being and life to us, but even more regeneration. Not merely being improved but being given new life by being *born, made, generated* anew and afresh.

And then it is described as a *new creation*, a term that is often used. "If any man be in Christ, he is a new creature," a new creation (2 Cor. 5:17). "God, who commanded the light to shine out of darkness, hath shined in our hearts, to give the light of the knowledge of the glory of God in the face of Jesus Christ," like the first creation (2 Cor. 4:6). It is comparable to that, something being made out of nothing. That is creation. It is also described as giving us a *new heart* or a *clean heart*. The heart is a very radical organ. Again it is said that we are made "partakers of the divine nature" (2 Pet. 1:4). James puts it in terms of our being begotten by God "with the word" (James 1:18). It is the same idea, but the variety of terms is interesting. John in his first epistle keeps referring to this as a "seed" of life, as if a seed were sown in our natures, in our hearts, a seed of new and divine life. "[The] seed," he says, "remaineth [or abides] in [us]" (1 John 3:9).

And then it is actually described as and compared to a *resurrection*. "You," says Paul to the Ephesians in the second chapter and the first verse, "hath he quickened, who were dead in trespasses and sins" (Eph. 2:1). He goes on to say that we have been "raised up together" with Christ. This is resurrection from the dead. And the same truth is worked out in the sixth chapter of the epistle to the Romans: "Planted together in the likeness of his death . . . also in the likeness of his resurrection" (Rom. 6:5). We have been "crucified with him," we have been "buried with him," we have been "raised" with him. These are terms that are used in order to bring home to us the greatness of this matter of regeneration. That is what makes people Christians, not anything they do—it is what is done to them. It is as profound as that. It is not an improvement; it is not just a trimming. It is a remaking, a reconstituting, the implanting in us of a new disposition, a new principle of life, which is a divine life.

Now that is what makes a man or woman a Christian. That is what our Lord is saying here to Nicodemus who was already religious, already moral, already able, already well versed in the Scriptures. Those other things do not make us Christians; it is new birth alone. And that is why some of us are so fearful about the emphasis on making a decision. You do decide, of course, but you can only do so after this has happened to you. "The natural man" does not want to decide; these things are "foolishness unto him" (1 Cor. 2:14). You do not decide for Christ and because of that become born again. As I have said, if that were the case you would not need to be born again, you would have already had the understanding. Regeneration is the first thing. All you can do is recognize, when the Spirit deals with you, that you are in this dead condition and cry out for life. This is the first essential, and without this there is no such thing as being a Christian. This is what makes us Christians; it is what God does to us, not what we do.

So obviously it is vital for us that we should all be perfectly clear as to this and know whether this has happened to us. "Ye must be born again." Are we born again? That is the question. It is no use saying, "I want these higher experiences. I want to get on. I have been reading about the saints, and that is what I would like to have and to be like." Before we go on, I must ask you the question, are you born again? Are you alive? You cannot know unless you are born.

Now in this eighth verse our Lord puts it like this: "The wind bloweth where it listeth, and thou hearest the sound thereof, but canst not tell whence it cometh, and whither it goeth; so"—like that, comparable to that—"is every one that is born of the Spirit." Now this word "so" contains everything that we are going to study together. Let me emphasize for a moment the words "every one." "So [like that] is *every one* that is born of the Spirit."

I want to clear up a point here. People are often in trouble because they find that they cannot make certain specific statements. There is wrong teaching here on both sides. Some people say that the "so" means that everyone's experience is identical in detail with everyone else's.

Now the natural process of birth varies greatly from case to case; sometimes it is sudden and dramatic, and one knows that it has happened. It is not always like that. Actually the act of regeneration, being God's act, is something that is outside consciousness. That is where our Lord's illustration here is such an important one. He says in effect, "You do not see the wind, and you do not understand it in an ultimate sense; but what you do see is the effects and the results." That is what he is concentrating on—"thou hearest the sound thereof." You can see its effect on the branches and on the leaves on the tree or on clothes hanging on a line. You can see what it is doing, but you cannot see it. The new birth is like that.

So the important thing for us to concentrate on is the manifestation of life. If I may press the analogy—that is a dangerous thing to do, yet surely in view of the terms used in the Scripture we are entitled to do so—a birth may take place quickly or it may be very prolonged and slow; it may be painful, or there may be no pain comparatively speaking. There are all sorts of variations here. I am, therefore, not asking if you can point to a particular second or moment or hour or service or particular text that was used; that is not the thing that is of importance. What is of importance is this: Do you have manifestations of this life within you? You are not asked to spend much time as to the process of how you were born, but what you are asked to be certain of is that you are born, that you are born again.

I trust that I have made that perfectly clear. The Devil always tries to confuse people. There are dramatic conversions, but a conversion is just as real when it is not dramatic. The important thing is that we know that this great act has taken place in us. That is the matter, therefore, to which we now turn.

What then are the characteristics of this life? How can you determine whether you are born again or not? There are a number of general characteristics that we must emphasize; they are very important. I sometimes think that these general characteristics are almost more important than the detailed characteristics with which we also have to deal. So the first thing I mean by general characteristics is this—family likeness. The Bible in its condescension and kindness uses these familiar illustrations, and therefore we are entitled to use them in exactly the same way. We are all familiar with the fact that when you have people who are born of the same parents and belong to the same family, though they may differ tremendously in many respects, there is generally a family likeness, there is something in common that you can recognize in all of them. Now that is profoundly true in the Christian life, and I regard this as one of the most important tests.

I put it therefore like this: when people are born again, that becomes the most obvious thing about them. Here is unregenerate mankind; then here are men and women who have now become regenerate as others have before them. My argument, and it is inconvertible, is that because they now have a seed of divine life in them because they now have become "partakers of the divine nature" (2 Pet. 1:4), that of necessity must be their chief characteristic. This new life, which is so much bigger and greater and more powerful than the other, becomes the predominating characteristic. They now begin to show and to display this feature, and this is true of all who are sharing the same life.

So I deduce from this that when people are truly Christians, that becomes the outstanding thing about them, more outstanding than their color or their nationality, more outstanding than the particular type of school they attended. It is more obvious about them than their profession, their ability, or anything else. You can work out this analogy for yourselves. Take people on the natural level; they are different in size, in the color of their hair or their complexion, in their abilities and many other ways, and yet there is this intangible something that tells you they belong to the same family. In many ways that is the first and greatest characteristic of the Christian.

Let me try to put this a little further in this way: this is one of those things that is difficult to put into words, yet one is always very conscious of it. There is a general impression that one gets, and that is what we are dealing with. The general impression that Christians give is that they are Christians, that they have this new life in them. How do they do that? Well, to put it in a very general way, they do it by giving you the impression that they are spiritually minded people. Spiritually minded! They must be. "They that are after the flesh do mind the things of the flesh," says the apostle Paul in Romans 8:5, "but they that are after the Spirit [mind] the things of the Spirit." He is arguing that there is this essential, fundamental difference that governs everything, and nothing does this more than this whole general impression.

Now—forgive me for putting it like this; I do not want to do this, and yet I must—I have often discovered this characteristic of which I am speaking in this particular way. I have known men who delight in talking about preaching. Alas, I have known preachers of whom this is true, and still know them. They talk about preaching, they talk about Christianity, they talk about the church; they are prepared to discuss these things and to ask about them. But one is always conscious that they are doing so with a kind of secular mind. You need not be a Christian to be interested in preaching or in the affairs of the church; you need not be a Christian to have an interest in the Bible. God knows there was a time when I was guilty of the very thing that I am describing. I have known what it is to be arguing about these things, but it was purely intellectual; it was not a matter of the Spirit, it was not because I had a spiritual mind. I did not; I had a carnal or secular mind.

So this matter becomes very subtle; it is not so much what a person says that matters as the way in which he or she says it. In a sense a man can be an expositor of the Bible and a teacher of the Bible, and yet you feel there is nothing spiritual about what he is doing. He can be giving you the letter but never the Spirit; there is no message. It is a mechanical, superficial, external attitude, and it can be most fascinating, but—and here is one of these subtle points that is difficult to put into words—you find that the attitude of a man to what he is doing and saying is much more important than what he is saying. You can even be a defender of orthodoxy and still have a secular mind. I have known many such men. This question of family likeness is a process of the

Spirit, and it is something that comes out in almost everything that a man or woman does.

So then, having put it like that in general let us go on and look at some other features and characteristics. Some of them are more subjective and some more objective, like the one to which I have just been referring. A man himself is not always conscious of this, but others are very conscious of it. You recognize it, you can sense it in others, and that becomes a very good proof of the fact that you yourself are truly a Christian.

But now let us consider another characteristic. It seems to me that a very valuable and thorough test in this matter is our consciousness of being dealt with. You cannot be born again without being conscious of being dealt with, without being aware that something has taken place within you. You are conscious of an interference in your life, not that you are doing things, but things are being done to you. "O Love that wilt not let me go," says one hymn-writer. Or take Frances Thompson's "Hound of Heaven": "I fled Him, down the nights and down the days; . . . I fled Him, down the labyrinthine ways of my own mind." That is it; that is the idea. It is Another dealing with you.

This is vital in this whole matter. It is not our action that we are most conscious of; it is that Another is dealing with us, coming into our life, disturbing us. We can do nothing better than take that great statement of it by the apostle Paul in the third chapter of the epistle to the Philippians where he puts it in a very striking way. He says his great desire is, "that I may know him, and the power of his resurrection, and the fellowship of his sufferings, being made conformable unto his death; if by any means I might attain unto the resurrection of the dead. Not as though I had already attained, either were already perfect: but I follow after, if that I may apprehend that for which also I am apprehended of Christ Jesus" (Phil. 3:10–12). Paul says, "I do not say I have arrived, but I am now try-ing to apprehend that which has apprehended me. I am trying to lay hold of that which has already laid hold of me".

That is a perfect expression of this particular point. Paul does not say, "Now I decided at a given point that I would take up Christianity. I decided for Christ." Rather what he says is this: "Christ had decided for me or decided on me. He had chosen me from my mother's womb. He laid hold on me, and I am now trying to lay hold on this marvelous thing that he has done to me." That is it.

And this, of course, by definition must be true. In the case of the apostle Paul one knows that it had all those dramatic elements that I say we must not overemphasize. He was a special man in the sense that he was given a special work to do, but his regeneration was no different. There were certain elements about his calling; he was to be an apostle, so he had to be able to testify to the resurrection, he had to see the risen Lord and so on. But that is not what he constantly refers to. It is this: "He has apprehended me. He has laid hold of me, and now I am trying to lay hold on him and what he has given me and what he has done to me." Now this is something that we can all only answer for ourselves. You are either living a self-contained life and are in charge of yourself, or else you have been disturbed, you have been interfered with, you are aware that something is happening to you, that God is dealing with you. You do not always understand that it is God at the beginning, but you are aware of something, and you might even fight against it, you might dislike it; you might "kick against the pricks" as Saul of Tarsus had done. That does not matter. The point is, "O Love that wilt not let me go." It is not you, it is the Love, the One who will not let you go. This is, I repeat, fundamental; this is something that is quite inevitable. The Creator is dealing with you. He is forming you, he has formed a new creature within you, and you are aware that it has been happening to you, that you have been dealt with by God.

Somehow or another this has gone out of even evangelical thinking. The emphasis is on man and man's decision. We must get back to the biblical position. When God deals with men and women, they know it is happening and that they must do something about it—"O Love that wilt not let me go"—and they come in the end and say, "I rest my weary soul in thee." There is nothing to me more fascinating or romantic than to find people coming, perhaps after months or even years, to tell me how this happened to them and when it did and so on, without any pressure from me or anyone else. It is God's work, and one knows when it is happening. That is the first thing.

A further really important test, therefore, is this one—we cannot be born again without being humbled. Our Lord humbled Nicodemus. Here comes the teacher, "a ruler of the Jews," an able, godly, moral, religious man. He essentially says with confidence, "Master, I want to know." And Jesus answers, "Verily, verily, I say unto thee, Except a man be born again, he cannot see the kingdom of God" (John 3:3). Nicodemus is humbled. And again this follows by definition. If we are in such a state and condition that nothing will suffice us except to be made anew, to be born again, if we are dead and need regeneration, that is a very humbling thought, is it not? Very humbling!

That is why people have hated the doctrine of regeneration. The two things that religious people hate more than anything else are the cross of Christ, seen truly as a substitutionary atonement, and regeneration. Why? Because they regard them as insufferable. They say, "I cannot believe this. It is impossible. Am I so wretched, so hopeless, so vile that I must be bought? The thing is insulting!" They hate the doctrine of regeneration, and they hate the substitutionary atonement in the same way, for they think they can do something, can make some kind of atonement themselves. So it is very humbling. And this is, I would suggest to you, the differentiating point over all others between those who take up Christianity, as they think, and those who have been taken up by it. The one who is taken up is always humble.

Now we must be clear in our definition of this. It does not mean that you are occasionally a little bit frightened when you are taken ill or have a serious operation or when a loved one dies or you are at a funeral. Ah, the natural man may be frightened by that and disturbed by it. I have seen that many times, and then it passes, of course, and you forget all about it. I am not talking about that. I am not talking about an occasional fearfullness. What I am saying is that no men or women are born again without some consciousness in some sense or another that they have been knocked down. Again the apostle Paul on the road to Damascus is a classic example of this, with all the dramatic elements—he was literally knocked to the ground, he fell flat on the road. It need not be physical like that, but there is always this knocking down, this humbling.

The apostle tells us in his autobiography in Romans 7 more or less how this happened to him. He says, "I was alive without the law once." And again, in Philippians 3, he says that with regard to the demands of the law, he was righteous, blameless. He was a happy, self-contained, self-contented man; he felt he was keeping the law. But then suddenly the Spirit began to deal with him and flashed upon his mind and heart and spirit the real meaning of the law—"Thou shalt not covet." "The commandment came, sin revived, and I died" (Rom. 7:9). He had to die; every man or woman has to die. You cannot be born again without dying—I mean in a spiritual sense, of course. You must undergo this death of self. You are knocked down, you are finished, you realize you are nothing.

Now this is inevitable; this is not a matter of argument or dispute. If you are conscious that you have new life that has been put into you, you have been born again. So what it tells you about what you had been is inevitable, and you are aware of it. You cannot have a new life without realizing the truth about the old. So the people who are born again, from whom self-reliance and self-confidence have gone, are no longer as *healthy* as they once were. "I was alive without the law once"; that is gone forever.

Or let me put it another way. Those who are born again are always humble because they know something about "the fear of the Lord." Here is the note that is missing nowadays, is it not? Here is the thing that we have somehow lost, "the fear of the Lord." The Old Testament is full of this: "The fear of the LORD is the beginning of wisdom" (Prov. 9:10). And as you read your Bible, Old Testament and New, there is nothing, surely, that impresses one so much and strikes one so much about these great heroes of the faith as this fear of the Lord that always characterizes them. Look at a man like Abraham. You see it in him; it was his outstanding characteristic. He was a great man in many ways, but the characteristic that always strikes one about him above all is his godly fear, the fear of the Lord.

You find exactly the same with Moses. Moses had to be taught this several times, but then it became his greatest characteristic. He was given the great lesson of the burning bush when he was about to look at it. The

Voice came saying, "Draw not nigh hither: put off thy shoes from off thy feet, for the place whereon thou standest is holy ground" (Ex. 3:5). When men and women are born again, they know something about this "holy ground." One cannot help it; it is inevitable. And so you find that Moses was ever aware of that. It does not mean he was perfect; he committed sins and was not allowed to go into Canaan, but "the fear of the LORD" was there during his whole life.

And take a man like David. David could be a great sinner, but if there is one thing that characterized David above everything else, it was his fear of the Lord, his reverence in the presence of God. We see it also in the call of Isaiah. He begins to feel, "Woe is me!" Why? It was because of the vision of God. And the implanting of this divine life in the soul does exactly the same thing. There is a very interesting phrase used about Hezekiah when he says after certain things had happened to him, "I shall go softly" (Isa. 38:15). He is going to walk softly for the rest of his life.

Now here is something that is a characteristic of those who are truly born again or born of the Spirit: they have been humbled. And this, I feel, is something that is often not seen in modern evangelicalism; there is no sense of being humbled. But it is inevitable in the light of this teaching. If you read the lives of saints in past ages, you will find that is what always characterized them; they were men and women who had been humbled. If you have ever met a person who has been through a revival, where the Spirit of God has been manifest in power, you will find that is always their outstanding characteristic—they have been humbled. It is "godly fear"—"reverence and godly fear." So they walk softly; they have felt the touch of the eternal. You find it even in the accounts of our Lord's miracles in the four Gospels. Even unbelievers were for the time being filled with a spirit of fear. This was certainly always true of the disciples. Our Lord performs the miracle that enables Peter and the others to catch a great haul of fish. Peter goes to him and says, "Depart from me; for I am a sinful man, O Lord" (Luke 5:8). Our Lord has not rebuked him, he has said nothing to him, but the miracle, the manifestation of the divine, the miraculous, the eternal power, is something that inevitably humbles Peter. And this touch of the Almighty, this recreating act, is something that humbles people; they are aware that they have been in the hands of God and that they are still there. Therefore this is something that is always a characteristic.

And this leads in turn to the next point. Those who are born again have always undergone a true repentance. Now you notice that I put my emphasis on *true* repentance. There is a counterfeit repentance that we sometimes call remorse and that often causes people to mistake the one for the other. The apostle speaks of this in 2 Corinthians 7:8–11. He has had to write to the Corinthians over a certain matter and to rebuke them, and he says, "Though I made you sorry with a letter, I do not repent . . . for I perceive that the same epistle hath made you sorry, though it were but for a season. Now I rejoice, not that ye were made sorry, but that ye sorrowed to repentance: for ye were made sorry after a godly manner, that ye might receive damage by us in nothing. For godly sorrow worketh repentance to salvation not to be repented of: but the sorrow of the world worketh death. For behold this selfsame thing, that ye sorrowed after a godly sort, what carefullness it wrought in you, yea, what clearing of yourselves, yea, what indignation, yea, what fear, yea, what vehement desire, yea, what zeal, yea, what revenge! In all things ye have approved yourselves to be clear in this matter." That is what I am referring to.

In other words, when people are born again, they truly repent in the sense that they have this "godly sorrow." They are not only sorry that they have done wrong things, they are much more sorry because they have a nature that ever made them desire to do such things. The "godly sorrow" is not the sorrow of those who have done something and know it is wrong; their own conscience condemns them, they are suffering the consequences, and they are uneasy. It is not that. The sorrow of those who are born again is the sorrow of men and women who have discovered that their hearts are evil and sinful. They are enabled to say with the apostle Paul, "In me, (that is, in my flesh) dwelleth no good thing" (Rom. 7:18). They are rotten, they must be made anew, they must be born again, and this is the thing that grieves them—the vileness of sin, the plague of their own heart. This is inevitable in anyone who has been born again.

Again then let me be clear—I am not postulating any intensity of necessity in the feeling; the intensity varies. All I am saying is that if they have not discovered that they have an evil heart, then they still have it, and they do not have a new heart and a clean heart; they have not been born again. But those who are born again not only know that they have an evil heart by nature, they mourn it and regret it and hate it and can say with David, "Create in me a clean heart, O, God; and renew a right spirit within me" (Ps. 51:10); they are the Christians. They have discovered this and henceforward with regard to everything wrong that they do say, with William Cowper, "I hate the thing that made Thee mourn and drove Thee from my breast." That is true repentance. In other words, they have seen why they had to be regenerated and why nothing short of regeneration would suffice for them or be of real value to them.

And that leads me to the last point which is more general, like the first point. I started with it, and I end with it deliberately. It is again one of those points that is rather difficult to put into words; yet the older I get and the more experienced I get in these matters, the more significance I attach to these general points. There is always a fundamental seriousness about the men and women who are born again. I mean something like this: they are never flippant, never light, never superficial. Have you known people like this? You are talking to them, and they are typical men and women. Then you or someone else introduces the subject of religion or of the faith, or you refer to a meeting, and suddenly they have to pull themselves together. They have to discipline themselves, change themselves as it were into something else, and there is a tremendous contrast; you feel you have two different people before you.

I cannot reconcile that with regeneration. If you have to put on a kind of mask and attitude when you deal with religious things, I say there is no life there. That is the kind of quick-change artist that masquerades as Christianity, as often happens. These people appear to be unnatural when they talk about these things, and if that is true of you when you are in the realm of faith, then you do not belong to it, you do not have the new nature. This is the native air of true Christians, and therefore I say that they are fundamentally serious people.

Let me hasten to add that I am not saying that they are solemn or pompous people. God forbid that anyone would think I am saying that! No, no, they are happy, they can even be humorous. But their humor never runs away with them. It is a manifestation of life; it is the showing of one of the attributes that they have received by nature. There is always control; there is always seriousness about them. In everything they do the controlling factor, the great principle, is that of people who are "partakers of the divine nature" (2 Pet. 1:4).

You find it exemplified to perfection in our blessed Lord himself. He is the Son of God, he knew a joy and an intimacy with God that no man has ever known, and yet he was "a man of sorrows, and acquainted with grief" (Isa. 53:3). Obviously there was a joy that radiated from him, and there are touches here and there, surely, of humor. There was nothing solemn, pompous, drab, or dull about him. No, no, quite the reverse, the eternal reverse of that. And yet he was "a man of sorrows, and acquainted with grief." Why? Because he was the Son of God, because he was holiness in perfection in an evil, sinful world such as this. And all I am arguing is that all who are born again of the Spirit, who have become "partaker of the divine nature," must have an element of that in them. They cannot be superficial or glib or flippant.

And when the flippancy and the lightness and the jocularity come into the realm of sacred things it is still more terrible. But it often does. Christians are serious. They say, along with the apostle Paul, "[We] ourselves also, which have the firstfruits of the Spirit, even we ourselves groan within ourselves, waiting for the adoption, to wit, the redemption of our body" (Rom. 8:23). Or take in 2 Corinthians 5: "For we know that if our earthly house of this tabernacle were dissolved, we have a building of God, an house not made with hands, eternal in the heavens. For in this we groan, earnestly desiring to be clothed upon with our house which is from heaven" (vv. 1–2). Can you imagine a more fascinating character than the apostle Paul? Does he strike you as being dull or pompous? No, no, there is a warmth, there is something lovable, there is geniality, and yet there is a fundamental seriousness. And those who are born again must be like this because, I repeat, they have discovered that by nature they could not be improved. "Ye must be born again." They see evil and sin, the state of the world, and all that it has involved and what is coming, and they are inevitably fundamentally serious people. Oh, get that right, my dear friends; serious—but not dull, pompous, heavy, unattractive. That is Satan's counterfeit, and it has done so much harm. There is no contradiction between joy and seriousness. The joy of the Christian is a holy joy, it is a pure joy, as are all the other characteristics that we shall go on to consider.

# 4

# The Sign of the New Birth

JOHN 3:8

Sunday morning sermon preached in
Westminster Chapel, January 30, 1966.

The wind bloweth where it listeth, and thou hearest the sound
thereof, but canst not tell whence it cometh, and whither it goeth:
so is every one that is born of the Spirit. (John 3:8)

Now we are dealing particularly with the word "so." "So [like that, comparable to that] is every one that is born of the Spirit." In other words, we are looking together at the characteristics of those who are "born of the Spirit," and our reason for that is that our Lord has been explaining to Nicodemus that unless a man is born again, he cannot even see the kingdom of God, let alone enter into it. The whole matter, therefore, becomes of great importance because so many fail to experience this new life in Christ. They fail to receive the fullness that is in him because they have made the same initial mistake that had been made by this great teacher of Israel, Nicodemus, this man who went to our Lord by night saying, "Rabbi, we know that thou art a teacher come from God: for no man can do these miracles that thou doest, except God be with him" (John 3:2). We have seen that his whole approach was wrong, his initial attitude was wrong, and we have seen why this was so.

Here was a man like so many people today who was trying to advance along a journey before he had ever really started. And he was told by our Lord, "Ye must be born again." So we are now looking at the characteristics of those who have been born again, "born of water and of the Spirit." We are doing this in terms of our Lord's illustration: he says this is like the wind. Nicodemus is trying to understand this. "How can these things be?" That is his great phrase, a great question. He is confusing flesh and Spirit, and he is marveling. So our Lord says, "Marvel not that I said unto thee, Ye must be born again." We must give up all this attempt to understand this and to get it within our comprehension. That is so common today, is it not? People say, "I don't understand," and because they do not understand, they think the teaching is wrong; so they are not prepared to believe it and to submit to it. These thoughts are utterly contradictory, of course. You do not understand electricity, but you use it; you do not understand the wind, but again you use it, and you see its effects and results. But here in this all-important matter people bring their understanding and say, *I am not going to believe a thing unless I can understand it.*

Now there is nothing as fatal as that very attitude, and that is why we are examining this matter in detail. It is so vital. We must all be "born again," and the first thing, therefore, is to discover whether we have been or not, and in order to do that we are looking at the characteristics of this new life in Christ Jesus, and so far we have discovered certain characteristics. We have suggested that when someone is born again, that is the most obvious thing about him; it must be, for it is the life of God in him. He is also conscious of being dealt with, of having been humbled; he is also aware of a true repentance, and he is characterized by a fundamental seriousness.

But now let us continue from that. The next characteristic—and I am trying to put these in a kind of order—is that the born again are aware of and conscious of a new life and a new nature within them. This again is something that needs no argument or demonstration; it is inevitable according to the teaching. Each of us is born what is called in the Bible a "natural man." But then the new birth happens to us in the way that we have been considering, and a new principle of life is put into us. Now my argument is that it follows of necessity that we are aware of this; we are aware that something has happened to us—not merely that we have been dealt with, but that something has actually happened. There is now an element within us that was not there before, and that can be expressed in many ways. The apostle Paul puts it, it seems to me, in a particularly clear way in Galatians 5:17: "For the flesh lusteth against the Spirit, and the Spirit against the flesh: and these are contrary the one to the other."

That is what I am describing, that the one personality is aware, as it were, of two beings within him and that they are in opposition and in conflict. Now a point that we must make clear at this stage in connection with this matter is this: someone may say, "How do you tell the difference between that and the conscience of the natural man?" Every man and woman has a conscience, and when we as natural men do something that we should not do, our conscience speaks, and the conscience speaks apart from us, we cannot stop it. We often wish that we could, and we try to, but we cannot; conscience is there, and it is independent of us, and it pronounces its judgments on what we do. So then, says somebody, what is the difference between what is described here and the conscience operating in a "natural man"? Is this not some kind of heightened conscience—why do you insist upon its being a new principle of life?

The answer, it seems to me, is this, and it is a very important point in this whole connection: conscience is always entirely negative. Conscience never acts in a positive manner; it simply delivers verdicts on what we have done or on what we have thought. It never initiates anything; it never promotes anything. It is not its function to do so. Conscience is a kind of legal court that is always trying cases. It is nothing more, and it delivers its verdict on what we have done and of what we have been guilty. But the whole point about this new principle of life within us is that it is positive, it is living, it is active, it is always initiating. So when I say that we are conscious of a new life and a new nature within us, I am not simply saying that we become aware that we are doing things that we should not do and come under condemnation. It includes that, but it is much more than that. It is that we are aware of something, to put it vaguely, within us that is urging us and calling us and stimulating us to something better, to something higher. It acts, as it were, independently of us; we are aware of it acting within us.

Again we can put this in the words of the apostle Paul, this time in Philippians 2:12–13: "Wherefore, my beloved, as ye have always obeyed, not as in my presence only, but now much more in my absence, work out your own salvation with fear and trembling. For it is God which worketh in you both to will and to do of his good pleasure." Now that is a very good statement of this very principle, that God works in us by the Spirit though this new nature. In other words, we are aware of this activity within us, and this is something that is peculiar to the man or woman who is born again.

Now I must watch my language because one can be guilty almost of a heresy, but this is how it appears to us at first sight. It is as if we ourselves were aware of two persons acting within us, what the Bible calls "the old man" and "the new man," but it is actually the old nature and the new nature. I am aware of one who acts in a manner that I do not like, and I am aware of another that acts in a manner that amazes me, because it is better than what I know myself to be by nature. And that is this new life that is in us, and this is something that only someone who is born again knows anything at all about. "Natural" men and women live and act and think, and then when they do something that is wrong, their conscience condemns them. That is all they are aware of, nothing else. And they have to decide to be better; they may read books and accept arguments. "Yes," they say, "This is right. I must do this."

But that is not what I am talking about. I am talking about those who are disturbed by someone else, as it were, within them. They are called to do certain things, and they find themselves being acted upon by this something else, and that is the principle of the new life. So whether one has this awareness and consciousness of a new life and a new nature within is a very good test of whether one is born again or not. It is not just one person succeeding or failing. It is two natures in one person—the old nature, the new nature—the divine life over and against and above that which one knew and still knows one's self to be merely by nature.

And that in turn leads me to the next test, which, of course, follows by an inevitable logic. It is that one is surprised at one's self. I have sometimes said, and I repeat it, that this may be the most subtle test of all in this matter. Christians are men and women who are surprised and amazed at themselves.

Does this need any demonstration? Does it not follow inevitably that when something of the divine nature enters into us, when we become "partakers of the divine nature" as Peter puts it, or when, as John puts it, this seed of divine life is put within us, when this new principle is implanted and acts in the way that I have been describing, then inevitably we must be amazed ourselves. And that is because this new life is so different, such a contrast to what we are by nature; you cannot imagine a greater contrast. It is the contrast between fallen human nature and God's nature. It is nothing less than that.

That change is exactly what is described in the New Testament. Man according to the New Testament is not only sinful, he is fallen. His nature is twisted, perverted, polluted, and that is what we all are by nature. Now this seed of divine life is put into us, and then that acts—and there is no need to argue this matter. And when we are aware of something like that happening within us, we must be filled with a sense of amazement and astonishment. The contrast is indescribable, and this is what we find referred to so often in the Scripture. There is no better statement of it than Galatians 2:20: "I am [have been] crucified with Christ: nevertheless I live; yet not I, but Christ liveth in me: and the life which I now live in the flesh I live by the faith of the Son of God, who loved me, and gave himself for me." There it is. "I live; yet not I." It is all there.

Paul has become an enigma, a puzzle to himself; in a sense he does not understand himself. He is the same man—Saul of Tarsus. Of course he is. And yet it is ridiculous to say he is Saul of Tarsus. Saul of Tarsus was "a persecutor," an "injurious" person, "a blasphemer," but here is "an apostle of Jesus Christ," and yet it is the same man. "I am!—I am not!" There you are. It is inevitable. You cannot argue with things like this. You cannot argue with life. You can argue with opinions, but you cannot argue with life. And when we are aware of this other life and its manifestations within us, we can scarcely believe it. Is it possible that we who were and are what we know to be true about ourselves are now like this?

What is this? We find now that we have a spiritual interest and a spiritual concern, and this is amazing. The world today outside Christ, outside the church, the unregenerate world, knows nothing about a *spiritual* interest. It has many other interests—political interests, interest in arts, music, drama. People are reading the critics in today's papers— "wonderful, intellectual"—books, plays, operas, concerts! That is all right, there are these interests; but they are not spiritual interests, and those who are unregenerate cannot know anything about a spiritual interest. Unregenerate men and woman are not interested in their souls. They never think about them; indeed they are not aware of them. They may talk about God when it is a question of having a religious argument or when they are listening to a so-called argument on television or somewhere else—this bit of entertainment today that passes for argument. That may make them think and speak about God for a moment.

But they know nothing about God, and they are not really interested; they do not really even think about their own lives. They think about activities in life, but they do not sit down and say: What is life? What is man? What am I? What am I here for? Where am I going? What is death? What lies beyond it? Not only do they not think about these things, they resent being made to think about them. So all these things become very good tests. Those who resent being made to think about death and those who simply want to go around and around in the whirl of life are just proclaiming that they are not spiritual men or women. They are not interested in the gospel or in the church as such. They are interested, perhaps, in making fun of the church, but they are not interested in what the church really is, how she came into being, what she is for. They are not interested in prayer, and they are not interested in the Bible.

Now that is "the natural man," but here now are men and women who were like that, but, to their amazement and astonishment, they find they have become interested in these things, and that is a very remarkable thing to happen. If you, my friends, are really interested in these things, take it from me you are born again.

What is the difference between you and others? This is the best way of looking at it: Does it all astound you? Does it amaze you? Have these things, these spiritual matters, become the chief thing in your life? I do not mean that it is just an item in your schedule: five days a week going to business or going to work, then Saturday sports, and on Sunday visiting a place of worship. I do not mean that. It is not just an odd item, the one that is dropped if anything has to be dropped. There are people like that. That is religion; that is church membership only. It is just an item in the schedule, easily eliminated and more readily eliminated than most of the other things.

That is not it. I am asking: Is this now the big thing in your life, the chief thing, the chief interest? If it is, you are born again—there is no question about it. And when you discover that, you are amazed and astonished at it. You say with Charles Wesley:

And can it be that I should gain
An interest in the Saviour's blood?
Died He for me, who caused His pain;
For me, who Him to death pursued?
Amazing love! How can it be
That Thou, my God, shouldst die for me?[1]

Do you know anything about that astonishment? It is inevitable if the life of God is in you. You see yourself with amazement and can scarcely believe that it is *you* of whom these things are true and that you now are delighting in these things that are so completely foreign to the life of the natural man.

But then I hasten to add the next test, which follows directly from that one, and I am always very interested in this one. Sometimes the first way in which one really discovers that one is born again is that *other people* let us know that we are. How do they do this? They do it in two ways. One is that they appear different to us. But still more important, I sometimes think, is that we appear different to them, and they let us know it, and they resent it. Our Lord himself prepared us for this. He prepared his own immediate disciples, and he has prepared all of us ever since. In Matthew 10 we read of his sending out his disciples, and he warns them that they will not be received gladly and with delight by everybody. He says, "Beware of men: for they will deliver you up to the councils, and they will scourge you in their synagogues; and ye shall be brought before governors and kings for my sake" (Matt. 10:17–18). And he goes on to say,

> For it is not ye that speak, but the Spirit of your Father which speaketh in you. And the brother shall deliver up the brother to death, and the father the child: and the children shall rise up against their parents, and cause them to be put to death. And ye shall be hated of all men for my name's sake: but he that endureth to the end shall be saved. (Matt. 10:20–22)

Then he puts it to them in a most striking phrase:

> Think not that I am come to send peace on earth: I came not to send peace, but a sword. For I am come to set a man at variance against his father, and the daughter against her mother, and the daughter in law against her mother in law. And a man's foes shall be they of his own household. He that loveth father or mother more than me is not worthy of me: and he that loveth son or daughter more than me is not worthy of me. And he that taketh not his cross, and followeth after me, is not worthy of me. (Matt. 10:34–38)

Now there it is in principle, and oh, how often has this been verified. The apostle Paul makes exactly the same point in his own way in these words: "He that is spiritual judgeth all things" (1 Cor. 2:15), by which he means, as I shall show you, that he has an understanding of these spiritual things. Then Paul adds hurriedly, "Yet he himself is judged of no man." He who is spiritual understands these things, but he himself is not understood by the other people who are not spiritual. That is the point that I am establishing.

And again surely this, like all these other points, needs no demonstration, no argument. Here are two men, take two brothers if you like. They are born of the same parents; they have the same essential characteristics, the same nature, and they have always done the same things together. One of them becomes born again, and the other does not. There is new divine life in the first; there is not in the second. Now I am saying that not only does the man who is born again become aware of the fact that it has happened to him, his brother also becomes aware that it has. He becomes aware that his brother is now somehow different. Now the brother who is born again is not trying to be different—he *is* different, and because he is different, of course, he thinks in a different way and behaves in a different way. But he is not deliberately trying to be odd and offensive; he is not condemning his brother who is unconverted. He loves him still and is more anxious about him than he has ever been and would do anything for him, and yet this unregenerate brother knows that something has come in that has put what he calls "a barrier between them." He says, "You are not like you used to be. This thing that has happened to you spoils everything; we are not like we used to be."

Now this is something that happens constantly. It happens not only between brothers but, as our Lord teaches elsewhere, between husbands and wives as well as between fathers and sons and mothers and daughters. One of the most striking examples of this I ever encountered happened in my own pastoral experience years ago. A man and wife (I had actually had the privilege of conducting their marriage service, though at that time neither of them was the kind of person I am describing) were both religious, nominal Christians like Nicodemus, but neither of them had been born again. After a few months the husband was truly regenerated and became a new man, and as the result of that he began to behave in the way that we are describing as being characteristic of this new man. And among other things this meant that he was at that place of worship to which we belonged, not only twice on Sunday and helping in the work of the Sunday school on Sunday afternoon, but also in the prayer meeting on Monday night, a fellowship meeting on Wednesday night, and the men's discussion group on theology on Saturday night. He never missed; he was always there. He still loved his wife, in fact loved her more than ever, and in a sense they were happy; but this thing had happened to him, and it had not happened to her.

Then one night this man was going home from a prayer meeting where we had been unusually conscious of the presence of God, and when he arrived home he was greeted by his wife who was in a flaming temper, and before he had had an opportunity of saying anything, she said to him, "You know I wish that you belonged to the Working Men's Club and not at that chapel. I would sooner see you being carried in here dead drunk than coming home every night from those prayer meetings and fellowships." Of course, she was very sorry afterward, and thank God, the rest of the story is that after a while she also received this same gift of life, and that very outburst was one of the things that brought her to see her need. She was appalled at this evil nature in her that could speak like that.

However, that is the point I am making. Here was a man who was a better husband than he had been before, and yet the unregenerate wife knew that there was now something in his life that continually came before her—God, the Lord Jesus Christ, the Holy Spirit—and she resented it. She was aware of this, and her awareness of it and her antagonism was the finest proof such a man could ever have of the fact that he had been born again. When this comes in, it is bigger than everything, and not only is the man himself aware of it, the unregenerate are aware of it. "He that is spiritual judgeth all things, yet he himself is judged of no man."

Now this is the contrast between being religious and being born again. If you are religious you will not be a problem to other persons because they may be religious themselves, and in any case the world never objects to a religious person as such. The formal religious person never gets persecuted. If you are the sort of person of whom it is known that you attend a place of worship occasionally or perhaps even every Sunday morning and no more, you will not get persecuted for that; that is quite a polite and nice thing to do. But if you give the impression that this is now the biggest thing in your life and it is affecting the whole of your personality, you will soon find that it makes a difference and that a kind of persecution will begin. The world never persecutes religion, but what it does persecute is Christlikeness. Our Lord said so himself. The more we are like him, the more the world will treat us as it treated him. "Yea," says Paul to Timothy, "And all that will live godly in Christ Jesus shall suffer persecution" (2 Tim. 3:12). "If the world hate you, ye know that it hated me before it hated you," says our Lord (John 15:18).

What a wonderful test this is. Are your friends, relatives, and associates, proving to you that you are born again? Are they aware that there is something in you now that is bigger, more important, more vital than the natural ties of blood and of birth and of everything else? Are they aware that you have become a different person, though you do not proclaim it or parade it? Then that is an absolute proof that you have received the life of God in your soul.

That leads me to the next characteristic, and the apostle Paul associates these things together. I have already talked about a spiritual interest. I must take that further and say that one of the best tests of having this life within is that one has a spiritual understanding—not only interest but understanding. This again is most important, and this is the way in which we differentiate not only between true Christianity and false Christianity—Christianity and religion if you like—it is the best way also of differentiating between knowledge that we have been born again and certain counterfeit spurious experiences that can be manufactured by the Devil. The Devil is always trying to counterfeit Christianity, and if he finds people who have been born again and who have certain experiences as a result of that, he will immediately proceed to counterfeit those experiences. He does not need to do that with the religious, but he does need to do that with Christianity because his kingdom is in danger when people are truly born again.

So how do you tell the difference between the true experience of regeneration and certain odd phenomena or experiences that people may have had as the result of cults or even as the result of spiritism or something like that? Here, I think, is one of the best ways of doing that. It is regeneration alone that can give one a true spiritual understanding. Those who are born again have a belief of the truth, they accept the truth, and by *the truth*, I mean the essential biblical message. Let us be clear about this. They believe it in the sense that it is clear to them; they have an understanding, an apprehension of it. Do not misunderstand me, I am not saying that everyone who is born again understands the whole of Christian truth. Of course not. That would be ridiculous. One goes on learning about these things throughout life; you can read books on theology and doctrine, and you can learn more and more. What I am saying is that those who are born again have an instinctive understanding of the truth in general, not all the particular details. They do not understand it all, but they now have an insight into these things that nobody else has.

Now I would emphasize the point that the believer's understanding is not perfect and entire because sometimes it has been represented as if that were the case, and Christian people have been grievously discouraged. The Devil has tormented them on that point. And that is why you will find that the church, when she has been alive throughout the ages, has always made different demands upon church membership and entering into the ministry. A man who is called to the ministry and who is ordained to preach should understand much more than a man or woman who just becomes a church member. This is obvious because he is going to be a teacher and a preacher and an expounder. But there is a basic minimum of understanding and comprehension that every born-again Christian has of necessity.

This, of course, is the difference between "the natural man" and "the spiritual man," and the second chapter of the First Epistle to the Corinthians is the most perfect exposition of this point that is to be found anywhere in the whole of Scripture. Again I would say that as I see things in this world at this present time and in the church in particular, I sometimes think that it is the most important chapter in the Bible at this moment. This difference between the natural man and the spiritual man is absolutely vital.

What does it mean? Well, here it is in 1 Corinthians, chapter 2, verse 14 in its essence: "The natural man receiveth not the things of the Spirit of God: for they are foolishness unto him: neither can he know them, because they are spiritually discerned." That is it. What is "the natural man"? The natural man is man as he is by birth, by nature. Who is the spiritual man? The spiritual man is the man who has been "born again," "born of the Spirit," the one in whom the Spirit of God resides. And what

Paul says is that the natural man *"receiveth not,"* he rejects the things of the Spirit of God, because "they are foolishness unto him." He cannot understand them, says Paul, because they are only "spiritually discerned," spiritually understood, and that is the very essence of this whole matter.

Then notice how the apostle works this out. "Which none of the princes of this world knew: for had they known it, they would not have crucified the Lord of glory" (1 Cor. 2:8). He means by "the princes of this world" the leaders, the top people of the world, not only in terms of royal or leading families but in terms of scholarship and learning and philosophy. He says they did not know Jesus Christ, they did not recognize him, they thought he was only a man. "Had they known it, they would not have crucified the Lord of glory."

What was the matter with them? It was not that they lacked scholarship. What they lacked was spiritual understanding, spiritual insight, spiritual discrimination. And not only does the natural man not have this, he can never produce it. You can pass through every university in the universe, and it will not help you in this matter, not at all; it will probably hinder you because it will give you pride of intellect. You are starting with your mind, you are out for understanding, and you cannot succeed; these things of God are foolishness to you.

Now do you see what a perfect test this is of the difference between being religious and being born again? You can understand religion in a sense, and I repeat, people are not troubled about you when you are religious. But that is not what I am talking about. I am talking about this spiritual life that leads to a spiritual understanding, and no one has this except a man or woman who is born again. None of the princes of this world knew of this. "As it is written, Eye hath not seen, nor ear heard, neither have entered into the heart of man, the things which God hath prepared for them that love him." Then Paul goes on, "But God hath revealed them unto us [that is to say, we who are born again, we who are truly Christian] by his Spirit; for the Spirit searcheth all things, yea, the deep things of God." Then he goes on to say, "Now we have received, not the spirit of the world, but the spirit which is of God, that we might know the things which are freely given to us of God." And he winds it up in this tremendous statement in verse 16: "For who hath known the mind of the Lord, that he may instruct him? But we have the mind of Christ," (1 Cor. 2:9–16). Those who are spiritual understand these things.

Now Paul is not only talking about apostles and leaders, he is talking about every single Christian, and this is the remarkable thing—and oh, how often has one seen it, and has seen it with rejoicing, in the life of the church: this spiritual perception is not dependent upon one's natural ability at all. The result is that you find unintelligent people with a greater spiritual understanding than great intellects who have not been born again. That is the amazing thing, and it is one of the most profound proofs, therefore, of the reality of rebirth in any single individual. There is, I say, a kind of intuitive knowledge that comes with this rebirth; it is inevitably a part of it, and it is a fact. It shows itself.

The poor "natural man," however, is fumbling and cannot understand. He is prepared to believe in religion, and he would like to be religious and may very well be religious. So he is reading books about religion and is delighted in the philosophical arguments and so on, but when you come to tell him about this rebirth and about the nature of Christ and the atonement, he says it is foolishness, it is rubbish. He cannot understand it; it seems immoral to him; he does not know what you are talking about. You suddenly have become ecstatic to him, and he does not like that sort of thing. He likes an orderly, refined, intellectual, intelligent, reasonable, logical religion because he can grasp that and handle it and master it. But of the other thing he says, "I don't understand," just as Nicodemus did. Of course he does not. "He that is spiritual judgeth all things, yet he himself is judged of no man." The natural man says that those who are born again are taking things a bit too seriously now, and he thinks they have gone soft—"They have a bit of a religious complex; they've gone psychological; they mustn't take these things too seriously; this is ridiculous." You are aware of all this, are you not? So if people are saying that about you, it is good evidence that you are born again.

Let us work this out just a little bit more. Those who are born again no longer spend the whole of their time just arguing about philosophy and science and things of that kind; they have passed all that. The man who is still arguing about preliminaries and a foundation and principles is a man who is telling us that he is not born again. So, you may say, is there any point in arguing? Yes, there is. You can show him very often that all his argumentation will lead him to nothing, that it will always bring him to that same blank wall, and then you pray that he may have the grace to submit and to see that his reasoning and arguing will never take him any further.

But now those who are born again have moved past all that. They are in no difficulty about preliminaries; their whole position is changed. They see that revelation is an absolute necessity. And they see that like this: they see the truth about their old nature, they see that they were blinded by sin and the god of this world and that in that condition they never could believe, and so of course these things were foolishness to them. But now they know that this operation of God has taken place in their souls. They do not argue about a miracle; they know it has happened to them. Miracles are facts—the supernatural, the miraculous. They do not argue about them; they know they are true. They are in the realm of the miraculous; they have been lifted to the realm of the supernatural themselves. So they do not argue about these things. They say, as an old hymn puts it, "Lord, I was blind: I could not see . . . I could not stir my lifeless soul to come to Thee." They know that nothing but the revelation of God can give them the knowledge of which they stand in need.

So this is a very good test. If you are still arguing—"Well, is this anything but . . . is the Bible anything more than men's thoughts and men's ideas?"—if that is your view, take it from me, you are not born again. Those who do not see the absolute necessity of revelation from God are not born again. Those who are born again have no difficulty about revelation and the miraculous and the supernatural. So they say, "I am dependent upon this." John Wesley used to say he had become a man of one Book. That is true, in a sense, of every born-again Christian.

Now this is the most remarkable thing: Christians do not have to argue with themselves to persuade themselves that they believe the Bible. They find themselves believing the Bible, and they only have to deal with residual problems and difficulties and the case put up against them. This is my way of putting in my language what John Calvin and others called *testimonum spiritus internus*. This how a man ever believes that the Bible is the Word of God. The Holy Spirit does two works: *testimonium spiritus externus* and *testimonium spiritus internus*.

It means this: in the Bible itself, if you take the trouble to go right through it, you will see evidence of a supernatural authorship and consistency in the message, though there are sixty-six books written at different times by different kinds of men with such long intervals between them. There is this tremendous argument that is in the Book itself. It is outside me, but it is there. There is the testimony of the Spirit in the Word if you like.

But then there is the testimony of the Spirit in me, inside me, and these two things meet together. In other words you never persuade a man to believe the Bible by arguing. The Holy Spirit alone can do that. You can marshal all these arguments, and to the one who believes the Bible they are very powerful and very wonderful. But you never get a man who is unregenerate to accept them.

But the first thing that happens to men and women who are born again is this: having this spiritual principle in them, this becomes open to them, it is inevitable, nothing else could be true, this is the Word of God: *testimonium spiritus internus*.

So those who are born again have no difficulty whatsoever about the broad doctrines of salvation. They do not understand them perfectly or fully, but they know that the biblical doctrine of sin is true—true of them, true of all. They have no trouble believing the doctrine of condemnation and of hell. If you still dislike the doctrine of condemnation and the judgment of the Law, I cannot see that you are born again; you are thinking as a natural man. If you are truly born again you say with Charles Wesley:

And can it be that I should gain
An interest in the Saviour's blood?
Died He for me, who caused His pain . . .[2]

That is born-again men or women speaking. Also they have no difficulty about the plan of redemption; they rejoice in it. No man could save them; no teacher could save them. There must be something divine, there must be incarnation, and it has happened. And our Lord must give perfect obedience to the Law; he must take my punishment and bear it in his own body. There is no trouble about these things to the one who is born again. These things are not only inevitable, they delight in them and in the Holy Spirit and in regeneration and in all these cardinal principles concerning the way of salvation, in our Lord and his work, in the Holy Spirit and this mighty act and event of regeneration.

These, then, are the tests and the signs. Are you aware of something new within you? Are you surprised at yourself? Do you surprise other people? And do you have this essential, new, intuitive understanding of the things of the Spirit of God? "God hath revealed them unto us by his Spirit: for the Spirit searcheth all things, yea, the deep things of God." Are you amazed at the fact that you delight in hearing about these things? Are you enjoying them? And are you amazed at the fact that you are doing so? If so you are born again and you are a child of God. You are no longer a natural person; you are a spiritual man, a spiritual woman. Give him, the author of it all, all the praise and the honor and the glory!

# 5

# Marks of the Spiritual Life

## JOHN 3:8

Sunday morning sermon preached in
Westminster Chapel, February 6, 1966.

*May the grace of the Lord Jesus Christ and the love of God and the fel-
lowship and the communion of the Holy Spirit abide and continue with
us now, throughout the remainder of this day, throughout this short and
certain earthly life and pilgrimage, and until we shall see him as he is in
all his glory and go to be with him throughout eternity. Amen.*

\*    \*    \*

The verse to which I should like to call your attention this morning is
the eighth verse in the third chapter of the Gospel according to St. John:

> The wind bloweth where it listeth, and thou hearest the sound
> thereof, but canst not tell whence it cometh, and whither it goeth:
> so is every one that is born of the Spirit. (John 3:8)

We are dealing particularly with this word *so*, meaning "like that,
similar to" that is everyone who is born of the Spirit. We are dealing, in
other words, with the marks, or the characteristics if you like, of the new

life in Christ Jesus, which is given to those who are born again. We are doing this because this is one of those foundational principles in connection with the Christian life, which the failure to understand must of necessity not only lead to trouble but to eventual disaster. This is the great thing, as we've been seeing, that is emphasized in this well-known story concerning Nicodemus, this ruler of the Jews who went to seek an interview with our Lord one night. Here was a man who was anxious to go on, seeing something in our Lord that he clearly didn't have himself. He was anxious to have this. But as the whole story indicates, recognizing exactly the man's position, knowing, as we are told at the end of the previous chapter what is in men, the truth about everyone of us, our Lord interrupts Nicodemus and points out to him that "except a man be born again, he cannot see the kingdom of God," let alone enter into it. He must be "born again," "born of water and of the Spirit" (John 3:3, 5).

Now here was the trouble with Nicodemus, and I've been suggesting that it is the trouble still with large numbers of people, especially perhaps those who have been brought up in a Christian atmosphere—home, church, Sunday school, and so on. It is this fatal error of assuming that we are Christians, which leads in turn, of course, to a desire to grow before we've been born, a desire to continue on a journey when really we're not on the right road at all. That's the great lesson of this story, and therefore we are interpreting it like this: the first thing we have to do is to discover whether or not we have been born again, as we see here in this great announcement of the way that leads to God and to heaven, and it informs us that except and unless we are born again we have no entry and we have no part or portion in the life of God. Therefore this is the most serious thing that people can ever consider together.

Now we've been looking at some of the characteristics of this life. I've said that a man who is truly born again reveals that. It is the most obvious thing about him. We read of our Lord in the Gospels that he could not be hidden, and the Christian can't be hidden. If there is this life of God in the soul, it makes itself known. It's the most obvious thing about us. There are other things still true of us, but this is the most obvious and outstanding thing. It's the thing that marks us above everything else. We've also seen that we are conscious of being dealt with. We've been humbled. We've truly repented. There is a fundamental seriousness about us, not a pomposity or a solemnity, but a fundamental seriousness, as there was in our Lord, who was described as "a man of sorrows, and acquainted with grief." That is because of the world into which he came. And it shall be true of us. We're all so conscious of the new life and the new nature within us, and that in turn leads us to be surprised at ourselves. I cannot see that a man can be a Christian without being amazed at himself. If you can understand yourself and all that you're doing, I say it's indicative of the fact that the new life is not in you. But when the new life comes and you become a partaker of the divine nature, you can scarcely believe that you are who and what you are. This thing is so astounding and so different. And in turn we saw that this leads to the fact that other people can see the difference. This life when it comes becomes a kind of sword separating us, dividing us, even from those who may be members of our families, as our Lord himself said. And everybody senses this, not only the man who has the new life; others who lack it are aware that there's something new and something different about this person.

And then finally we ended the last sermon by indicating that this also and of necessity involves a spiritual understanding. That was the thing poor Nicodemus didn't have. He couldn't understand it. "How can a man be born when he is old?" he says. That's the rationalist. That's the natural man with his own powers. How can these things be? But once a man receives this life, it leads to understanding. The apostle Paul is able to claim for himself and for all who are born again, "We have the mind of Christ." Very well. But he doesn't stop there. The next thing I want to direct our attention to is this, and the analogy of God makes this obvious and inevitable: once one has this life that leads to spiritual apprehension and understanding, one always desires more and more of this knowledge and understanding. There is this principle of growth in life. You see it in the seed. You put the little seeds into the ground, but there's a germ of life there that's always expanding and growing, stretching out, seeking more and more. That is the great characteristic of life. This is what differentiates something living from an inanimate object. And this is very true of those who are born again. The Scripture reminds us that we go through these stages. We are born. We are babes in Christ. Then we begin to grow. We become children. We become young men. This is John's specification in his first epistle. Children—young men—old men. There's this growth and this development. That is the nature of this life, just as it is of every other kind of life. Therefore we are entitled to deduce from this that one of the marks of the man who is born again is that he desires more—more of this food, more of this drink, more of this nutriment that is going to feed his mind and enable it to understand more and better and to go on and to grow in grace and in the knowledge of the Lord.

Now let's be clear about this. This obviously is something that varies. I'm not saying there's a standard that one must always desire in every particular case. Obviously not. As you get variations in growth between members of the same family, and as you get variations in the rate of growth in every one of us, so it happens in the spiritual life. All I'm contending for is that there is this element of desire for more. Now this is put to us in many ways in the Scripture. Take that verse from the First Epistle of Peter, the second chapter: "As newborn babes, desire the sincere milk of the word, that ye may grow thereby: if so be ye have tasted that the Lord is gracious" (1 Pet. 2:2). Now you see the supposition. If you have tasted that the Lord is gracious, he's arguing in a sense, though he puts it in the form of an exhortation, you *will* desire more of this unadulterated, pure word. That is true. He gives a picture of a newborn baby who desires milk, and so we desire the sincere milk of the Word. The apostle Paul puts it in terms of his own experience. This is, it seems to me, is the norm that we should always be recognizing and by which we should evaluate ourselves. The apostle, in spite of his amazing experiences, his unusual attainments, the work that he had been privileged to do as the Apostle to the Gentiles, can still say in Philippians 3:10 (this is his desire), "That I may know him." You see, concerning the things he used to glory in and boast of he now says:

> I have suffered the loss of all things, and do count them but dung,
> that I may win Christ [that's what he's after], and be found in him,

not having mine own righteousness, which is of the law, but that which is through the faith of Christ, the righteousness which is of God by faith: that I may know him, and the power of his resurrection, and the fellowship of his sufferings, being made conformable unto his death; if by any means I might attain unto the resurrection of the dead. Not as though I had already attained [he's not satisfied; he hasn't arrived; he hasn't reached the goal], either were already perfect: but I follow after, if that I may apprehend that for which also I am apprehended of Christ Jesus. Brethren, I count not myself to have apprehended: but this one thing I do, forgetting those things which are behind, and reaching forth unto those things which are before, I press toward the mark for the prize of the high calling of God in Christ Jesus. Let us therefore, as many as be perfect, be thus minded. (Phil. 3:8–15)

That's it. You see, he's not satisfied with what he has. He has a great deal. He knows so much. He thanks God for all that. But he's not satisfied. He desires more, and he's pressing after it. He can never have too much of this.

Now the very nature of the life principle within us produces that desire. In other words, a very good test of life is an awareness of our ignorance. The more a man knows in any realm, the more he's aware of his ignorance. And it's very true here. With this life you're given spiritual apprehension and knowledge, and that in turn makes you aware of your ignorance. You become aware, for instance, of your past ignorance, and you're amazed at yourself. How often have I been told this, and there's nothing that rejoices the heart of a pastor more than this. People come to me and say, "You know, I simply cannot understand how I was so slow in seeing it. I'm amazed at myself." They remained in such ignorance perhaps for years, but now they see it. And they see, of course, the terrible danger of ignorance. That is the ultimate trouble with the unbeliever—he's ignorant. You see, the gospel of Jesus is truth, and truth gives light and instruction and knowledge to the mind and to the understanding. When a man is born again, he begins to realize that he had been dwelling in the ignorance of darkness. The apostle Paul says that about himself, you remember. He's amazed that he's a preacher at all, that this grace should be given to him who was before, he said, "A blasphemer, and a persecutor, and injurious." But he says, "I did it ignorantly in unbelief" (1 Tim. 1:13). The moment a man receives life and light and knowledge, he sees his former ignorance, and he's appalled at it. He's horrified at it. Fancy a man persecuting Christ, hating him, regarding Christ as a blasphemer. He sees it now, and he's appalled at the terrible dangers of ignorance. And that, of course, stimulates at once the desire to receive greater and greater knowledge. He realizes what he's missed in the past, and he doesn't want to go on missing this.

Now this argument works unconsciously, subconsciously, but it does work. And the man, therefore, desires greater and greater knowledge. And on top of that he begins to realize the dangers of ignorance. He's been given the mind of Christ; the Spirit has revealed the deep things of God to him. And he's clear, as we indicated earlier, on the fundamental doctrines of salvation. But he also becomes aware, as he never was before, of the adversary, of the enemy, of the accuser of the brethren, of the subtleties of the Devil. He knew nothing about that before. The unbeliever, you know, not only doesn't believe in the Lord Jesus Christ, he doesn't believe in the Devil. And whether a man believes in the Devil or not is a very good test of whether he is a believer or not. The unbeliever ridicules the doctrines of salvation even though he knows nothing about our conflict, which is not against flesh and blood, but against the principalities and the powers, against our adversary the Devil. But the believer has this knowledge. And so a man who has new life and has this spiritual apprehension and understanding realizes that in a sense he's in a very dangerous position. He's going to be the special object of the attacks of the Devil. What will the Devil do with him? Well, the Devil will not try to ridicule the whole of Christianity. What the Devil will now do with him will be to try to insinuate certain heresies, certain errors, certain doubts and queries and questions about particular matters. That's what the Devil did in the early church, as we see in the New Testament, and that's what he's been doing ever since. He's very active at the present time among evangelicals. They are looking again at the early chapters of Genesis. Have they been wrong all these years? They've been looking anew at evolution and so on, the supernatural. This is the subtlety of the Devil.

Now the man who is truly spiritual and does not merely have an intellectual knowledge of the Bible recognizes these subtle dangers. And therefore he has a fear of going astray, of being led astray into error, into heresy, into mistaken notions. He can see from the New Testament that this happened to the early Christians. The history of the church confirms that; so he's aware of this terrible danger as it confronts him. And therefore his very instinct urges him to have more and more of this knowledge.

You see what I'm trying to suggest to you, my dear friends. If you are one of those people who said, "Oh yes, I made my decision, and I've been a Christian ever since," and you don't want very much more, well, that tells us a lot about you. The people who think they have it all, that they've arrived, don't. What you find about them is that at the end of fifty years they're exactly as they were at the beginning. They don't know any more, they don't understand any more, they have no deeper experience. They started as babes, and they ended as babes. Though they may be old in years, they're still spiritual babes. And you find oftentimes that such children are fractious, and they dislike learning. They dislike knowledge; they don't want further understanding. The suggestion that they are not complete they dislike very much indeed. Children often don't want to go to school. Well, that's sometimes true in the spiritual realm. But when there is true life, one begins to understand these dangers and desires more knowledge, more instruction, further light on these spiritual problems in order to be saved from these various errors and dangers.

But let me put this positively, because it's much more wonderful when you look at it in the positive way. The man who really has this life in him and has this spiritual understanding realizes that he's like a man who has been brought in from the street into a great palace. There he was in the street with the rain and the mud, lacking food and lacking anything that gives real delight and satisfaction. Suddenly he's taken hold of and is brought in. He's given new clothes. He's cleansed in the vestibule, and he's ushered into this great palace. And there is food, and there are treasures of art and of knowledge and of everything good. Now the Christian is a man who realizes that's the truth about him. The Christian is not merely a man who knows now that he's been forgiven, and that's the end of it all. Not at all. That's merely the introduction. He's been ushered into a great treasure house. What is he facing? Well, the apostle Paul speaks of this in writing to the Ephesians in chapter 3. He says that he is commissioned now to go to declare "among the Gentiles the *unsearchable* riches of Christ" (Eph. 3:8). Later on in that same chapter he states that his business is to make known unto people what is "the breadth, and length, and depth, and height; and to know the love of Christ, which passeth knowledge, that ye might be filled with all the fullness of God" (Eph. 3:18–19). Now the moment a man gets any sort of inkling of that, he's stretching every nerve. He wants to get at this and after it. He sees all this tremendous treasure, and he is anxious to partake of it.

Do you know anything of this eagerness? Do you know anything of this hunger and thirst after this? Are you delving into the mystery, the profundities of this great Word of God? You see all the treasure that is here, and you're following it, and you can't keep up with it because it's ever going ahead of you and eluding you as you press toward the mark. You're not satisfied. How can you be? What you have is wonderful. Of course it is. But you don't stop there. It's like a man at a great banquet, if you like. You don't spend the whole of your time just drinking soup. That's merely an appetizer. That's merely something to stimulate your appetite. Look at the menu, my dear friend. Look right through it. There's an order in these things, but it gets more wonderful as you go on. The man who is born again is a man who has some consciousness of this, and there is a deep desire within him to have more and more of the sincere milk of the Word, to grow in grace and in the knowledge of the Lord.

Now let me put this still more particularly in this way, and I am doing this because I am trying to be very practical in this matter. This, I believe more and more, is a valuable and subtle test. Let's test ourselves by it. The man who has true spiritual life is always a man who is not content with the preliminaries. What do I mean by that? Well, as I've been saying, there are steps and stages in this truth. There is foundational truth. That's not my term; it's the apostle's term. "Other foundation can no man lay than that which is laid" (1 Cor. 3:11). But then, you see, you build on the foundation, and you go on. Or, to use the language of the author of the epistle to the Hebrews, there are what he calls in the first verse of chapter 6, "The principles of the doctrine of Christ." "Therefore leaving the principles of the doctrine of Christ, let us go on unto perfection" (Heb. 6:1). What does "principles" mean? It means first principles, the elements, the beginning, the simple foundational truths. But that is only the introduction. They lead to others, and these, of course, because they're deeper, are more difficult. And they in turn lead to others that are still deeper and still more difficult. As you go on, you have to use your mind more. You have to make a greater effort. Well, this is something that we all surely agree with. Anybody who's ever studied any subject knows that. During preliminary lectures, as you read the early chapters of a textbook, it's fairly simple and plain sailing. But as you go on it becomes more involved, it becomes more difficult, and you have to make more effort. Yes, but you're going on, and you're grasping it more and more. And you're hoping eventually you'll get right into the depths. It's exactly like that in spiritual life.

And this, I say, is a most important test. Take it in terms of the Bible itself. I think it's quite right that children should only read a few verses of the Bible every day. They're children, and you treat them as children. But when people in older age later on in life who have been Christians for many years are still only reading a little section, surely there's something wrong. Or take books that help you understand the Bible. If you're a child, you want just a little comment. A series of books were published called Told to the Children. They abstracted stories from the whole Bible to make them easy for the children. That's sound method and good teaching. But, of course, as you get older you don't read Told to the Children. You read the whole thing. You have to wade through a lot of stuff that may appear to you very uninteresting. But the more you do it, the more you appreciate it, and the more you enjoy it.

Now there's something wrong when people keep reading the Told to the Children edition of the Scriptures and the simple comments on the Scriptures there. As one goes on, one should be aware of the depth of the

Word. One should be aware of the struggle to apprehend it and be ready to make the effort and to desire to do so in order that one may enter into this apprehension of something that is bigger and deeper and still more difficult. Now let me show you how the author of the epistle to the Hebrews makes this very point. You see, he's writing to these Hebrews to comfort them and to encourage them in a time of tribulation through which they are passing, and he wants to unfold the great truth to them, particularly the great truth about the person of the Lord Jesus Christ. That was their initial trouble, indeed their central error. And after putting it in various forms comparing and contrasting him with the prophets and with the angels and with Moses and Aaron, the author comes to this great truth concerning the Lord Jesus Christ as our great High Priest after the order of Melchizedek. And this, he says, is the most wonderful thing of all. But then he has to put it like this in chapter 5, verse 11:

> Of whom we have many things to say, and hard to be uttered, seeing ye are dull of hearing. For when for the time ye ought to be teachers, ye have need that one teach you again which be the first principles of the oracles of God; and are become such as have need of milk, and not of strong meat. For every one that useth milk is unskillful in the word of righteousness: for he is a babe. But strong meat belongeth to them that are of full age, even those who by reason of use have their senses exercised to discern both good and evil. (Heb. 5:11–14)

That's the position. And I'm arguing that a man who truly has this life within him, who has been given this apprehension of deeper truth, is anxious to obtain it and is therefore anxious to make this effort. He wants to go on and to appropriate this. He's no longer childish, almost babyish.

Christian people, are we still taking Christian truth in a tabloid form, or are we facing it and tackling it on a deeper level? We're living in an age, of course, that wants everything in tabloid form. It's the age of digests. Even in biographies they no longer write a full biography. It's a sort of study, a kind of picture. This is the tragedy, I feel, of the hour. People want everything short, snappy, simple, in a digest, in tabloid form. They start like that, and they go on like that throughout the whole of their lives. As we read the lives of our spiritual fathers, we find that they struggled with the Word. They read massive commentaries, and they struggled with them. They read books on doctrine and on theology, and thus they deepened and developed a deeper understanding, and they were bigger men and women as a result. And they began to know something about the higher reaches of the spiritual life, the possibilities in the life of grace. You don't enter in and then just maintain that the rest of your life. You must go on, launch out into the deep. You press forward after the mark, the prize of the high calling of God in Christ Jesus our Lord.

My friends, is there evidence of growth and of development and of enlargement in your life? Do you resent the effort, or are you making an effort? Do you say, "Ah, well, I have all I want. That's enough for me. I don't have time for more"? If you don't, that just means you don't know what's in the treasure house. You've just poked your head in through the door and said, "That's all right. As long as I'm nearby . . ." I say, look at each item. Stand back. Have another view of it. Examine it closely. You have your guidebook. Go around the exhibition. You haven't much time, you know. Time is passing. It's fleeting. There are treasures here—"the unsearchable riches of Christ," the truth of God, the mind of Christ, the love of God in Christ, which passes knowledge.

Are we satisfied with first principles, the beginnings, the elementary statements, the childish position? I say, if we are, we'd better examine ourselves again very thoroughly, because there is an instinct about life that makes one desire more and more. The man who truly appreciates is the man who wants more. He can't be satisfied.

As a final argument under this heading, the man who really has this life in him desires more and more of this knowledge and of this truth in order that he may help others. You see, he's not living for himself any longer. He has understanding, and he wants to help others. How can a man help others if he doesn't know, if he can't explain? The apostle Peter in his first epistle, in the third chapter says, "Be ready always to give an answer to every man that asketh you a reason of the hope that is in you." Or as a hymn puts it:

Men die in darkness at your side,
Without a hope to cheer the tomb;
Take up the torch and wave it wide,
The torch that lights time's thickest gloom.[1]

The apostle Paul in Philippians 2 says we are like the lights in the heavens, luminaries shining in the darkness of the night. The world is in darkness, and because we've been born again, we have become the light of the world, because we belong to Jesus, the light of the world, and reflections of his light shine through us as we "hold forth the word of life" amidst "a crooked and perverse nation." The man who has spiritual understanding and apprehension feels this. He says, how can I help these people? Well, he can't help them if he doesn't know the truth himself. Experience is essential, but merely to relate your experience doesn't answer people's questions.

So we feel the desire to know the truth and to have an understanding of it so we can explain it and expound it to others and give them answers to their questions and help them in every conceivable way. Those are the things that urge a man to desire more and more of this spiritual apprehension that he has received as the gift of God.

But let me work out that last statement in a little more detail. I'll put it as a separate principle, a tenth test of this new life in Christ Jesus. The regenerate has a concern for the unregenerate. Surely this follows and doesn't need any proof. We've have a great demonstration of this in the first chapter of John's Gospel, where we find cameos of the first disciples whom our Lord called. John the Baptist was standing one day with two of his disciples, and he pointed out Jesus and said, "Behold the Lamb of God." And they went and spoke to our Lord, and he took them to his house. "They came and saw where he dwelt, and abode with him that day: for it was about the tenth hour." And we read that one of the two who heard John speak and followed Jesus was Andrew, Simon Peter's brother. "He first findeth his own brother Simon, and saith unto him, We have found the Messiah, which is, being interpreted, the Christ. And he brought him to Jesus." And Philip did exactly the same. "Philip findeth

Nathanael, and saith unto him, We have found him, of whom Moses in the law, and the prophets, did write, Jesus of Nazareth, the son of Joseph" (John 1:36–45).

This is the sort of instinct that is the characteristic of this life. And later on we read in a most interesting way about the ordinary Christians in Jerusalem. A great persecution broke out in the early church right at the beginning. You read about it in chapter 8 of the book of Acts of the Apostles. "As for Saul [the one who became Paul], he made havock of the church, entering into every house, and haling men and women committed them to prison. Therefore they that were scattered abroad went every where preaching the word" (Acts 8:3–4). Now the word translated *preaching* is a most interesting one. Somebody suggested that a good translation would be, "Therefore they that were scattered abroad went everywhere gossiping the word." Gossiping it. We are told in the next verse, "Philip went down to the city of Samaria, and preached Christ unto them" (Acts 8:5). He was an evangelist, a preacher. That's proclamation. These didn't preach in that sense. The two words are different. They spoke the gospel in conversation. They explained it. They gave others an understanding. They said, "We are persecuted for this reason," and they began to tell people about the truth everywhere they went. As a result of this, the apostles alone were left in Jerusalem (v. 1), but these others were scattered abroad throughout the regions of Judea and Samaria. So here are ordinary Christian people, and they tell others about the gospel. Why? Because they have a concern for them.

Now this, again, I want to try to show is a really subtle test. It's a good test to differentiate between a religious person and a truly Christian person. The religious person does not have this concern about the unregenerate. He is religious, and he's generally satisfied with his religion, and he's self-satisfied. Not so with the Christian, with the spiritually minded person. You see, the religious man not only does not have a concern for others, he has nothing to offer. He's a good man. He lives a moral life, and he's amazed that others don't, and he looks at them and despises them. He's like the Pharisees. You can't give your morality to somebody else. You can't give your rectitude to another man. He sees a man in the gutter. How terrible. But he can't help him. But the Christian doesn't look at the man in the gutter like that. Remember the parable of the good Samaritan.

Here's a very good test then. There is in the man who has new life a concern about those whom he sees to be lacking it. But a problem arises just here, and I think it's an important one. I think it's one of those more or less subtle distinctions that nevertheless is really important. Somebody may say to me, "But you can't be right in what you're saying. I know many people at the present time whom I don't regard as Christians. I can't regard them as born-again Christians, but they are manifesting a great proselytizing zeal. They don't believe the gospel as you and I do, but they come to our doors, and they give up their Saturday afternoons, and they're selling literature and distributing leaflets and tracts." This tremendous zeal of the cults and these aberrations from the Christian truth are admired by many. "Oh," says somebody, "surely your point therefore collapses. You are saying that one of the tests and signs of the fact that a man has this new life of God is that he has a concern about others and does something about it. What about these people?" I grant this is a most important point, and it seems to me that the answer to the question reveals the true nature of this spiritual life, which is from God. There is such a thing as carnal zeal, even in connection with Christianity, for we see carnal zeal in these cults and false religions that are round and about us at the present time.

How can we tell the difference between the two? I will now suggest some of the tests. With the false, the carnal, here are the characteristics. It is invariably suggested to people to do this because of the authorities over them. It isn't that a man feels the desire to do it—he's told to do it. He's in; now he's told to go get another. He's put into it at once. The man doesn't work it out, as it were. It doesn't come from his heart. It's imposed upon him. He becomes part of a system. It's the thing to do, and the moment you're in you start your activity and your working. Now the very way in which these people do their work and the way in which they talk about it always seems to me to betray them completely. There is a lightness, there is a glibness, there is a mechanical element about it that marks it for what it is. In addition there is generally an element of excitement. Anything that's organized and worked up and done in this way always has this element of excitement. Carnality is always excited, and you see it coming out in this kind of activity.

Another way of putting it is, perhaps, that the technique is always so obvious. They all do it in almost exactly the same way. They almost look the same and appear the same, and they speak in the same way. It is a technique, and it's always characterized, of course, by clichés and by certain pet phrases and expressions. And you're always given the impression that what they're really up for is the success of the cause. Their interest is always in numbers. Interest in numbers is always indicative of carnality. And they're impatient with you. They want to get adherence. They want to get a large number of converts. They want to be able to state how many have been obtained. That's the whole attitude. It's mechanical. It's carnal. It's worldly minded. It's the method of big business rather than what we are talking about. And so you get this element of impatience manifesting itself.

But what of this other thing of which I am trying to speak? It's much more difficult to put into words, but it's very real and very different. It is the difference between life and mechanism. It's the difference between fruit growing on a tree and the manufactured counterfeit. Oh, how subtle this is. I am pressing this because, alas, I am old enough to have seen a great deal along this line in my pastoral life and experience. You've seen people like this. They come into the Christian life, and they've been so busy and so active you rather felt you'd never been a Christian. But where are they now? What's happened to them? Outside the church and the Christian life. It was nothing but carnal zeal. The Devil will persuade us to do that even in the Christian life, this counterfeit of his. You can have this great zeal, proselytizing zeal, but it's false, and it tries to insinuate itself into the true. But the characteristic of true zeal is the element of spontaneity. It's something that arises within. It isn't that a man is told, "Get out there; do this, that, and the other." No, no; here's a man who has become conscious of this life of God in his soul, this spiritual apprehension, and he begins to think, and he begins to observe others. He realizes the darkness they're in, and he begins, therefore, to be conscious of a concern within him.

I almost always prefer a Christian who's afraid at first to try to win another rather than the Christian who does it with extreme ease. There's a sensitiveness about this. Respect for another's personality is a good sign. The man who does it in spite of initial difficulty is the one who, to me, is demonstrating the truly spiritual life. Here's a man who because he has an understanding of the truth begins to feel a deep concern for others. He's not anxious to get proselytes, but he's troubled about them. He's worried about them. He knows grief of soul concerning them. Paul talks about making up in his own body what remains of the sufferings of Christ. Jesus came into the world because of his grief for our lost souls, and he grieved at the grave of Lazarus and again in the Garden of Gethsemane. Now the man who has Jesus's life in him is a man who doesn't do things mechanically. The Devil can produce that, and man himself can arrange and organize that. But here is a man who knows something of a soul agony for the souls of others. He feels something of the compassion that our Lord felt.

We are told that when our Lord looked out on the multitude, he saw them as sheep without a shepherd, and he had compassion upon them. The man who has something of Jesus's life in him knows something of this compassion, and he's not lighthearted, setting out to get new converts. There's a deep seriousness in him. And in this matter, in this seriousness is something that runs right through the life of the man who is truly born again. He realizes what he's doing and knows it is not something light and glib and easy. He's dealing with souls. Eternal destinies are involved. The Holy Spirit is engaged. So there is this deep seriousness.

I've heard men talking glibly about handling souls. I remember one poor man, it seemed to me, who when he talked about souls was talking in much the same way as when he talked about handling fish. But the man who has this life in him realizes that the thing is serious, profound; it's an eternal matter. So he's a man, I say, who prays about this. The soul is on his heart, and he prays to God. He may be in agony. This is the truth of spiritual things. And above all he has great patience. He knows that he would not be what he is were it not for the patience of the Lord with him. So if a man doesn't accept his witness immediately, he doesn't leave the other in disgust and go on to the next. He's patient. He's long-suffering. He's ready to bear with him. He has such a concern for the man's soul that he will not let him go, because he himself belongs to the Lord who would not let him go. And thus in his life, in his attitude toward the unregenerate he is reproducing, or rather there is reproduced in him, the life of his blessed Lord and Master.

My friends, do we know much about this concern, real deep concern for the souls of others? Does it weigh upon us? Do we know something of this burden? Does it grieve you? Does it trouble you? Are you praying about it? Do you realize that nothing but a great outpouring of the Spirit of God can deal with such a situation? Or are you still in the realm of organizing? What can we do about it? These are the tests. The spiritual outlook is one that realizes the depth and the gravity of the problem, but also the heights and the endless limits of the grace of God.

Well, God willing, we'll go on with this examination in the next sermon. May he give us grace to examine ourselves in the light of some of these thoughts.

We praise and bless Thee, gracious Lord,
Our Savior, kind and true,
For all the old things passed away,
For all Thou hast made new.[1]

6

# The Christian and the World

JOHN 3:8

Sunday morning sermon preached in
Westminster Chapel, February 13, 1966.

We continue our study of this great verse, this most vital and momentous statement. We have been considering the essence of the teaching, and the important thing, therefore, is that we should appreciate something of the content of this little word *so*. "So is every one [like that, in the case of every one] that is born of the Spirit." You do not understand this regeneration, this rebirth, but you see its results, the effects that it produces, and that is what we are engaged in studying now.

I am laying down as a fundamental proposition that the most important thing for any one of us in this life is to know whether we are born again or not. There is nothing more important than that. This is the dividing line between being religious and being truly Christian. Those who are truly Christians are men and women who are "born again," "born of the Spirit." A mighty act of God has taken place in their souls, and according to our Lord's illustration, this is something that can be known. It can be known by its results, by its effects, and that is what we are considering. We are examining ourselves in the light of the biblical teaching with regard to the manifestations of the life of God in the souls of men.

Now we have already considered a number of things. We have said that when people are born again, that is the most obvious thing about them. It strikes you at once; it is the biggest thing in their lives. Many influences have made them what they are, but this, because it is the life of God, is obviously the outstanding one. The other manifestation is that they are conscious of being humbled; you cannot be a Christian without being humbled. To be a Christian means that you realize that you were so hopeless by nature that nothing but a new birth could put you right. You cannot be improved—you must be born again; so you are humbled. So you know what it is to be truly repentant, what it is to have a fundamental seriousness in a world like this, and you are obviously conscious that there is new life within you.

You are surprised and amazed at yourself. You say, "Is it possible? Am I the same person? What has happened to me?" You cannot be a Christian without being surprised at yourself. Something new has come into your life, new life from God, and you cannot have that without being astonished. And indeed, as I pointed out, others are equally aware of it and are equally surprised. If we do not surprise other people who are not Christians, there is something wrong with us, if we are Christians at all. The people who lack this life recognize when we receive it; they are conscious of something new, and a kind of division comes in between us and them. It is inevitable. Our Lord said it would happen. He said he had come to bring a sword that divides a man from his father, and the mother from her daughter, and so on. This new life differentiates us, and everybody is aware of it, not only us but others also.

Then we have seen that it gives us a spiritual understanding and a desire for more and more of that. As a newborn babe desires milk, so we "as newborn babes, desire the sincere milk of the word, that [we] may grow thereby" (1 Pet. 2:2).

And this new life also invariably inevitably creates within us a desire that others may have it also. You cannot have new life from God in your soul without immediately desiring that everyone you know and especially those who are nearest and dearest to you may have the same. This has come to you, and it is so marvelous, so wonderful that by an inevitable instinct, you feel concerned about others.

Let us now then go on to the next point, and I am trying to put these in a kind of spiritual, logical order. So the next result of the new life in the soul (a test that we apply to ourselves) is this: when people are born again, for the first time in their lives they begin to see through the world. They begin to understand the world in which they live and what it is.

Now this, again, is very important; it is one of those points that helps us draw the distinction between being religious and having the new life. That is what this story of Nicodemus illustrates to perfection, so that we can test ourselves by it. The story of Nicodemus is invaluable to those of us who were brought up in a religious atmosphere. We went to church as a custom and habit, part of the social routine or whatever, and we thought we were Christians. But we were not. We discovered we had never been Christians; we were only religious.

Now religious people have their morality, of course; they recognize certain things as being wrong and condemn them. They try to avoid them, and they are troubled when they commit such acts or thoughts, whatever they may be. But they never get beyond that. What they are not aware of at all is what the New Testament calls "the world."

Now men or women who are not born again, those who are just good, moral, religious people, know nothing about the world in this New Testament sense. To illustrate what I mean, let me read some of the statements that are made about this, particularly in the first epistle of John. Listen to John writing to these early Christians:

> Love not the world, neither the things that are in the world. If any man love the world, the love of the Father is not in him. For all that is in the world, the lust of the flesh, and the lust of the eyes, and the pride of life, is not of the Father, but is of the world. And the world passeth away, and the lust thereof: but he that doeth the will of God abideth for ever. (1 John 2:15–17)

And again there is a statement toward the beginning of the fifth chapter of that epistle where we read, "For whatsoever is born of God [that is it; that is what we are dealing with] overcometh the world: and this is the victory that overcometh the world, even our faith" (1 John 5:4). That is what I am talking about, and this is something that no one knows anything at all about until he or she is born again. Religious people know about particular things that are wrong, but they never know anything more than that. But when someone is born again and is given this spiritual insight and understanding, he or she begins to recognize what the Bible calls "the world."

What is "the world"? Of course, John does not mean the physical universe. In the Scriptures "the world" is the whole outlook of mankind upon life without God. It is everything without God. So this can include being good, it can include being religious, because there are many such people. They are very good people on one level, but God really does not come into their thinking or living at all. If it could be proved—which it cannot and never can be—that God did not exist, it would not make any difference to them at all. They have thought in terms of their moral codes and their sense of right and wrong and so on, but they have never thought in terms of God. It is all human thinking, human philosophy, human understanding. They have never considered life in terms of God, the unseen, the spiritual, the eternal.

That is what the Bible means by "the world." It means man's thinking apart from God and the way in which the world is organized without him. So it is a very comprehensive term. It includes what people call "good" as well as what they call "bad." "The world" is not confined to gross, flagrant, obvious, vile sin; it includes that, but it also includes that which may be highly cultural, that which may be interested in beauty and in art and in quite a number of benevolent things, but God is not included. "The world" includes all of that. Worldliness means thinking of yourself and your life in this world, and the whole of life in the world, without God.

And beyond that this world mind, this world outlook, this worldliness, is entirely due to the influence of the Devil. The Bible calls the Devil "the god of this world"; it calls him "the prince of the power of the air, the spirit that now worketh in the children of disobedience." That is what the apostle Paul tells the Ephesians in chapter 2 of his letter to them: "You hath he quickened, who were dead in trespasses and sins." And then he goes on to elaborate that by saying, "Wherein in time past ye walked according to the course of this world" (Eph. 2:2)—that is it, the same idea, the way of the world, the mind of the world, the outlook of the world, the thing to do according to the world, and it includes good things as well as bad. It includes the whole of thinking that is not dominated by God but is dominated, according to this teaching, solely by the Devil. The Devil will make people good if he can keep them from Christ. He is very subtle; he can transform himself into an angel of light. Take the apostle Paul himself. He was always a good man; he was a Pharisee, a moral man, a religious man, a teacher of the law and zealous. And yet he was a Christ hater; he was really opposing God though he thought he was pleasing him. The Devil will encourage us to do that.

This is one of the most excellent differentiating points, therefore. The man or woman who is merely good and religious and moral never has awakened to the fact that he is dominated by the world, which is dominated by the Devil; he has only the mind, the outlook of this world. But the new man, on the other hand, the man who is born again, has had his eyes opened to all this. That is why John puts it like that. "Whatsoever is born of God overcometh the world" (1 John 5:4). We are all by nature overcome by the world. We are born into it, we are taught, we inherit traditions, and it is all of this world. We become victims of it, slaves of it. We are not allowed to think freely; the Devil sees to that. And the mind of the world with all its books and literature and all these things will keep us in captivity. We are overcome by the world, we are slaves, we are under the dominion of Satan, and we are not aware of it. But the moment we are born again, our eyes are opened to this. And this is one of the most subtle tests as to whether we are born again or not. Those who are born again begin to see the world for what it is; they see it with new eyes.

I have often used that old quotation about the two men in the prison: "Two men looked out through prison bars. The one saw mud, the other, stars." Beauty is in the eye of the beholder, and being born again gives us new eyes and new understanding. We look out on the things we have always seen, but we do not see them as we have always have done. We no longer see them as others see them; we have a new outlook, a new understanding. "If any man be in Christ, he is a new creature: old things are passed away; behold, all things are become new" (2 Cor. 5:17). They have not passed away in the sense that they are not there, but we do not see them as we used to see them—that is the thing. This is an absolute proof of being born again; this is what happens when we have the Spirit of God within us. And if we do not have this new view, the question is, are we born again at all?

Now Christian men and women looking out at all this see through it, by which I mean that they are no longer deluded by it, they no longer judge by outward appearances. Our Lord said that very thing: "Judge not according to the appearance, but judge righteous judgment." Christians, with new eyes, see that all that they thought to be so wonderful before is nothing but a vain show. In *The Pilgrim's Progress* John Bunyan described what the Bible calls "the world" and worldliness as "Vanity Fair," and that is exactly what it is. It can be very attractive, it can be very beautiful, but it is "Vanity Fair." Why? Because it is opposed to God. It has nothing solid and real and lasting to give to us. It appears to be wonderful, but when you examine it and when you need it most of all, you find it is tinsel; there is nothing there. It is all show, it is all appearance, it comes to nothing.

And John has put it, again, so plainly and so clearly—"The world passeth away, and the lust thereof"(1 John 2:17)—and that is what happens to it. The world at its best does not last. As an old hymn says, "Change and decay in all around I see."[1] You realize it on your deathbed. You cannot take it with you. It has gone; it was only temporary. It seemed so marvelous, but in the hour of your greatest crisis you have nothing—nothing at all. It was an empty bubble. Beautiful, iridescent, but only a bubble; it explodes, and you are left with nothing.

Now Christians begin to see this, and as the result of that—notice what a delicate test this is—the next thing is that they find they are beginning to lose their taste for it. It is very difficult to put this into words, but it is this spirit that is in a man or woman that proves whether they are born again or not. The moral man will say, "This is wrong, that is wrong," and you get moral people who are not Christians at all denouncing certain things that are disgracing the life of the community today. But they still belong to the world themselves, and they do not know it. The world can be very decent as well as indecent. It is only Christians who know what it is to lose their taste for all this. They are not merely looking at it objectively; something has happened inside them, and they have lost their taste for the world.

Now let me be careful about this, lest I may discourage anyone. When I say you have lost your taste for it, that does not mean that the world cannot tempt you; sometimes you may have quite a fight. All I am saying is that though that is true, fundamentally you have lost the taste, you are a different person. Before you were part of it; now you are aware that it is outside you, but it is trying to get into you again. This is a subtle thing, but it is very important.

Or let me put it like this: people who are born again do not have to force themselves to not belong to the world in its practice. Moral men and women are always having to force themselves; they have to exercise great willpower. They are always having to take themselves in hand and compel themselves. But because of their changed disposition Christians are not like that; their taste has changed. There is not this forcing; there is rather a new principle working in another direction. They see through the world, they lose their taste for it, and they do not have to force themselves against it. And it leads to this in the end—and this is where growth in grace comes in—it invariably ends with a hatred of the world. Not a hatred in a physical sense, but a hatred of what the world stands for and a hatred of sin.

Now there is nobody who can ever know this hatred of the world except a Christian. As Christians grow in grace and in the knowledge of the Lord, they will know what it is to hate this great devilish organization that is opposed to God, that is holding the masses of the people in its thralldom, in its tyranny and dominion. As William Cowper puts it:

I hate the sins that made Thee mourn,
And drove Thee from my breast.[2]

Here is a man who is born again. He hates this evil influence. It is all round and about him, and it is temping him as it tempted our Lord himself, who "was in all points tempted like as we are, yet without sin," but he hates it (Heb. 4:15). He hates it because it is against God, because it is against the interests of the soul. He sees—oh, he sees through it now, all this appearance that is so wonderful and so thrilling—he sees the ugliness, he sees the rags beneath the surface, he sees the rottenness at the center of the apple that looks so beautiful on the outside. He realizes, therefore, that fundamentally the world is altogether bad, and he hates it, even as God himself does.

But then I must add this, and this is on the positive side, the fact in which one rejoices and glories: those who have been born again not only see and feel all of that with respect to the world, they are conscious of having been delivered from it. This is wonderful. You are *in* the world still, but you are no longer *of* it.

Now this again is expressed by the New Testament writers in various ways. Listen to the apostle Paul in the opening of his letter to the Galatians:

> Grace be unto you and peace from God the Father, and from our Lord Jesus Christ, who gave himself for our sins, that he might deliver us from this present evil world, according to the will of God and our Father. (Gal. 1:3–4)

Jesus has delivered us not only from the condemnation of the law, not only from punishment, but "from this present evil world."

Or take another way in which he puts it in a glorious statement in the first chapter of the epistle to the Colossians:

> Giving thanks unto the Father, which hath made us meet to be partakers of the inheritance of the saints in light: who hath delivered us from the power of darkness, and hath translated us into the kingdom of his dear Son. (Col. 1:12–13)

Now, my friends, here is the test: Are you aware of this deliverance? Do you know that you have been translated from the kingdom of Satan or of darkness and into the kingdom of God's dear Son? Are you aware of this? When men and women are born again, they cannot help being aware of this; they must be aware of it. They know that whereas they were entirely dominated by the world and its mind and its outlook and its influence, they are no longer in that position; they do not belong to it anymore. They are in the same world, they are mixing with the same people, but there is a difference. They do not belong, and they know they do not belong. They have been separated. They have been translated into the kingdom of God's dear Son. They belong to a different realm. They are aware of it deep down, in the very vitals of their being. They may have to do business and so on or work in a profession in that same atmosphere, but they know they do not belong to it. They were in it before, that was everything, that was life—they were gripped and ruled by it. But no longer! They have been set apart; they have been moved entirely out of it.

Now again I would emphasize that I am not saying that a person who is born again and has the life of God in his or her soul is not conscious at times of the attraction of the world. Of course, there is temptation. But temptation and sin are not the same thing. You can be tempted without sinning. So in order to clear up this point and in order to comfort somebody who may be distressed—someone maybe feeling, *Well, if I were truly born again, surely I would not feel the temptation as I do*—let me raise this question: What would you say is the difference between the religious worldling and a backsliding Christian? It is possible for a Christian to fall into sin and to become a backslider. There is such a thing as a backsliding saint, a backsliding child of God. What is the difference between such a person and what I have called "the religious world"?

If you look at it merely in terms of actions, you might very well come to the conclusion that the religious worldling is very much the better person, and people have often used that argument. They say, "There cannot be much in your Christianity after all. I know many men who are not Christians at all, but as far as uprightness and morality and justice, why, they are altogether better than your supposed Christians. I see your Christians failing and doing things that are unworthy"—and they think they have solved the problem! That is exactly where they show that they know noting about the doctrine of the rebirth and that they know nothing about the Spirit and that, really, they know nothing about the world itself. You judge these things not in terms of actions, but in terms of a fundamental relationship and a fundamental Spirit.

Let me put it like this. What determines whether we are children of God or not is not what we do—it is the spirit and the life that is in us. It may be possible—and often in history has been the case—that ordinary people may have greater ability and may live a better life than members of the royal family. But that is not what determines whether we belong to the royal family or not; it is a question of blood, a question of birth. And this is the great distinction between the religious worldling and a backsliding, failing saint. The saint may appear to be much worse. That is not the test. The test is something internal; it is a test of the spirit.

I will put it like this therefore: the backsliding saint is always miserable. That sounds contradictory, but it is true, and it is true to experience. The saint may sin, but he is miserable as he does it, and he is always miserable in it. He cannot help himself. He knows he is wrong. Like the Prodigal Son of old, there is that within that is always telling him that he has sinned against his father and his home and so on. So the backsliding saint is always miserable.

But the thing that I would emphasize is this, and this is the whole matter: when saints sin, they know they are not sinning against law but against love. Consider good religious men, Nicodemuses. When they do things that are wrong, what troubles them is that they have broken a law, they have let themselves down, they have failed to keep up their code. It is always legal; they have done something bad, they have done something wrong, and they cannot get out of it. But the thing that characterizes a child is always that he knows that his misdeed went much deeper than doing what his father told him not to do. He is not sinning against law, he is sinning against love, and that is what breaks his heart. That is what makes him feel that he is a cad: he is offending love! This is not something mechanical or legal but a violation of relationship.

Now only the man or woman who is born again knows anything about that or could ever feel that, and that is the difference between remorse and repentance. Good moral religious people feel remorse when they fall into sin, but they know nothing about repentance. Repentance involves the feelings; there is a hatred of the sin. There is consciousness of having wounded the loved one who has given birth to us and has given life to us, and that is the thing that hurts and grieves and breaks our heart. That is repentance. And only the saint, the born-again person, knows anything about that.

So when you are born again, your whole relationship to the world is absolutely changed. It is changed deep down within you; it is changed in principle. It may take time to show itself in action and in particulars, but the great thing is this consciousness of no longer belonging to it; you have been taken out of it. You are in it, but you are not of it. There is this essential distinction.

Let me take that a step further with my next test: men and women who are born again not only hate the world, but they hate themselves and their life in this world. Here again is a very important matter, a matter that we must handle carefully because it can be so misunderstood. It has been often misunderstood in the past by people who have become monks or hermits; it has been misunderstood by people who have gone in for a kind of false asceticism or for "mortifications of the flesh" as they call them, but these really have nothing to do with scriptural teaching. That very thing is condemned in the teaching of the Scripture itself. So let me give you the words of our blessed Lord himself: "He that loveth his life shall lose it; and he that hateth his life in this world shall keep it unto life eternal" (John 12:25). That is what I am talking about. "He that loveth his life" means the worldly outlook upon life, his life in this world; he is going to lose it. And that is, of course, the tragedy of everybody who is not born again. They have held on to this life; they have rejected Christ, and they think they have made a good bargain. But they will find they are going to lose it all; they will have nothing at the end. "What is a man profited, if he shall gain the whole world, and lose his own soul? Or what shall a man give in exchange for his soul?" (Matt. 16:26). They are going to lose this "life" that they have imagined they have enjoyed, and they then will have nothing. But "He that hateth his life in this world shall keep it unto life eternal." That is what I mean by hating one's self and hating one's life in this world.

There is discussion along the same lines in the seventh chapter of Paul's epistle to the Romans. A man or woman who is born again at some time or another has passed through the experience of Romans 7. The apostle says there—it is a tremendous bit of analysis and autobiography,

> Was then that which is good made death unto me? God forbid. But sin, that it might appear sin, working death in me by that which is good; that sin by the commandment might become exceeding sinful. For we know that the law is spiritual: but I am carnal, sold under sin. For that which I do I allow not: for what I would, that I do not; but what I hate, that do I. If then I do that which I would not, I consent unto the law that it is good. (Rom. 7:13–16)

Then he says,

> Now then it is no more I that do it, but sin that dwelleth in me. For I know that in me (that is, in my flesh,) dwelleth no good thing: for to will is present with me; but how to perform that which is good I find not. For the good that I would I do not: but the evil which I would not, that I do. . . . For I delight in the law of God after the inward man: But I see another law in my members, warring against the law of my mind, and bringing me into captivity to the law of sin which is in my members. O wretched man that I am! who shall deliver me . . . ? (Rom. 7:17–19, 22–24)

That is what I am talking about. You see what you are, you have understood your own nature at last, and you hate it.

Now nobody knows anything at all about that experience except a man or woman with whom the Spirit of God has dealt in a living, real manner. This is to me the beginning of conversion. Your mind is illuminated with regard to the law, and that is the inevitable result. And as you go on that becomes increasingly true in the sense that you are amazed that you can still sin at all; you are still more amazed that you ever want to, and yet you know it is true. In other words you have become aware of the fact that there is still this old nature within you. You are not the old man, but the old nature is still there. And yet when you feel that it is there—this is the marvelous and the wonderful thing to me—you have a feeling that it is in you, but it does not really belong to you; you know that you have this new life. This is the real you now, this new life, this new person, this new being. But you are aware of this other thing, this other pull, this thing in you that can still respond to temptation and may occasionally lead you to fall. And yet, I repeat, you have this extraordinary feeling that it no longer belongs to you.

Do you know what it is to feel that sin is a nuisance and an annoyance? That is the kind of thing, it seems to me, that the apostle is teaching in Romans 6:14: "Sin shall not have dominion over you: for ye are not under the law, but under grace." There is a kind of divine impatience with it all, and it is only those who are regenerate and have new life in them who know anything about what it is to feel like that. And this is therefore a peculiar characteristic that belongs to the man or woman of God. And so looking at themselves, they have lost that old self-confidence that belonged to them and that belongs always to the good, religious, moral, unregenerate people, who are always self-satisfied. The apostle Paul as Saul of Tarsus was a most self-satisfied man. Religious people are always pleased with themselves. They are religious when so many are not! They go to church, and others do not! Wonderful!

Ah, but when people are born again that is gone forever. So they are driven to say with the apostle Paul, and they know it is profoundly true, "By the grace of God I am what I am." Were it not for the grace of God they would not be what they are, they would not have this new outlook, they would not have this new feeling, they would not be seeing through the world, they would not be aware of this difference, this having been moved. It is all due to the grace of God. There is nothing in themselves of which they can boast; boasting is excluded. They hate themselves; they hate this "life in this world" as it were (John 12:25). The old nature still reminds them of it, what they once were and what they still would be were it not for the grace of God and this action of drawing them out and putting new life into them and making them different. "By the grace of God I am what I am."

Or they put it like this, and here I think is another test of the born-again man or woman:

I dare not trust the sweetest frame,
But wholly lean on Jesus' name.

In other words, Christians, saints, those who are born again, know that they cannot even trust their feelings. They know that feelings are so treacherous, and the Devil is so subtle and can counterfeit them. So they dare not trust their "sweetest frame, but wholly lean on Jesus' name."

On Christ, the solid Rock, I stand;
All other ground is sinking sand.[3]

Everything is taken from them; all that they used to rely on or boast of has gone. There is only one solid foundation—it is Jesus Christ. Or as it was put by Lavater, that Swiss man and saint who had experienced these things:

That I am nothing, Thou art all,
I would be daily taught.

That is the Christian.

O Jesus Christ, grow Thou in me,
And all things else recede.[4]

That is the heart's desire of the Christian. They have understood this thing within them that made them self-confident and boastful and self-righteous, and they hate it. They know it is deceitful and deceptive. "The heart is deceitful above all things," as Jeremiah puts it, "and desperately wicked" (17:19). They have come to see not only the world but the world that was in them, this evil principle, the world in their heart and soul and mind and spirit, and they hate it. "That I am nothing, Thou art all, I would be daily taught."

My dear friends, these are some of the tests. Is there anything that compares in importance with the great question, have you been born again? "Except a man be born again, he cannot see the kingdom of God." "Except a man be born of water and of the Spirit, he cannot enter into the kingdom of God." Has God the Spirit done this mighty act in you? Has he created you anew? Do you see the effects and results? "So is every one that is born of the Spirit." "Let a man examine himself" (1 Cor. 11:28).

7

# Righteousness

JOHN 3:8

Sunday morning sermon preached in
Westminster Chapel, February 20, 1966.

We have been considering how Nicodemus is taught in John 3 that he must understand that this life that the Son of God has come to bring into the world is indeed entirely new. It is to be "born of the Spirit"; it is to be made "partakers of the divine nature."

Now here is a great lesson for all, and especially for those who, like Nicodemus, have been brought up in a religious manner. There is no question that the New Testament itself reveals this, and the subsequent history of the church ever since reveals it, and perhaps never more so than today. Ultimately the greatest enemy of the Christian faith is religion. It happened in the time of our Lord when the publicans and the harlots went into the kingdom of God before the Pharisees and the scribes. That is the terrible fact that is depicted in the pages of the four Gospels, and I maintain that it has been the case ever since. So there is nothing more vital for us to realize than this very thing: the Christian life, the Christian faith, is not something that we add on to what we have; it is something that is done to us. We need to be "born again." It is a mighty operation of the Spirit of God, and it is nothing less than giving us a new life, a new disposition, a new nature, a new heart. These are the terms that are used. A man or woman becomes a "new creature," a new creation. That is Christianity, and nothing less than that will do. Therefore, we are trying to discover whether this is true of us. The way to do that, of course, is to discover the characteristics of this new life that is in Christ Jesus. This is so vital and so urgently important that we are going through it at our leisure, looking at the different aspects.

We have done a great deal already. We have seen that obviously this is the most outstanding characteristic about anybody who has received it. You cannot receive life from God without its being evident. It is the life of God in the soul, and therefore, it is more obvious about us than anything else that may be true of us. We have also looked at many other characteristics.

Last time we were dealing in particular with the fact that when a man or woman receives this new life it changes his or her attitude completely toward the world. They no longer love the world. They may be still attracted by certain aspects and at certain times, but they no longer love it. "Love not the world, neither the things that are in the world . . . the lust of the flesh, and the lust of the eyes, and the pride of life" (1 John 2:15–16). These are the things that belong to the world; they are not the things that belong to God. Or as the apostle Paul says in writing to the Romans, "They that are after the flesh do mind [are attracted by, are interested in, are engrossed in] the things of the flesh; but they that are after the Spirit the things of the Spirit" (Rom. 8:5). This is a tremendous test, and we saw together how it works out in practice. These are not things that you have to do yourself; you just find that you are doing them. This new nature has changed you, and therefore your instinctive reaction to things becomes different. And we ended by pointing out how this happens even in your view of yourself and of your life in this world. Once you get this new life, you see yourself as you never have before, and you hate what you see. You do not love yourself or your life in this world any longer.

But that was more or less negative, and we must proceed now to look at this selfsame thing in its positive aspect, because it is important that we should do both in order to make it comprehensive. And let me remind you, I am not saying that we must have all these manifestations of this new life completely or perfectly. Nobody does. If we were to set that up as the standard, we might well come to the conclusion that no one is a Christian at all! All I am saying is that if there is evidence of this kind of thing, then this life is essentially there; it is all in this seed of life. But, of course, there is to be growth and development and enlargement as we go on in our study of these things and our understanding of them and as we "grow in grace, and in the knowledge of our Lord and Saviour Jesus Christ" (2 Pet. 3:18).

So now I come to this next test, which is a love of righteousness. Now here again is one of those tests that differentiates so clearly between the cults and their teaching—and that of other religions too—and true Christianity. This is the great and vital contrast. It may be strange that one is saying all this about religion at a time like this; there are not many religious people left. But I have this terrible feeling, and I have it increasingly—it is a terrible thing to say, but I think we must face this—that the main obstacle to the people who are outside the church today is very often the people who are inside the church. It is so clear in the Scriptures and, I repeat, has been clear ever since then that it is the false so-called Christians within the church who are the problem. We see this in John 2 when our Lord cleansed the temple, and all the great histories of reformations and revivals illustrate the same thing. The church herself has been the problem. Why? Because she has lost her Christianity and has just become a religious institution.

So many evidences suggest that is true today that we must make clear the difference between religion and Christianity. Nothing is of any value except the true Christian faith, this new life that comes from God into the soul. And, therefore, this is a particularly valuable test at this point, because religion is always concerned with morality only. It *is* concerned with morality, of course, but that is its only concern. Religion is concerned with behavior; it is much more concerned with a man's behavior than it is with the man himself, and that is why it is finally useless. Religion looks at a man on the outside, and as long as he looks fairly good and clean and respectable, it is very satisfied with him. But it does not look at the inside. Our Lord said, in speaking to the Pharisees one day, "Now do ye Pharisees make clean the outside of the cup and the platter; but your inward part is full of ravening and wickedness" (Luke 11:39). Religion puts up a respectable appearance, but it is never really interested in the person as such, in the texture of the personality through and through. And because it is only interested in behavior, I have always felt that the final charge against morality is that it really insults us by telling us that what we do is more important than what we are. That is a terrible insult.

But that is true not only of religion; it governs so much of life and of behavior, does it not? It is the outward show, the outward appearance, but on the inside there are horrors. But cults and religion and social codes and agreements are not interested in that; it is all about appearance, "What does it look like?" The man himself is more or less forgotten.

In other words morality is entirely negative. As long as a man is not a drunkard or a murderer or an adulterer, morality and religion are very pleased with him; he is doing very well. The outward appearance is entirely negative and interested only in the absence of certain things. Religion is the enemy of this glorious truth that we have here in the New Testament, because this is essentially positive, and that is its glory.

Our Lord himself put this for us in one of his beatitudes: "Blessed are they which do hunger and thirst after righteousness" (Matt. 5:6). Do you see the positive character of this? They are not blessed who merely are concerned not to do this and that. That was the Pharisee: "Ye pay tithe of mint and anise and cummin, and have omitted the weightier matters of the law, judgment, mercy, and faith" (Matt. 23:23). That is the contrast. But those who are truly blessed, Christian men and women, are those who "hunger and thirst after righteousness"; they want this positively.

The apostle Paul expresses the same thing in Romans 14:17: "The kingdom of God is not meat and drink; but righteousness, and peace, and joy in the Holy Ghost." The difficulty was that certain people in Rome, even members of the church, were being tempted by the Devil. False teaching had been coming in, and they were becoming a little legalistic. So there was a great argument going on in the church as to which day they should observe as the Sabbath, whether they should observe the seventh day or the first. The same was happening about meats, what meats should you eat and so on, and the whole of the church in Rome seemed to have been arguing about this. And that was how the apostle finally put it to them—"The kingdom of God is not meat and drink." Whether you do not eat certain meats or do not drink certain drinks is not what decides whether you are a Christian or not; that does not make a person a Christian. It can make one a religious or a moral man or woman—he does not get drunk, he does not do this and that, therefore he is all right. But he is not! "The kingdom of God is not meat and drink," a mere correctness in certain external matters and conduct and behavior. That is included, but that is, as it were, just the introduction to it. Rather it is "righteousness," positive righteousness, "and peace, and joy in the Holy Ghost."

Now I am taking up this whole statement as it is put by our Lord and by the apostle, and we can sum it up by saying that the people who are merely religious are concerned about not doing certain things, and then they are satisfied. But those who are truly Christians, who have the life of God in their souls, have a great desire and longing to be holy, positively to be holy; they hunger and thirst after righteousness.

So how does this work itself out? How can we test ourselves in detail? There it is in principle, but to be practical, how do we apply that to ourselves and to our condition? Many things are told to us about this in the Scriptures. Let me give you one from the apostle John in his first epistle (5:1–3).

> Whosoever believeth that Jesus is the Christ is born of God: and every one that loveth him that begat loveth him also that is begotten of him. By this we know that we love the children of God, when we love God, and keep his commandments.

But then:

> For this is the love of God, that we keep his commandments: and his commandments are not grievous.

That is it. That is our first test.

John is there describing the people who are born of God, and he says to them, "His commandments are not grievous." The point is that they are grievous to everybody else, and that is how we are able, therefore, to test ourselves. In the New Testament we read about the Christian life and its characteristics. We get great doctrine; then we get the appeal to work that out in practice, and we get pictures and portrayals of Christian people and how they live. Of course, we see what they do not do, but above all we see what they do do and what they are like, and we find that there is a type of life depicted. We see it in perfection in our Lord himself, but we see it also in the apostles and in the early Christians and the saints.

There are certain characteristics of that life. So the question for us is, what do we feel about that life? Christians do not do certain things, I repeat, but they do other things. So the whole test here is, what is our reaction to that? Do we feel that the Christian life is narrow? Do we feel that it is against the grain? Do we wish that it were not like this? If we do, we are just saying that God's commandments to us *are* grievous. If we are always coming up against them as it were and starting back and being somewhat annoyed, and if we use that term *narrow*, that is a very bad sign. When someone brings in that term, it tells us all about him or her, does it not? And that is the point—the commandments to such people are "grievous." And many people, religious people in particular, always find the commandments of God grievous. They often have to readjust themselves, and they try to make themselves conformable to this. The whole thing is outside them, not inside them; so it is always grievous. It is a kind of "yoke" as the apostle Peter put it in the council at Jerusalem in Acts 15. "The old Jewish system," he said, "was a yoke, and it was grievous to be borne, and our forefathers found that so just as we have found it."

There are people who find the Christian life to be like that; they regard it as something that is against them. They would like to do so many things on Sundays and other days, but they cannot because they are Christians. That is a kind of stumbling block to them; it becomes a law. Now that is not Christianity. Law is always grievous. But the Christian life is not grievous because this is life, not law, and therefore this to me is a tremendous test. If we have objections to the Christian life and wish it was not like this and wished it allowed this or that—if we are always up against it, it just means that it is grievous to us. And John says that to the man who is born of God and has this life of God in him, God's "commandments are *not* grievous." Of course not, because "his delight is in the law of the LORD," and he "hungers and thirsts after righteousness," so it cannot be grievous to him.

Or let me put it like this: those who have this life of God in them, who are born of God, who are children of God, are instinctively anxious to please their Father. They are aware of this relationship, and they feel this desire, therefore, to be "wellpleasing in his sight" (Heb. 13:21). As we have seen already in some of the other tests, the glory of this life is that it is always personal. God is no longer merely the Lawgiver—he has become our Father. We pray, "Our Father," and immediately we are in a new realm. We are no longer governed by rules and laws and regulations but are governed by this personal relationship. We have within us a desire to please him. This is inevitable; it is natural. That is why this truth is so important. It is *life*, not merely taking on a point of view, not taking on a new code, not taking on a religion. It is something within us, and it inevitably leads to that result.

Or let me put it like this—and this is where one sees the fascination of the Scriptures, how it all works out in so many different ways, but comes to this point: men or women who are born of God, those who are truly Christians, come to the realization that really the whole object of salvation, ultimately, is to make us righteous. Now when we first get to know these things, and perhaps partly because of the evangelistic form in which the truth is so commonly presented, we tend to think of salvation as almost exclusively forgiveness of sins, something that delivers us from the guilt and the condemnation and the punishment of sin. We are forgiven—we are all right—we are saved.

Of course that is there, but that is not the real object of salvation. What is then? The apostle Paul has put it in a very memorable statement in his epistle to Titus:

> For the grace of God that bringeth salvation hath appeared to all men, teaching us [what does it teach us?] that, denying ungodliness and worldly lusts [that is the negative that we were dealing with last

time; we start with that], we should live soberly, righteously, and godly, in this present world; looking for that blessed hope, and the glorious appearing of the great God and our Saviour Jesus Christ; who gave himself for us [why?] that he might redeem us from all iniquity, and purify unto himself a peculiar people, zealous of good works. (2:11–14)

That is it. That is the characteristic of his people, the people for his own possession, a people who are redeemed not only from the guilt and the punishment of their sin, but "from iniquity," and purified unto him as a people who are "zealous of good works."

That, as the apostle puts it there—and it is not the only statement by any means to that effect—is the ultimate object of salvation. It must be, for this reason: God made man in his own image, and that means that man was originally *righteous*. Now we all unconsciously tend to absorb pernicious teachings—evolution and so on, that man was once an animal, and then he became a man after a long process and gradually developed a moral sense; this insinuates itself into our thinking. But it is all wrong. It is a complete contradiction of the Scriptures. Man was created perfect—righteous. God is righteous, and if he puts something of his own image on man—which he did; man was created in the image and likeness of God—then man was endowed with this original righteousness, and salvation is that which brings a man back to that.

Man in his rebellion and disobedience not only broke commandments, he lost his righteousness, and he lost his love of righteousness. We are all born lovers of sin and of evil. We are all born lawless by nature; there is no question about that. We are all against God and against God's holy law, and that is why we need the new birth. So those who have this life in them soon come to see that they do not stop at their forgiveness; they do not say, "I am safe now, and I can do what I like. I have only to plead the blood of Christ, and then I am all right." They cannot do that. Those who do are people who make light of the blood of Christ, as Hebrews 10:29 puts it. But not so the Christian. True Christians realize that all that has been done in Christ has been done in order to make us positively righteous: "A peculiar people, zealous of good works."

Or consider the apostle Paul's words it in 2 Corinthians 5:21: "He hath made him to be sin for us, who knew no sin." What for? Here is the answer: "That we might be made the righteousness of God in him." We see this again in Romans 8:3–4: "What the law could not do, in that it was weak through the flesh, God sending his own Son in the likeness of sinful flesh, and for sin, condemned sin in the flesh [why?] that the righteousness of the law might be fulfilled in us, who walk not after the flesh, but after the Spirit." This is the teaching of the whole New Testament. Why did Christ die? He did it in order that we might be made righteous. As Cecil Francis Alexander wrote in her hymn "There Is a Green Hill Far Away":

> He died that we might be forgiven,
> He died to make us good.

If we leave that out, we have not really understood the ultimate object and objective of our great and glorious salvation.

Let us take it even a step further. Surely we cannot be in this new life very long or have this life in us without realizing that righteousness is clearly the basis of our communion with God. Now here is something that is of vital importance. The Christian is conscious that what really matters is this personal relationship. In other words, the object of this new life is not merely to deliver me from hell; it is not only to make me righteous. Why should I be made righteous? There is only one answer. I should become righteous in order that I may have communion with God. In the original creation man had constant communion with God. God had made him in this way in order that man might be his companion; there was fellowship between God and man, and the basis of that was *righteousness*. But we have lost that through sin, and that is why men and women by nature do not know God. Furthermore, the God they think they believe in is not God but is merely a creature of their own creation. But when they become truly Christian, they realize that the ultimate object of it all was to bring them back to communion with God.

This is the constant teaching of the New Testament. We have become so legalistic in our outlook that we persist in thinking of it just in terms of forgiveness and being put right with the law and so on, and we leave it at that. But the ultimate object is to bring us back into fellowship and communion with God. Listen to Peter: "Christ also hath once suffered for sins, the just for the unjust, that he might bring us to God" (1 Pet. 3:18). That is the meaning of the word *reconciliation*. It does not mean that you are merely reconciled in terms of the law; it means that you are restored to fellowship, to communion, to a knowledge of God. We must get rid of this merely legalistic aspect. It is there, and you must start with it, but it does not stop there. This is the result that the whole salvation is intended to produce—we are brought back into this condition and relationship in which we know God and know him as our Father. Jesus prays in John 17:3, "This is life eternal, that they might know thee the only true God, and Jesus Christ, whom thou hast sent"—not know about him, but to know him with a prominent element of intimacy.

Now here is something that obviously becomes true of those who have this new life from God in their souls. They have this new nature, and it is a righteous one, and this is something that seeks communion with God. But as Amos had put it in the Old Testament, "Can two walk together, except they be agreed?" (3:3). It is impossible. Two cannot really walk together in fellowship and in communion except or unless they be "agreed."

Or if you like it in a still more logical form, consider the argument of the apostle Paul in 2 Corinthians 6. He is putting this whole question to the Corinthians, and he winds it up by saying, "Be ye not unequally yoked together with unbelievers" (v. 14). Why? We have already seen that there is an essential separation. The "sword" has come down dividing a man even from his father or his mother and so on. There is a division, and yet because of the weakness of the flesh and because of the Devil and his inducements and enticements, we are foolish enough at times to try to keep up this communication between ourselves and the life out of which we have been brought and from which we have been separated. So Paul says, "Do not be unequally yoked together with unbelievers." Why not? "Because," he says in effect, "if you are, you are contradicting the very thing that has happened to you; you are showing a failure to understand that you have received new life from God." "For what fellowship hath righteousness with unrighteousness?" There is really none at all. You cannot mix these things. Righteousness and unrighteousness are eternal opposites, by definition. Their whole nature, their whole character is different.

Paul also says, "And what communion hath light with darkness?" (2 Cor. 6:14). None at all; they are altogether different and separate. "And what concord hath Christ with Belial? or what part hath he that believeth with an infidel? And what agreement hath the temple of God with idols?" (2 Cor. 6:15–16). The answer in all these cases is, none whatsoever. So those who have this new life in them realize that righteousness is the very basis of communion with God, and as that is what they desire above everything else, the commandments of God are not grievous. Rather they are the means that point them to the way of communion, leading to the fellowship that they desire. They cannot go on doing the things they have been doing and still say that they seek fellowship with God.

Next we will note what John says in his amazing and almost startling manner.

> This then is the message which we have heard of him, and declare
> unto you, that God is light, and in him is no darkness at all. If we
> say that we have fellowship with him, and walk in darkness, we lie,
> and do not the truth. (1 John 1:5–6)

But in the second chapter of that first epistle he puts it still more strongly when he says, "Hereby we do know that we know him, if we keep his commandments. He that saith, I know him, and keepeth not his commandments, is a liar, and the truth is not in him" (1 John 2:3–4). And that is all that can be said of him—he is a liar. A man who claims to be a Christian and yet is altogether against the things this great salvation has come to produce is just a liar; he does not know what he is talking about. He is contradicting himself, and he is misleading others. The thing is inevitable; there is no need to argue about it at all. As God is righteous, the man who desires communion with him obviously is a seeker after righteousness in order that he may enjoy that fellowship and communion.

So I can put it like this: this new nature that we have been given, this new life of God, life from God, creates within us a desire to be like him—not only to know that we may enjoy the communion, but because we know that it is his nature and we are meant to be like that. Because we were created in his image and likeness, we desire to be like him. Therefore we see the point of the statement that goes running through the whole Bible in different places: "Be ye holy, for I am holy." And we feel this new holy nature that is within us. This is an incorruptible seed; this is a pure seed. Peter again stresses that very point when he reminds Christian people of this very thing.

> Seeing ye have purified your souls in obeying the truth through the Spirit unto unfeigned love of the brethren, see that ye love one another with a pure heart fervently: being born again, not of corruptible seed, but of incorruptible, by the word of God, which liveth and abideth for ever. (1 Pet. 1:22–23)

It is an incorruptible seed, and as it grows and develops it creates within us this desire for incorruptibility, for righteousness, for positive holiness, to be like the sons of God that we were meant to be, that we may glorify our Father who is in heaven.

So I put it finally like this (this is perhaps the ultimate test that we must apply to ourselves in this matter): is our desire for righteousness and holiness greater than our desire for happiness, greater than our desire for experiences? I have to put it like that because of the subtlety of the Devil. When the Devil has failed to keep us from taking any interest in these matters, he will come as our would-be friend, as "an angel of light," and he will quote the Scriptures and will say to us, "Now the thing above everything else that you want, of course, is happiness," and he will fix our eye on happiness. But we must not. Remember the beatitudes quoted earlier: "Blessed are they [happy are they] . . ." Oh yes, they are very happy people, they alone really are happy; but who are they? "Blessed are they which do hunger and thirst after happiness"? No!

"Blessed are they which do hunger and thirst after righteousness." That is the whole secret. It is a subtle point, and yet it is a very important one. Are we really concerned to be happy, or are we concerned to be holy? Is righteousness the thing we are seeking, or is it really happiness?

Or I could put it in terms of experiences. The Devil comes and tells us, "Ah well, of course you are quite right. Go in for this, and you will have the most thrilling, marvelous experiences," and you whole attention is on the experiences and the thrills and the feelings and the excitements and so on. Yes, there are great experiences in the Christian life. All I am saying is this: Which comes first with you, righteousness and holiness or experiences? There is no more urgently vital test that we can apply to ourselves than that. The proof of the life of God in the soul is that we say, "Though he slay me, yet will I love him." I do not care what happens to me. If all goes wrong with me, it does not matter. I still desire him above everything else. That is the test, and it is greater than anything else, it is above everything else. Everything else has to take second place to this. If you can say with confidence that you are hungering and thirsting after righteousness beyond everything else in the world, my dear friend, you have the life of God in you, for no man or woman is ever in that position except the one who has been born again, born of the Spirit, born of God. That is a great and a vital test.

Let me supplement that by putting it in another way—this is virtually the same, but it makes it yet more positive. I am suggesting that another whole group of tests is that men and women who have the life of God in them will show some evidences of the fruit of the Spirit. Read the description of that in Galatians 5 in order to concentrate your attention on this. You find exactly the same in 1 Corinthians 13: "Though I speak with the tongues of men and of angels, and have not charity [love], I am become as sounding brass, or a tinkling cymbal." It is this quality of life, this "love," that matters. And we see it too in Galatians 5:22-23.

It is the principle here that is of first importance to us. You notice that it is called "the *fruit* of the Spirit." Now you cannot manufacture fruit. You can manufacture things that look remarkably like fruit, and you have to look a second time to make sure whether it is real or artificial, but it is not fruit. With all their cleverness today, and they are very clever, men cannot make life, they cannot make fruit. Fruit is never manufactured. You cannot add on fruit; it is not added on to the branches of a tree. It comes from within; it is a manifestation of life, a manifestation of nature. That which is within comes out.

That is the principle, and that is the whole difference between religion and Christianity. The religious man is like an artificial Christmas tree. It is manufactured; you add things on to its branches, and you paint them, and you make them look however you wish. That is similar to people like Nicodemus, who was confused on these things, and many others have been in the same position with him. Religion and Christianity are not the same; they are essentially, vitally different. They are as different as mechanics and divine life in the soul.

All I am saying is that when the seed of divine life is put in a man or woman, the fruit will appear; it must appear. But you never get true fruit with religion and morality. You can be religious, you can be orthodox, you can have it all, as it were, and yet have nothing. If you do not have the life of God in your soul, there is no fruit. Matthew Arnold once defined Christianity, wrongly, as "morality tinged with emotion." He was defining religion, and he confused religion and Christianity. Christianity is not merely "tinged with emotion"; it is vibrant with emotion. It is life that includes emotion, and here in Galatians 5 the apostle gives us a great list. There is no need for me to go through the list in detail. I will only mention them so we can test ourselves.

'The fruit of the Spirit is love." Love to God, love to man. The Pharisees talked a lot about God, but they knew nothing at all about love for God. Oh, my dear friends, the question is not merely, do you believe in God, but rather do you love him? How do you think instinctively of God? God is love, and if we have something of his life in us we will have love in us. "Thou shalt love the Lord thy God with all thy heart, and with all thy soul, and with all thy strength, and with all thy mind; and thy neighbor as thyself" (Luke 10:27). That is one of the fruits of the Spirit.

Then secondly, "joy." "Love . . . joy." This is one of the best tests, again, to differentiate between religion and Christianity. We see it in Romans 14:17: "The kingdom of God is not meat and drink; but righteousness, and peace, and joy in the Holy Ghost." How much joy is there in you? If you do not know anything about this joy, you are just religious; you are not a Christian. This is a joy that enables us to rejoice even in trials. "We glory in tribulations," says Paul in Romans 5:3. This is a joy that, as our Lord puts it in John 14, the world can neither give, nor take away. It is his joy. He says, "My peace [my joy], give I unto you," and you can have this joy irrespective of your circumstances and conditions. It must be so because if your joy depends upon your circumstances and conditions, it is going to be very variable, and you will sooner or later be in a position when you cannot have any joy at all. But that is not joy. Joy is a great principle that is within; it is a condition of soul that is inexplicable. One just knows that one has "joy unspeakable and full of glory." The religious man never knows joy. I believe that the deadness in our churches and in much of the world today is entirely due to the fact that religion—joyless, cold, and lifeless—has been pushing itself in and true Christianity has gone out. I am not talking about an artificial joy, a mechanical joviality that makes one more miserable than anything else. Joy is an inner quality of soul; it is a glow in the soul that nothing but the Spirit of God can produce.

Next is "peace!" "Peace . . . like a river" (Isa. 66:12)!

> Be careful [anxious] for nothing [it does not matter what it is] but in every thing by prayer and supplication with thanksgiving let your requests be made known unto God. And the peace of God, which passeth all understanding, shall keep your hearts and minds through Christ Jesus. (Phil. 4:6–7)

My friends, do you know anything about that amazing peace? Are you amazed that you can be at such peace? This is what happens to you when the life of God is put within you. It is one of the fruits of the Spirit.

"Love, joy, peace, longsuffering . . ." This is seen in your attitude toward other people. ". . . gentleness"—not flabbiness, but "gentleness." The stronger the man, the more gentle he is likely to be. He is not a spineless individual. That is not gentleness. Only a really strong man can be really gentle. Look at the apostle Paul. He could be stern, he could be strong, he could be logical, he could condemn and rebuke, but was there ever such a gentle soul? Gentleness is something of the character of our blessed Lord himself within us.

Next comes "goodness." That means essential goodness—not merely not doing things that are wrong, but positive goodness. "Faith" means faithfulness, being reliable and trustworthy. "Meekness" is not mock modesty, which would go against one of our Lord's own beatitudes. "Temperance" means self-control, self-discipline. But the thing we must emphasize here is that this is not merely discipline that is based upon observance of rules and regulations; it is instinctive.

Let me use an illustration as I close. You know the difference, do you not, between a real gentleman and a man who is trying to behave as a gentleman? The religious man has his own kind of discipline, but it is not an internal discipline, it is not instinctive. The Christian has this instinctive self-control; he is dominated by this desire to know God and to be righteous and to be like him. So in all things—food, drink, and everything else—there is this instinctive balance—discipline, self-control. He is not just trying to be something, he knows he is something, and that is what controls him and disciplines him in all his ways.

What we are talking about is a life. Let us forget legalism and mechanics. True life is given by God, and it is miraculous and supernatural. You cannot add it to yourself; rather you go to him and you say, "I realize I am not able." *"Thou must save, and thou alone. God, you must work this operation in my soul. You have said, 'Ye must be born again.' I cannot give birth to myself. Grant that your blessed Spirit may do this to me."* That is it. And once this life is put into you, these are the things that inevitably begin to show themselves.

# 8

# Loving the Brethren

### John 3:8

Sunday morning sermon preached in
Westminster Chapel, February 27, 1966.

We are continuing our study of Jesus's basic foundational statement with
regard to the whole condition and position of the Christian. The Christian, as our Lord here teaches Nicodemus, a "ruler of the Jews," is one
who is "born again." So we are looking at some of the many and varied
expressions of this new life of God that comes into all who are truly born
again. We have seen that these are negative and positive, and they are
all important.

Now let me remind you once more that I am not postulating that we
must all be able to discover these things I am describing in their fullness
in us. That would be unfair; it would be wrong. None of us is perfect. All
I am saying is that this life does always manifest these features. I am not
concerned as to the amount, as it were, of the manifestation; all I am
saying is that these manifestations are there, that this is something that
is inevitable.

The human analogy helps us here again. We know how certain characteristics of the life of a family are present in some shape or form in all
the members of a family, but they vary in degree, some more, some less;
and so it is with all the other manifestations of life. We vary in size, in

appearance, in brainpower, understanding, and so on, but everyone has a certain amount of this. The most ignorant person knows something; the person least gifted intellectually does have a brain and shows that he has a brain in certain respects. That is the kind of principle that I am laying down. I am not asking for a 100 percent standard; no one can provide that. But I am saying that these things should be clearly present and that as we test and examine ourselves we should be able to discern them.

Now we are trying to move in a logical sequence as we look at these various tests, and in the last sermon we were looking at that characteristic of this life that always shows itself in a hungering and thirsting after righteousness. To this new man in Christ, righteousness comes before happiness; he is more concerned about holiness than he is about happiness, and we ended by glancing at some of the manifestations of "the fruit of the Spirit." As our Lord says here, this man who is "born again" is "born of water and of the Spirit." And the apostle Paul reminds us in Romans 8:9, "If any man have not the Spirit of Christ, he is none of his." You cannot be a Christian without having the Holy Spirit in you. That is true of every Christian. I am not talking about the baptism with the Spirit. I am talking about having the Spirit of Christ within you and being "born . . . of the Spirit." So we are entitled to look for the manifestations of the fruit of the Spirit in every Christian.

That leads us to the next step, which was mentioned in "the fruit of the Spirit." "The fruit of the Spirit is love, joy, peace, longsuffering, gentleness, goodness, faith, meekness, temperance" (Gal. 5:22–23). Now there are three groups there, and one of them very clearly has reference to our relationship to one another as Christian people—"long-suffering, gentleness, goodness." We are put into relationship with one another, and these characteristics are always put like this in the New Testament teaching. Take, for instance, the way Peter puts it in his second epistle, in the first chapter: "And beside this, giving all diligence, add to your faith virtue; and to virtue knowledge; and to knowledge temperance; and to temperance patience; and to patience godliness; and to godliness brotherly kindness; and to brotherly kindness charity [love]" (vv. 5–7). So the next test for we who have this life in us is our relationship to one another. We find this in 1 John 3:14: "We know that we have passed from death unto life, because we love the brethren," and he elaborates on that in the whole of that section of his first epistle.

Now here is a categorical statement, "*We know*." It is an absolute proof "that we have passed from death unto life." We have been born again. How do we know? "Because we love the brethren." There it is stated in a doctrinal form. If you want it put in a more natural, human, historical form you will find it at the end of the second chapter of the book of Acts when the apostle Peter preached his sermon on the day of Pentecost. There were about 120 Christians until that point, but Peter preached in Jerusalem and three thousand people were added to the church. What was the characteristic of these people?

> Then they that gladly received his word were baptized: and the same day there were added unto them about three thousand souls. And they continued stedfastly in the apostles' doctrine and fellowship, and in breaking of bread, and in prayers. (Acts 2:41–42)

Later on we read,

> And all that believed were together, and had all things common; and sold their possessions and goods, and parted them to all men, as every man had need. And they, continuing daily with one accord in the temple, and breaking bread from house to house, did eat their meat with gladness and singleness of heart, praising God, and having favour with all the people. (Acts 2:44–47)

There it is in its historical form. That is how Christian people immediately and instinctively began to behave. And surely here again is a matter that needs no arguing, no demonstration. This is something that is quite inevitable. We are all familiar with this in terms of the human analogy. This is something that is always true of a family. We have a saying that "blood is thicker than water." Something draws together people who have the same blood, who partake of the same particular nature. That is true in the natural realm; members of a family are instinctively bound together in a way that they are not bound to everyone else. And the argument is that this is equally true in the spiritual realm, and indeed, not only equally true, but even more so, because the quality of life is a greater one; it is a purer, more powerful one, and therefore this must of necessity be true.

Now I want to hold this before you because I think that at the present time this is perhaps one of the most important principles for us to consider in this whole matter that we are dealing with together. There is a great deal of talk today about church unity and so on, and in connection with that nothing is more important than this. And it is there, it seems to me, that so much trouble is being caused. Everyone is talking about church unity, but surely, before you do that you must find out what a church is and what a Christian is. That will determine your idea of unity. The tendency is to approach these things as the world does or as big business does. This is a day in which small businesses, the small man, the private man is disappearing; everything is being amalgamated, and the church seems to be thinking in much the same way. Political parties form their coalitions. But I want to try to show that all *that* is entirely wrong in the spiritual realm and that to think in that way about the Christian church is not only to confuse the issue but is to go sadly astray and to be quite unscriptural.

So we see something of the urgent relevance of all this. It is not only important for us individually, therefore, it is important for the whole state and condition of the church. So let us define our terms. "We know that we have passed from death unto life, because we love the brethren" (1 John 3:14). Here is the definition. What does he mean by saying, "We *love* the brethren"? Let me define it negatively, and I feel that this again is most important. It is a distinction I have often emphasized, and it seems to me it is more and more necessary. Remember, loving and liking are not the same thing. We are not told, "We know that we have passed from death unto life, because we *like* the brethren." That is not what we are told. We are told that "we *love* the brethren."

What is the distinction? Liking is something natural. You either like a person or you do not; we do not all like the same people, and there are some people we like more than others. There is nothing wrong with that. You do not do a person any harm by not liking him. This is beyond our control; it is part of our makeup and a part of their makeup. There are elements that attract one another, and there are elements that tend to repel. That is the realm of liking. You find that in the animal world as clearly and patently as you do in the human realm. There are certain attractions and the absence of attractions in other cases. So we are not told that we must like one another. But we are told to love one another and that it is our duty to love one another, and there at once you see the difference between these two things.

What does it mean to "love the brethren"? I sometimes think the best way of defining it is this: you love the brethren when you treat people whom you actually do not like as if you did like them. That is loving them. If you, as a Christian, allow your likes and dislikes to govern your conduct, especially negatively, then you are not behaving as a true Christian. Christians, though they do not like a person, do not allow that to make any difference. They go out of their way to treat that person as if they did like him, because he is a brother and because he is bound by the ties that I shall put before you.

There, then, is the difference between loving and liking. You can be commanded to love but not to like. We are not meant to like everyone in the same way—I mean Christian people—because Christians are not all exactly alike. Our temperaments are not changed when we are born again. There are certain things that are basic and fundamental to our personalities that are not only not changed but are not even meant to be changed. It is a dangerous thing when you find a number of Christian people all alike in every way, in their manner of speech and everything else. That is wrong; that is psychological. Christianity does not do that. You can see the variation in the disciples and the apostles. It is wonderful, and this has continued ever since in the history of the church. As God varies everything in nature, and it all ministers to his glory, so it is with Christian people. We have our different natural gifts and capacities and personalities, and all these remain in the new birth and add a variety and glory to it all. And for that reason it still follows that we do not like everyone equally. But we are told that we are to love everyone equally.

This is one of the proofs again that people are born again. They discover the difference between liking and loving. "The natural man," the man who is not born again, is governed entirely by his likes and dislikes, and he acts accordingly. But when a man becomes a Christian he sees all these things in a different way. He now *loves* those whom he actually does not like. He likes some more than others, but he treats those whom he does not like as well as others, and thereby he is loving them. That is a most important point, because if we are not clear about that, we may condemn ourselves wrongly.

Now *loving* is not merely a matter of having a nodding acquaintance with other Christians, and this is where all this is so relevant to the modern talk of "we love the brethren." You must not think of that in an institutional sense. Institutionalism has always been a great curse in the history of the church. In some great organizations the people are more or less ciphers. That is not the picture of the New Testament church. It is a gathering of brethren. So it is not just a question of social fellowship with people or just a recognizing of certain people in that kind of way. It is not merely being members of the same church and having your names on a certain list. That is not the New Testament picture at all. There is a "love" here; it is something deeper, it is something that is much more positive. It is a very real and a very living fellowship, and therefore we must be clear as to whether this relationship with other Christian people, the brethren, is true of us. It is one of the most subtle and delicate tests of the new birth.

Now why do I say that it must of necessity be the case that those who are born again love one another? There are many reasons for this. They have, I repeat, fundamentally the same life in them, and life always attracts. It is inevitable. Work it out again in terms of the analogy of the family. It is very difficult to define it in words, but we all recognize it. There is something unseen that you cannot put your finger on, but you know it, you feel it instinctively. It is this same nature that is manifesting itself. Now that is true of all who are born again. We are all born of the same Spirit; we have all become the children of God. And, of course, this means that we have the same outlook on life, the same understanding of life. These are the things that bring us together and make us love one another. People who have the same interests are always drawn together. "Birds of a feather flock together." Of course! Having the same community of interest brings them into a more intimate relationship, into community, and though many other things tend to separate them, this is something that cements them together.

Now this is very true in this particular realm, and of course, especially at a time like this. We have already considered our relationship to the world. When people are born again, they are taken out of the world, out of "this present evil world," and are "translated into the kingdom of [God's] dear Son." All those who are born again have had that happen to them, and, therefore, they have this same view of life. And that immediately not only separates them from others, but it brings them together, this unity of outlook and of understanding of everything that is happening.

So I venture to put it like this: people who are born again really speak the same language, and the older I get, the more significance I attach to this particular test. Now that is an expression that is used, is it not, in secular life and in the natural life. Here again is this community of interest and particularly a given point of view. You say, "I get on well with that man; he and I speak the same language," and you know exactly what that means. And that is infinitely more true in the spiritual realm; this, again, is something that comes from the life that is within. The outlook determines the very language that is spoken.

Now the apostle Paul, again, has put this in his usual exceptionally clear manner in 1 Corinthians 2 where he says, "We have received, not the spirit of the world, but the spirit which is of God; that we might know the things that are freely given to us of God. Which things also we speak, not in the words which man's wisdom teacheth, but which the Holy Ghost teacheth; comparing spiritual things with spiritual" (vv. 12–13). In other words, those who are born again begin to speak in a certain language, and it is a spiritual language. They use the same words that they used before, but there is a difference in their use of words and in their manner of speech. They have a kind of new language, and therefore those who are born of the same Spirit understand this language.

I do not want to overrefine this, but I think it is an important point. Have you ever noticed the difference between someone born again using the language and someone who is not born again trying to use the same language? What a revealing test that is! I have known people like that. They use the terms and the phrases, the clichés, the terminology, but somehow you have the feeling that they are not really speaking the language; it is an imitation. But the children of God, those who are really born again, speak the language; it is their natural way of speaking. It is the essence of hypocrisy when someone who really does not have the life speaks as if he or she does have it and uses the language and the phrases and the terminology. What I am concerned about is this reality of the language. You recognize it instinctively, and heart speaks to heart.

Then we can go on from that and point out that we have the same interests, the same concerns, the same desires. The analogy of the family puts it all before us. There are family interests, and they do not need to be put down on paper. Everyone knows that the fact that you are a member of the family means that automatically these things become a concern of yours. This is the fundamental factor, ultimately, that makes the family one and will unite a family as against all others if their fundamental interests are in jeopardy or in danger in any respect. The children, of course, are inevitably concerned about the well-being of the family. They do not want the family to suffer but to succeed. Now transfer all that to the spiritual realm and the children of God. They will always have these family concerns, family desires; they all have the great concern for the family name, the family of the Father, the success of the kingdom.

In other words, you test yourself like this: How do you react to the world and the life of the world as it is at the present time? It is one thing to be appalled at the immorality and the vice and the mounting moral problems in this country and in other countries, but that is not the way the Christian looks at it. Christians look at all this from the standpoint of men and women as souls and the kingdom of God and the glory of God; they are grieved about the godlessness. That is how they react to it all because they are children of God and because they are members of his family. A man or woman cannot be born again without being grieved about the present state of the Christian church, her weakness in this country, her perilous condition. Naturally the children of God feel this and are deeply concerned about it, and they are anxious for the success of the kingdom of God as a result.

Or take it like this: we love the brethren because we share certain secrets with them. There are things that are said within the family circle that you do not say outside. You keep family secrets, things that are not noised abroad. Oh, how true this is in this realm! Have you not often found that there are certain things you cannot talk about in the presence of other people who are not Christians? You know for one thing that they will not understand them; they will not know what you are talking about. You are told not to "cast . . . your pearls before swine"; you know that they are liable to misunderstand them. You can only speak about these things when you are with the family, when you are among the brethren. You know that you are a sharer of the secrets; you do not need to be told them, you know them. All this is summed up in many hymns. For example:

The love of Jesus, what it is,
None but His loved ones know.[1]

To them you can talk about these things freely as you do in a family circle, but you cannot do this with anyone else. So this again brings us together.

If we had nothing else, this would be enough to make us love the brethren. We are all fighting the same enemy. If you read through the Bible, you will find that. Read through the subsequent history of the Christian church, and you will find that God's people in times of persecution have always been driven together and cemented together in a much closer manner than they had ever been at any other time. They are fighting the same common foe, so they draw together. And as Christians become fewer in number year by year in this country, it should have this effect upon us: we are aware of one another, and we draw closer together; our love for one another is increased because of our circumstances.

And lastly, Christians are those who have the same "hope of glory." They are all looking forward to that same glory. They have been born into this new realm; they have been translated into the new kingdom. This world is only temporary, it is not complete; we are going on to the final fulfillment, "the hope of glory." We are people who are aware of this, but no one else is. The world does not know about this; the world does not believe it, in fact. The world probably believes that there is nothing after death; that is the end. It does not believe in the final glorious appearing of our blessed Lord and Savior and his eternal kingdom. But if we are born again we do; it is a part of our whole belief and faith, and naturally, therefore, we are conscious of being "strangers and pilgrims" in this world. That fact draws us together; we recognize one another, and so we love the brethren. In other words, the community and the commonness of the outlook and belief, the same desires and same hopes and fears and battles and problems, all these things drive us together and therefore lead to this conclusion: "We love the brethren."

But if those are the reasons for this love, how does this show itself in practice? I am concerned to be most practical. The difficulty is that the Devil will delude us and persuade us that we are children when we are not. So we must be equally subtle, and in the teaching of the Scriptures we are given the means whereby we can be. How do I know that I love the brethren? I see that I ought to; that is inevitable if I am truly born again. But do I? How do I test myself? Well, here are some of the tests. I suggest again that the first—and it works out from the human analogy—is this: one becomes aware of the relationship at once; you recognize it immediately in the other. This is something intuitive, something instinctive, and it is one of the most marvelous and thrilling experiences in the Christian life. I think I can say quite honestly in the presence of God that I have not known more thrilling experiences than those that I often get in my vestry at the close of a service, and have done so throughout the years. Strangers come in to see me. I have never seen them before, and they have never seen me, but at once I know that they are brethren. There is no need of any introduction in a sense. The name, well, all right—but it does not matter at all; you are aware that you have here a Christian, someone who is a child of God, and there is an immediate affinity.

I could show you a subtle difference at that point. I sometimes get people coming in from other countries, and they announce themselves to me immediately and say, "I am a So-and-so." They come in and say, "I am a Congregationalist" or "I am a Methodist" or whatever, and my suspicions are immediately aroused when they emphasize that. That is not the language of the children of God. What matters to the children of God is not primarily the denomination to which they belong; it is the fact that they are children of God, and they are more interested in the truth to which they have been listening. That is what reveals itself immediately. Instinctively you recognize one another. There is something about this family relationship that shows itself. I do not want to go too far in this matter, but I have said it before and I am conscious more and more how true it is. Something happens to the very appearance of the Christian that marks him out, especially in the eyes. Do not ask me to define it, I cannot. Would you not expect that? Does not the inner nature show itself? Is it not bound to show itself? It does, and I maintain that in these strange ways, these signals, as it were, are given, these indications, these manifestations, and the child recognizes the child.

So I would put it to you that this relationship of being brethren is something that counts with us more than anything else, that we are more pleased about this when we meet one another than with anything else. Now we are testing ourselves: What is it that I look for in other people? I suggest that the child of God is one who looks more for the marks of the child of God in the other than any natural gift—looks, charm of personality, ability, powers, anything you like. I say the children of God are more interested in this subtle, almost indefinable something that claims that the other is a Christian than in anything else whatsoever; he is more interested in this than in nationality.

Now that is something that a man like the apostle Paul came to understand, and how he gloried in it! He was a Jew. He had always been narrow, nationalistic; he despised everyone else and regarded them as dogs. But here is a man who came to glory in the fact that he was an apostle to the Gentiles. Here is a man who now rejoices above everything in this: "The middle wall of partition" has been broken down, Jew and Gentile have become brethren, and by one Spirit and as one body they preach the same Lord and the same Savior. To Paul this was the most tremendous thing that had ever happened to him. All the old prejudices were gone; he did not care what a man's nationality was now. "There is neither Greek nor Jew, circumcision nor uncircumcision, Barbarian, Scythian, bond nor free" (Col. 3:11). The color of the skin does not matter; nothing like that matters. Accent? Irrelevant! A fellow Christian is a brother, and he loves him. This comes before anything else.

I have illustrated this especially in the matter of nationality, but it applies to everything else too. Class, color, ability—all these things recede and pale into insignificance when put into the light of the common life that we share from our blessed Lord and Savior.

I must take this step further: when men and women are born again, they love others who are born again more than they love their own flesh and blood who are not born again. It goes as far as that, and it must. You are, after all, tied to those who are related to you by flesh and blood in a natural sense. But here is something divine—love to God, a purer nature, a purer love, a purer seed. It is a divine seed, and this obviously is more important than anything else. This takes precedence over everything else, and it is a simple fact of experience that you become aware of a deeper tie, a deeper attachment to a child of God to whom you are not related in a physical sense at all, more than you do to those to whom you are bound by ties of blood and flesh. This is a very deep test, a profound and true one, and we can know exactly whether we are Christians or not by this one test even if we had no other.

And then I go on to other things that follow out of all this, and this again is a wonderful test. Do you feel awkward in the presence of Christian people? Perhaps you have known this. Do you feel awkward in the presence of saints, do you feel like a fish out of water, do you feel you do not belong? If you do, it is a sign, my dear friend, that you are not born again, you are an outsider. It is a terrible thing to feel you are an outsider in any realm, and one knows it at once in this realm. But those who are born again never feel awkward in the presence of others in a spiritual sense. They may feel they are young and immature, but they like to be with others who are born again because they want to be like them. They are aware, of course, of feeling humble and meek and inadequate, but that does not mean that they feel awkward. They know they belong, and although they do not understand fully, they have an understanding of these matters.

And then I go on and put it like this: those who prefer the society of the brethren to the best society that the world can afford belong to the children of the heavenly King, and the least in that kingdom is greater than the greatest outsider. David has put that once and forever in that immortal verse in Psalm 84: "I had rather be a doorkeeper in the house of my God, than to dwell in the tents of wickedness" (v. 10). Of course he would! The children of God prefer the society of the children of God to the best, the greatest, the most exalted society that is not Christian, and if you gave them a choice of spending their day with a simple illiterate saint or the most sophisticated and brilliant worldling, they would inevitably and unhesitatingly choose the simple Christian. They love believers.

They enjoy the society and conversation of the children of God. We read in the book of Malachi, "Then they that feared the LORD spake often one to another" (3:16). They liked to come together, and as we saw in Acts 2, the first Christians immediately did this. "They continued stedfastly in the apostles' doctrine and fellowship, and in breaking of bread, and in prayers." They met with one another daily. You did not have to force them to come to one another, and they did not come to God's house so that they might go out of it, hoping that the thing would not last too long—that is a sign that something is wrong. Christian people delight in these things, and they want to talk about them, they want to learn about them. They enjoy one another's society and fellowship; they have experiences to share with one another. They cannot do this outside, and if a man of the world came into such a service, he really would not know what I am talking about.

Do you know what I am talking about? Here is the test. To the children of God there is nothing like the society of the brethren when you can be talking about these things; these things are more valuable than life. Life may end at any moment, but here is something that goes on for all eternity. We are talking about our Father and our elder Brother, and we are thinking of those who have gone on and who are near the throne, and we are going to be with them. There is nothing comparable to this. These are the ways in which you can test whether you have this life or not.

Let me draw to a close by putting it like this: we have sympathy with one another and concern for one another, concern for our happiness and well-being. The Bible is constantly illustrating this. We read in Acts 12 that the king called Herod arrested the apostle Peter. First of all he took James, the brother of John, and beheaded him for no reason whatsoever, and then he threw Peter into prison. He intended to behead him, but he could not do it at once because it was Eastertime. So he put Peter in prison and assigned four quaternions—four squads of four soldiers each—to guard him day and night, and all the prison doors were guarded as well. "Prayer was made without ceasing of the church unto God for him" (Acts 12:5). Peter was in prison, but the whole church was in prison in spirit! Only one man was actually suffering and bound with chains, but all the church was conscious of the fetters and the dungeon and the cruelty in the prison, and they were praying for Peter.

Why was this? He is their brother; he belongs to them. One cannot suffer without all suffering, and Paul says that in 1 Corinthians 12: "Whether one member suffer, all the members suffer with it." "Bear ye one another's burdens" (Gal. 6:2). This is a thorough test of our whole position. Many Christian brethren in this and other lands are suffering grievous persecution. Does that trouble you? Does it worry you? Or do you say, "Well, it is all right as long as I am not concerned"? That is the spirit of the world, but it is not the spirit of a Christian. The man who is not concerned when his family is in trouble is unworthy of the family. You belong to the family of God, and many of God's children are suffering in many respects at this present time. Does that burden you? Does it lead you to pray about them? Do you feel with them? Do you sympathize with them? I say that the fact that we have this same life within us, the same blood in us, should lead to that inevitable conclusion.

And lastly I end with the thing that John was emphasizing when he said, "We know that we have passed from death unto life, because we love the brethren" (1 John 3:14). How do you know whether you love the brethren? Here is the test: Can you bear with them? Are you long-suffering; are you patient? It is very difficult at times, is it not? We are all very difficult people. By nature we are all impossible! Paul writes to Titus in the third chapter that we were all at one time "hateful, and hating one another," (v. 3) and you know that is the simple truth about men and women by nature. What a vile lot we are, and so we are impatient with one another. But when you are born again you are "born of the Spirit," and the fruit of the Spirit is "love, joy, peace, longsuffering, gentleness, goodness, faith, meekness, temperance." So the children of God, knowing one another, are ready to bear with one another. You do that in your family, do you not? You will forgive things and bear with things in the family that you do not outside. Multiply that by infinity and you have the children of God, the born-again people, the family of God. You not only bear one another's burdens, you bear with one another.

So if you say that you are born of God, but you hate your brother, it is a lie; it is impossible. But if you are born again, you bear with one another and are ready to forgive one another. Why? Because you know that you have been forgiven when you did not deserve it at all. There is a new logic that comes into the thinking of the Christian. The other man, the man who is of the world and is not born again, says he has done no wrong. "Why should I forgive? Why should I always be giving in?" The Christian does not speak like that. The Christian says, "What if God handled me as I handle others?" and he is immediately humbled. He says, "I was forgiven when I was a rebel, when I was vile, when I was a sinner, when I was an enemy of God. God forgave me freely in spite of it all, and if God so forgave us, we ought to forgive and love one another." So if you are aware of this attitude in you toward your brethren, if you are ready to be long-suffering and patient and to forgive your brothers, you have proof positive that you are loving the brethren.

My dear friends, may God give us grace to apply all this to ourselves. It is one thing to say, "I am a child of God." What we are concerned about is *knowing* that we are. "We know that we have passed from death unto life, because we love the brethren." This is infallible proof!

# 9

# Knowing God

## JOHN 3:8

Sunday morning sermon preached in
Westminster Chapel, March 6, 1966.

The wind bloweth where it listeth, and thou hearest the sound
thereof, but canst not tell whence it cometh, and whither it goeth:
so is ever one that is born of the Spirit. (John 3:8)

We are studying this verse because it deals with a crucial matter. There
are so many who spend a lifetime seeking blessings, trying to advance in
the Christian life, but who are always in trouble because they have never
really started in it. They have been acting on certain assumptions, and
almost invariably one of them is the one that was true of Nicodemus, this
fatal confusion between religion and the Christian faith.

We have seen how this shows itself in so many different ways, and
we have therefore come to the conclusion that the most important thing
for any of us is to make certain that we have been born again. We do
not have to understand fully what that means; that was the blunder of
Nicodemus who keeps on saying, "How can these things be?" We must
get beyond that stage and realize that by definition we are in the realm
of the miraculous, the supernatural, and the divine, and our Lord sums
that all up so perfectly in this eighth verse: "The wind bloweth where it

*wishes*

listeth, and thou hearest the sound thereof, but canst not tell whence it
cometh, and whither it goeth: so is every one that is born of the Spirit."
This is a mystery, and we are not to waste time trying to unravel or dis-
sect the mystery and bring our foolish, puny understandings to bear. We
are in a realm altogether above and beyond that. But it is not irrational;
this is the true rationality. What we regard as rational is not rational,
and what we regard as irrational is God's rationality. The essence of the
teaching is that what makes us Christian is that we are given new life,
being born again.

Now the whole history of the church shows so clearly the importance
of this distinction. Throughout the centuries religion has been the greatest enemy of the Christian truth and the Christian faith, and the tragedy
is that you can have religion in the church. The Christian church can just
become a form of religion, an institution that deals solely in the realm
of religion. In the epistle to the Philippians, chapter 3, there is another
perfect statement of all this. The apostle Paul had been a bitter opponent
of the Christian faith. He had been a persecutor, he regarded the Lord
Jesus Christ as a blasphemer, and he had done his utmost to exterminate
the Christian church. Why? Simply because he was religious. He was
holding on to his religion, and he felt that was sufficient. He was quite
sure that God was well-pleased with him; he tells us that he acted "in
all good conscience" (Acts 23:1). Nothing is so inimical to the true faith
and the true Christian position as religion and a reliance upon religion.
So it is vital to draw the distinction between these two things, and our
method of doing that is to look at some of the characteristics of this true
life when we receive it. Life always expresses itself, and therefore we can
test ourselves, and as we do so, we are showing the striking difference
between religion and true Christianity.

Now I have been trying to put these things in an experimental order
starting with experience and going on to more objective statements of
truth. I have also been trying to put them in a kind of rising, ascending
order, because I think that is the right way to approach it. You start with
a very general examination, with broad, obvious, outward things, and
you gradually narrow it down. So the tests become more subtle, more

accurate, and more searching as we go along. But as we are doing this, we are just showing the difference between religion and this divine life that is given to us in Christ Jesus. As Peter puts it, the Christian is a person who has become a "partaker of the divine nature" (2 Peter 1:4), or as John puts it in his epistle, there is a "seed" in him, a seed of life, and that is a part of the divine life.

Let me put it like this before we go any further. We have been looking at these various tests, and what is so wonderful about it is that we know at once what these emerging differences are. We see the difference between religion and Christianity. If we do not, it just means that we are not born again. But the moment we are born again we see it at once. The apostle Paul puts it in a striking manner: "What things were gain to me . . ."—the things he had gloried in; he had not only relied upon them, he had gloried in them. But he came to see that they were useless, refuse, and there is no question about it. The moment we receive this life we see the difference between this and everything that we formerly regarded as Christianity (Phil. 3:7). And, therefore, as I am drawing these distinctions and showing these differences, that in and of itself is a test as to whether we have life or not. If all this seems meaningless to you, if you think I am trying to draw distinctions where there is no real difference, if you feel that I am just splitting hairs, that just means you do not have the new life. The moment you have this life you *know*. "He that is spiritual judgeth all things, yet he himself is judged of no man" (1 Cor. 2:15).

Let us, then, go on with these tests. Previously we considered this test: "We know that we have passed from death unto life, because we love the brethren" (1 John 3:14). What follows that? It seems to me that what follows inevitably is this: we know that we have passed from death to life also because we love God and because we have an increasing desire to know God—God the Father, God the Son, and God the Holy Spirit. We saw in dealing with the brethren that one of the inevitable expressions of this family consciousness was that we desire to be in their presence; we desire to know them more; we desire to love them more and to spend our time with them. This is natural and inevitable in terms of the analogy. And it is exactly the same here.

I wonder if anyone has a query in his or her mind as to the order in which I am taking these things. Is there someone who feels like saying, "But surely you should have put this love of God and this desire to know God before the love of the brethren"? There is a very complete answer to that. It is what John says in his first epistle: "If a man say, I love God, and hateth his brother, he is a liar: for he that loveth not his brother whom he hath seen, how can he love God whom he hath not seen?" (4:20). So if you have such an objection, it is because you take a theoretical view of these matters and not an experiential one. If you take it experientially, then you will have to do what John says there. The first test is: Do you love your brethren? If you do not, there is no need to discuss as to whether you love God. If you do not love your brother whom you have seen, how can you love God whom you have not seen? So we take them in that order—love for the brethren first, then the love of God.

We are going from broad, general objective tests to the more inward and delicate and sensitive tests, but oh, how vital this is! These, after all, are the final proofs. If this is true of us, then we can be absolutely certain. The others are all true, but here, as we advance, they become more delicate and therefore give us a yet greater certainty. What I am talking about is this: a desire, an increasing desire, for a personal knowledge of God. Now I do not mean by that a desire to know more _about_ God. That is all right, but the merely religious man is interested in knowing about God; that is why he is religious. The distinction I am drawing is the difference between desiring to know things about God and the desire to know God himself.

Now here it is not only the difference between religion and Christianity—it is the difference between philosophy and true Christianity. I have said that religion is the greatest enemy of Christianity; next to it I would undoubtedly put philosophy. Philosophy has been throughout the centuries one of the greatest enemies of the Christian faith, and it is the curse of this present age in which we live. Many religious books are gaining great popularity and notoriety and are advertised because they are daring and unusual. But the real trouble with all these is that they are simply interested in God intellectually and philosophically, and their terms always betray them. That is the exact opposite of the biblical teaching. They talk about "the Absolute," "the Uncaused Cause," "Ultimate Reality," or "the Ground of Being." They are always impersonal, whereas the very essence of the Christian position is that it is personal.

Now the whole analogy of life and of being born again, becoming a child, being in a family, insists upon this, and that is why this is such an important test. We are dealing, therefore, with something internal instead of external. We must be careful over this. We are all always liable to go from one extreme to another, and you will find that the philosophers often do that. Having spent years trying to understand with their minds and having failed, they suddenly stop that altogether and turn to what is called *mysticism*. They abandon intellect, as it were, and now dwell solely in this realm of internal experience. Having tried to find a God outside them, they now try to find the God who is within them. There are many notable examples of this. Let me give you just one. Take the late Aldous Huxley, for instance, a brilliant intellect, a man who up to a certain point indulged in a search in this way, philosophically and scientifically. He was a typical representative of the outlook of the twenties of the twentieth century. It was all intellect. But in the latter part of his life he abandoned that completely and said that the only hope of the world is mysticism, and he began to dabble with Buddhism.

Many intellectual people are doing that at the present time. They see the futility of the external, and they turn to the realm of the subjective and the internal and the mystical. Now I say that we must avoid that particular danger, but there is an emphasis there that is absolutely right. They detect this, of course, as they read about people in the Bible and as they read the life history of the saints in the churches since then. They see that these men had something experiential, something internal. It was an inner knowledge of God and not merely some intellectual, objective, academic, theoretical interest in God and all that belongs to him.

So here is a very great test, and this has been the great characteristic of God's children throughout the centuries. The true Christian faith is always *inner*, it is internal, it is vital, it is experiential; it is not entirely objective. But let me elaborate on that. When men or women are born again, not only can it be said of them that they have this desire for this inner, personal direct knowledge of God, but this desire becomes their chief object; it becomes more important than everything else. More important than what? More important (I have to put it first again) than religious interests. That is what our Lord is really saying here to Nicodemus. Nicodemus comes as a religious man out of a religious background and religious training. He was a Jew, and he had come with all the background of the Jews' religion—the temple and its worship, burnt offerings, sacrifices, the ceremonies, the rituals, and all that belongs to that—and it was a most imposing fabric in every sense. But he has been told that is of no use here.

This is true always of those who are born again; they realize that their religious interests are not sufficient. How easy it is to rely on religious interests, still more on religious activities and religious duties. You find it in this man Nicodemus; you find it equally in the case of the apostle Paul. That bit of autobiography in Philippians 3 is so valuable in this respect. There was a man who really lived for his religion. He did it with his mind, and he did it with his heart and his will. He went all out—the interests, the activities, and all the various duties were the things on which he lived. And many have lived on them.

Now this, alas, is encouraged by the church herself. The church always tends to become a great institution, presenting her organizations and her services, and there is nothing so simple as just, as it were, to become a candidate for all this. You are told exactly what to do, and you become a part of a great system. You are told you have to get up at a certain time in the morning, go to your Mass or whatever before breakfast, and so on. Your whole day and in a sense your whole life is planned. You are told what to read, what to eat and not to eat at Lent and at other times, and how to confess your sins. You have become part of a great religious system and organization—it is all outside you. Many people are genuinely persuaded that they are Christians because of this, but it is all a reliance upon what they are doing. That is what I mean by religious interests, activities, and duties.

But the moment a man or woman truly becomes a child of God, he or she sees through all that. This becomes very obvious when it happens. I remember a particular case of a lady and her husband. The lady thought and claimed herself to be an exceptionally fine Christian, and she was regarded as such by everyone else. But her husband was not a Christian. Indeed he was a cynic, and while in a sense he admired his wife and would boast of her as being a highly religious person, he himself was not interested. This lady was of the type I have just been describing. She went every morning to a very early communion, and she seemed to be one of the finest Christians you could ever imagine. Well, in a very remarkable manner her husband came under the sound of the gospel and was truly born again, and what astounded everyone was that the lady herself, after a few months, became terribly convicted. She knew that the husband had something vital inside him that she did not have. Seeing the change in him, she realized that all she had was the religious actions she did herself, and at first she was bitterly antagonistic toward what her husband had. But the Spirit of God opened her eyes, and she saw that all she had was religion. She did not have the true Christian experience; she was not a child of God and was not born again. She was just a religious person, and that led eventually to her conversion and to her rebirth.

Now do not misunderstand me. I have had occasion to say, in dealing with a statement in Romans 12, that you must of necessity have a minimum of organization, but that is very different from institutionalism and the whole religious system.

Christianity simplifies all that. Every great reformation and revival has always been a great simplification, bringing believers back to the New Testament. Our Lord sits on the side of a mountain, sits in a boat, and there he preaches, and the unction and the power are there. It happens in the same way with the apostles. That is true Christianity. The Christian puts this inner knowledge of God not only before religion in its various manifestations but (I want to take it a bit further than that) the Christian puts it before an interest in theology and doctrine. Now there are those who say, "I quite agree with what you have been saying about religion, and I have long since seen through that." But now their position is that they are interested in theology, in doctrine, in understanding the truth and reading about it. They say, "Those other people, of course, are ignorant; they are just slaves, as you have described them, slaves to a mechanical system. They do not know what they are doing, and they leave it all to the church and so on; but we have seen that is all wrong." They now have become theologians, and they are reading books about doctrine.

Now I have spent a good deal of my energy in my pastoral life advocating that people should become theological and doctrinal, but what I am trying to say now is that you can be interested in theology and doctrine without being born again. It is a wonderful system; it is an intellectual system as opposed to a more practical one (religion). Religion is on the practical level; theology and doctrine are on the intellectual level. I have known many men whose hobby was to read theology—some Protestant, some Roman Catholic. It was their great interest to read it and discuss it and to go to meetings together and argue final, subtle points. You can do all that and still not be born again. God knows this is a very real possibility. I passed through that stage myself.

Now the one who has been born again sees that all that is not an end; it is only a means to an end. The purpose and function of all knowledge and understanding is to bring you to a knowledge of God himself. If you want to be introduced to the queen and have an audience with her, you do not stop at reading the books and the etiquette and the court procedure; the object of those is just to bring you into the presence of the queen. You are not content merely to say, "Now I know exactly what to do when I go to Buckingham Palace." You want to see the queen; you do not want mere theoretical knowledge so you can discuss it. That is just foolish, you will say. Yes, and it is infinitely more foolish when you come to the spiritual realm. So those who are born again say, "I thank God for all knowledge, but I see the danger even of that knowledge if it is only theoretical. I want to know God, the living God, the personal God." Now if someone comes to that conclusion, he or she is born again—that is the only explanation. But if he she does not, then he or she is not born again.

Or take it another way: those who are born again desire this personal knowledge of God even more than they desire the blessings of God, even more than they desire experiences that are given by God. This is a test that works everywhere; that is why it is so wonderful. It is because of a divine seed, being "born of water and of the Spirit." This life is bound to express itself. It always does, and it always will, and it will expose everything else. These things are subtle, but this is something about which I am sure we all know something, the danger of desiring only God's blessings.

Or put it in the form of desiring certain experiences. There is nothing more wonderful about the Christian life than the blessings to which it leads, and it does lead to experiences. You cannot be a Christian without some kind of experience. But the danger is that people are more interested in the blessings and the experiences than in God; they are interested in the gifts rather than in the Giver. This is very dangerous and very subtle. The Devil will try to keep us on that level.

Do you see the importance of this distinction? There are many teachings and agencies in the world that can give people experiences and apparent blessings. The cults would never flourish were it not for this. That is what makes them successful; they can produce certain results. Now the Devil takes hold of this and does exactly the same thing, but he makes use of Christian terminology, anything to keep people from the person. He will keep the interest on the level of the blessings and the gifts, and some people spend a lifetime seeking these.

So the way to look at this is: having life you will have experiences and blessings, but if you reverse the order and put all your emphasis upon the blessings and the experiences rather than upon the knowledge of God, you have it all wrong. A human analogy proves this to perfection. What is the difference between a child and an adult? Or take one person as a child and then look at him when he is grown after many years into maturity and judgment. The difference is that the child is not very interested in persons as such; he is interested mainly in what the person can give. That is why the judgment of all of us at that age is not to be relied upon. I am sure that I am giving the experience of all of you when I say that one finds that one's evaluation of people has undergone a very great change since childhood. I can think of certain persons, uncles and others, who, when I was at a given age, I thought were wonderful, and I much preferred them to certain other uncles or people.

But "when I became a man," if I may use the apostle's language, my judgment was entirely reversed. What made the difference? It was that the ones I thought so much of as a child were good at entertaining children; they would amuse and make me laugh, and they would give me gifts and presents. But others seemed cold by contrast, and I was a little bit afraid of them. When one gets older, one sees that the heroes of one's childhood were very nice, but there was very little in them. They were not the sort of people you want to go to for advice and for knowledge; actually you did not find them very interesting. They were experts at entertaining children but had not much to give one when one got older. This is something that you all must have experienced, and you will find it more and more true.

Now the cause of all that trouble is that the child tends to judge in terms of benefits or enjoyments received, gifts and experiences. The child does not judge in terms of the value of a character and of a personality. But as you get older you begin to do this, and you now become interested in persons because they are what they are—not because of what they can give you, but because you are interested in them as people. This is a sign of maturity in life. What are your standards of judgment? The child tends to resent discipline and order and firmness and understanding; he always wants to be on the level of entertainment and amusement, with accompanying gifts. But that is not the real test to apply, and as you grow older you begin to value people who help you discipline yourself. You see that they were the ones who really loved you. They did not always say yes to every request. They did not always give you what you wanted. They were not always giving in, and later you begin to appreciate this and you say, "Fancy my ever resenting that!" You begin to admire it now. This is what you want above everything else, and you blame yourself for having taken so long in coming to this appreciation of these persons and all that they have for you.

Transfer all that to the spiritual realm, and it is equally true. It is a sign of life and a sign of growth in life, particularly in this matter of desiring to know God himself more than one desires to be blessed. As Job put it, "Though he slay me, yet will I trust in him" (Job 13:15). That is it.

Nearer, my God, to Thee, nearer to Thee!
E'en though it be a cross that raiseth me.[1]

That is it. That is what comes first. One has now come to this place of realization that nothing matters ultimately save this. So this new nature, this new life, this new crying out for the Father becomes the chief, the supreme object in life.

Let us put it like this: those who are born again realize that this is really the chief end of salvation. Our Lord himself put this for us plainly in the seventeenth chapter of the Gospel of John, in verse 3. He said, "And this is life eternal, that they might know thee the only true God, and Jesus Christ, whom thou hast sent." He is defining eternal life. The one who is born again is one who has received eternal life. "God so loved the world, that he gave his only begotten Son, that whosoever believeth in him should not perish, but have everlasting life." This is life eternal. It is not merely continuing existence. Eternal life is knowing God. That word *know* is the vital word, and we can never repeat this too often. It is not a knowing about; it is to know him in an immediate and in a personal direct sense, the knowledge of God.

Our Lord puts it like this in that same seventeenth chapter of John's Gospel, in his High Priestly Prayer: "O righteous Father, the world hath not known thee: but I have known thee [he does not mean knowing about, he means *knowing*], and these have known that thou hast sent me" (v. 25). Indeed in the third chapter of John's Gospel our Lord says the same thing. He says to Nicodemus, "And no man hath ascended up to heaven, but he that came down from heaven, even the Son of man which is in heaven." He also says, "Verily, verily, I say unto thee, We speak that we do know, and testify that which we have seen; and ye receive not our witness. If I have told you earthly things, and ye believe not, how shall ye believe, if I tell you of heavenly things?" (vv. 13, 11–12). This is what is meant by knowledge, and again it is not merely knowing about. You can get knowledge about God in books, you can get it in the Bible, and you can get it in nature and creation. The philosophers spend the whole of their lives arguing about these proofs of the being of God. I am not saying those are of no value at all, but I am saying that those who have life in them realize that the ultimate end of being given this, and of the whole of salvation, is to bring them into a personal knowledge of God.

Now they realize that this is something that is possible in this life and in this world, and here again is one of these great differentiating points between religion and Christianity. You can come and apparently worship God in a formal, external manner with your mind and with your will and yet not feel anything at all. But that is not true worship. Worship really means a communion, an exchange, a consciousness of the presence of God. If you read the lives of the saints, you will find that they have all concentrated on this. I think it was George Müller of Bristol—that man so famous for his prayer and his confidence in prayer and who had such a gift of faith that his prayers were answered in phenomenal ways—who used to teach that the first thing one does in prayer is to realize the presence of God. You should not begin to think about petitions until you know you have realized the presence of God. How? Start, says Müller, with the realization that you are in the presence of God and that he is looking upon you and is listening to you.

Now that is possible in this life and in this world, and no one is interested in that except the man or woman who is born again. Others are satisfied with getting on their knees, saying their prayers, reading a small portion of Scripture, and so on and think, "Ah, I am a Christian." But my dear friend, do you know God? Do you know anything about personal communion with him?

The Bible itself is full of this. For example, "Enoch walked with God" (Gen. 5:24). That does not just mean that he lived a godly life; it includes that, but it goes well beyond it. "Abraham . . . was called the Friend of God" (James 2:23). You cannot read about these men without finding that they had direct and immediate experiences, that God spoke to them as a man speaks with his friend. Think of Jacob running away that night from his brother. Weary and tired he put himself down to sleep, with his head on the stone as a pillow, and there God began to deal with him, and

Jacob realized what had happened: "This is the none other but the house of God, and this is the gate of heaven" (Gen. 28:17). He realized that he had had communion with God, and he never forgot that.

Of course, Jacob did many things afterward that he should not have done, but he always came back to that experience. And when he eventually went back to his own country, he referred to it. That was the crucial moment in his life; it was the central thing. So in the next great crisis he had to face when he was going to meet his brother, on his way to his own country and he feared he might lose everything, what he was concerned about above everything else was that God who met him there at Peniel should again assure him that all was well, and he struggled with him during the night. "I will not let thee go," he said, "except [until] thou bless me" (Gen. 32:26). That is the experience.

You find the same with Moses, not only at the burning bush, though that was his first great experience of it—God addressing him, God dealing with him personally, and he knowing that he was in the presence of God. In the same way, at another time he was in a position of great crisis, when he came down from the Mount and found the people making a golden calf and worshipping it. God punished the people and said to them, "I will send an angel before thee." But Moses said in effect, "If you will not come yourself, we will not go." That is what I am talking about. So many of us are content to go on with the leadership of the angels, something distant and indirect. But Moses said, "If thy presence go not with me, carry us not up hence." He insisted upon this personal knowledge and this personal experience of God (Exodus 33).

In the sixty-third Psalm you find the same expression of this. Here is poor David facing the insurrection and rebellion of his own son Absalom and having to escape from Jerusalem for his life, and there he is in a wilderness. Everything has become doubtful, he may be killed, everything may be lost, but notice his prayer. "O God," he says, "thou art my God." That is the thing. Not "Whatever gods may be," but "my God." And he can groan, "O God, thou art my God; early will I seek thee: my soul thirsteth for thee, my flesh longeth for thee in a dry and thirsty land [he is in a wilderness] where no water is" (v. 1). What does he want? "To see thy power and thy glory, so as I have seen thee in the sanctuary" (v. 2). David had had experiences in the sanctuary. We meet with God in the sanctuary; that is why we come to church. God has promised to meet with his people in the sanctuary, and David, as he puts it in the eighty-fourth Psalm, had found "grace and glory" in the sanctuary. He had had experiences in the house of God when he knew that God was his God; he had seen something of the glory.

So now, when he is out in the wilderness, there is no building, there is no ceremony, but David knows that God is as real here as he is in the sanctuary. And what he wants here is not an assurance that he is going to be given power to defeat Absalom and his armies—all he wants to know is that God is still his God. "I want to know you," he says, "as definitely and as truly here in the wilderness as I ever have in the sanctuary," that is the supreme thing. He knows it is possible anywhere; it is possible everywhere. The eighty-fourth psalm is just a variant on this same theme. He is prevented from being in the house of God, but that is where he wants to be. He thinks of people going up to meet with God—"grace and glory"—and he longs to have this more and more.

The point I am making is simply that this is an absolute proof of divine life in the soul. The apostle Paul says in Philippians 3:10, "That I may know him"—the same word again—"that I may *know* him." Here is the man who has preached about him, the outstanding apostle, the Apostle to the Gentiles whose knowledge and information about the Lord Jesus Christ had surpassed everyone, and likewise his knowledge of God. But that is not what he is talking about. "That I may know him." "I do not have a full apprehension," he says, "I have apprehended a great deal, but I have not fully apprehended." That is what he is talking about. It is not theoretical knowledge; he is here concerned about experimental knowledge, heart knowledge, inner knowledge.

This is Paul's great desire, and this is because of the life that is in him. Life cries out for life. There is nothing that can satisfy it save life, and this is therefore one of those ultimate and final proofs of the new life. When men and women have this longing for God, books will not satisfy them. Books will help them up to a point, but they cannot stop there. There is still dissatisfaction, longing, searching, hungering and thirsting after the living God, knowing in a direct and immediate sense.

All I am saying is that men or women who are born again know that this is possible. They have that within them that cries out for the knowledge of the Father, the Son, and the Holy Spirit, and they are no longer content with anything less than that. They thank God for every experience they have had; they thank God for every manifestation, for every blessing that has come into their life, material and spiritual. But oh, above and beyond all, and even beyond the gifts of the Spirit, what is central and primal to them is personal, immediate, direct knowledge of God.

May God have mercy upon us! So many of us are children and are only interested in the presents and the gifts and the entertainments. That is not proof that we are truly born again. The Devil can counterfeit experiences and gifts and most other things, but there is one thing the Devil cannot do, and that is give us a desire for a personal knowledge of God. The Devil can give you an interest in theology and encourage it; as you go on, you become more and more proud of your vast knowledge. That is not what I am talking about. I am talking about the crying out of a child's need for his or her Father, the true filial cry and desire. The Devil cannot counterfeit that; he knows nothing about it, and he cannot produce it. Only one person can produce it; that is God himself through the Spirit as he implants within us a seed of this living life.

# 10

# A Personal Knowledge of God—God the Father and God the Son

## John 3:8

Sunday morning sermon preached in
Westminster Chapel, March 13, 1966.

We have been considering what we are told in the Bible about the manifestations of this new life from God that is given to those who are Christians, and we have seen that there are many, many tests. We have arrived now at one of the most important of all. We are trying to proceed on a kind of ascending scale, taking the big, broad, obvious things first and then narrowing it down in one sense, but only in the sense that we are concentrating more on this vital matter of a personal knowledge of and a personal relationship with God.

We began doing this in the previous sermon, and I have said that there is no better test than this. This, indeed, in many ways is the ultimate test, that we have an increasing awareness that the ultimate end and object of salvation is to bring us to this direct and immediate and personal knowledge of God. The great characteristic of the Christian faith, as against all other religions, is that it is internal, not external.

Of course, there is the objective aspect, but the mark always of a truly Christian life is this inner life, this inner growth. The apostle Paul, in the third chapter of Ephesians, refers to "the inner man": "strengthened with might by his Spirit *in the inner man.*" That is it. Or to put it another way, one becomes aware of the fact that one has an inner man. Christians are aware of this; nobody else is. The life of those who are not Christians is in one sense all of one piece. They are each just one man, and that is the same man whether outward or inward. Indeed the whole tragedy of men and women who have not received this new life is that they are not aware of this inner life, this inner being.

The New Testament describes the Christian in this way: it is the inner man that matters, and the body is nothing but a kind of tent in which we live for a while. It is not the body that is important; it is merely the place in which this inner man of ours dwells while we are here in this world of time. But those who are not Christians know nothing about this life; to them their life is all in the flesh. The body is essential; they cannot conceive of themselves apart from it. The only life they know is this kind of soulish psychical life, call it what you will, the life that is entirely made up of relationships with men and women and is entirely dependent upon that. They are dependent upon them for their interests, their happiness, their pleasure, for everything. And when they are bereft of these things they are completely lost and are without any comfort or consolation. But the moment they become Christians a new man comes into being, an inner man, this spiritual man.

Now this new man, of course, is concerned about having a knowledge of God. The apostle Paul says of the Christian, "Though our outward man perish, yet the inward man is renewed day by day" (2 Cor. 4:16). That is what I mean by saying that this is internal, not merely external. Religion is always external, as morality is external; it is always interested in the surface. But the spiritual, the unseen, is always internal, and the great characteristic of this "inner man" is that he desires this personal knowledge of God. That is what he is most interested in, even more than in religious duties or theology, more than in blessings. This is the chief end of salvation. Christ died for us, says Peter, "that he might bring us to God."

"This is life eternal," says our Lord again, "that they might know thee the only true God, and Jesus Christ, whom thou hast sent" (John 17:3).

Now Christians realize that this is possible in this life, that the knowledge of God is not something postponed until life after death. It starts here. One of the old Puritans of over three hundred years ago left as his dying statement something he wanted to bequeath to all his relatives and all who knew him, this statement: "God dealeth familiarly with men." He only discovered that at the end of his life. He had been preaching these things, but then he had a great experience and said, "I leave this as my dying gift—God dealeth familiarly with men." In other words, though he is a God far off, he is a God who is also near. As the hymn puts it:

Center and soul of every sphere,
Yet to each loving heart how near.[1]

Men and women with this new life, this inner man, this new man, have discovered that God, the everlasting and eternal, is in this sense near. He is "the high and lofty one that inhabiteth eternity, whose name is holy," but he also dwells "with him also that is of a contrite and humble spirit," as Isaiah puts it.

This is regarded by them as the highest privilege in their lives, and it therefore becomes the chief object of their lives. We all know what it is to desire to have more and more of the company of certain people, the desire to talk to people, to mix with people who are in exalted and high positions, and so on. And if that is so on the natural level, it is infinitely more so on this level. So you will find that the great characteristic of the people of God in the Old Testament as well as in the New—but more in the New than in the Old, as one would expect because of all that has been done in and through our blessed Lord—is this desire. David, for instance, says, "As the hart panteth after the water brooks, so panteth my soul after thee, O God. My soul thirsteth for God, for the living God: when shall I come and appear before God?" (Ps. 42:1-2). That is a desire for communion with God, "the living God."

Let us be quite clear about this—the God of the theologians may very well be a dead God. That is the whole danger of a purely intellectual approach. The God of the philosophers is certainly a dead God; he is an abstraction. "The Absolute," "the Ultimate," and the other terms they use about him display the fact that they do not know the living God. But here is a man who with the whole of his being is longing for the *living* God. He is not concerned about an intellectual knowledge and apprehension. His heart is involved; his feelings, his sentiments, the whole of his being is crying out, "My soul thirsteth for God, for the living God"—nothing is more important to him than that.

Blaise Pascal said exactly the same thing when he had a great experience: "The God of Abraham, and of Isaac, and of Jacob; not of the philosophers." Now Pascal was a brilliant philosopher, an astounding thinker, a brilliant mathematician; he had philosophized a lot about God and about these matters. But when he had this experience of the living God, then he was overwhelmed and knew that he was having the kind of experience that had been vouchsafed to Abraham and to Isaac and to Jacob. He knew his Old Testament, and he knew how God had appeared to these men, and they knew they had been in contact with the living God.

Take the experience of Jacob at Peniel in Genesis 32. There is a man aware that he now is really dealing with the living God, and he will not let him go. This is the greatest thing he has ever known. He'd had a great experience before at Bethel, but here is something that goes even further, and this gives us an insight and an understanding into the whole life and character of that man Jacob. Pascal realized that he now lived in the same dimension, no longer theorizing, philosophizing, talking and arguing about God and concerned about the proofs of the being of God. They are all right as far as they go, but once a man has had an experience with the living God, he does not need the other proofs; he *knows* God. There is nothing that is comparable to this immediacy. As Job cried out, "Oh that I knew where I might find him!'"

I am putting these phrases before you in order that we all may ask ourselves certain questions. Have you ever asked that question like Job? Have you ever felt like that? Have you ever uttered the ejaculation, "Oh that I knew where I might find him"—seeking him, searching for him?

O Love Divine, how sweet Thou art!
When shall I find my willing heart
All taken up by Thee?[2]

That becomes increasingly the deepest and greatest desire of Job's life.

Now you see the importance of asking these questions; you see the difference between religion and this vital, true characteristic that is always a manifestation of life. On Sunday morning we come to the house of God, but my dear friends, do we not all know from experience and must we not all admit and confess that we have often done that quite mechanically because we believe in general that worshipping God and so on is the right thing to do? But the question is, do we come to meet with him, do we come because of this desire to find him? Do we come with that kind of eagerness with which Jacob struggled and wrestled on that occasion at Peniel because he wanted the blessing that God alone can give? This becomes the chief thing. Jacob had many other concerns on that occasion (read the history for yourself). He was going to meet his brother Esau, and he might lose all his goods and possessions, which meant a great deal to Jacob. But the moment he meets with this Other, he forgets all about his goods and possessions and everything else; nothing matters but this. All I am trying to say is that one of the tests, always, of the possession of this life is that it becomes the supreme aim; it is bigger than everything else in our lives. I have quoted to you the apostle Paul at the height of his experience crying out, "That I may know him, and the power of his resurrection, and the fellowship of his sufferings" (Phil. 3:10).

Now the danger is that the Devil may come to us at this point and say, "Well, that is all right for the people in the Bible, but it has nothing to with you." We often fail to know these things because we listen to that suggestion, and there is a great tendency to do this. "All that was only for the patriarchs—they were special people; only for the apostles—they were special people; only for the first Christians—they were special people." And thus we exclude a great deal of the Bible. But it is not true. This is something that God's people have gone on experiencing throughout the centuries, and it is not confined to any particular type. The psychologists will tell you, "Ah yes, that is all right. We like to read about these things. There is that mystical type of person, but we are not all like that, you know. There is such a thing as a religious complex, a religious temperament. Certain people are so constituted by nature that naturally they go in for that kind of thing. It is all right for them, but you must not say that we are all to know that."

And that again is a lie of the Devil. This has nothing to do with natural makeup. We are "born again"; the others are "born of the flesh." There are such differences, and I am very ready to grant it, all sorts of types and kinds. You get your mystical type in a natural sense, a psychic type, the phlegmatic type, the scientific type, and many others. But what we are discussing goes beyond all that—"Born, not of blood, nor of the will of the flesh, nor of the will of man, but of God" (John 1:13). New birth! "Born of the Spirit." It is the work of the Spirit, it is the life of the Spirit, and this is available for all of us. So you must not avoid it by trying to explain it away in clever terms. This is something that is to be true of all God's people. Listen to a man living in the last century who put it like this:

I see Thee not, I hear Thee not,
Yet art Thou oft with me;
And earth has n'er so dear a spot,
As where I meet with Thee.[3]

That is it. He has not had a vision, he does not hear words from heaven, and yet the experience is real. I could give many other quotations indicating the same thing. All I am saying is that if you know anything at all about such a desire or are able to utter such a sentiment, that is an absolute proof that you are "born of the Spirit," that you have the life of God within you. The thing is obvious, is it not? The man of the world is not interested in knowing God. "I never think about it. God is an abstraction; everything is so vague." This is only something that is known by those who truly have been born of the Spirit.

This "inner man" also finds in himself an increasing interest in the three blessed persons of the Holy Trinity in and of themselves and for their own sake. Now here I am developing the point that I mentioned in passing in the previous sermon when I said that this man is even more concerned about this personal knowledge than he is about receiving blessings. This is a most important point—he has an increasing interest in the divine persons as such, the persons for themselves.

Let us start therefore with the Son of God, the second person in the blessed Holy Trinity. Here is a very good way of testing ourselves. Are we interested in our Lord himself? We are all interested in the benefits of salvation. We all want forgiveness, we want to be delivered from sins, we want happiness and so on. That is perfectly legitimate. I am not saying anything against that. But what I am saying is that if you stop at that you may be deluded, because in various ways that can be counterfeited by the enemy. But he will never create an interest in our Lord himself.

Now the Holy Spirit was sent to glorify the Lord Jesus Christ, and therefore the ultimate test of a work of the Spirit within—indeed all the work of the Spirit—is that it leads us to a greater interest in the person of Christ himself. You find this increasing interest in the glory of his person in the Scriptures, and you will find it particularly in the hymnbooks. The man or woman of God, the saint, likes to dwell upon and to meditate upon the very glory of the person of the Lord Jesus Christ. They think often about him. They like to think of him in his eternal and everlasting glory with the Father before time; they like to read the descriptions of him that are given in the Scriptures. "In the beginning was the Word, and the Word was with God, and the Word was God" (John 1:1). They turn to the first chapter of the epistle to the Hebrews and they find, "God, who at sundry times and in divers manners spake in time past unto the fathers by the prophets, hath in these last days spoken unto us by his Son, whom he hath appointed heir of all things, by whom also he made the worlds; who being the brightness of his glory, and the express image of his person, and upholding all things by the word of his power . . ." (vv. 1–3). They like to meditate about that and to think about it.

Now these are the marks of this new life, and they are surely inevitable if we really do believe the message of the Christian gospel that all has come to us through the Lord Jesus Christ. So we want to know something about him. Take the human analogy once more. If someone is being kind to you or you have heard of someone who has done you a kindness, or if you have heard of someone who has done something wonderful in any realm, the first thing you say is, "I would like to meet that person. I would like to get to know him." You know what he has done, but you are not content with that. Knowing what he has done creates a desire within you to know what he is like, to know what kind of person he is. That is what we do on the natural level. It is exactly the same here. So one becomes interested in the glory of this blessed person. You cannot grasp it all, of course, but you take these descriptions, and you realize that they are true, and you are amazed at them. And then you go on and begin to ask yourself, "Is the Lord Jesus Christ the one who died for me on the cross? How did this ever come to pass?" So you begin to think of and to rejoice in the marvel and the glory of the incarnation.

Now we are obviously doing something here about which the natural man, however clever, however brilliant he may be, knows nothing at all. He may be interested in the subject as an item in theology or a philosophical argument, but he does not have this personal interest. But those who are born of the Spirit, because they have this life in them, do have this personal interest. So they now like to look at and to meditate upon the incarnation. So they read Philippians 2, and they are astounded at it and revel in it. They read, "Who, being in the form of God, thought it not robbery to be equal with God; but made himself of no reputation" (vv. 6–7). "What does that mean?" they say. They want to analyze it, and they find that what it means is this: he was in the eternal glory, the second person in the blessed Holy Trinity; that was his right, his prerogative. He was the Son of God. "All things were made by him; and without him was not any thing made that was made" (John 1:3). But—this is the point—for us and for our redemption and in order that we might be made the sons of God he did not hold on to all that. The real meaning of the sentence, "[He] thought it not robbery to be equal with God" is, he did not regard it as a prize to be held on to, to be clutched at. He did not say, "I can't leave this; this is so marvelous, and I cannot leave the enjoyment of it." Instead "he humbled himself." He laid aside the signs of that glory and came to earth. He "made himself of no reputation, and took upon him the form of a servant, and was made in the likeness of men" (Phil. 2:7). "The Word [the everlasting Word] was made flesh [literally], and dwelt among us" (John 1:14).

Now for men and women who are born of the Spirit, this is the most amazing and astounding thing. They like to think about it; they like to meditate about it and to dwell upon it. And then they watch this blessed person in his life and in his works. They read the Gospels with an entirely new eye—not merely as a matter of history, for they now have a living interest in it. There is all the difference between reading about someone who belongs to history and who does not belong to your family and reading about someone whom you know and love intimately and who belongs to you and you to him. Now you are reading the Gospels with a new interest, his life and works, and you like to watch him as he deals with people, as he deals with the poor, the publicans and sinners and the reviled, and as he deals with the Pharisees and scribes and the authorities, and you are watching him the whole time.

And then you look at his dying upon the cross and you meditate about these things. Consider the apostle Paul: "God forbid that I should glory, save in the cross of our Lord Jesus Christ." The distinction I am trying to draw is this: it is one thing to believe the theory about the death of our Lord or to believe it as a fact and to glory in it. You can believe in it intellectually, but you will never glory in it intellectually, and those who have life in them know something about glorying in it. They can say:

Were the whole realm of nature mine,
That were an offering far too small;
Love so amazing, so divine,
Demands my soul, my life, my all.[4]

Now this is something that only those with new life in them know anything at all about. It is no longer external. You do not need to put up crosses, therefore, in your churches; you have the cross of Jesus in your heart. You are looking at it spiritually; you are looking at it internally. This has become everything to you, and this is the characteristic of God's people throughout the centuries. And then we can think of him not only dying and being buried but rising again, the glory of the resurrection. And then we think of him reigning in heaven. Does that thrill us? Does it amaze and astound us? Does it lift us up and put us into a kind of ecstasy?

We sometimes try to bring ourselves into a belief of these things. This the cause of many of our troubles. There is no verse, I sometimes think, that is so misinterpreted as Romans 6:11: "Reckon ye also yourselves to be dead indeed unto sin, but alive unto God through Jesus Christ our Lord." People have turned that into a psychological process; they see *reckoning* as *persuading* themselves. It does not mean that at all. It means to realize that it is true, it has happened, and it thus becomes something vital.

And then you go on and you realize that Jesus Christ is at the right hand of God, seated there in the glory everlasting. You are in trouble, you are in difficulties, and there you are, trying to work up faith, trying to apply something. Do not do it, my friend. Go to him; realize he is there. It is not a matter of self-persuasion; it is going to him, glorying in the fact that he is there and remembering that he said, "All power is given unto me in heaven and in earth" (Matt. 28:18). He is seated at the right hand of God, waiting until "his enemies be made his footstool" (Heb. 10:13).

This is really the great argument of the epistle to the Hebrews. Why was that epistle ever written? There is only one answer. These people had become depressed and unhappy. They were being persecuted, they were having a very hard time, and they were beginning to become shaky in their faith. They were becoming doubtful of everything, and this man writes to say one big thing to them, though he takes thirteen chapters to do it. He works it out in detail to drive it home to them at every point.

This is what he is saying: all your troubles are due to the fact that you are not clear about the person of Christ. So he bursts out without any introduction, "God, who at sundry times and in divers manners spake in time past unto the fathers by the prophets, hath in these last days spoken unto us by his Son [that is what you have forgotten, he says], whom he hath appointed heir of all things, by whom also he made the worlds." He is saying, you are looking at your persecutors; you are saying, "They have robbed us of our goods, they are treating us very harshly, they are very unkind to us." "Listen," he says, "[He] who being the brightness of his glory, and the express image of his person, and upholding all things by the word of his power, when he had by himself purged our sins, sat down on the right hand of the Majesty on high" (Heb. 1:3). Look at him, he says. "Looking unto Jesus"; dwell upon that. Do not look at your enemies and your difficulties and your problems; realize that he is there and that he has all power. He is waiting until he makes his enemies his footstool.

Are these the things that occupy your mind and your heart and your interest? It is a sign of being born again and having life that you meditate upon your High Priest above and that you realize that he is there in all his glory at this present hour. You see the difference, do you not? You might say, "Ah yes, I took my salvation. I responded to the appeal. I went forward. I took Christ as my Savior. My sins are forgiven. I am all right, and now I will just go on." Is it only that? It sounds as if you are doing everything and that you are resting on something you did in the past. Where is Jesus? Where does he come in? Where is your personal relationship with him? Where is your personal reliance on him? Where is your personal glorying in him? It is a mark of the new life that this personal aspect becomes more and more evident.

Look at this matter in the writings of the apostle Paul, and you will see exactly what I mean. The apostle may be engaged in a bit of argumentation. He has to do this because of the state of the people, and he is working something out. Then in doing it he mentions the name of Jesus or of Christ or of the Lord Jesus Christ, and invariably it fires him up, and off he goes to some great ascription of praise and glory and worship and adoration. He forgets all his grammar, forgets his own argument, and has to come back to it by putting in a dash as it were. "Oh," say the experts, "he is guilty of incoherent syntax." Thank God he is! It is because he is in love with the person of the Son, and everything else is forgotten. If you like to use such terms, you can call it a Christ mysticism. I said in the last sermon that one of the greatest enemies is mysticism, and it is. I mean by that a philosophic mysticism. But here you have what you may call a Christ mysticism, and the apostle Paul, whenever he thinks of this blessed name, this blessed person, is transported, he bursts out, he cannot contain himself. His language becomes inadequate because of the glory and the blessedness of the person.

But again let us be very careful that we do not allow the enemy to sidetrack us by saying, "Ah yes, but after all the apostle Paul was a very exceptional person." That is the argument, is it not? We tend to evade all these things by saying things like, "Of course, this is always meant for someone exceptional, but not for me." My dear friends, that is the lie of the Devil; there is no such distinction in the Scriptures. The apostle is always at great pains to say that he is a man saved like everyone else. He has said that he is "less than the least of all saints." He says in writing to the Corinthians that he is not worthy to be called an apostle at all because he persecuted the church of Christ. What he is always telling us is that everything that he has known, we can also know. That does not mean that we shall see the Lord with the naked eye; that was peculiar to him because he was an apostle, a witness of the resurrection. But otherwise his argument is always that this is something that we are all to enjoy together because it is God's giving that matters, not our receptivity or any ability that is in us.

Now that is of the very essence of this matter, and thank God it is. We must get rid of this carnal thinking. We must not bring in here our various natural gifts. Here we are in a realm where they do not matter. That is what makes the worship of God such a unique thing. In the world your natural gifts and abilities, your intellect and so on all have great importance and great value. But the moment you come into the church they are not only of no value, they can be your greatest danger. No one has an advantage over anyone else here. Why? It is all the free gift of God; it is all the grace of God; it is all the operation of the Holy Spirit. It is all the seed of divine life that is put into us. The life is in the seed; so this is equally possible to all. And when you come down the centuries you find this testimony coming out, this repetition of the experience and the bursts of worship and of adoration that we find in the apostles. Read your hymnbooks and you will find this.

How sweet the Name of Jesus sounds
In a believer's ear!
It soothes his sorrows, heals his wounds,
And drives away his fear.[5]

Is that true of us? "How sweet the Name of Jesus sounds." Does it? Now I am not talking about repeating it mechanically. I am saying that it sounds so sweet at times that one is rendered speechless. Or listen to another:

Jesus, the very thought of Thee
With sweetness fills my breast;
But sweeter far Thy face to see,
And in Thy presence rest.[6]

Is this true of us? Have we this interest in the person? Not just what he has done for us, but the person himself—do we seek him? Listen again to another, Charles Wesley:

Thou, O Christ, art all I want,
More than all in Thee I find.[7]

Is that true of us? Do we know anything about that? Does he satisfy us? Have we such a knowledge of the person? Is that true of our experience? Is that how you feel at this moment? Does he give you complete satisfaction?

My Jesus, I love Thee, I know Thou art mine;
For Thee all the follies of sin I resign.[8]

The saints have cried out like this throughout the centuries.

O that I could forever sit
Like Mary at the Master's feet;
Be this my happy choice;
My only care, delight, and bliss,
My joy, my heaven on earth, be this,
To hear the Bridegroom's voice.[9]

You can read of some people at different times in the history of the church in whose case all this was so true that they dwelt so much upon the person and the glory of the person, upon the wonder and the amazement of what he had done and especially on the cross, that it is said of some of them that they developed what are called *stigmata*. Some are said to have meditated so much upon the cross and the nails in his hands and so on that marks appeared on their own hands. Do not be concerned about that. I simply mention it to show you that ordinary people, Christian people, once this life grows and develops and matures in them, are brought into the position in which they not only desire this personal knowledge but have it to such a degree that Jesus is so real to them that they do enter into the fellowship of his sufferings.

That is what the apostle Paul was talking about in Philippians 3:10: "That I may know him, and the power of his resurrection, and the fellowship of his sufferings, being made conformable unto his death." You enter into such a union with him that you partake, as it were, of his sufferings. Indeed the apostle in the first chapter of the epistle to the Colossians even talks about making up what remains of the sufferings of Christ. Here is an identity in which one really enters, even into a sharing of his sufferings. I leave it at that, but I leave it in the form of a question. How long have you been a Christian, how many years? Do you have an increasing interest in the person of Jesus Christ, an increasing desire to know him personally, and do you glory more and more in him as a person?

And then we go on and say the same thing about the Father. Here is a great mystery. Many saints in the church have testified that they know what it is to have separate communion with God the Father, God the Son, and God the Holy Spirit. All I am asking is, do we have this personal interest in the Father, do we like to think about his being and his attributes? Again the Bible is full of this, the thought of God and the glory of God and the being of God. "No man hath seen God at any time." But the Christian knows that God is personal. He is not an abstraction, not just a "ground of being" or even "love." God is personal. The men in the Bible met him, the living God; they came near him. Moses was given a view of his "back parts" as the Scripture puts it. God placed his hand upon him when he was in the cleft of the rock and passed by, and Moses was given just a glimpse of the back parts of God. And so the Christian, this new man, likes to think about this and to meditate about it. You no longer think of God as just some sort of agency that gives you blessings or someone to whom you turn when you are in trouble. You delight in him, you want to know him, and you delight in thinking about him and all his infinite attributes.

What has gone wrong with us Christian people? Three hundred years ago people used to write books on the attributes of God. They preached on them for months, and the people were delighted to hear them. But today we are so practical, we want short cuts. We do not think about God in his glorious attributes; we are just interested in blessings and experiences and in our own activities. We have gone seriously astray. Do we like to think of the everlasting and eternal God, existing in eternity, deciding for some amazing reason to create the world and to create man and to have man as a companion for himself? Do you mediate upon this glorious God and all his great purposes—how he governs by his providence, how he has provided for us? The psalmists write many psalms about this. Read Psalm 104 and you will see the psalmist glorying in the providence of God in nature and in creation.

And then you come to God in history and to God in redemption—the plan and the purpose of God before the foundation of the world. Note how the apostles deal with that, reminding themselves of it, being amazed at it. Paul says to the Corinthians who were boasting about their wisdom, their philosophy, and their cleverness, "Howbeit we speak wisdom among them that are perfect: yet not the wisdom of this world, nor of the princes of this world, that come to nought: But we speak the wisdom of God in a mystery, even the hidden wisdom, which God ordained before the world unto our glory" (1 Cor. 2:6–7). See how he has gone off into his ecstasy! Do we know what it is to accompany him there? Do we think of this "hidden wisdom, which God ordained before the world unto our glory"? I am simply asking as I close whether this is true of us—the worship of God, the contemplation of God, the adoration of God. "Immortal, invisible, the only wise God." Great hymns should be sung thoughtfully, with meditation, giving full value to every word and every phrase, to the glory of the eternal God.

> The God of Abraham praise
> Who reigns enthroned above;
> Ancient of everlasting days,
> And God of love.[10]

Listen to him as he puts it at the end: "Hail, Abraham's God, and mine!" Abraham's God is my God, and I glory in him as Abraham, Isaac, and Jacob did.

> O worship the King, all-glorious above,
> O gratefully sing His power and His love. . . .
> Pavilioned in splendor, and girded with praise.

Language becomes totally inadequate.

> O measureless might! Ineffable love!
> While angels delight to worship Thee above,
> The humbler creation, though feeble their lays,
> With true adoration shall all sing Thy praise.[11]

Oh my friends, all I am asking you is, do you delight in singing his praise? I do not mean being carried away by a tune. I mean that the words are so glorious to you that you thrill with the thought of them and that this has become your knowledge and your heart is possessed by these things. These are tests of life. No longer the cold, intellectual abstractions, no longer the distant thoughts of a legal God who is interested in moralisms, but "Abraham's God, and mine"—my God.

We shall go on to consider this further, but these are the things by which we who have received the life of God in our souls as the result of being born of the Spirit.

# 11

# The Fellowship of
# the Holy Spirit

## JOHN 3:8

Sunday morning sermon preached in
Westminster Chapel, March 20, 1966.

The wind bloweth where it listeth, and thou hearest the sound
thereof, but canst not tell whence it cometh, and whither it goeth:
so is every one that is born of the Spirit. (John 3:8)

We are now considering whether we have new life in us, whether this
great thing has taken place in us, whether by the Spirit of God we have
been born again, and there are many ways in which we can test that.
The test we are dealing with at the moment is one of the most wonderful of all, and that is our relationship to God and our knowledge of God.
This is something, as I must keep on reminding you and myself, that
is internal. Our Christian faith is not something outside us. That is always true of morality and law. But this is inside us, something spiritual,
something not only for the mind but for the heart. The whole person is
engaged and is involved. And as we have been seeing, one of the leading characteristics, therefore, of this life is this increasing desire for a
personal knowledge of God. It is expressed in that hymn of Toplady:

"Object of My First Desire." That is it! The hymn goes on, "Jesus, crucified for me."

Now I have been trying to show that this is one of the most wonderful
proofs of all of the fact that we are born again. We desire this personal
knowledge of God—God the Father, God the Son, and God the Holy
Spirit—more than anything else, more than we desire a knowledge of
theology and knowledge of the Scriptures, more than to be moral and
good, more even than we desire experiences as such. Above all is concen-
tration upon this person.

Let me sum it up by putting it like this: this is the thing that one
sees so clearly in the human analogy. The child, without understanding
why or how, desires the parents, particularly in times of grief or sorrow
or trouble. Everything else is thrown aside, and nothing will do but the
person. I remember once this being brought home very forcibly to me by
an old friend of mine who was also a great saint. He and I were talking,
and a little child was with us who was tending to disturb the conversation. So I turned rather impatiently to the child and said, "What do you
want?" The child answered, "I want Mother." And the old saint rebuked
me. He said, "There you are, you see. You say *what* do you want, and the
answer is who, a person—not *what*, but the person, the mother."

That is what is being put before us here, and it is therefore one of
the most delicate tests we can ever apply to ourselves. We can become
involved in a routine—that is always the danger with religion. We can
be content with church membership and things like that, but this is the
ultimate test. When there is life, it cries out for life, and the true Christian
cries out for this intimate knowledge of the Father and of the Son and
of the Holy Spirit.

Now we have considered in a general way our desire for the Father
and our knowledge of him in that way, and, too, the Son, though I took
them in the opposite order. We started with the Son because we are dealing with this matter experientially. Then we arrive at the knowledge of
the Father. And that brings us now to a consideration of this knowledge
that is possible to us of the Holy Spirit. I do not want to go into this in
too much detail, but I have already reminded you that many saints have

testified that it is possible to have this separate knowledge of the Father and of the Son and of the Holy Spirit.

Now in connection with our knowledge of the Holy Spirit, there is a term that is used in the New Testament itself that gives us the key to the understanding of this matter. It talks about "the communion of the Holy Ghost." Take what is called the apostolic benediction at the end of Paul's second letter to the Corinthians: "The grace of the Lord Jesus Christ, and the love of God, and the communion [or fellowship] of the Holy Ghost, be with you all" (2 Cor. 13:14). That is the key to the understanding of this matter. It means fellowship, cooperation. These are all meanings of the term that was used by the apostle in that benediction. But it also includes communication *from* and communication *with*; it is all included in this word that we translate as "fellowship" or "communion."

It can also sometimes be used for a kind of partnership; it is often used in that sense in the New Testament. We read that some of the disciples were "partners" in fishing, and that same term is used to describe our relationship with the Holy Spirit. The apostle can wish nothing greater than that for the Corinthians, so he puts it there at the end of his second epistle to them. Now we must try to discover something of the content of this great term. How may we know this? How may we know whether we really are enjoying the fellowship, the communion, of the Holy Spirit? I suggest that we can know it in the following ways.

The first is that we are definitely aware that in our (to use the term generally) religious life we are not doing everything ourselves. The religious man does everything himself. He is in charge; he takes up his religion and puts it down again. The religious man is not aware of anything apart from himself and his own activity. He believes it is a good thing to worship God on Sunday morning, so he does so, and if he feels he will not do so one Sunday, then he does not. He is in charge; he does everything. He believes in a certain amount of religion, but he misinterprets a text that says, "Be not righteous over much," (Eccles. 7:16) which he interprets as meaning, you must not take these things too seriously. He is in charge of these things and in control. That is always the characteristic of the religious man, and he believes, therefore, that all depends upon his faithfulness, his activity, and his zeal. That is always the characteristic of the religious and moral person. It is always a very self-contained life and a generally self-satisfied one for the same reason. It sets up its own standard and is satisfied that it is keeping it up; other people, of course, do not, but this person does.

We need not waste our time on this. Our Lord has described this perfectly for us in his famous parable of the Pharisee and the publican who went up into the temple to pray. The Pharisee goes right to the front and says, "God, I thank thee, that I am not as other men are . . . or even as this publican. I fast twice in the week, I give tithes of all that I possess." That is typical. He does not ask for anything; he does not need anything. He is so perfect; he is doing it all. He just thanks God that he is as he is, unaware of any need, not aware of anything dealing with him at all. He is in charge of the whole situation and is very pleased with the result. That is the Pharisee, the religious man. He is not aware of any outside influence, but he has chosen to believe certain things, and he now puts them into practice. It is all very neat and tidy, and all is well. Read again what our Lord says about him and how he contrasts him with that poor publican, who feels that he is scarcely worthy to enter into the place at all and beats his breast and can simply cry out for mercy and for compassion (Luke 18).

The apostle Paul gives us an equally clear picture of this in his own bit of autobiography in the third chapter of his epistle to the Philippians. He describes what he used to be and how *he* was doing it all; he had happened to be born a Hebrew and was proud of it—"circumcised the eight day, of the stock of Israel, of the tribe of Benjamin, an Hebrew of the Hebrews; as touching the law, a Pharisee; concerning zeal, persecuting the church; touching the righteousness which is in the law, blameless" (vv. 5–6). That is the same picture. And that is the characteristic of the merely religious person, but it is never the characteristic of the men and women who are spiritual and who are aware, above everything else, that they are what they are by the grace of God.

It is difficult to put these things into words. One either knows them or one does not. If, I repeat, you can explain what you are and why are you what you are, you are religious. But if you are amazed at it, you are spiritual. That is the first characteristic, therefore; that is quite obvious.

But the second step is to assert that the one who is born again, the spiritual person, is aware of the presence of the Holy Spirit. Religious people are not aware of any presence; they just have a system, and they live within that and try to fulfill it and to carry it out. But the essence of true faith is an awareness of the presence. Or let me put it still more generally: it is the awareness of Another. You cannot get rid of this mystical element in the Christian faith. This is not mysticism alone, which is philosophical, but a mystical element. In other words this is experiential, this is personal. And if it is not personal, it is not true.

Not only do you see this personal element in the Scriptures, you find it also in the great hymns. The greatest hymns always have it. Look at them and always notice the dates. You will find that the hymns that are composed in periods of revival and awakening and reformation always have this personal experimental element very prominently. You can almost tell by the hymn when it was composed. If you read the hymns in the Victorian era when they did not know much about revival, you lose this, and they sentimentalize about their own inward moods and feelings—morbid, introspective sentimentality. The really great hymns always have this objectivity, this awareness of the Other.

Therefore we are aware of being dealt with by him; that is what I am emphasizing. In contrast to those who do it all themselves, the thing that Christians, spiritual men and women, are most conscious of is that they are being dealt with and that they are in the hands of Another. You find (in the Bible) terms like this in connection with our relationship to the Holy Spirit—"resist the Spirit," "grieve the Spirit," and so on. And I am trying to establish the point that it is only the spiritual man or woman who knows the meaning of those terms. They know what it is to resist this Other or to grieve him. Now the religious man does not know that. All he knows is that he may not have come up to his own standard now and again, or he may have done things that he regards as wrong. But he is still judging it entirely in terms of his own standard. He is annoyed with himself, he feels that he has let himself down and that he must do better, but it is all in terms of himself.

But the whole point about spiritual men and women is that what troubles them is that they have resisted the Spirit. The Spirit was operating upon them, and they were rebellious, they were resistant, and they are aware of the fact that they have grieved and hurt and wounded the Spirit. Many hymns express this. Take a hymn of William Cowper, for instance, in which he puts it so clearly. After such a period in his life, he cries out:

> Return, O holy dove, return,
> Sweet messenger of rest!
> I hate the sins that made Thee mourn
> And drove Thee from my breast.[1]

You see the personal reference and the personal relationship, and this is of the very essence of this new life that is in Christ Jesus. It is a communion with God. "This is life eternal, that they might know thee, the only true God, and Jesus Christ, whom Thou hast sent," and know him in this experiential manner. So when Christians fall or fail or sin, this is what they are most acutely aware of, that they have hurt, they have wounded the Holy Spirit. So they plead with him to return.

You will find this in the experience of the saints down through the centuries. Something has gone wrong in their lives. It may be due to some sin or it may not be due to that, but for some reason or another they pass through a period of trials or aridity. It does not mean they are no longer living the Christian life; they are, and this is what really troubles them. They describe how though they are still doing everything they did before—reading the Scriptures, praying, doing good, refraining from evil, living the Christian life as far as their will and their willpower are concerned—and everything is all that could be desired, yet they are unhappy. And when you ask them why this is, they tell you they are unhappy because for some reason or another, "I am aware of a dryness. I do not seem to be realizing his presence." Some of them will struggle for long periods in this condition, and nothing can satisfy them until they are aware again of the old relationship, until they have renewed the relationship that somehow or another has become clouded. William Cowper, again, reminds us of this:

> Behind a frowning providence
> He hides a smiling face.[2]

But there are times when Christians only see the clouds, and what they are most concerned about is that they should now again enjoy this relationship that they have temporarily lost. This is a most important point because the Devil comes and suggests to such people that they might as well stop praying. No! The thing to do is to go on praying, and to keep on, knowing that he is there. And then, in his own good time, he will grant you again this realization of his presence and of your relationship to him.

I do not want to elaborate on this now, because it would take us too far away from the immediate object that we have in view, but let me say in passing that those who know something about the ways of the spiritual life know this experience. The old experts in this, the old teachers, used to talk about periods of desertion. They used to teach about how God averted his face, as it were, and there is no doubt that this is true. It is part of our whole understanding of the Christian life. God, for our good, sometimes seems to withdraw himself and avert his face. I believe he does so to make us grow. We would remain children if he did not do that. He wants us to become people who trust him, as it were, in the dark, who trust him in spite of feelings, who trust him in spite of everything, who rest on his bare Word and say, "Though he slay me, yet will I trust him" (Job 13:15). But the thing that comes out of all this is that Christians are aware of this relationship, and therefore they are grieved and troubled and unhappy when for the time being they lack it.

There then is the second step, our awareness of God's presence. But let me go even beyond that. Christians—spiritual, born-again men and women—are therefore aware of their dependence upon the Spirit, and this, of course, takes it yet further. In other words, they have discovered that they cannot rely upon themselves, and they learn to rely more and more upon the Holy Spirit and his presence and his power. The whole of the Christian life is really life in the Spirit; that is the great contrast that the apostle Paul draws, for instance, in chapters 7 and 8 of the epistle to the Romans, and particularly in chapter 8: "Ye are not in the flesh, but in the Spirit" (v. 9). "The law of the Spirit of life in Christ Jesus hath made me free from the law of sin and death" (v. 2). That is the great contrast. "Ye are not in the flesh, but in the Spirit, if so be that the Spirit of God dwell in you. Now if any man have not the Spirit of Christ, he is none of his" (v. 9). So it is a life in the Spirit, and this governs one's entire outlook.

Let me work it out like this very briefly. It is still this contrast between the religious person, religious practices, and conforming to religious forms and this living relationship, this living worship. Those who are spiritual, who are "born of the Spirit," are no longer content with merely following the forms, because to them that can be empty and can mean nothing. They are concerned about this spiritual element. Our Lord himself taught that. He taught it to the woman of Samaria—it was the whole essence of his discussion with her. She was a religious woman, she was "worshipping in this mountain," as she essentially said. In summary she said, "My forefathers taught that you should worship God in this mountain, but you Jews say that God should be worshipped in Jerusalem," She was tied to places and forms and so on. But our Lord answered and said, "God is a Spirit: and they that worship him must worship him in spirit and in truth" (John 4).

The test, therefore, that we apply to ourselves is this: the character of my worship, the character of my reading the Bible, the character of my prayer life. There is nothing to prevent you from sitting down and deciding to read the Bible. You may have a lexicon or a concordance, you may look up the meanings of words, and indeed, it may be very wonderful. It is like a crossword puzzle, and you become expert on the letter and the details. You may have it all at your fingertips, and you may read your Bible like that. But what a world of difference there is between that and reading the Bible in the Spirit. By that I mean that you realize it is not the letter that matters but the spirit of it all; it is not the words but the message. You realize that it is not the actual material content, but it is that which is life and speaks to you. It is very difficult to put this into words. I could tell you a great deal about this. I know what it is to spend hours reading the Bible as it were in the flesh, not that I want to do so, but I cannot do anything else for the time being. And then the Spirit comes, and the whole thing changes.

That, of course, is the romance of the Christian life, and if I may say so it is particularly the romance of the life of the preacher. A man, another minister incidentally, said to me yesterday, "How much longer are you going to remain at Westminster Chapel?" I said, "What do you mean by that?" He said, "Well, how long have you been there?" "At this moment," I said, "I have nearly finished my twenty-eighth year." "Well," he said, "I don't know how you do it." And I said, "That's the whole point. I don't know how I do it either." What I mean is this: the man was arguing—and we have all thought like this—that you would have thought that a man, after a given number of years, would have gone through the whole Bible. He is, therefore, finished and must move on! That is not the spiritual approach. The marvel and the wonder and, I repeat, the romance of it all is just this: you find yourself reading something that you have read dozens and dozens of times before, but suddenly it is new, it is illuminated, it is glorious. It speaks to you, it ravishes your heart, it puts you on your feet, and it goes on expanding. And it illuminates, as it were, the whole of the rest of the Bible in a way you have never seen before.

That is what I am talking about. One learns that what really matters in this realm is the communion of the Holy Spirit. It is not natural ability. That soon comes to an end; one becomes tired and jaded. I have often heard of men saying they have left the ministry. Why? "I have preached myself out," they say. What a terrible thing to say. If *you* are doing it, you are bound to preach yourself out; your themes are limited and so on. But when the Spirit is there dealing with the Word with you, there is endless possibility.

It is exactly the same with prayer. What a difference between a man praying because he wants to pray and because he believes it is right for him to pray and a man praying "in the Spirit." I cannot find words to express the difference, but it is one of the most real things one can ever know. I remember two particular prayer meetings that I have been privileged to attend. One was a regular weekly prayer meeting, and one went to the prayer meeting on this particular occasion not expecting anything at all. It started at 7:15 as usual; it was in the summer, and everything seemed to be against us. Two people prayed; they were good people, and they were doing their utmost. Then another man got up whom one never regarded as a particularly spiritual person. But somehow, in the mystery and the marvel of God's ways, the Spirit of God chose to come upon that man just as he was starting to pray, and he prayed in a manner that was amazing and astonishing. He began praying in the Spirit. His very voice changed; everything changed. He was using English. It was the same language we all understood, there was no question of speaking in tongues, but it was true praying in the Spirit, a man being taken up and lifted up. And as the result of what happened to him it happened to the others, and on and on they went praying without any intermission till about ten o'clock. Now that was praying in the Spirit. One was aware of the reality of the spiritual realm and of the presence of God, something indescribable. You cannot describe these things; you can simply give an account of them in that way.

Now this can happen to us individually, and by the grace of God it does happen to us individually. So there is praying, and there is praying. All I am saying is that if you know anything about this "praying in the Spirit," it is because you are "born again"; it is because you have been "born of the Spirit." And this is what the New Testament is always exhorting us to. Do not be content, it seems to be saying, with the ordinary level, do not be content in life on the human level; do it in the Spirit, rely upon the Spirit, look to the Spirit. The same applies to preaching and to every single activity in the Christian life. The test, therefore, is our awareness of our dependence upon him. So we seek him, and we pray for him.

> Come, Holy Spirit, come;
> Let Thy bright beams arise;
> Dispel the darkness from our minds,
> And open all our eyes.[3]

That is the kind of prayer I am talking about. You realize that without him you cannot do these things properly.

Breathe on me, Breath of God,
Fill me with life anew,
That I may love what Thou dost love,
And do what Thou wouldst do.[4]

That is it!

Do you know anything about that kind of longing? You feel that you are lifeless; you feel that you are dead. These are all experiences that God's people have to go through. We are still in the flesh, and this inter-relationship between the body and the mind and the spirit is a very real and a very subtle thing. And because of physical conditions at times we feel lifeless; we have to drag ourselves through our duties. It is right that we should do so. Do not sit down and wait for something to happen; go on, but do not rely upon your going on. Turn to him and pray, "Breathe on me, Breath of God, fill me with life anew"—that is it. So spiritual men or women know that nothing is right until that is true of them. They are aware of this profound dependence upon the Holy Spirit, who is their partner, their co-operator; they are in fellowship, in partnership with him. They are doing business with him, if you like, and he is the senior partner. Without him we really can do nothing.

We are aware, therefore, of his activities within us. I have put it generally by saying that we are aware of the Other and of his influence, but I want to mention certain particular activities of this inner life. The Spirit is in us. You cannot be a Christian without having the Holy Spirit in you. I am not talking about the baptism with the Spirit. I am talking about having the Spirit within you, as the disciples had him before the day of Pentecost. Our Lord breathed on them in the upper room and said, "Receive ye the Holy Ghost" (John 20:21). That was several days before the day of Pentecost when he came upon them in the form of a baptism to give them power. I am talking now about how born-again Christians have the Spirit in them, and they are aware of the workings and the activities of the Spirit within them. What the baptism does is to make them still more aware. The Spirit heightens the awareness.

What are these activities? Well, take the promptings of the Spirit.

Look at this again as expressed by the apostle Paul in Philippians 2:12–13: "Work out your own salvation with fear and trembling. For *it is God which worketh in you* both to will and to do of his good pleasure." Now I put that under the heading of promptings, and here is a test we apply to ourselves. It is again just an elaboration of this point that you are not doing it all yourself. Religion is something that you have in a bag, and you pull it out, use it, and put it back again. But here are men or women who are aware of promptings quite apart from their own decisions. One of the most dangerous things in the spiritual life is a timetable. There are, of necessity, loose ends in the spiritual life because it is life in the Spirit. I have illustrated that often in the writings of the apostle Paul, how the pundits get annoyed with him for breaking the rules of grammar, breaking into a new thought halfway through a sentence, and forgetting what he had started to say, and so on. That is the Spirit's doing.

But the other way is so nice and neat and tidy; people talk about "burning a beautiful phrase" or something like that. That is literature, but that is not preaching, that is not Christianity, and that is no good. Here is the dynamic power of the Spirit, and he breaks in upon us and all our timetables, and he urges us, he moves us, and he stimulates us for prayer, for Bible study, for meditation about these things. This only happens to those who are "born of the Spirit"; it is the divine partner dealing with us. His desire is to bring us to ultimate perfection, so he will not leave us alone. There is a hymn that expresses this. Though the writer did not mean the same thing, because he was further back in experience, it is equally true at every level in this experience. He says, "O Love that wilt not let me go." Sometimes we are almost annoyed with him. We want to be doing something else, but he keeps on interfering, prompting, urging, and we resist, we fight with him. That is it. The fighting is a proof of the fact that we know that he is there, and we know what we are doing. Afterward we feel what fools, what cads we were, and we mourn as William Cowper did ("I hate the sins that made Thee mourn and drove Thee from my breast"). There it is, an awareness of these promptings.

Or let me put it a stage beyond that—not only promptings but leadings and guidance. There is nothing plainer in the New Testament than the way in which these Christian people, these early Christians particularly, were led and guided by the Holy Spirit. Take Philip. After he had been preaching in Samaria,

> The angel of the Lord spake unto Philip, saying, Arise, and go toward the south unto the way that goeth down from Jerusalem unto Gaza, which is desert. And he arose and went. (Acts 8:26–27)

Then we read that another man, an Ethiopian, a eunuch with great authority under the queen of the Ethiopians, was returning from Jerusalem and was sitting in his chariot reading Isaiah the prophet. "Then the Spirit said unto Philip, Go near, and join thyself to this chariot. And Philip ran thither to him" (vv. 29–30). Here is the point: "The Spirit said unto Philip." He did not just decide, "Ah, I wonder what that man is doing there. I think I'd better go and have a word with him." Not at all! "The Spirit said unto Philip"—and Philip knew it was the Spirit. There was no difficulty about understanding this. This is what I call *leading*.

Or take what we read of the church at Antioch in Acts 13:

> Now there were in the church that was at Antioch certain prophets and teachers. . . . As they ministered to the Lord, and fasted, the Holy Ghost said, Separate me Barnabas and Saul for the work whereunto I have called them. (vv. 1–2)

That was not an audible voice, but they were absolutely certain that it was the Holy Spirit who had spoken to them: "The Holy Ghost *said* . . ." But if you want a still more striking example go to the sixteenth chapter of the book of Acts of the Apostles, verses 6–7:

> Now when they had gone throughout Phrygia and the region of Galatia [this is Paul and his companions], and were forbidden of the Holy Ghost to preach the word in Asia, after they were come to Mysia, they assayed to go into Bithynia: but the Spirit suffered them not.

There you have this contrast stated very clearly. They decided to go, they had purposed to go, but they were not allowed to go. They were "forbidden of the Holy Ghost," and "the Spirit suffered [allowed] them not."

Here are spiritual men who are in such fellowship with the Holy Spirit that they know both when he tells them to do something and when he tells them not to do something. We see the contrast between that and the natural man's thinking. Paul was a great man and a great genius, and it seemed to him that the right thing to do was to go and preach the word in the province of Asia; it seemed to be the obvious next step. But he was not allowed to do it, and he was sufficiently sensitive to know this was not the will of the Spirit. Then he says, "If I am not to go there, then obviously I am meant to go to Mysia and Bithynia." But the Spirit did not allow them to do so. "And they passing by Mysia came down to Troas." The point was that the Spirit's plan was that Paul should come to Europe, to Philippi. So he stops Paul from going here and he stops him going there, so that there is only one thing left—he must go straight on, and he comes to Troas. But he does not know why he is there. Then that night he has the vision of the man from Macedonia, and then he understands. He did not at first, but he is so sensitive to the presence and the working and the leadings of the Spirit that he knows the prohibition from the right hand and from the left and gives obedience to this.

The same thing runs right through Paul's story. In the lyrical account in Acts 20 of his bidding farewell to the elders of the church at Ephesus, he says in verses 22–23, "I go bound in the spirit unto Jerusalem, not knowing the things that shall befall me there: save that the Holy Ghost witnesseth in every city, saying that bonds and afflictions abide me." The Holy Spirit was witnessing through the people and was giving them this understanding, and they were able to tell the apostle these things. In Acts 21:4 it is still more specific. Paul arrives again in another place and we read, "And finding disciples, we tarried there seven days: who said to Paul through the Spirit, that he should not go up to Jerusalem."

There it is, leadings and guidance of the Spirit. And as you read the literature of the lives of the saints through the centuries you will find their increasing sensitivity to this. Indeed, some of them arrived at a stage in which they would scarcely move apart from this. It can be carried to excess, but the question I am putting to you is this: Are we aware of this partnership, "the communion [fellowship] of the Holy

Ghost," and are we so aware of him that we are aware of his leading and his guidance.

And then think of the way in which he can give us special and unusual power and authority to perform various tasks that he himself has allotted to us. Here is another wonderful test, the test of power, the power of the Spirit, and we find this in many, many places in the New Testament. Let me give you just one instance in order to illustrate what I mean. Take the story that we are given in Acts 4 of how the apostles Peter and John were arrested and were arraigned before the court in Jerusalem (the Sanhedrin) because of their healing of the man who was born lame who was placed daily at the Beautiful Gate of the temple. As the result of their preaching afterward, they were arrested and put on trial. The authorities speak first of all and they say, "By what power, or by what name, have ye done this? Then Peter, filled with the Holy Ghost, said unto them . . ." (vv. 7–8). Now do not misunderstand that as many people do. They say, "A man is only filled with the Holy Spirit once." Some say that that happens to everyone at regeneration; others say that happened only once to the apostles, on the day of Pentecost. But it goes on being repeated; you can be filled with the Holy Spirit like this many, many times over. Here is Peter, in a difficult situation, fighting, in a sense, for his life and that of John and of the whole church, fighting for the whole future of the Christian faith. It is a most serious and momentous occasion, and no doubt Peter is acutely aware of his inadequacy. But he is a man who was filled with the Spirit on the day of Pentecost. He knows the realm in which he is now living and his dependence upon the Spirit, and there is no doubt that he uttered up a prayer that he might be guided aright. And what happens is that he is filled with the Spirit. He is given words of wisdom, words of understanding; he is given power, he is given authority, and it impresses the authorities when they speak with him. We are told, "When they saw the boldness of Peter and John, and perceived that they were unlearned and ignorant men, they marvelled; and they took knowledge of them, that they had been with Jesus" (v. 13).

But they were wrong. They were right that Peter and John had been with Jesus, but remember, these same apostles had been with Jesus when they denied him at the time of the crucifixion. Their "being with Jesus" does not explain the boldness of these men; it is only the beginning of the explanation. This same Peter had been with Jesus for three years when he denied him to that servant girl at the trial and even denied him with oaths and curses. Yes, he had been with Jesus, but that is not the explanation. These authorities were wrong. That was the introduction—to what? Well, being with Jesus, eventually believing in him, having his own explanation of his death and resurrection, being told to tarry in Jerusalem, then the baptism with the Holy Spirit, and the knowledge of this spiritual realm, and the fulfillment of the promise that "the Spirit shall be in you." Peter knows this now, and therefore he realizes his need and depends on the Spirit and is filled with this clarity, this understanding, this power of speech, this ordering of language, this presentation of his case. He speaks as he is "filled with the Spirit." And as you go on in the book of the Acts of the Apostles and keep your eye on that, you will find that was constantly repeated. Whenever these men are called to work a miracle, you generally get this idea of being filled with the Spirit.

This is something that all of us should know in experience, an ability given, an understanding given. I have already mentioned it in connection with reading the Scriptures, but it also has to do with speaking to others. There is a word of wisdom and of understanding, knowing how to present yourself and your case, and this power, this authority, this freedom that the Holy Spirit of God alone can give. "Where the Spirit of the Lord is, there is liberty. But we all, with open face beholding as in a glass the glory of the Lord, are changed into the same image from glory to glory, even as by the Spirit of the Lord" (2 Cor. 3:17–18). It is the power and the activity of the Spirit upon us.

There, then, are some of the ways in which we can know that we know the fellowship and the communion of the Holy Spirit. That is the Christian life! Not men or women in their own strength trying to do something painfully, wearily as a matter of duty. Rather it is life from the Spirit, the Spirit entering in, giving them life anew, working in them, leading, guiding, prompting, giving power and authority and understanding, but above all an awareness of himself. "Now," our Lord essentially says to Nicodemus,

It is no use you asking me questions as to how I work miracles and preach as I do. Verily, verily, I say unto you, you must be born again. A man who is not born again cannot see the kingdom of God. Except a man be born of water and of the Spirit, he cannot enter the kingdom of God.

So realizing our utter nothingness and our complete helplessness, we offer this prayer:

Breathe on me, Breath of God,
Fill me with life anew,
That I may love what Thou dost love,
And do what Thou wouldst do.[5]

And we will never offer that prayer in vain.

# 12

# Heavenly Things

## JOHN 3:8

Sunday morning sermon preached in
Westminster Chapel, March 27, 1966.

We have been considering together the marks and characteristics of the new birth in order that we may know for certain whether we are truly Christians or not. The Bible exhorts us to "examine" ourselves, to "prove" our own selves, whether we are in the faith or not. It is possible for us to imagine that we are Christians without being so. Because there is much teaching about that, we have been looking at the manifestations of this new life from God in the souls of men that result from the new birth, regeneration. It is essential that we should do that, and we have been doing so in terms of the great statement and illustration that our Lord himself used: "The wind bloweth where it listeth, and thou hearest the sound thereof, but canst not tell whence it cometh, and whither it goeth: so is every one that is born of the Spirit" (John 3:8). You see the effects, the results, and we have been examining them and looking at them, but now the record takes us further and beyond that.

Nicodemus is still in trouble. "Nicodemus answered and said unto him, How can these things be?" So our Lord deals with that, and his answer will occupy us now. I am concerned to show and to emphasize that the great obstacle that prevented Nicodemus from entering into life still prevents so many people from ever becoming Christians. It is, at the same time (it seems to me) the chief hindrance that keeps Christian people themselves from receiving "his fullness . . . and grace for [upon] grace."

Read the descriptions given in the New Testament of Christian men and women and the possibilities for them while they are still in this world of time. Then examine yourself in the light of that. We are offered "the exceeding riches of [God's] grace" (Eph. 2:7). We are offered the "unsearchable riches of Christ" (Eph. 3:8). We are told that we can be "filled with all the fullness of God" (Eph. 3:19). That is what is held out before us. That is what we are meant to be as Christian people. I repeat, let us examine ourselves. Do we correspond to that? Are we like that? If not, one of the main causes is the very thing that stumbled Nicodemus. There is an adversary and an enemy who is always trying to stand between us and the receiving of God's fullness and grace. And the weapon that he uses most frequently (it seems to me) is the very one that he used here in the case of Nicodemus.

What is it? Let me put it as a principle to you. The supreme hindrance to our receiving the fullness of this life is pride of intellect and confidence in understanding. That is the greatest enemy in these spiritual matters from the beginning to end. And the fact that we may be converted and are Christians does not mean that we have finished with that particular problem. It is a problem that dogs our footsteps all the way through. You find illustrations of that even in the New Testament itself. In a sense the apostle Paul had to write his epistle to the Galatians simply to deal with this. He says in effect, "Having started in the Spirit, are you going to go on in the flesh?" It was the same trouble in the church at Corinth. This enemy keeps creeping in. It has dogged the footsteps of Christian people throughout the centuries. There is always a tendency to fall back on works and human ability and understanding. So I lay it down as a proposition that this is the supreme hindrance to our receiving God's fullness and grace upon grace.

This is, of course, implicit in our Lord's teaching about the new birth. It is essential, just as he says it is: "Ye *must* be born again"; "Except a man be born of water and of the Spirit, he cannot enter into the kingdom of God." So the fact that a man *must* be born again is in itself sufficient to prove that as he is with all his powers and propensities, he can never enter into the kingdom of God on his own.

This truth was implicit before, but now our Lord makes it perfectly clear and explicit. That is the particular and peculiar value of these few verses that we are looking at together. "How can these things be?" That is the difficulty.

A man of the world comes into a Christian church, hears an exposition of the Scripture, and is bewildered, baffled. Why? Because it is totally unlike everything he has ever heard before, everything that is outside. It is odd, it is mysterious, it is unusual, and he is troubled because he cannot understand. But he *wants* to understand. Man, by nature, always wants to understand. The third chapter of the book of Genesis tells us that was the first sin. It is indeed the original sin. Man wants to be as God, and the Devil tempts him along that line. "Has God said? Don't listen to him," says the Devil to Eve. "If you eat of this fruit, you will be as gods, and you'll understand everything." And that is what man wants. He starts with that. This is innate within him, this desire for full comprehension.

That leads to the next step, which is this: man says he will not believe anything unless he can understand it. That, as you know, is the common position and argument put forward by the person who is not a Christian, by humanists and others. "I'm not going to believe a thing unless I understand it."

Let me just say this in passing: people who take that position are not only being foolish, they are being utterly inconsistent with themselves. Let me use the argument I have often used. Do you understand electricity? The answer is you do not. The greatest scientists do not understand electricity, but they use it. They are prepared to use it though they do not understand it. They are prepared to harness its effects and its results though they do not understand the thing itself. To be consistent they should never use electricity because they do not understand it, but that is the point of inconsistency when it comes to unbelief and sin.

But this tends to follow us even into the Christian life itself, and this is where it becomes most serious. The next step, then, is to limit the truth of God to the measure of our understanding. So when we come to the gospel and say that we believe it—we believe in God, we believe in salvation in Jesus Christ—we tend to put our limits on what that means. To me this is perhaps the greatest sin in the Christian church today. We have reduced the infinite, glorious, everlasting gospel to the measure of our understanding. We do so in so many different ways. We do so even in our very definitions, in our outlining of what truth is. This is the common tendency at the present time. The moment you put the authority of the Bible to one side and refuse to submit to revelation but say that truth is only that which you can understand and comprehend, you are guilty of this very thing. That is what is being done today. People are no longer governed by the Scriptures. They sit in judgment upon it. They say, "This is right; that isn't right." Revelation is no longer the authority. What is the authority? Man's understanding and philosophy—and philosophy is nothing but man's human understanding—and that is the tragedy today. The gospel is being limited to the measure of man's mind and comprehension. They throw out the miraculous and supernatural. They say, "Modern scientific people can't possibly believe this." So out it goes. This is happening even among those of us who are in the church. The glory of the gospel is being limited and lowered and narrowed, and this, I repeat, is probably the greatest hindrance of all to our receiving God's fullness and grace upon grace.

What is your view and mine of the Christian life? Far too often it is just this: "Oh yes, I believed in Jesus Christ at conversion. I made a decision and accepted him." You have relied upon that. You have stopped doing certain things, and you begin to do others, and you have it all nice and complete. You do your duties, and you may be active in work, and there you are. You are self-content, and you think that is Christianity. But, my dear friends, is it? Have we received his fullness and grace, ever expanding until we know something of the fullness of God himself? I feel this has been one of the great troubles perhaps in the present century— and I am talking to evangelical people in particular. I feel we have made the gospel something small, sometimes even something glib, something that we can handle, so that we are afraid of yielding ourselves to the possibilities that are put before us in the New Testament Scriptures.

Now this is something that is quite fatal, this limiting of the gospel to the level of our understanding and comprehension. There is a danger that many today are even interpreting the Scriptures in terms of their little experience instead of judging their experience by the teaching of the Scriptures. There are people who are afraid of the Holy Spirit and his power and do not do anything about it. Because they have not experienced it, they would even limit the teaching of the Scripture. It is all interpreted in terms of their own understanding. It is so nice and neat. Nothing unusual must happen. They are afraid, as it were, of the breaking in of the supernatural. Here is the great danger that is exposed and denounced in the New Testament. Our Lord does it here with Nicodemus at the very heart of his message to him, but he did it in many other places also.

Look at the end of the eleventh chapter of Matthew's Gospel. Our Lord breaks out into prayer and says, "I thank thee, O Father, Lord of heaven and earth, because thou hast hid these things from the wise and prudent, and hast revealed them unto babes. Even so, Father: for so it seemed good in thy sight" (Matt. 11:25–26). There it is, once and forever. It is hidden from the wise and prudent, people with understanding, but it is revealed to babes. The apostle Paul, giant intellect though he was, keeps on making the same point. He puts it clearly at the end of 1 Corinthians 1:

> Ye see your calling, brethren, how that not many wise men after the flesh, not many mighty, not many noble, are called: but God hath chosen the foolish things of the world to confound the wise; and God hath chosen the weak things of the world to confound the things which are mighty. (vv. 26–27)

And again in the second chapter in verse 14 he says, "But the natural man receiveth not the things of the Spirit of God: for they are foolishness unto him: neither can he know them, because they are spiritually discerned." These are great statements, yet people seem to fail to grasp and understand the truth. They say, "How can these things be? I can't understand it. I can't follow this." And because they cannot, they hold back and limit the possibilities of grace and of glory.

Now let me, in expounding our Lord's teaching to Nicodemus, show you in the second place the folly of this as well as its utter uselessness, the folly of trusting to human wisdom and of wanting to understand. Our Lord ridicules it here in handling Nicodemus, and he reprimands him. He says,

> Art thou a master of Israel [a teacher of Israel], and knowest not these things? . . . If I have told you earthly things, and ye believe not, how shall ye believe [how can you possibly believe], if I [should] tell you of heavenly things? (John 3:10, 12)

Here is the message to so many of us at this present time: the utter folly of always putting forward the question "How can these things be? I'm not going to believe unless I understand." Oh, the folly, the tragedy of this. This is the curse of man! This is why the world is as it is today. It is rejecting God and his teaching and his government because of this. It is just a repetition of the chaos that resulted at the fall, man's original disobedience.

This folly can be shown by the fact that man cannot really understand earthly things. What does our Lord mean by "If I have told you earthly things, and ye believe not . . ."? He is undoubtedly referring to what he has just been saying in his illustration about the wind. He has just put it bluntly to Nicodemus by saying, "Verily, verily, I say unto thee, Except a man be born again . . ." Then he repeats it, "[You must be] born of water and of the Spirit."

And Nicodemus is baffled. "Well," says our Lord, "it's like this. You hear the sound of the wind. You can't see it. You don't understand it or the rules that govern it, but you hear the sound. You see the clothes flapping on the line. You see the branches of the trees swaying. You see the effects. You don't understand what's happening or how it's produced, but you see its manifestations, and you're content with that, and you use it. What I'm talking about is like that. There is a mystery about it, but you see the effects and the results."

But Nicodemus still does not understand. He goes on saying, "How can these things be?" So our Lord puts it like this to him: "You can't even understand earthly things as I have put them to you." Being interpreted, that means we are incapable of really understanding either what we see or the workings of the gospel in human life, in the life of this world.

These things have been prophesied in the Old Testament. Our Lord reprimands Nicodemus for that reason. He says, "You are a master of Israel. You ought to know these things. Haven't you read the prophets? They have said that when the new age comes, the lame man shall leap as the hart, the blind shall be enabled to see, and the deaf to hear. The new age is coming, and the Spirit will be poured out. That's the teaching. Are you ignorant of all that? You have that in your Scriptures. As a Jew you should have been prepared for this kind of thing. Don't you see? Don't you understand? You've noticed me. You've seen my power to work miracles. You've expressed your amazement at my teaching. You've come to the conclusion that I must be a teacher sent from God. Well then, why don't you listen to me? Why don't you follow out your own logic? Why are you still baffled?"

That's what is meant by "earthly things," and, of course, that is equally applicable to us at the present time. No one can understand the facts of Christian history—the lives of the saints, the greatest benefactors that the world has ever known, the amazing things that have happened to them, the astounding things they have been able to do. These are earthly things. They belong solidly to history. Can anybody understand them? They cannot. The wise people of today do not understand these things.

In this present century of ours [the twentieth century] we have been making great efforts to do this. Psychology with its analysis claimed at first it was going to explain everything, and it tries to explain the Christian man, but it cannot. It is totally inadequate! And again the apostle Paul has put this very clearly in 1 Corinthians 2:15 where he says, "He that is spiritual judgeth all things." He means by "spiritual" that the man who is born again, the man who has the Spirit within him, has an understanding of these matters. "He that is spiritual judgeth all things, yet he himself is judged of no man." That means that when people are born again and become Christians, they have the Spirit in them; they have an understanding, but other people cannot understand them.

The true Christian is a problem to everybody who is not a Christian, and this again, of course, is one of the best tests we can ever apply to ourselves. If people can understand you in total, you are not a Christian. The Christian is a mystery. The Christian is an enigma. He must be. You cannot have the life of God put into you and remain as you were. You become strange. There is a difference; something has happened. "How can these things be?" they say. They do not understand you. They see what has happened to you. They see what you are, but they do not understand. They do not understand these earthly things, and that is the whole position with the world today. And the tragedy is that you and I tend to bring that even into the realm of the Christian life. Unless we have full understanding, we are not prepared to believe, we are not prepared to yield ourselves, and so we put our limits upon God's blessing to us and the possibilities of grace.

But let us go on to the bigger argument that our Lord uses. "If I have told you earthly things, and ye believe not"—here's the question—"how can you possibly believe if I tell you heavenly things?" And here are the things that we need to spend more time contemplating and considering. What are they? Well, our Lord puts it like this: "No man hath ascended up to heaven, but he that came down from heaven, even the Son of man which is in heaven." These are the heavenly things. "Look here, Nicodemus," says our Lord to this great teacher, "give up this attempt to understand. I've come down to your level and have used a human, earthly illustration, but you still can't follow. Well then, do you think you can possibly understand if I begin to tell you about the other things, the upper limits and reaches of this great salvation that I've come to bring? Man, see at once that is utter folly. Give it up."

I feel that is what our Lord is saying to us. Here are some of the heavenly things. They are revealed in the Scriptures. First, there is the teaching concerning the blessed Holy Trinity, God in three persons and yet only one God—Father, Son, Holy Spirit. Think of the glory of God if you can. This is what we are concerned about. This is what Christianity is. Christianity is not just about being nice and good and moral and a little bit better than obvious sinners. It is not expressing your opinions on the current political problems of the day. Those are earthly things. The content of this, the real basis of this, the real essence of this is the heavenly things.

What is Christianity? Christianity is that which brings a man or woman to a knowledge of God. Take our Lord's own definition of eternal life: "This is life eternal, that they might know thee the only true God, and Jesus Christ, whom thou hast sent." That is Christianity—knowing God, not just believing a few things about God and living a nice little life. That is not Christianity. That is often nothing but morality or mere religion. The essence of this is entering into this realm into which you begin to know and have communion with the Father and the Son and the Holy Spirit.

Where's your understanding now? Are you still saying, "How can these things be? I can't understand three persons and one God." Of course, you cannot. Are you ever fool enough to think that you could or that anyone else could? That is what our Lord is ridiculing! You who are a finite little person who cannot understand yourself or the phenomena that are round and about you, are you going to try to measure the inimitable and eternal God? God who is from everlasting to everlasting, without beginning or end—do you think you can understand him? Are you mad enough to bring such a term into this realm? These are the heavenly things.

Or try to think about the glory of God and the glory of heaven. Read the sixth chapter of the book of the prophet Isaiah, because there we get a glimpse of it. Isaiah was a very great and a very able man, but being called to his great task and mission, he was given just a glimpse into the glory, and you remember what happened. The glory of God appeared, and the posts of the door begin to shake, and the place was filled with smoke, and he felt completely shattered and undone. He has not seen God. He has had only a glimpse of him, as it were, in the distance, and his reaction is, "Woe is me! for I am undone; because I am a man of unclean lips, and I dwell in the midst of a people of unclean lips" (v. 5). He does not say, "What is happening? What is this phenomenon? How can these things be? Can I understand this scientifically?" He does not think of such things. He is not mad enough to do so. It is the glory of God, and he is humbled to the ground and to the dust.

My dear friends, this is Christianity, not something that you and I can have in a neat little packet so we can explain everything and control everything. Do you want to know something about these heavenly things? It is when you and I and all Christians are lifted up in this realm that God will begin to smile on us and use us and we will see this whole world shaken again in a great revival.

Listen to the apostle Paul in 2 Corinthians 12:

> It is not expedient for me doubtless to glory. I will come to visions and revelations of the Lord. I knew a man in Christ above fourteen years ago, (whether in the body, I cannot tell; or whether out of the body, I cannot tell: God knoweth;) such an one caught up to the third heaven. And I knew such a man, (whether in the body, or out of the body, I cannot tell). (vv. 1–3)

Understanding has been dropped, you see. He cannot tell; of course, he cannot. He does not ask, "How can these things be?" It is happening. He is there! He is lifted up. But he does not understand. "God knoweth . . . how that he was caught up into paradise, and heard unspeakable words, which it is not lawful for a man to utter. Of such an one will I glory: yet of myself I will not glory, but in mine infirmities" (vv. 3–5).

That is a glimpse of the heavenly things. Do we know anything about these things? Can you explain everything? Is Christianity just a little system that you have worked out? O God, have mercy upon us! We shall not all of necessity be given that privileged experience of the great apostle, but in a measure it is open to all of us to be lifted up into this realm that is entirely beyond all human understanding.

Listen to it again as it is put in the book of Revelation:

> After this I looked, and, behold, a door was opened in heaven: and the first voice which I heard was as it were of a trumpet talking

with me; which said, Come up hither, and I will shew thee things which must be hereafter. And immediately I was in the spirit: and, behold, a throne was set in heaven, and one sat on the throne. And he that sat was to look upon like a jasper and a sardine stone: and there was a rainbow round about the throne, in sight like unto an emerald. And round about the throne were four and twenty seats: and upon the seats I saw four and twenty elders sitting, clothed in white raiment; and they had on their heads crowns of gold. And out of the throne proceeded lightnings and thunderings and voices: and there were seven lamps of fire burning before the throne, which are the seven Spirits of God. And before the throne there was a sea of glass like unto crystal: and in the midst of the throne, and round about the throne, were four beasts full of eyes before and behind. . . . And the four beasts had each of them six wings about him; and they were full of eyes within: and they rest not day and night, saying, Holy, holy, holy, LORD God Almighty, which was, and is, and is to come. (Rev. 4:1–8)

That is Christianity—knowing something about these heavenly things, being in the presence of God, realizing God. Cannot you see the utter futility of asking your foolish, little question, "How can these things be? I don't understand. I don't know that realm. I'm afraid."

Listen to our Lord's teaching to Nicodemus. Drop your petty little understanding. You cannot even understand earthly things, still less these heavenly things. Can you understand the whole scheme and plan and purpose of redemption? Of course, you cannot. Who could try to understand such a glorious, amazing scheme? The apostle Peter tells us that not only can no man ever understand the plan of redemption, even angels cannot. Peter puts it like this in his first epistle, the first chapter, verses 10 and following:

Of which salvation the prophets have enquired and searched diligently, who prophesied of the grace that should come unto you: searching what, or what manner of time the Spirit of Christ which was in them did signify, when it testified beforehand the sufferings of Christ, and the glory that should follow. Unto whom it was revealed, that not unto themselves, but unto us they did minister the things, which are now reported unto you by them that have preached the gospel unto you with the Holy Ghost sent down from heaven; which things the angels desire to look into.

The apostle Paul again says this in writing to the Ephesians in the third chapter, verse 10. He says this is God's great plan, "To the intent that now unto the principalities and powers in heavenly places might be known by the church the manifold wisdom of God." The angels do not understand this! This is the mind of the eternal and everlasting God. This is something that God has planned and purposed, and man says, "I don't understand this. How can these things be? I'm not going to believe unless I understand."

Oh, fool! You will spend eternity trying to understand the incomprehensible, and that is hell. You have shut yourself out from all the glories and the blessings of God's eternal grace in Jesus Christ, his Son. Or are you still foolish enough to try to understand the person of our Lord himself? He says this to Nicodemus, in this way: "And no man hath ascended up to heaven, but he that came down from heaven, even the Son of man which is in heaven." Do you understand that? "No man hath ascended up to heaven." You do not understand that because nobody has. No man has ever ascended into heaven. "Wait a minute," says someone, "haven't you heard about the Sputniks?" What utter nonsense that is. "No man hath ascended into heaven, but he that came down from heaven, even the Son of man which is in heaven." He has come down, but he is still there. How can these things be exactly?

If you are going to rely on that little bit of brain you have, you will be the miserable wretch you are, and always have been, forever and ever. You need to be born again, my friend, and you need to realize that these things are beyond understanding. The person of Jesus Christ, in heaven, God, has descended. He is both man and God, yet only one person, not two persons; two natures but one person.

Are you seriously trying to understand that? These are heavenly things.

This is the glorious gospel of salvation. It is the only hope for the world today. If the future of this world is in the hands of men, we are already undone. But it is not. Here is the message: "For God so loved the world, that he gave his only begotten Son" (John 3:16). This the incarnation—the eternal son of God being born as a man, the Word being made flesh and dwelling among us and yet still in heaven while he was on earth. God and man in two natures in one person and yet unmixed. This is the very essence of the gospel. He has come to give us a life that corresponds to that.

When will we have the wisdom to understand that we must not attempt to understand these things? Listen to Charles Wesley's great hymn "O Love Divine, How Sweet Thou Art":

> Stronger his love than death or hell;
> Its riches are unsearchable;
> The first born sons of light
> Desire in vain its depths to see;
> They cannot reach the mystery,
> The length, and breadth, and height.

Only God knows the love of God. That's the answer to all our foolish questioning and to all this utterance of, "How can these things be?"

> 'Tis mystery all: the Immortal dies:
> Who can explore His strange design?
> In vain the firstborn seraph tries
> To sound the depths of love divine.
> 'Tis mercy all! Let earth adore;
> Let angel minds inquire no more.[1]

These hymn-writers have all seen this. Isaac Watts wrote:

> Almighty God, to Thee
> Be endless honors done,
> The undivided Three,
> And the mysterious One:
> Where reason fails, with all her powers,
> There faith prevails, and love adores.[2]

That is the true Christian experience. You realize that the heavenly character of these things is such that you are in a realm altogether above and beyond man at the very tiptoe of his achievement. You are face-to-face with the everlasting God. "Great is the mystery of godliness."

And that is not only true of the being of God in three persons, it is true of the whole of the salvation that is given to us. That is the glory of this message. It is not human or earthly; it is divine! It is God's way of salvation. It is life that is life indeed. It is eternal life, life in the Spirit beyond not only the understanding but even the imagination of man. There is only one thing to do: submit in utter ignorance and helplessness and hopelessness to this One who is speaking.

"No man hath ascended up to heaven," and no man ever will if you are trusting to modern knowledge and modern understanding, or if you are hoping that it will increase and that, perhaps by the middle of the next century, if there is such a time, if man has not already blown this world to nothing, man will have arrived at a great knowledge of ultimate truth. You are the biggest fool in the universe if you trust to that.

"No man hath ascended up to heaven," and no man ever will on his own. It is impossible. He cannot even understand himself, let alone ascend into heaven. We are utterly and entirely dependent on this One. Why? Because we are concerned about heavenly things. We do not know, we have not seen, we have never been there, and we can never arrive there, but he has. "Verily, verily, I say unto thee, We speak that we do know" (John 3:11). Jesus is not a philosopher; he is not a speculator. He is not a seeker and searcher after truth. He is not engaged in scientific experimentation.

"We speak that we do know, and testify that we have seen." "No man hath seen God at any time" (1 John 4:12). People speculate about him. They say he is "the Crown of Being," "the Absolute," but what does that mean? It is meaningless. There is no sense there. They have never seen him, and they never can. "No man hath seen God at any time." No man can see God and live, but here is One who says, "[We] testify that we have seen."

Why can he say this? Because he is the eternal Son. He has come out of the bosom of the Father. "He hath declared him" (John 1:18). He is one who has looked into the face, into the eyes, of God. He is a witness! He has come from heaven! He is not trying to get up there. He has come down, and he is telling us, he is reporting to us, he is leading us out and manifesting God to us.

There is only one thing for us to do, and that is to receive him and to receive his witness and his testimony. He tells us that we must be born again. He tells us that we *can* be born again. He has come in order that it might be possible. He has come to reconcile us to God, to take away the sin that blinds us. He has come to make us the children of God, to introduce us into the presence of God. He has given us his Spirit, and the work of the Spirit is to give us this understanding and this knowledge, this enlightenment, this experience, to lift us up into the realm of heavenly things and to enjoy them more and more.

Oh, my dear friends, my one appeal to you is just this: beware of setting limits to the possibility of the Christian life. The apostle Paul prays for the Ephesians that they may be "strengthened with might by his Spirit in the inner man." What for? In order that they may begin to learn and "to comprehend with all saints what is the breadth, and length, and depth, and height; and to know the love of Christ, which passeth knowledge, that ye might be filled with all the fullness of God" (Ephesians 3:16–19).

I am not asking you whether you believe on the Lord Jesus Christ. I am assuming that you do. What I am asking you is this: What do you know about these heavenly things? Do you have communion with heaven and with God? When you get down on your knees to pray, are you talking to yourself or to God?"

Oh, the supreme importance of heavenly things, "life eternal . . . know[ing] thee the only true God, and Jesus Christ, whom thou hast sent" (John 17:3).

Beloved people, if only we knew something of the possibilities of this life of grace, this life in the Spirit, our whole condition would be changed and that of the church, and through us the blessing would spread to the perishing masses that are dying in the ignorance and darkness of sin and evil.

# 13

# Assurance

## JOHN 3:8

Sunday morning sermon preached in
Westminster Chapel, April 3, 1966, Palm Sunday.

The wind bloweth where it listeth, and thou hearest the sound
thereof, but canst not tell whence it cometh, and whither it goeth:
so is everyone that is born of the Spirit. (John 3:8)

We are considering this great statement that our Lord and Savior made
to this man Nicodemus, this ruler of the Jews who came to him by night
seeking, obviously, to know from our Lord what it was that he must do in
order that he might advance to the position that our Lord so clearly occupied. But our Lord teaches him, as we have been seeing, that his whole
understanding of these matters is entirely wrong, and he goes on to tell
him that "as Moses lifted up the serpent in the wilderness, even so must
the Son of man be lifted up: that whosoever believeth in him should not
perish, but have eternal life" (John 3:14). No man saves himself by his
life, by his works, by his actions. The Son of Man had to be lifted up, to
be crucified on the tree, and to die and be buried and rise again before
any man could be pardoned and be saved from perishing.

But we are particularly concentrating at the present time on what
results after that. The first thing we all need is to be reconciled with God,

and that was the primary work of our Lord. He came to keep the law for us, to satisfy the demands of God's holy law. But that was not merely a matter of active positive obedience. It necessitated also his bearing on our behalf the punishment of the law, and there we see his passive obedience on the cross—how he was led as a lamb to the slaughter and nailed to the tree. His body was broken; his blood was shed. He *had* to be lifted up: "Must . . . be." There is no salvation apart from Jesus Christ and him crucified. It is the only way of salvation. There is no reconciliation between man and God and between man and man apart from this mighty act that took place on the cross on Calvary's hill.

But thank God, it did not stop merely at reconciliation and pardon and forgiveness, vital and essential as they are as preliminaries and as foundations. Beyond that he gives us *life*. And that is what we are considering. That is what our Lord is telling Nicodemus here. "Except a man be born again, he cannot see the kingdom of God." Natural ability and human understanding in this realm is perilous. Indeed it can be a great hindrance because we all tend to trust in it. Religion is of no value in this regard; morality is of no value; nothing is of any value. We must be born again, born of the Spirit.

So we are looking at the characteristics of this life that he came to give us. He died not only that we might be forgiven ("He died to make us good," as the old hymn says), he died to give us life. He says, "I am come that they might have life, and that they might have it more abundantly" (John 10:10). This is the great New Testament message, and we are trying to make sure that we are possessors of this life. This is what matters—that we have received this life anew, that we have been born again, born of the Spirit. And we have seen that in the Scriptures there are many tests given to us whereby we may know for certain that we really are the children of God, the heirs of God, and joint heirs with Christ. We have been looking at a number of them, and now we have arrived at the point at which we are dealing with our sense of communion with the three blessed persons of the Holy Trinity—the Father, the Son, and the Holy Spirit. Christians do not merely believe things about God. Because of new life, and because they have been adopted into God's family, they are children of God, and they have a personal knowledge of God. And we are dealing in particular now with our communion with the Holy Spirit. Here is a test: if we know anything about this, we are children of God. All that sinners, unbelievers, know of the Holy Spirit is his convicting power, and it is terrifying. They do not know communion and fellowship with him.

Christians are delivered from a spirit of bondage, and not only that, they are aware of peace with God. We ended last time by saying that they have within them what the apostle calls "the Spirit of adoption, whereby we cry, Abba, Father" (Rom. 8:15). We cry with this elemental heart cry of the little child who does not understand human relationships, but he knows his father and mother and cries out after them in his need and his trouble. This, as we have seen, is a fundamental test—the spirit of adoption. The Devil can never counterfeit that. He can counterfeit peace and many other things, but he can never counterfeit the spirit of adoption.

But now we move to a great test, and it follows logically from that last one—the Spirit bearing witness with our spirit. This is all part of assurance of salvation, assurance of the fact you are born again. You are not just hoping, you *know*. And that is the position in which all Christian people should be. John, this same man, writes a letter when he is an old man, and he says, "These things have I written unto you that believe on the name of the Son of God; that ye may know that ye have eternal life." My friends, we are meant to *know* it. We are meant to enjoy it while we are still in this world. Anything short of that is really the spirit of bondage.

And that, as perhaps we must remind ourselves more and more in these days, is the spirit of Catholicism. Catholicism does not believe in assurance. You can never be sure. That is why people have to pray for you even when you are dead, to pay money for indulgences, and to light candles. Catholicism and all forms of Catholicism are opposed to the teaching of assurance. The whole system of the priesthood depends upon the absence of assurance: you need them in life, you need them in death, you need them in purgatory. You can never be sure of your salvation. But that is the antithesis of the New Testament teaching. We are meant to have assurance and knowledge and certainty while still in this world.

So the teaching is that not only do we have this filial spirit within us that cries unto the Father, but over and above that we have the Spirit "bear[ing] witness with our spirit, that we are the children of God."

> Ye have not received the spirit of bondage again to fear; but ye have received the Spirit of adoption, whereby we cry, Abba, Father. The Spirit itself [himself] beareth witness with our spirit, that we are the children of God: and if children, then heirs; heirs of God, and joint-heirs with Christ. (Rom. 8:15–17)

That is New Testament Christianity—no fear, no bondage, but great assurance, confirmed by the testimony and the witness of the Holy Spirit himself. Now this I have often described as the highest form of assurance. And what it means in its essence is this: the Spirit's bearing witness with our spirits means that quite apart from all we feel and all we can deduce from the Scriptures, there is an immediate and direct witness given to us by the Holy Spirit. Another way of looking at that is the way the apostle puts it in the fifth chapter of the epistle to the Romans and especially in verse 5, where he says, "Hope maketh not ashamed; because the love of God is shed abroad in our hearts by the Holy Ghost which is given unto us."

People often misunderstand that statement. They think "the love of God . . . shed abroad in our hearts" is our love to God. It is not! It is God's love to us. And this means that we are given this assurance by the Spirit that God loves us, that we are his children, that our sins are forgiven. There is nothing on earth or in heaven that is higher than this—the knowledge that God has set his heart upon us, that God loves us. The love of God to us is shed abroad in our hearts. All the clouds have dissipated and vanish, all uncertainty is gone, and we are amazed at the fact that God not only loves us but has troubled even to tell us so.

How does God do this? Well, the great characteristic of this is that it is something immediate and direct. It is not our action. You can get assurance by reading the Scriptures and looking at what they tell you. There are several of them in this third chapter of John's Gospel alone.

> God sent not his Son into the world to condemn the world; but
> that the world through him might be saved. He that believeth on
> him [Jesus Christ] is not condemned: but he that believeth not is
> condemned already, because he hath not believed in the name of
> the only begotten Son of God. (vv. 17–18)

If you truly believe, therefore, there is your assurance. Even more than
that, you will have this filial spirit, this spirit of adoption, sealing it all,
guaranteeing it. "The Spirit itself [himself] beareth witness with our
spirit, that we are the children of God" (Rom. 8:16).

Sometimes the Holy Spirit may do this through a word of Scripture.
Let us be clear about these things. You need not have a vision. Very few
people have had visions, and you should always be very careful when you
feel you have had one. The Devil can counterfeit visions, so do not seek
visions or something like hearing an audible sound or an audible word.
It does not mean that. What it means essentially is an impression upon
the spirit. The Spirit acts upon our spirit; he "beareth witness with our
spirit." It is an impression he makes upon our spirit that is absolutely certain, stronger than any evidence we can ever see. He may do this through
the Word. He may take a word of Scripture one day and bring it to you
anew: you may feel that you have never seen it before, and it speaks into
you, "Son, your sins are forgiven; you are my child."

I have given you great evidence from time to time from the writings of
saints and martyrs and confessors throughout the centuries testifying to
this, and God's people are still privileged to know this sense of the glory
of God. This is the highest gift in the baptism of the Spirit, far and away
above any particular gifts you may receive; this is the highest thing of all,
that he is speaking directly to you and telling you that you are his child.
This is, I repeat, the highest form of assurance. It might be accompanied
by gifts, or it might not be. But what matters above everything else is this
certainty, this assurance that makes one a living witness, that gives one
power to witness and to testify to him and to the Word and to his grace.
Furthermore, it is important that we should realize that this is not just
some vague feeling of happiness. It is beyond that. Many of us—all of us,

I trust—have known what it is to have a vague feeling of happiness in a church service or at other times. That is all right, and that is often God-given (not always; remember, that is something the Devil can counterfeit up to a point). But what we are considering now is something that the Devil cannot and would never desire to counterfeit. This is something beyond a vague feeling of happiness; it is this specific matter of God making known his love to us in a direct, immediate manner. It is not general, it is not vague, but it is specific. He is addressing us as our Father, and he is making known to us that we are his children.

This is something that many have testified to in their accounts of it and in their autobiographies. D. L. Moody used to say that he rarely referred to this great experience when it came to him because there was something so sacred about it that almost defied description. It is, of course, comparable in a lesser degree to the experience that the apostle Paul describes as having had himself when he was lifted up into the third heaven and heard things that could not be described. It is a touch of heaven, and language is inadequate to describe a touch of heaven. "The love of Jesus, what is it, none but His loved ones know," and they have always found it difficult to describe it. They can only humbly testify to the fact that God, in his infinite love and mercy and compassion, has been pleased to grant it unto them. That is the testimony of the Spirit with our spirits. That is what I call the baptism by the Holy Spirit; that is what I mean by being "sealed with the Spirit." This is given to believers to assure them that whatever may happen to them in this world, they are children of God and therefore are joint heirs with Christ.

Now that is a realm that the man who is merely religious never enters; he knows nothing at all about it. The man who is merely religious is of all men the one to be most pitied, because he is concerned about these things and yet he is robbing himself of their real and essential glory. There is nothing more tragic than the man who is trying to live the Christian life himself, trying to make himself a Christian, and who believes he has done so. That is the greatest tragedy of all, this Nicodemus type of person. They never know anything about things like this. They never know anything in reality and in experience of the spiritual realm, always dwelling in the realm of moralities and their own activities, robbing themselves in their self-righteousness of the highest blessing that God gives to a human being in this world.

But now I want to show you some of the things that result from this great assurance in all its forms. These results are quite inevitable, but they provide us with very valuable tests whereby we can examine and prove to ourselves as to whether we are in the faith or not. Let me put it to you like this: our blessed Lord went deliberately to Jerusalem to be crucified. He did it in order that we might have the great enjoyment of this blessing. And the best way to thank him for what he did and what he suffered on your behalf is to enjoy these things that he has given you. Do not pity him; pity yourself that you do not know the blessings he has bought for you. That is why I am stressing all this, and here are things that are invaluable as tests because they are absolute proofs of the fact that we are born again, that we have received this new life, that we are born of the Spirit. (1)

Here is one: a spirit of rejoicing. This is something that runs right through the whole New Testament. For example, Peter says, "Whom having not seen, ye love; in whom, though now ye see him not, yet believing, ye rejoice with joy unspeakable and full of glory" (1 Pet. 1:8).

He is writing to ordinary Christian people. He does not even know their names. He has to address them as "strangers scattered throughout Pontus, Galatia, Cappadocia, Asia, and Bithynia" and so on. He is not writing a circular letter to apostles; he is writing to unknown ordinary Christians, and he says, "I know this about you—that you are rejoicing in Jesus with a joy that is unspeakable and full of glory." Philip Doddridge, interpreting that verse, said, "Joy unspeakable and full of glory means that there is a touch of the glory of heaven upon your joy. It is a picture of the joy that the blessed spirits in glory are privileged to know." Peter assumes that about these Christian people, and it results from the love of God being shed abroad in their hearts.

The apostle Paul, in his Philippian epistle in particular, keeps on saying this. "Finally, my brethren, rejoice in the Lord" (Phil. 3:1). Go on to the fourth chapter and the fourth verse and there it is again: "Rejoice in the Lord always: and again I say, Rejoice." It is the great note of the New Testament Scriptures. John writes his last letter, as I have reminded you, as an old man, and he tells us why he writes it. He knows he is going to die, and he is leaving these people. "And these things write we unto you, that your joy may be full" (1 John 1:4). Full! Why did our Lord die for us? Was it to make us miserable? Some people give the impression that the main effect of their being Christians is that they are miserable. They seem to know enough about these things to spoil everything else for them; they have no positive joy. If what you have is something that makes you unhappy and miserable, if it just robs you of things, and you feel you are always making great sacrifices, my dear friend, you know nothing about it! Your joy is meant to be a full and positive joy that is unspeakable and full of glory.

And this, again, is something that the world and the Devil can never counterfeit. Religion can never produce this. Religion never makes people happy, and that is one of the best ways of differentiating between religion and Christianity. Religion is always a task, a burden, a knowledge of God that makes one fear; religion always depresses, always makes us unhappy. That is why we must be careful lest we be led back into some organized, institutional religion that keeps people priest-ridden and depressed and in the fear of God in the wrong sense, a craven fear. When Martin Luther understood in a flash the doctrine of justification by faith, he began to sing; he was filled with a sense of joy. This is New Testament Christianity. The other is not. It is merely religion; it is a conglomeration of Old Testament religion and mystery religions and paganism, all amalgamated into a horrible system, and it is the very antithesis of Christianity. It is a miserable, wretched religion that robs people of true joy. Of course, there have been cases—and thank God for them—even among such people when God has visited souls and has given them this great experience. There are saints and mystics among them who have known this joy, but it has been in spite of the system, and they have generally been persecuted by the system and by the authorities that control it.

Religion can never give such joy. It is the very essence of this new life in Christ Jesus; this is being born of the Spirit. But let me put this to you in its fullness. I have already quoted Peter to you from his first epistle, and I must complete my quotation because it is important that we should understand fully what he says. I quoted the eighth verse to you. But this is how Peter puts it in full:

> Blessed be the God and Father of our Lord Jesus Christ, which according to his abundant mercy hath begotten us again [that is being born again] unto a lively hope by the resurrection of Jesus Christ from the dead, to an inheritance incorruptible, and undefiled, and that fadeth not away, reserved in heaven for you, who are kept by the power of God through faith unto salvation ready to be revealed in the last time. (vv. 3–5)

But listen to this:

> Wherein ye greatly rejoice, though now for a season, if need be, ye are in heaviness through manifold temptations: that the trial of your faith, being much more precious than of gold that perisheth, though it be tried with fire, might be found unto praise and honour and glory at the appearing of Jesus Christ. (vv. 6–7)

What a combination! "Wherein ye greatly rejoice, though now for a season, if need be, ye are in heaviness through manifold temptations."

Then listen to Paul saying the same thing in Romans 5: "Therefore being justified by faith, we have peace with God through our Lord Jesus Christ: by whom also we have access by faith into this grace wherein we stand, and rejoice in hope of the glory of God." But then he adds, "And not only so, but we glory in tribulations also: knowing that tribulation worketh patience; and patience, experience; and experience, hope: and hope maketh not ashamed; because the love of God is shed abroad in our hearts by the Holy Ghost which is given unto us" (vv. 1–5). Here is the key phrase: "not only so." We not only "rejoice in hope of the glory of God," we do so, says Paul, in the midst of tribulations. When everything is going against us, when circumstances are mocking us and jeering at us and going against us, when all the enemies seem to have risen against us, when hell seems to have been let loose round and about us—tribulation.

We are rejoicing not merely in spite of them but in the midst of them. Did you notice that extraordinary logic? We see the value of these things; we glory in tribulations *knowing* that tribulations produce patience.

The sort of Christian who looks back to his conversion constantly and who is always talking about that seems to me to be utterly unscriptural. The Christian life is a life that grows and develops and becomes more wonderful as you go on. People say, "Oh, that I might have again that first flush of joy." My dear friend, if your joy is not greater now than when you first believed there is something radically wrong with you. We need to be taught that "tribulation worketh patience" and that patience works experience and that experience leads to hope. "Hope maketh not ashamed"; of course not! So the rejoicing that Christians know, the joy of men or women who are children of God, is a rejoicing that never fails them. And that is how to differentiate between the true and the counterfeit. There are people who have a manufactured joy that can be worked up. Psychologists in public meetings often know how to do this, and they work people up with hymns and choruses and various other forms of manipulation, and people think they are filled with this joy.

But I can tell you how to discover the difference between the true and the false: false joy goes out the window the moment you are in trouble. It is a fair-weather friend. When the tribulations come, when the trials come, you are utterly cast down, your joy is gone, all your happiness has disappeared, and you are grumbling and complaining and wonder why God is dealing with you like this. You have a false joy. A true joy is the joy of the child of God who rejoices in tribulations, in the midst of them, in the depths or the height of them. "Rejoice in the Lord always: and again I say, Rejoice," whatever the circumstances and the conditions. This is a valuable test: knowing that when everything has gone against you, you still have a spirit of rejoicing within you. This joy is in Christ, of course. It is not vague and general. The test of whether we are true Christians or not is this: we "worship God in the spirit, and rejoice in Christ Jesus, and have no confidence in the flesh" (Phil. 3:3). The true Christian says, "In the cross of Christ I glory," in the words of an old hymn. Paul says, "God forbid that I should glory, save in the cross of our Lord Jesus Christ" (Gal.

6:14). So whatever your circumstances are, however great the tribulation, you go on rejoicing, because you are rejoicing in the Lord Jesus Christ, in his cross, in everything that appertains to him. And that is a joy that is "unspeakable and full of glory." It is a joy, if I may borrow the words of Wordsworth and lift them up into infinity, that is "too deep for tears." That is the joy we are describing. The joy of rejoicing.

And then there is that which follows immediately from this—praise and thanksgiving. Here is a wonderful test. Praise and thanksgiving were the characteristics of the true Christian followers. And we must test ourselves by these things. This is something that is universal in the New Testament. And again it is one of those things that can never be counterfeited. Now praise and thanksgiving does not just mean singing hymns that you like and being carried away by the tune. I am talking about praise and thanksgiving welling up from the very depths of our hearts. We find the beginnings of this even in the Old Testament. The Old Testament saints were aware of all these things in a measure, but only in a measure. They never enjoyed the fullness. The Spirit was not yet given because Jesus was not yet glorified, as John puts it in the seventh chapter of his Gospel, verses 38–39. But they knew something about it. Read what one of the psalmists says. The time of harvest was a happy time for farmers, and they had their feast and their wine and their rejoicing. It was the highest moment of the year, for all the labor was now giving its return; the fruit was being gathered in, and they could face the winter. It was a time of great rejoicing. But listen to the psalmist: "Thou hast put gladness in my heart, more than in the time that their corn and their wine increased" (Ps. 4:7).

We find many similar expressions of joy in the Old Testament Scriptures. But, of course, when you come to the New, and after the day of Pentecost, we see this coming out in all its fullness. You begin to read about the early church in Acts 2, and this is the note that strikes you immediately: "Then they that gladly received his word [the word of Peter] were baptized: and the same day there were added unto them about three thousand souls." It was a dangerous thing to be a Christian in those days. It would mean persecution from your fellow Jews, ostracism from the family, and so on. But let us read the story that follows:

And they continued stedfastly in the apostles' doctrine and fellowship, and in breaking of bread, and in prayers. And fear came upon
every soul: and many wonders and signs were done by the apostles.
And all that believed were together, and had all things common;
and sold their possessions and goods, and parted them to all men,
as every man had need. And they, continuing daily with one accord
in the temple, and breaking bread from house to house, did eat their
meat with gladness and singleness of heart, praising God, and having favour with all the people. And the Lord added to the church
daily such as should be saved. (vv. 41–47)

That is Christianity, that is the Christian church—a rejoicing, praising
church that is filled with thanksgiving.

So it started, and it continued like that. In the introduction to his first
epistle Peter bursts out, "Blessed be the God and Father of our Lord Jesus
Christ" (v. 3). Read the epistles, note the introductions, and immediately
you will find them starting off with praise and thanksgiving, magnifying
the grace and glory of God. They were a thankful people.

But why was this? There is no need to argue about this, is there? How
can anyone be a Christian without being thankful and grateful? What is a
Christian? Well, Christians are men and women who know that they are
what they are by the grace of God. Their sins are forgiven. Why? Is it because of their good life or because of their religious duties? Is it because of
the gifts they give to others? No, that is religion. Christians know that they
owe everything to the grace of God in our Lord and Savior Jesus Christ.
They have received it all as a free gift. They know they are what they are—
they have forgiveness, new life, everything—because the Son of God gave
himself for them on the cross on Calvary's hill and endured the shame, the
suffering, and the agony of it all in order that they might be forgiven and
become children of God. Now if you can believe a thing like that and not
feel grateful and thankful, then I do not understand you. It is impossible.

If there is no thankfulness, there is no value in the belief. It must be
purely intellectual. When a human being does you a kindness, how careful
you are to thank them. You write a letter; you go and see them; every time
you meet them, you thank them; you pour out your thanksgiving upon

them for what they have done for you. And, of course, that is right, but look at what the Son of God has done for us: he died for us, suffering all that he endured during that week from Palm Sunday to Good Friday so that you and I might be what we are. "Thanks be unto God for his unspeakable gift" (2 Cor. 9:15). The apostle Paul cannot think of Jesus or mention his name without bursting forth into thanksgiving and praise and worship and adoration. It is inevitable. But the religious man knows nothing about this; everything is somber and dark. He is just praying for strength and forgiveness, and there is no thanksgiving; he does not know anything about it.

Let me end then on this note, and this is again a most wonderful test: resting in God and in his promises and in our great salvation. It is the other side of the rejoicing in tribulations that I mentioned earlier, but it is a very important one. There are times when we are so hard-pressed that our joy is apparently, for the time being at least, blunted somewhat. But there is a depth in joy that shows itself in just resting quietly. Again you cannot analyze or explain it, but you know that it is there and that it is true. It means that you so know the love of God to you and so know that you are a child of God that even when you do not quite understand what he is doing to you or what he is doing with you, you still trust him, you still love him, you still leave yourself in his hands. You would rather be in the hands of God and in the dark than anywhere in the blazing light. This is something that only the child of God knows; it is ultimate, final trust. Let me put it to you in the words of the apostle Paul in Philippians 4:6–7: "Be careful [anxious] for nothing." Don't be overanxious, he says, about anything, no matter what your circumstances are. This is all-inclusive: "Be careful for *nothing* [nothing at all]; but in every thing by prayer and supplication with thanksgiving let your requests be made known unto God. And the peace of God, which passeth all understanding, shall keep your hearts and minds through Christ Jesus."

"The peace of God, that passeth all understanding"! And he goes on a little later:

> But I rejoiced in the Lord greatly, that now at the last your care
> of me hath flourished again; wherein ye were also careful, but ye

lacked opportunity. Not that I speak in respect of want: for I have learned, in whatsoever state I am, therewith to be content. I know both how to be abased, and I know how to abound: every where and in all things I am instructed both to be full and to be hungry, both to abound and to suffer need. I can do all things through Christ which strengtheneth me. (Phil. 4:10–13)

That is it, my friends. In prison he writes things like "I have learned, in whatsoever state I am, therein to be content." Nothing matters to Christians except that they know that all is well between them and God. So they can say:

When peace, like a river, attendeth my way,
When sorrows like sea billows roll;
Whatever my lot, Thou has taught me to say,
It is well, it is well with my soul.[1]

They can also sing:

My heart is resting, O my God—
I will give thanks and sing;
My heart is resting at the source
Of every precious thing.[2]

That is it—a heart that can rest, that can rest from itself and rest from the world. A heart that is resting in the Lord fulfills in practice the commandment of the Old Testament: "Rest in the LORD, and wait patiently for him" (Ps. 37:7). The children of God are always ready to do so. They know intuitively, instinctively as only a child can know—they cannot prove it in logic, but they know—that "all things work together for good to them that love God, to them who are the called according to his purpose" (Rom. 8:28). Oh, the poor religious man! He knows nothing about that, and he is devoid of one of the most glorious, blessed experiences that can ever come to a human being in this world of sin and shame, trial and tribulation—the peace of God that passes all understanding but is a glorious reality.

# 14

# Alive in Christ

## JOHN 3:8

Sunday morning sermon preached in
Westminster Chapel, April 10, 1966, Easter Sunday.

The wind bloweth where it listeth, and thou hearest the sound
thereof, but canst not tell whence it cometh, and whither it goeth:
so is every one that is born of the Spirit. (John 3:8)

The great fact that is impressed upon us in these verses is the mysterious
character of this Christian life. It is a mystery from beginning to end. Poor
Nicodemus! His trouble was that he was trying to understand things that
cannot be understood, and we have been considering the essential difference between merely being religious and being Christian. Before men
and women can be Christians they must be born again. They are brought
into a new realm, the realm of the miraculous, the supernatural. It is folly
to bring in your natural human understanding as Nicodemus did. Those
who try to understand these things are of necessity baffled, and they will
never experience their grace and glory and power.

So that is the great and essential message of this passage, and it leads
us very naturally into what we are now considering together. There is an
ancient tradition that when the first Christians used to meet one another
they greeted one another with the phrase, "Christ is risen." That was

their ordinary form of salutation. The Jews used to greet one another by saying, "Peace be unto you." But the Christians had this new salutation, and they said it to one another whenever they met and whatever their circumstances might happen to be. They said it with joy and with rejoicing. It was not just a password. It was that incidentally because they were often persecuted. It was a dangerous thing to be a Christian in those early centuries. But, of course, there was a deep significance in it; they said it with joy, with rejoicing, with confidence.

This, after all, was the basis of their whole position; they were what they were because Christ is risen. If he had not risen there would never have been a Christian church, there would never have been a Christian individual. This was the basis and the foundation of all their assurance and of all their hope, so they said it to one another whatever the circumstances might be. When things were going well they said, "Christ is risen, and so things are going to be even better." When things were going badly, when they were persecuted, harassed, hunted, driven to dwell in caves and in rocks, whenever they met one another they said, "Christ is risen." They were saying in effect, "Whatever these enemies may do to us, because the ultimate Victor is on our side, nothing can make him forgo his purpose or frustrate him in his endeavor."

So "Christ is risen" summed up their whole position. I now want to bring a question to you: Is that our position? Is that the thing by which we live?

Let me put it in another way. There is no better test as to whether we have been born again or not than this very thing. To men or women who are born again, this is everything. *Christ is risen!* But if they are not born again, this is certainly not the center of their life or the basis of their hope. That is why this is such a thorough test; it cannot be counterfeited. The Devil can counterfeit many of the things that we experience as Christians, and that is why we are always told to prove the spirits, to "try the spirits," to test them to see whether they be of God or not. But here is something that cannot be counterfeited. The Devil is never anxious for people to say, "Christ is risen!" He received his greatest defeat there, and this is something that he tries to get people to deny, even those who call themselves Christians. Many are denying this today; they say the literal, physical resurrection is not true. But this was the basis of the hope of the early Christians, and so they greeted one another with the salutation "Christ is risen!" I repeat, the vital question that comes to us: Is that the basis of our hope and of our whole position?

Now I want to try to show you that this means two essential things. The first is, of course, an acceptance of and a belief in the fact of the resurrection of Jesus. You must start with that. It is not just an idea; it is not just another way of saying, "Spring has come again, and the flowers are blooming and blossoming." That is not what is meant. This is a statement to the effect that the Son of God who was crucified on the cross on Calvary's hill has risen from the dead. They had taken down his body and put it in a grave; they had rolled a stone over it and put seals on the stone and guarded the stone with soldiers. Nevertheless the stone had been rolled away by angels, and he had literally, bodily come out of the grave. That is the statement, and it is the basis of our whole position.

Of course, the world, like Nicodemus, says, "How can these things be? Nobody rises from the dead." Or they try to explain it away. They say he never really died but only swooned—he only fainted on the cross. Or they say that his disciples stole the body in order to give the impression that he had risen from the dead. There are various theories. Some say that it was just the chemical constitution of the earth round about him that led to an unusually rapid dissolution of the body. That is the kind of thing that the world and, alas, many in the church are saying today in order to deny the resurrection. And why do they deny it? Because they are trying to understand the resurrection, the greatest miracle of all—one being raised from the dead!

But the whole of our Christian faith is miraculous. The virgin birth is a miracle. We are in the realm of the supernatural. As our Lord said to Nicodemus, "If I have told you earthly things, and ye believe not, how shall ye believe, if I tell you of heavenly things? . . . Marvel not!" (John 3:12, 7). Those who are foolish enough to try to understand the resurrection and who do not believe it as a historical fact because they cannot understand it and because modern science cannot explain it are just telling us that they are not Christians, they are not born again. All who rely on their own understanding are proclaiming that they are not Christians. The essence of Christianity is that we are given power to believe the impossible, the supernatural, the miraculous—the literal, physical fact of the resurrection of the Lord Jesus Christ in the body out of the grave and his manifestation to his chosen followers. That is the first part of the significance of "Christ is risen," and it is an essential part. There is nothing if that is not true.

But what I am more anxious to do now with you is to invite you to examine yourselves as I examine myself as to whether we know something of the consequence of the resurrection in our personal lives. It is possible for us to accept the resurrection as a literal, historical act and still know nothing about it in experience. There is something wrong with people who do not accept the fact intellectually. Their arguments against it are so patently false, they contradict one another. The New Testament itself tells us how even at that very time the Jews and others tried to concoct stories to explain it away, but this just cannot be done. There would never have been a Christian church were it not for the resurrection. But what I am much more concerned about is this: the real test as to whether we are born again is that we know something of the consequences of the resurrection in our personal lives and experiences. This is certainly something that the Devil can never counterfeit—never. This is something that only belongs to those who, as our Lord says, are "born of water and of the Spirit," born from above, who have experienced the miracle of the new birth, regeneration.

What, then, are these consequences? They are laid before us in the New Testament in many places. Indeed this is one of the leading themes of all the epistles, as you would expect it to be. What do we know of the power of the resurrection, the fact of the resurrection as an experimental fact in our own lives? Well, here is the first thing. Those who are born again, born of the Spirit, those on whom God has worked this blessed miracle, know that they are dead to the world, dead to sin.

What do I mean by that? Let me first of all give you a number of statements in which this is presented to us. We read in Galatians 6:14, "God forbid that I should glory, save in the cross of our Lord Jesus Christ, by whom the world is crucified unto me, and I unto the world." You find the same thought in a remarkable manner in Romans 6:6, where the apostle Paul puts it like this: "Knowing this, that our old man is crucified with him." That is a most important statement. A better rendering would be, "*was* crucified." It is an aorist; it is in the past. It has happened once and forever. When he was crucified, we were crucified. So the appeal goes on, "Likewise reckon ye also yourselves to be dead indeed unto sin, but alive unto God through Jesus Christ our Lord," and "Sin shall not have dominion over you: for ye are not under the law, but under grace" (vv. 11, 14). Or again, "If ye then be risen with Christ, seek those things which are above, where Christ sitteth on the right hand of God" (Col. 3:1, 3). Why? "For ye are *dead*, and your life is hid with Christ in God." "I am [have been] crucified with Christ," says Paul in Galatians 2:20.

What do these statements mean? They are of the very essence of the Christian faith. The Christian is "in Christ," joined to him, and the result of that is that everything that happened to our Lord has happened to us who are in him. "If we have been planted together in the likeness of his death, we shall be also in the likeness of his resurrection" (Rom. 6:5). These are the arguments. What a wonderful test this is. So I ask you the question, are you dead? Do you know that you are dead?

This means that we are conscious that man by nature, man as he is born, man in Adam, the man that belongs to the world and its way, to the life of sin and the dominion of sin and Satan, that is the man we all are by nature. We were "born" in sin; we were "shapen in iniquity." We were born belonging to the world. Nobody is born a Christian. There is no greater fallacy than that. It does not matter who your parents were—you were not born a Christian. You are born a sinner; you are born a child of Adam; you are born belonging to this world and its life and its way.

What the apostle is saying is this: if you are a Christian, if you have been born again, the you that you were is dead; it is gone. That "old man" died with Christ upon the cross on Calvary's hill; it was "crucified with him." Now Romans 6:6 and the following verses are not an appeal to us to die with Christ (there is no more tragic misinterpretation of Scripture than that); they are telling us that we have already done so. There are those who say, "Ah well, you believe that Christ died for you? Now you must die with him." You cannot do that. As Romans 6:6 tells us, you *have* died with him, you were "crucified with him." He does not tell you to die. If you are in Christ you have already died with him; the "old man" is already dead.

Now let us be clear about this. It does not mean that the old nature is dead; it is "the old man" that was crucified with Christ. There are relics and remnants of the old nature still left in us. That is why Paul has to tell us, "Let not sin therefore reign in your mortal body" (6:12). It is there, but do not let it reign. Why? Because you are dead. You once were one, but you are now two as it were; you are a "new man." You are aware of the old nature in you, but you know for certain that as a being you are no longer what you were born as.

Is this clear to you? This is what gives you an assurance that you are a Christian. You are imperfect still, you sin still, you fail still. There are many things about you that are wrong, but you know that the man you once were is dead; you are not that man. You are not a perfect man yet in Christ, but you are not that "old man." The old man has died; he has been crucified and buried with Christ. You no longer belong to the world; you are no longer under the dominion of sin and Satan. Oh, the apostle Paul has again summed it up by saying, "If any man be in Christ, he is a new creature: old things are passed away; behold, all things are become new."

And so it comes to this: taking oneself as one is, one is able to say, "Whatever may be true or not true about me, I know I am not as I used to be. I am dead to that. The world may still attract me, but the world does not dominate me any longer. I do not belong to it any longer. I may be an unworthy Christian in this new kingdom, but I certainly do not belong to the old kingdom. I am dead." You are dead! You are finished with that. Isaac Watts put it so well in his hymn:

> His dying crimson, like a robe,
> Spreads o'er His body on the tree;

Then am I dead to all the globe,
And all the globe is dead to me.[1]

Let me put it very simply. Do you know that you no longer belong to this world? Have you undergone that essential death once and for all? Do you no longer belong there? The man that used to be there is not there any longer; he is now in Christ. You have died with Christ.

There, then, is the negative; the first step is negative. But obviously we do not stop there; we go on to the positive. Those who are born again, therefore, know that they are alive and are risen to a new life with Christ. There are these two aspects, and they are vital, and it is important that we should be aware of both of them.

Now let me again show you the apostle saying these things and working them out. "Knowing this, that our old man was crucified with him, that the body of sin might be destroyed, that henceforth we should not serve sin. For he that is dead is freed from sin." He does not mean that Christians do not sin. He means they are freed from the demands and the dominion of sin; they do not belong to the realm of sin. When a man is dead you cannot prosecute him for debt or for anything else.

Now if we be dead with Christ [which is what is true], we believe that we shall also live with him: knowing that Christ being raised from the dead dieth no more; death hath no more dominion over him. For in that he died, he died unto sin once: but in that he liveth, he liveth unto God. Likewise reckon ye also yourselves . . . (Rom. 6:8–11)

Realize that this is true of you. Do not just persuade yourself that it is; believe and know that it is true. "Likewise reckon ye also yourselves to be dead indeed unto sin." This is not pretending there is no sin in you. That is mere psychology, but this is Christian teaching. It means that you are dead as far as the dominion and the whole territory of sin is concerned.

Realize that you are "dead indeed unto sin." And you are "alive unto God through Jesus Christ our Lord." I especially like the way in which Paul puts it in his next appeal:

Let not sin therefore reign in your mortal body, that ye should obey it in the lusts thereof. Neither yield ye your members as instruments of unrighteousness unto sin: but yield yourselves unto God, [how?] as those that are alive from the dead, and your members as instruments of righteousness unto God. (vv. 12–13)

There it is. We must realize that we are "alive from the dead."

Oh, let the apostle expound himself to us; he can do it better than any of us can! In Ephesians 2, verse 1, he describes how we were: "And you hath he quickened, who were dead in trespasses and sins." That means that men and women are not aware of the fact that they have souls. They are dead to God, dead to the spiritual realm. They come with their clever scientific knowledge and say, "How can these things be?" Poor things! They are

dead in trespasses and sins; wherein in time past ye walked according to the course of this world, according to the prince of the power of the air, the spirit that now worketh in the children of disobedience: among whom also we all had our conversation in times past in the lusts of our flesh, fulfilling the desires of the flesh and of the mind; and were by nature the children of wrath, even as others. (Eph. 2:1–3)

That is the unregenerate, the man of the world, the one who has not become a Christian and been born again.

But God, [here it is!] who is rich in mercy, for his great love wherewith he loved us, even when we were dead in sins, hath quickened us together with Christ, (by grace ye are saved;) and hath raised us up together, and made us sit together in heavenly places in Christ Jesus." (Eph. 2:4–6)

So I put this again to you in the form of a question: Is that true in your experience? Do you know you have been quickened? Do you know that you have been raised with Christ from that death of sin, that absolutely utter deadness to spiritual realities and to God the Father, God the Son, and God the Holy Ghost? Do you know that you have been made alive? Have you been quickened, have you been raised? The apostle Paul never tired of saying this; he keeps on repeating himself. In the great prayer that he offers for the Ephesians he says he is always praying for them, and this is what he prays:

> The eyes of your understanding being enlightened; that ye may know what is the hope of his calling, and what the riches of the glory of his inheritance in the saints, and [notice this!] what is the exceeding greatness of his power to us-ward who believe, according to the working of his mighty power, which he wrought in Christ, when he raised him from the dead, and set him at his own right hand in the heavenly places, far above all principality, and power, and might, and dominion, and every name that is named, not only in this world, but also in that which is to come. (Eph. 1:18–21)

Do you know anything of that power? Paul says in essence, "I am praying that you may know the exceeding greatness of his power to us-ward who believe." What sort of power is that? It is the same power, he says, according to which he raised up his Son from the dead. That is the power that is working in you. Are you aware of the working of that resurrecting power in you? That is the truth about the man or woman who is born again. You can accept these things as historical facts, but if you do not know any of the power, you are lacking in spiritual life, you are not born again. We are united to Christ—crucified with him, buried with him, raised with him, given life with him.

Here again the apostle keeps on saying this. I have already quoted Ephesians 1 and Ephesians 2 to you. Then again in Ephesians 3 he prays that they "may be able to comprehend with all saints what is the breadth, and length, and depth, and height; and to know the love of Christ, which passeth knowledge, that ye might be filled with all the fullness of God." Then he adds, "Now unto him that is able to do exceeding abundantly above all that we ask or think, according to the power that worketh in us" (vv. 18–20). That is it. Is that power working in you, my friend? "The power that worketh in us" is the power of the resurrection. That is the power that is working in everybody who is born of the Spirit, who is born again. They do not live in the energy and the power of their flesh and their own mind and understanding and all that the world can give them to help them along that line. They are living a new life. They are living by the power of the life of Christ. They are living by resurrection power, the power of God, the power that raised Christ from the dead!

The apostle Paul when he comes to express his innermost, dearest heart's desire puts it like this:

That I may know him, and the power of his resurrection, [that is what he wants to know] and the fellowship of his sufferings, being made conformable unto his death; if by any means I might attain unto the resurrection of [out from among] the dead. (Phil. 3:10–11)

"The power of his resurrection"! The apostle knows about this. He says, "Not as though I had already attained [to a full, perfect knowledge], either were already perfect: but I follow after, if that I may apprehend that for which also I am apprehended of Christ Jesus" (v. 12). The power of the resurrection!

I asked you earlier, do you know that you are dead? I now ask you a second question: Do you know you are "alive from the dead"? Do you know that in you there is a principle of life? Do you know that though you are still in this world you do not belong to it? You have a different character, quality, and type of life in you. It is a new life, it is a resurrection life, it is life given by God. Do you know something of the working of God's almighty power that raised up Christ from the dead? Do you know something of that working in you, thrilling your nerves, energizing you?

This was the common experience of the apostle Paul. This is how he puts it to the Colossians:

We preach [Jesus Christ], warning every man, and teaching every man in all wisdom; that we may present every man perfect in Christ Jesus: whereunto I also labour, striving *according to his working, which worketh in me mightily.* (Col. 1:28–29)

That is it. We are not all apostles, we are not all great men like the apostle Paul, but he was no more a Christian in the fundamental sense than we are. He had to be "born again," he had to "die," he had to be "raised" with Christ. The same power was working in him as works in us. It was greater in degree in him perhaps, but it was the same power. All who are born of the Spirit have been raised again with Christ to newness of life, and they know it—they are "alive unto God." God is no longer just a philosophic $x$ to them. God is not just an "absolute" or an "uncaused cause" or any one of these terms that are used by clever philosophers. He is the living God. He is their Father; he is related to them. They have been raised, and they are "alive unto God through Jesus Christ their Lord."

It was because they knew they were alive in Christ that the first Christians looked at one another in the prisons or wherever they met in days of persecution and said, "Christ is risen!" And the moment the other heard it, a smile came over his face. "He is risen indeed," he would say. "Christ is risen! He has risen in me. I know his rising within me. I have felt the presence and the power. I know I am dead, but I am alive."

Let me add to that. Because of this, the third thing that is true of Christians is that they know they are always safe, and they must know this. They cannot know the things of which I have been reminding you without knowing that they are safe. Consider what Paul tells us about ourselves in the light of the resurrection. "But God, who is rich in mercy, for his great love wherewith he loved us, even when we were dead in sins, hath quickened us together with Christ, (by grace ye are saved;) and hath raised us up together, and made us sit together in heavenly places in Christ Jesus" (Eph. 2:4–6). Now that is a statement of fact. It is true not only of Paul and the other apostles but also of these Ephesian Christians who had been born and brought up as Gentiles, as you and I have. We have not only been "raised" with Christ; we have been made to sit together with him in the heavenly places. That is a fact! It is true now. If I am "in Christ," where he is I am. He is seated there, and so am I, in the spirit. I am still on earth in the body, but in Christ I am seated with him in the heavenly places.

But let me give you what is to me a still more beautiful expression of this in Colossians 3:3: "For ye are dead, and your life is hid with Christ in God." "Your life"! My friend, if you are born again, if you are a Christian, if you are in Christ, "your life is hid with Christ in God" now, this minute. We Christians ought to be ashamed that we are apologetic and afraid—afraid of science, afraid of philosophy, we of whom these things are true! Shame on us! "Your life is hid with Christ in God." It is there because you are born of the Spirit and are "in Christ," and in him you are with God.

Here again is an explanation of why those early Christians saluted one another by saying, "Christ is risen!" That meant "*We* are risen." Christ is at the right hand of God, and so are we, seated in "heavenly places." "Your life is hid with Christ in God." Therefore we are safe and have nothing to fear. Why? Because he is on the throne of the universe. "He . . . sat down on the right hand of the Majesty on high" (Heb. 1:3), and his last word, as it were, to his disciples, to all his followers, were the words recorded at the end of the twenty-eighth chapter of the Gospel according to St. Matthew. "Jesus came and spake unto them, saying, All power is given unto me in heaven and in earth." "All power"!

Paul tells the Ephesians of their position and of this power that works in them. "God," he says, "raised him from the dead, and set him at his own right hand in the heavenly places, far above all principality, and power, and might, and dominion, and every name that is named, not only in this world, but also in that which is to come." Christian people are afraid of materialism, Communism, and much more. Oh, miserable Christians, when will you realize the truth about yourselves? Jesus Christ is "far above all principality, and power, and might, and dominion . . . and [God] hath put all things under his feet, and gave him to be the head over all things to the church, which is his body, the fullness of him that filleth all in all" (Eph. 1:21–23). All power is given unto him. He has already conquered our every enemy; not a single one is left.

So the apostle Paul again is reminding the Romans who were passing through a time of trial and tribulation that they need not have any sense of fear, still less of despair. "Who shall lay any thing to the charge of God's elect? It is God that justifieth. Who is he that condemneth? It is Christ that died, yea rather, that is risen again, who is even at the right hand of God, who also maketh intercession for us. Who shall separate us from the love of Christ?" Who can do so? "Shall tribulation, or distress, or persecution, or famine, or nakedness, or peril, or sword? . . . Nay, in all these things we are more than conquerors through him that loved us" (Rom. 8:33–35, 37). Then comes the final assertion:

> I am persuaded, [which means "I am absolutely certain"] that nei-
> ther death, nor life, nor angels, nor principalities, nor powers, nor
> things present, nor things to come, nor height, nor depth, nor any
> other creature, shall be able to separate us from the love of God,
> which is in Christ Jesus our Lord. (Rom. 8:38–39)

Why cannot these things do it? It is because we are "in Christ" and because our lives are "hid with Christ in God," and the Devil cannot get there, still less earthly authorities and powers. Nobody can get there. Nothing can ever "separate us from the love of God, which is in Christ Jesus our Lord." This the final perseverance of the saints! Saved and safe, secure and certain because our lives are "hid with Christ in God." Beloved people, this is the message of the resurrection. You have been "raised" with him; you have been elevated. You are seated in "heavenly places," and nothing can ever bring you from there. That is why these early Christians looking at one another said, "Christ is risen!"

And lastly, it follows, surely, from all this that men and women who are born again, who are born of the Spirit, know that they are alive unto God and that their life is hid with Christ in God. This follows by a logical necessity. They look forward to the glory of his coming and his appearing and to that glory that awaits them. This is the final proof of the fact that we are truly Christians and are born again and born of the Spirit. Here again is something that the Devil can never counterfeit and will never want to because he knows that will be the occasion of his finally being cast into eternal destruction. He is already defeated; he has already been "cast out" as "the prince of this world." That happened at the crucifixion. "Now is the judgment of this world: now shall the prince of this world be cast out" (John 12:31). And he was! But he will finally be cast into the lake of destruction at the blessed appearing of our great Lord and Savior.

Now here again is something of which the religious person knows nothing at all. Of all the fools in the world, those who are only religious are the biggest fools of all. They only have hope of Christ as they understand him in this life, and they rely upon their goodness and their religion and their performances, but they do not have joy, they have no happiness. But above all things else what they lack is this: they know nothing abut "blessed hope." You have never seen a religious person looking forward, as the apostle Paul did, to death. He said, "I am in a strait betwixt two, having a desire to depart, and to be with Christ; which is far better" (Phil. 1:23). He said in essence, "For your sakes it is better for me to stay here." "As for myself," says Paul, "I have 'a desire to depart, and to be with Christ; which is far better. . . . For to me to live is Christ, and to die is gain'" (v. 21). Religious people have never said that. They hold on tenaciously to all that they have in this world. Why? Because they know no other. They do not know that they are "in Christ"; they do not have the life of Christ, the life of God, in their soul. They are not aware of their life being "hid with Christ in God." They do not know this mighty power working in them. But those who are born again do. The degree, again, may vary tremendously, but it they know anything about this, then they must inevitably know something about this desire, the full perfection of the glory.

The apostle Paul spoke of this in his letter to the Romans. They were in trouble; so he reminds them that they are "children of God: and if children, then heirs; heirs of God, and joint-heirs with Christ; if so be that we suffer with him, that we may be also glorified together." Then he adds,

> For I reckon [again he means "I am sure, I am certain"] that the sufferings of this present time are not worthy to be compared with the glory which shall be revealed in us. For the earnest expectation of the creature waiteth for the manifestation of the sons of God. For the creature was made subject to vanity, not willingly, but by reason of him who hath subjected the same in hope, because the creature itself also shall be delivered from the bondage of corruption into the glorious liberty of the children of God. For we know that the whole creation groaneth and travaileth in pain together until now. And not only they, but we ourselves also, which have the firstfruits

of the Spirit, even we ourselves groan within ourselves, waiting for the adoption, to wit, the redemption of our body. (Rom. 8:18–23)

That is it. "The sufferings of this present time are not worthy to be compared with the glory which shall be revealed in us."

Christian people, do you ever think about this glory? Is that the thing that sustains you? Is that the thing that holds you up in moments of trial, disappointment, unhappiness, illness, when you are face-to-face with death? Have you the victory that overcomes the grave, even the last enemy? Do you know that you are going to this glory and do you say, defying everything, "I reckon that the sufferings of this present time are not worthy to be compared with the glory which shall be revealed in us"? Oh, let Paul add even to that:

Our light affliction, which is but for a moment, worketh for us a far more exceeding and eternal weight of glory; while we look not at the things which are seen, but at the things which are not seen: for the things which are seen are temporal; but the things which are not seen are eternal. (2 Cor. 4:17–18)

It does not matter what happens to us, says Paul, and he has given a terrifying list there in 2 Corinthians 4:17 of the trials and tribulations he was enduring. And he smiles at them. "Our light affliction, which is but for a moment, worketh for us [and produce in us] a far more exceeding and eternal weight of glory." Some suggest it should be translated "an exceeding exceedingly abundant weight of glory." "Weight of glory"! ". . . while we look not at the things which are seen." Those who are in Christ Jesus do not spend all their time looking at the things that are seen; they are passing away, they are temporary. "But at the things which are not seen: for the things which are seen are temporal; but the things which are not seen are eternal."

Jude sums it all up for us in his benediction at the end of his little letter. Here again were people passing through terrible trials, not only persecution but false teaching in the church—and that is something that grieves the Christian even more than persecution—false teachers claiming the name of Christ and yet denying the essential gospel or adding to it. They came in the early days, and this is the way Jude comforts them:

> Now unto him that is able to keep you from falling, and to present you faultless before the presence of his glory with exceeding joy, to the only wise God our Saviour, be glory and majesty, dominion and power, both now and ever. (Jude 24–25)

Christian people, if the life of the resurrection is in you, then it must create within you some faint longings and desires after that perfection. We are still in the body, and we are waiting for the redemption of the body. We are saved, but the body is not yet. But the body is going to be saved. It is going to be changed "in the twinkling of an eye"; it is going to be glorified, made perfect. There is a glory awaiting us, and if the life of God and of Christ is in our souls, that life will cry out in various ways in longing for that great and glorious day that is to come, when he will appear and when even the whole creation will be filled with amazement as it looks at "the manifestation of the sons of God." And it will be so wonderful that even nature and creation itself will be transfigured and transformed. It will be the Grand Apocalypse! The Great Regeneration! All things shall be new, and all things shall manifest the glory of God. We shall see him, and we shall be like him, and we shall reign with Christ. We shall be his people and rejoice in the sunshine of his face forever and ever.

Those it seems to me are some of the inevitable consequences of the resurrection. How are things with you, my dear friend? "The heart knoweth his own bitterness." Have you trials, troubles, tribulations? Is everything against you and trying to drive you to despair? Child of God, I say to you, Christ is risen! Whatever this world may do to you, it can never rob you of that glory that awaits you, for even now your life is hidden with Christ in God.

15

# The Love of God in the Salvation of Men and Women

## JOHN 3:16

Sunday morning sermon preached between
April 10, 1966, and May 15, 1966.

Let me begin by saying that while this is possibly the most familiar and well-known verse in the whole Bible, it is nevertheless true to say that perhaps no verse is so frequently misunderstood and misinterpreted as this one. Nothing is therefore more fatal than just to repeat it generally, as if it were some kind of incantation. It is a verse that must be examined and observed carefully, because it is a verse that is packed with fundamental and vital Christian doctrine. The very fact that it is connected with the previous verses should open our eyes to that at once, but it is extraordinary how people almost invariably isolate this verse. The Bible in front of me, for instance, starts a new paragraph here, which is obviously quite nonsensical; you should not start a paragraph when the first word of the verse is "for." It is a continuation of what our Lord had been saying in verses 14 and 15, but really all the way from verse 11.

Now it is not my intention to deal with the great doctrines that are contained here one by one. We have already been looking at several of them as we have been working our way through this great chapter. I am rather anxious to look at what is, after all, the central theme of this verse, and that is the love of God as it is displayed in the salvation of men and women. Our Lord was anxious that Nicodemus should grasp this above everything else. Now again we must not lose sight of this point: these words were spoken to that great man Nicodemus, a Pharisee, a ruler, a teacher of the Jews, and we bear that in mind because there are certain aspects of the statement that we cannot fully grasp unless we realize that they were spoken in particular to this learned and religious Jew.

Our Lord was anxious that Nicodemus, who had such an entirely wrong notion as to the Messiah who was to come, should grasp the true idea and that, therefore, he should realize to whom he was speaking and what was the purpose of the coming of the Son of God into this world. The great theme is the love of God as manifested in his Son and in the salvation that the Son has made possible. We can spend considerable time looking at the degree of this love. "God *so* loved." "So" is the expressive word, and it is the content of that little word in which we are interested. What is "the world"? It is man in sin, man fallen away from God, man living a life outside God and all the glorious possibilities that God originally placed in man when he created him. But God loved the world—man—in that condition. And not only that, he so loved man that he sent his only begotten Son into such a world. There is nothing so moving and so wonderful in the whole of Scripture as this—"God so loved the world, that he *gave*." He delivered him up for us all. He delivered him up to all the suffering and the agony that you and I merit because of our sin and disobedience. He bore our sins in his own body on the tree. It is by his stripes that we are healed. He received the stripes; he suffered under them. God gave him over to that, and there we see something of the degree of God's love.

But now I want to consider the *manner* of God's love, and that still has to do with this little word *so*. It is, of course, defined by our Lord himself in certain words that are actually used by him in this particular verse. I regard it as a great privilege to hold before you the manner of

God's love, and I do so for two very special reasons. I pray that God may look upon us and have mercy upon us all together and give me power to put this before you in such a way that it shall be plain and clear to all of you at this moment. Why do I feel this in an unusual manner? Let me put it to you like this: all of us are living a life in which we never quite know what is going to happen next, and nothing is so important, as we listen to the gospel, as that we should listen to it with that in our minds. If all of us only realized the truth about life in this world, we would consider this gospel in a very different manner. The trouble with us—and we are all guilty of it—is that we tend to act on the assumption that we are on earth forever and that we can afford to listen to these things in a detached manner. If only we saw ourselves as strangers and pilgrims and sojourners, which is what we are. Only during this past week I heard that a man, who I have known for some thirty-odd years, suddenly, while speaking in a meeting such as this, collapsed and died. "Ah," you say, "we're all familiar with that sort of thing." Yes, we are, so familiar with it that we forget it! But we are all in that kind of situation.

One disadvantage about living in a big city like London is that things like that are not brought home to us as they are in smaller communities. If you happen to be living in a village and a man suddenly dies, you cannot help thinking about it. Everybody talks about it; it is the great topic of conversation for a week or longer. But in London so many things happen that we tend to forget about these things. It is a dangerous thing to live in a great city. So I mention a fact like that to you in order that we all may remember that we are just human beings like everybody else, and all of us can say, "Here today and gone tomorrow." The gospel addresses us in that way, as men and women who are here and listening and have that opportunity. But it may be the last, and every man who preaches should preach in that way, as a dying man to dying men. So as we consider these gracious words uttered by the Son of God, may we note them in that way.

My second reason for solemnly calling your attention to these words is that again very recently I have had abundant evidence that many people stumble with respect to the Christian life at this very point. It is my privilege on Friday nights to be working through the epistle to the Romans, and recently in doing so we have come to the apostle's great and mighty and moving statement of the doctrine of justification by faith only. We have been going through it and trying to expound it. And to me it has been wonderful to see how God has used a service like that, which one would have thought was primarily a teaching service, as a means and an instrument of conversion and of bringing at least three people out of darkness and into the light, bringing them to a knowledge of the truth. Every time the gospel is presented it is an evangelistic service. We have gone sadly astray to think that only certain services in the church are evangelistic. This division is not scriptural, and God has corrected our notions in that way by using such a service to bring people to a knowledge of himself. Whenever his truth is expounded and preached we proclaim the *evangel*, and we can expect conversions in every meeting. How easy it is to miss this central point, this preliminary point of the gospel. So I want to try and put it to you now in as practical and as simple and as direct a manner as is possible.

How does God manifest his love to us? First he does so in what he *gives* to us. "God so loved the world, that he gave his only begotten Son." Why? "That whosoever believeth in him should not perish, but have everlasting life." That is what the gospel is about. Nicodemus had never realized that. He thought that it was about miracles and certain aspects of teaching and so on, but it is not. The gospel includes all of those, of course. It has the most amazing ethic; it preaches the highest morality that has ever been held before men; it has a social application, an industrial application—endless applications. Yes, but if you spend your time with the applications but miss this, what a tragedy it is. The great object and purpose is to give men and women everlasting or eternal life.

Had you realized that the gospel is offering you everlasting life, that the Son of God came into the world in order to give it to you? What is it? Well, as our Lord makes quite plain and clear here and in the previous verses, it is the opposite of perishing. "Should not perish, but have everlasting life." What, then, does he mean by "perish"? It is defined elsewhere in the Scriptures in this way: it is to be dead in trespasses and sins. The one who is dead in trespasses and sins has perished, and that is the condition of all men and women by nature. That is how we are born into this world. This means that we are outside the life of God and that we are living a life that is entirely confined to the human and to the temporal level and sphere. It means that instead of belonging to God we belong to this world, and we all know perfectly well what that means. It means that our ideas are bounded by life in this world, the ideas and the thoughts and the capacities of men, and that we can never go outside that and never get beyond it. That is what it means to be perishing.

Life is found only in God. God alone is immortal. God alone has life, and apart from God there is no life. That is why the apostle Paul calls our natural condition "dead in trespasses and sins." That is our state by nature. How evident it is that such is the condition of so many in this world today. They are not alive to spiritual things at all. They do not seem to realize that they have a soul within them, something that is altogether bigger than this world, something that will go on when their body is dead and buried in a grave, something that is imperishable, something immaterial. They never stop to think about it; they are not interested in it. Why? Because they are perishing, they are spiritually dead. The only life they know is the life that belongs to the body. That is their realm, their sphere, and of course they are always talking about it and getting excited about it, spending their money and their time. I need not waste your time telling you in detail what I mean. We are all perfectly familiar with it. You simply need to read a newspaper or listen to the radio. Now I am not criticizing these things as such, but I am saying that it is rather odd or strange that people are prepared to give such time and money and enthusiasm to things that belong only to their animal and bodily and physical part and none at all to the highest part. That is what it means to be perishing. Not to be alive to and alert to the highest and the noblest and the most wonderful things, but to get so excited about the other. Surely that is a sign of death, a sign that we are in a perishing condition.

And I think you will agree that is the state, alas, of the majority of people today—food, drink, clothing, games, sports, excitement. Look at them by the thousands at their various sports events, the distances they will travel, the way they will talk about it before and afterward and spend money and all the excitement about it. "But," you say, "there's nothing wrong with a game of football." I quite agree. That is not what I am talking about. I am not talking about the people who play football but about the people who get excited about it just watching it and things of that sort. It is a good thing to exercise your body, but I am talking about the whole personality living for that or living for any one of these things that are purely on the animal and physical level—having no interest at all in, indeed despising, this other kind of life in which one reminds oneself of the something within that links one to God and enjoys him and his life. Not alive at all to the things of God but living only and entirely bound and circumscribed by these things that belong not only to the body but to time and to this world.

And what makes it more tragic is this: even as people are doing so, they are literally and physically dying. Every day we live we get older. Every day we live we are losing something in our faculties. Now this is not being morbid. This is facing facts. The gospel is not soft stuff. The soft stuff is the talk that does not face the facts and tells you, "Leave it alone. Let's go and have a good time." That is the soft stuff because it is not honest; it is not facing facts. I believe in facing facts, and I therefore know that every one of us is getting older every single day, and it can happen to us without our knowing. So a man who appears to be full of health and vigor and strength can suddenly drop dead. He has never felt that pain before; his first attack killed him. Why? Well, there was a process going on in his arteries. He did not know, nobody knew, but it was there, and he was dying, and suddenly everybody knows that he is dead. What is so terrifying and so awful is the message of the Scripture that anybody who dies in that state and condition goes on like that through all eternity. "I don't believe hell is a place," says someone. All right, my friend, I am not asking you to believe that at the moment. All I am asking you is this: Would you like to spend eternity as you are now and even worse? With no hope, no prospects, nothing to relieve it at all? That is the condition of mankind.

Now the love of God is seen in this way: "For God so loved the world, that he gave his only begotten Son, that whosoever believeth in him should not perish, but have everlasting life." That is the exact opposite of all that I have been describing to you, and this is the most amazing thing in the world. The apostle Paul says to every Christian, "Reckon ye also yourselves to be dead indeed unto sin, but alive unto God" (Rom. 6:11). That is what is meant by eternal life. One comes out of that condition of perishing and begins to live in a real and in a spiritual sense. In the Bible life always means a participation in the life of God. And that is Christianity. A great Scotsman called Henry Scougal who lived nearly three hundred years ago wrote a book with the title *The Life of God in the Souls of Men.* That is eternal life. That is Christianity. Christianity is not just morality. It is not just goodness. It is not just doing certain things and not doing others. It includes that, but it goes beyond it. The real heart and call and center of Christianity is the life of God in a man's soul. Eternal life.

So then we must define this term *eternal* or *everlasting* in a twofold way. It first of all means a particular quality of life. It means, in other words, that we are made spiritually alive. It means that whereas we had always been living in the way that I have been depicting, suddenly we awaken to the fact that "Dust thou art, to dust returnest, was not spoken of the soul."[1] We are aware of the fact that there is something in us that is bigger than all the physical, the material and is earthly. There is an immaterial, invisible something that is a part of us and is the greatest part of us. We begin to awaken to that fact and we say, "I've never considered it. I've never thought about it. I've done nothing about it. I've been neglecting the most priceless thing of all." But now we are made alive spiritually; we awaken. And so we begin to think about God. The way to measure life, or any view of life, is just this: How does one spend it? What is it we do with our activities? So I put it to you as a simple, reasonable question: Which is greater when you come to assess and to measure—to be thinking upon the mere use of the body in various ways or to be thinking about God, the Lord God Almighty, the everlasting and the eternal, and our relationship to him? Thinking of men in the context of God and of eternity and of all that is glorious and wonderful, that is what happens to those who are given eternal or everlasting life. They become spiritually awake, and they now begin to think along this line.

Our Lord himself on one occasion said, "And this is life eternal, that they might know thee the only true God, and Jesus Christ, whom thou has sent" (John 17:3). That is what is given to us by believing on the Lord Jesus Christ—knowing God, knowing God's love to us, knowing God's care for us, his solicitude with respect to us. Suppose that we find ourselves suddenly stricken by an illness and no longer able to follow our usual profession or business or whatever it was and no longer able to go after our excitements and our interests and our pleasures. Suddenly all that is stopped, and we are lying helpless on our back in bed and left to ourselves and do not know what to do with ourselves. Before we knew Christ we were wretched and miserable and disconsolate in such circumstances, but now we are not alone. We know that God is with us. He manifests himself to us, and, indeed, we may find ourselves even thanking God for an illness. We may say with the psalmist of old, "Before I was afflicted I went astray. . . . It was good for me that I have been afflicted; that I might learn thy statutes" (Ps. 119:67, 71). But now we have come back, and we are enjoying a life of communion with God, and we know that God will never leave us or forsake us.

And other things follow as well. We begin to experience a peace and a joy we had never known before. It is difficult to find peace in this world with its rush and its bustle and its noise and its clatter. Oh, where can one find peace and rest and quiet? Here it is as a part of everlasting life, and joy too. Indeed, I can sum it up by putting it like this: to have eternal life means that we become the possessors of exactly the same life that the Son of God himself had when he was in this world. Read the four Gospels for yourself; look at his life. Everybody admires that life. That very type and quality of life is offered to you by Christ himself. You and I can have the life of Christ within us. And we can go through this world exactly as he went through it, living above it, living on a higher plain and on a higher level, knowing a peace that nothing can disturb, knowing a joy that even the cross could not rob him of! That is the quality of life.

But eternal life is not only a quality of life, it also has the element of quantity to it. Note the difference in the wording of the fifteenth and sixteenth verses: "That whosoever believeth in him should not perish, but have *eternal* life" and "Whoever believeth in him should not perish, but have *everlasting* life." The life that is given to the Christian in this world is a life without end. It not only lasts in time, it lasts throughout eternity. Indeed, what we are given in this life is merely the firstfruits, merely the foretaste. In ancient times when the crop had become ripened, the farmers used to go and reap just a little. That was called the firstfruits, the first pickings. For example, you take the first ripe apple from the apple tree and eat it. Then you say, "Isn't it marvelous?" and you see the crop that is coming. The firstfruits, the foretaste—that is all we are given here. It is marvelous, it is wonderful, but after death we receive it all in its fullness and in all its glory. That is everlasting life. God puts his life into our souls here. It lasts through life, it lasts through death, and it will go on lasting throughout eternity itself. And that is the prospect as our Lord puts it here for everyone that believes upon his name. That is the gift. Oh, is this not an amazing love? The love of God for man is as great as this. This is its method, that he comes to ransom sinners who are dead and perishing and gives them life, God's life. Thus we realize that we can begin to enjoy the life of God in our souls in this present world. That is the very message of the gospel.

But then notice the way in which God gives this life. This is what astounded Nicodemus most. Nicodemus, as a Jew and as a Pharisee, believed that God rewarded men for the good life they lived and for their prayers and for all their religion and so on. They said, "If I do this much, then God will give me the reward." The apostle Paul once believed that doctrine, as he tells us in writing to the Philippians. He was proud of his own life, his own godliness, his religion, and all his own effort, and he believed God would reward him, that he could put in his bill, as it were, and ask for the reward. That is the natural man's view, if he believes in God at all. But notice what the Lord Jesus Christ said to Nicodemus. "God so loved the world, that he gave his only begotten Son, that whosoever believeth in him should not perish, but have everlasting life." Now this is what I am anxious to make so plain and clear. You receive this gift of eternal life; you receive salvation entirely and only and utterly as a gift from God. It is the result only of believing on him, of faith in him. You do nothing at all for it. It is not the result of good works or of your good life; it is not the result of your efforts or your striving or any of your achievements. That has nothing to do with it; it is entirely the result of believing in the name of the Son of God.

It is here that people persist in going astray. There is no greater fallacy than to think that you can make yourself a Christian. No man has ever made himself a Christian; no man ever will. Indeed, I go so far as to say this: the man who thinks he has made himself a Christian is proving and asserting that he is not a Christian. It is an impossibility, and there is nothing that so prevents men and women from becoming Christians as their own efforts to make themselves Christians. It simply cannot be done. The history of the church is strewn with evidence about this. Was that not the whole trouble with Martin Luther before his conversion? He was trying to make himself a Christian, and he realized it was a tremendous test. He became a monk, he turned his back upon the world and upon prospects in a profession, and he went into a cell, and there he was, fasting and sweating, praying and doing good. What was he trying to do? Trying to make himself a Christian. Trying to work up a righteousness that would satisfy God so that God would look on him and say, "Well done, Martin Luther. You've done so well that I give you the gift of eternal life as a reward." Then his eyes were suddenly opened, and he saw that it was all tragically wrong. So he turned right about, and he saw that that was the way to hell and that there was only one way to God and to heaven, and that was the way of faith. "The just shall live by faith" (Heb. 10:38).

What does that mean? Let me put it simply like this: what obtains this gift of eternal life is that a man *believes* in Jesus Christ. "God so loved the world, that he gave his only begotten Son, that whosoever *believeth in him* should not perish." It means, as our Lord has already been expounding to Nicodemus, that you must believe in his person. It means that you accept scriptural testimony and evidence that Jesus of Nazareth was none other than the eternal Son of God, the only begotten Son of God. It just means that you believe this record, that at that given point in time, which happened when you turn from BC to AD, the Son of God came out of heaven and was born of a virgin's womb. You believe that Jesus is the Christ, the Son of God. You believe that the person who appeared to be just a man and who worked as a carpenter in Nazareth for all those silent years was none other than the Everlasting Word of whom it is said, "All things were made by him; and without him was not any thing made that was made." You believe on the person of the Son of God.

Yes, but you believe not only on his person but also on his work. You believe that he came into this world in order to save men from perishing and that he did not come into the world just to give us a moral teaching, just to give us an example and to add to our efforts and endeavors. No, no, you believe him when he says, "The Son of man is come to seek and to save that which was lost" (Luke 19:10) and "the Son of man came not to be ministered unto, but to minister, and to give his life a ransom for many" (Mark 10:45). You believe that. Believing on him means that, and you must put that into the context. In other words it means this: if you say truly that you believe in the Lord Jesus Christ, what you are saying can be put in these terms: "I see that I am a sinner. I see that I am perishing. I see that I'm outside the life of God. I see that all my goodness about which I've boasted so much is nothing but filthy rags or what the apostle Paul calls 'dung,' refuse, manure. I see that I can never put myself right, and I see and believe that the Son of God came from heaven to earth in order to save me. I believe that he took my sins upon himself and bore the punishment, that he has done for me what no one else could do."

That is what believing in him means, but I want to emphasize the believing aspect. What does that mean? Obviously it must mean in the first instance recognition of the truth. An interesting statement is made about the woman Lydia, a seller of purple [cloth] from Thyatira who lived in the city of Philippi. The apostle Paul and his companions went and sat down among some women at a prayer meeting, and the apostle began to speak to them the words of the Lord. Then notice what happened: ". . . whose [Lydia's] heart the Lord opened, that she attended unto the things which were spoken of Paul" (Acts 16:14). She paid attention for the first time in her life. And here is the first thing always in belief. You may have had an open Bible in your possession all your life. You may have read it when you were a child; you heard it read in chapel or in church. You say, "I've always been familiar with the Bible." But have you *attended* unto it? Have you said, "This word is speaking to me. When I read what our Lord said to Nicodemus, I'm reading what he said to me"? This is not simply about people who lived two thousand years ago; it is about people today, it is about men and women always. This word is speaking to me. How can it be that I have lived all these years and I have never attended unto it? I have never paid attention, I have never concentrated, I have never said, "What does this mean, what is it saying?" Have you attended unto this word? You cannot believe it without attending unto it. You cannot take it for granted. You must pay attention.

The next step is accepting it with your mind. But believing goes a step further than that. It means that you begin to trust it, that you have confidence in Jesus and in what he has done for you. Indeed, I can define believing on the Lord Jesus Christ like this: it means resting yourself and your soul and your eternal destiny entirely in him and upon him. I can therefore test you very easily at this moment as to whether you believe in the Lord Jesus Christ or not. This is the test: Are you still looking to yourself in any way? Are you still saying, "Ah, yes, I'm now going to decide that henceforward I am going to do this or that"? If you speak like that, you do not believe in the Lord Jesus Christ. To believe in the Lord Jesus Christ means that you are finished with yourself and your own efforts forever, that you say, "I see clearly that it doesn't matter what I do, it doesn't matter how long I may go on doing it, I can never do enough. Therefore, I'm not going to rely on myself and my activities anymore. I am now going to rely entirely on him and what he has done for me." That is to believe on the Lord Jesus Christ.

But I have a further test. It is something that once you see it, you do it at once. You do not say, "I'm going to." What's the point of saying that? Why not do it *now?* What can you do by waiting? What difference is it going to make if you wait twenty-four hours? What can you do between now and this time tomorrow night that will make a difference to your relationship with God? The moment a man or woman believes on the Lord Jesus Christ he or she says, "I will do it now. I won't wait for a second. I want nothing more; nothing else can make a difference. I take Jesus now."

There is an immediacy about belief. That comes out in the story about the Philippian jailer in Acts 16. The Philippian jailer did not have to undergo a course of instruction before he became a Christian. He had the Word preached to him, and he believed it. He believed Paul and Silas, he was baptized, and he rejoiced there and then, in the middle of the night. This thing happens at once. If you see it, there is no point in delaying. You say at once, "I can trust him now as well as tomorrow or in a thousand years time. I believe *now*." You will never be any better or any more qualified than you are now. Belief is immediate. To see the truth is to accept it and to trust it. I even go further and say, do not worry about your feelings for the moment. Do not worry about your assurance for the moment. Believing on the Lord Jesus Christ is accepting his testimony, setting your seal to it that the word is true, saying, "If I do not believe it I am making him a liar. I do not understand, but I have believed. I see that when he spoke to Nicodemus he is speaking to me, and he tells me this. I believe him. I'll trust my all, my everything to him." Oh, what a wonderful love this is—God giving us this gift of everlasting life, his own life in that way.

> Nothing in my hands I bring,
> Simply to the cross I cling;
> Naked, come to Thee for dress;
> Helpless look to Thee for grace;
> Foul, I to the fountain fly;
> Wash me, Savior, or I die.[2]

Believing in the Lord Jesus Christ—there it is. Have you done this? Without a second's delay, without waiting to rid yourself of one dark blot, you come to him just as you are and believe him when he tells you that he can wash you and make you whiter than snow.

My last word is on the other word that is here and in which you can see again the love of God so gloriously—the word *whosoever*. "God so loved the world, that he gave his only begotten Son, that *whosoever* believeth in him should not perish, but have everlasting life." Do not forget that this was spoken to Nicodemus, who thought that only Jews were to be saved and that all Gentiles were to be condemned. "No, no," says our Lord, "you're quite wrong. It's for Gentiles as well as Jews. It is for all who believe, whoever they are, from any nation or tribe or language." It does not matter whether we are British, African, Japanese, Chinese, or American—we are all human, and we are all in sin. "Whosoever believeth."

A verse in a hymn seems to me to sum it all up: "Today thy mercy calls me to wash away my sin." The hymn continues, "However great my trespass"—do you get that? "Today thy mercy calls me to wash away my sin, however great my trespass." There is no limit to that. Have you understood this, my friend? It does not matter what you have been; it does not matter what you have done. "Ah," people have said to me, "if you but knew the life I've lived, if you knew the sins I've committed . . ." I always reply, "I'm not at all interested in your sins. I don't care what you've done or what you've been. We're all sinners." It is we who draw these distinctions between big sins and little sins. God does not. One sin is as bad as another in the sight of God, and one sin damns the soul as much as another. It is quite immaterial to the preacher of the gospel whether you have committed murder or not. If you are a murderer you have the same sins as anybody else. Put whatever you can into the list—murder, drunkenness, adultery, immorality, vice. List the foulest, most fiendish, most perverted, horrible things beyond description and imagination, put them all in. "However great my trespass, whate'er I may have been"—it does not matter.

Then listen: "However long from mercy I may have turned away." It does not matter at all. Perhaps you have been reading the books of the psychologists in which they say that if you are not converted in your adolescent stage, you never will be. Nonsense! I do not care how old you are. I will let you into the secret of the essential difference between the life as a doctor and the life of a preacher and evangelist. When the doctor is handling people, he wants to know their past history, about the father and the mother, what they died of and so on. He must have the patient's history. He cannot do anything without it. I am not interested in histories. I am not interested in testimonies of people describing the sins they have committed, and so on. It is a waste of time because everybody is a sinner and everybody needs the same salvation. The particular sins you have committed do not matter at all, and it does not matter what you were. You are a soul; you are a human being. No one case is any more wonderful than another. Each one is a miracle, and it is God alone who could do it. You may be an octogenarian, trembling at the brink of your grave. Or you may be only eight years old. It doesn't matter.

> However long from mercy I may have turned away,
> Thy blood, O Christ, can cleanse me and make me white today.[3]

The only thing that matters is, do you believe on the Lord Jesus Christ? Every objection is answered, every obstacle is moved. If you really see this and believe what he says, you can believe it now and know that your sins are forgiven, that you are not perishing any longer, but that you have received everlasting life. Have you done so? Do so now. If you begin to say, "Ah, but . . ." you have not seen the truth, you have not attended unto it, and you do not believe it. On the other hand, if you believe what he says, every "but" is withdrawn. Nothing matters. I just go to him as I am and confess my sin in the knowledge that I deserve hell and eternal punishment because of my folly and arrogance and sin. But I believe that because of what he, the Son of God, has done for me, it is all canceled and from this moment I am a child of God and an heir of eternal bliss with the Father. If you do not do this now, you have not believed. If you have believed, you will do it at once. I therefore leave it with you. "That whosoever believeth in him should not perish, but have everlasting life." And that is life indeed.

If you have not believed and have never done so before, confess your sin to him now, tell him that you believe, and cast yourself upon his love and mercy. Do so now.

*May the grace of our Lord and Savior Jesus Christ and the love of God and the fellowship and the communion of the Holy Spirit abide and continue with us now and throughout the remainder of our short, uncertain earthly life and pilgrimage, until we shall be with him in glory sharing his eternal life without end. Amen.*

# 16

# Darkness and Light

JOHN 3:19-21

Sunday morning sermon preached in
Westminster Chapel, May 15, 1966.

In the first chapter of this Gospel, the apostle John says, "Of his fullness have all we received, and grace for grace" (v. 16). The great question is, Why do we not know more of that? It is a continuous process and ever increasing, and the question we are confronting is, Why is this not true of all of us, as it should be? Why is it that so many Christian people are half-hearted and apologetic and unhappy, perhaps even defeated? That is a contradiction of the whole message of the gospel. It brings the gospel into disrepute. It is a very poor recommendation for the Christian faith, and we are concerned about this for two reasons. First, it is tragic that with all this offered to us and possible for us, we should be living as paupers instead of as princes.

But still more urgently the world will only become interested in Christianity when it sees Christian people really reproducing what you read of in the New Testament. The world is not interested in ecclesiastical systems and institutions, and rightly so. It is concerned about something living and vital, something that really does to a man or woman what our Lord told Nicodemus it can do and always does.

There are many hindrances to this, and these exist because we are all sinful and because we have a mighty adversary against us who is always out to confuse us, to muddle us in our thinking and our whole attitude. And he is so resourceful that he can turn himself, says Paul, into "an angel of light." He can quote Scripture—anything to keep us from this living, vital relationship with the Lord Jesus Christ, anything that will keep us from receiving his fullness.

Our essential trouble is that we know so little about the love of God that we read about in the sixteenth verse of John 3. If we only knew that, most of our problems would immediately be solved. So it is our business to discover that love in the Scriptures and to discover it by seeking God in prayer and in communion and fellowship.

But that is not the only trouble, and here in these three verses we are brought face-to-face with yet another difficulty, another obstacle, another problem. This is what is put before us in these words, showing us how we tend to fool ourselves and allow the Devil to fool us in our whole approach to this very matter. It is put explicitly in the nineteenth verse: "And this is the condemnation, that light is come into the world, and men loved darkness rather than light, because their deeds were evil," and the exposition of this follows.

What is the principle taught here? I suggest to you that there are really two principles. It is in a sense one, but it is better to subdivide it. It is the danger of seeking and looking for something that is already there instead of submitting ourselves to it. Or if you like, it is the whole trouble of mistaking the real nature of our problem. "And this is the condemnation, that light is come . . ." In a sense men and women are looking for, seeking for, hoping that the light will appear. Yet they refuse the light God sends them.

Why do they do so? Because "men loved darkness rather than light, because their deeds were evil" (John 3:19), but they do not know that, they do not realize it. In these two ways, we are constantly fooling ourselves, and that is why we know so little about this "fullness." It is extraordinary how mad mankind has become as the result of sin. We are like Hagar, that servant maid of Sarah, the wife of Abraham, with her boy in the wilderness and almost dying of thirst. They did not know what to do, and in her desperation she cries out to God, and God says, "Look, there is a well there by your side." It had been there the whole time, but she had not seen it. We are all like that. Why have we not received "his fullness"? That is the question.

I will try to deal with this statement here by putting it to you under the following headings. Consider for a moment the way in which we delude ourselves in this matter of seeking. "And this is the condemnation. . . ." Now this is true primarily, of course, of all who are not Christians. Many people are disturbed about life, disturbed about themselves as Nicodemus was, dissatisfied, aware that something better is possible and having a longing within them for it.

So they set out in a great quest for this, and they can go to the ends of the earth and come back and never find it. Why? Because it is only possible in one place and in one person. That is what our Lord was really saying to Nicodemus. Here is a questioning man; he comes at night and seeks an interview. Our Lord says in effect, "It is your attitude that is wrong. You are looking at the Light, and you need not seek any further. I am the Light; all that you seek is in me." That is what our Lord was really saying to him.

That is always the trouble with the unbeliever. Many of us know this from experience, and this is the point to which you have to come in the end. You give up, and you see that the whole time it was there facing you.

Now that is not only true of the unbeliever, it is equally true of believers when you put them face-to-face with this statement about "his fullness." The same thing that holds us back from entering this life holds us back from receiving "his fullness . . . and grace for grace" (John 1:16), "that ye might be filled," as Paul puts it to the Ephesians, "with all the fullness of God" (3:19). Why is this? It is because we fall into this error; our whole approach to it becomes wrong. Many of us seek it and have sought it perhaps along some intellectual route. We spend our time reading books about the holy life, the devout life. We study it, philosophy comes into it, and we philosophize about the love of God, and we feel that by doing this and going along that intellectual route we will eventually arrive at this fullness that we are desiring. We can spend many years reading many books, hoping that a new book is about to appear that will give us what we seek.

This is a real danger. One can do it not only with manuals like that but even with biographies. I have known people who have spent their lives in this way; their great interest was to know this fullness, to enter into this intimate relationship with God, and yet they have never had it. Why not? It is often because they have just been reading about it and are interested intellectually, and it becomes almost a lust. You read book after book after book, and you see it happening in others; you read the descriptions, but you never get it yourself, and this is because you formed this bad habit of regarding the whole thing from the intellectual stand-point. You think all along that it is more knowledge you need and more information, so you go on collecting more and more.

Now I know one has to be careful in saying a thing like that. The Devil will make you do everything to excess. You can learn a lot through reading biographies and the lives of saints, but there is a danger of living on your knowledge and information concerning them and never really applying it to yourself.

Another error is the danger of waiting for some climactic experience. Here again we see the subtlety of it all. You cannot be a Christian without an experience. It is not what you do—it is what happens to you; being "born again" leads to experience. And it is right that we should realize that being Christians means that we have a definite experience of the action of God upon our souls. But then the danger comes in that when we are facing this whole question of his fullness, we are just waiting for some experience or seeking it, going to meetings trying to get it, people putting their hands on us and various other things. And there are, again, people who spend a lifetime doing that; many have done so. That is how they go astray.

And then there are others who regard this solely from the standpoint of the will—mind, heart, will. They think that the whole secret of this teaching is that you have to take yourself in hand, and with a great and a mighty effort of will you drag yourself along the mystic way or some other way. Again history is full of important instruction concerning this.

People have segregated themselves from society. Some have become monks and hermits and anchorites and put on camel-hair shirts. Various people used to flagellate themselves and lacerate their flesh and do all sorts of things in this endeavor to receive God's fullness. They have worked so hard; they have sacrificed so much. There is something very heroic about so many of them. But according to the teaching of the New Testament they have been all wrong. And we find this in various forms at the present time. There are people who are spending their time trying to be "willing to be willing," trying to force themselves. This is the result of teaching that tells us that we can get all this in one act or one experience or something like that.

So there are some of the ways in which we spend time seeking this fullness. But here comes the answer: "And this is the condemnation, that the light is come" (John 3:19). What are you looking for? What are you striving after? What are you struggling about? The second principle has do with all that is wrong because the light *has* come. It is all there, and this is what the Gospel of John, above the others perhaps, puts so plainly before us in that great verse, the sixteenth verse of the first chapter. But he goes on repeating the idea—"eternal life," "everlasting life," and so on. "That whosoever believeth in him should not perish, but have [and have more and more of it] everlasting life" (John 3:16), eternal life, "his fullness," call it what you will (John 1:16).

This means that all we need is in the Lord Jesus Christ. It is all there in him. That is the teaching of the whole New Testament. All we need to do is to receive him, to take of him and of his fullness. Our Lord put this in many different ways. He will describe it later on as "a well of water" that he puts within us, and so on. But here is the great message: there is nothing we can ever need in this respect that it not already provided for us. Everything is in Christ Jesus. "Of him," says Paul to the Corinthians, "are ye in Christ Jesus, who of God is made unto us wisdom, and righteousness, and sanctification, and redemption" (1 Cor. 1:30). He is "all, and in all" (Col. 3:11). He is all-sufficient. All the treasures of God's grace and wisdom are treasured and stored up in him for us. That is the teaching—nothing less.

Again let me remind you of Paul's prayer for the Ephesians. He says he is praying for them that they "may be able to comprehend with all saints what is the breadth, and length, and depth, and height; and to know the love of Christ, which passeth knowledge, that [they] might be filled with all the fullness of God" (Eph. 3:18–19). There are people who cannot read books on philosophy; they cannot enter into this great intellectual quest. They have not had the education or the culture for this. So is there no hope for them? Thank God, there is. The light has come; it is in Jesus Christ. It is just a question of looking at the light, turning to his face. It is the same for salvation. He says himself that he is like the brazen serpent lifted upon a pole. You just look at him, and you look at him in this respect as in every other respect; it is all found in him. Oh, the tragedy of the wasted and lost years that so many of us are conscious of along that intellectual line or along the line of experience, waiting for something. You feel you need further light, further instruction, further knowledge; so you spend a lifetime and end as barren as you were at the beginning.

That is all wrong; that is "the condemnation"; that is where we have gone astray. You must not plead for more light; it has all been given. You do not need to wait until some great book comes out next month or next year; the truth is all here already. There have been Christians now for nearly two thousand years—how have they done it? They did not have wonderful modern knowledge and all the rest of it, but look at the heights they have reached, look at the experiences some of them have had. How did they do it, simple ordinary people and geniuses as well? The answer is that it has come to all of them in exactly the same way—through the realization that everything we need is in Christ. There is nothing we can ever need that is not already present.

> Plenteous grace with Thee is found,
> Grace to cover all my sin;
> Let the healing streams abound,
> Make and keep me pure within.
> Thou of life the fountain art,

> Freely let me take of Thee;
> Spring Thou up within my heart,
> Rise to all eternity.

That is it! That is how Charles Wesley came to see it, and it is right.

> Thou, O Christ, art all I want,
> More than all in Thee I find;
> Raise the fallen, cheer the faint,
> Heal the sick, and lead the blind.[1]

It is all in him. The light has come! You do not need some special new instruction that the modern man alone has discovered. Oh, the nonsense of this! What a denial of the whole of the Christian faith it really is. All we need came in him, and there it has been ever since.

So here is the question: Why do we go astray like this? What makes us do it? Why do we fool ourselves in this way? We seem to be so good; we are seeking the higher reaches; we are on the quest; we are wonderful people—but we are all wrong! Why is this? We are told here exactly why we are wrong. The answer is that the trouble with all of us in these matters is never intellectual but is always moral. Here is the trouble. This is where we fool ourselves. That is where we fail to realize the essential nature of our problem. We think it is intellectual, that we do not understand. We are like Nicodemus—we want light and insight. But we do not! That is the camouflage. "And this is the condemnation, that light is come into the world." So why does not everybody turn to it and bask in it and be renovated and rejuvenated spiritually by it? Here is the answer: "Men loved darkness rather than light, because their deeds were evil." And this is still true today.

That is true of all, and that is where this argument about intellectualism and so on is so specious. If this were an intellectual problem, it would only apply to certain people. As I have said, there are some people who cannot handle intellectual problems. So do they come into this at all? Of course they do! There is only one common denominator to the whole of mankind, and that is an "evil heart." And that is as true of geniuses and great philosophers as it is of the most flagrant and violent sinner. There are no special cases in the spiritual realm, but we like to think there are, do we not? We all try to make a special case of ourselves. Nicodemus was doing it, and we have all done it. We say, "Of course, I am an intellectual person, and I have special difficulties."

There is only one answer to that. Rubbish! Hypocrite! That is not your trouble at all. Nobody has a special problem. We all think we have. People have often come to me and have tried to show me how because of something or other, their heredity or something else, they have a special problem. Again there is only one answer to that. There is no such thing. Everyone has something peculiar to fight with. We all have some skeleton in the closet. We all have special problems, but they all come to the same point; they all come back to this one thing that is stated here so plainly and so clearly for us, and this is the point therefore at which we start.

My dear friend, the form of the sin does not matter at all. It is the fact of sin that matters, and that is something that is true of every one of us. "All have sinned, and come short of the glory of God" (Rom. 3:23). "There is none righteous, no, not one" (Rom. 3:10). That is what infuriated the Pharisees about the teaching and preaching of our Lord. He made them see and feel that they were sinners, and they hated him for it and killed him because of it. But he did that because he knew this is the truth about everybody. It is common to the entire human race.

How does this show itself? Here is our problem. It is not intellectual at all. It is that we love darkness. "This is the condemnation" (John 3:19). There is the light; it is all there, that fullness in him that the saints of the centuries have received and in which they have rejoiced. Why do we not have it? It is not because of these problems—"I want more light, more instruction." The real trouble is that by nature we love the darkness. That is the very essence of sin, and here, of course, is where we go wrong. We tend to think of sin as merely doing wrong. Of course, that is included, but that is not the real essence of sin. It is not the wrong things we do; the real trouble is the fact that we ever *desire* to do them. That is the trouble—whatever made us desire to do such things? And there is only one answer; it is this love. "Men loved darkness. . . ." It is not merely that they live in it and do things that are characteristic of it. They love it, they like it, they gloat in it so much that they will not turn to the light.

That is where all moral systems are so superficial; they are only interested in behavior, in conduct. They never touch the real source of the trouble, which is what the Bible calls lust, inordinate affection, desire, concupiscence. This is what the apostle Paul tells us that he was so ignorant of, until he was enlightened by the Spirit. He thought he was all right. But "the commandment came, sin revived, and I died" (Rom. 7:9). He says that when he understood the meaning of "Thou shalt not covet," he was finished (Rom. 7:7). He knew he had coveted. The Pharisees all thought as long as you had not done something, they had not sinned. But Christ says, "Whosoever looketh on a woman to lust after her hath committed adultery with her already in his heart" (Matt. 5:28). It is a matter of desire; it is the love of darkness.

Many people have not done these things, because—dare I say such a thing?—they have not the courage, as it were, to do them. That is what made Martin Luther once say to such people, "Sin strongly, don't sin politely." The greatest fool in the universe is the man who sins politely. If a man sins strongly and violently, he will soon knock his head against a brick wall and come to his senses. This is the sham; this is the deceit. The *love* is there, and that is what is damnable—loving darkness rather than light. Sin is not a matter of the will—it is a matter of the heart, and the first thing we must realize, as is put so plainly here, is the terrible power of sin over us. The New Testament talks about being under the "dominion" of sin. "Listen," says Paul to the Romans, "sin shall not have dominion over you: for ye are not under the law, but under grace" (Rom. 6:14). Sin shall not have dominion over us; but it has dominion over everybody else. That is what salvation means—we are delivered from the dominion of sin and evil and Satan.

Or take other ways in which this is put. Paul, in the second chapter of the epistle to the Ephesians, says, "And you hath be quickened, who were dead in trespasses and sins; wherein in time past ye walked according to the course of this world, according to the prince of the power of the air, the spirit that now worketh in the children of disobedience" (vv. 1–2).

That is the dominion, the tyranny of sin, and it works in us as a lust, a desire, a love of evil. And the first thing we must realize is that we love evil; we love sin. That is why we keep on doing things that we are sorry about afterward. That is the meaning of remorse, of all the accusations of conscience, which can ultimately lead to repentance.

Or take the way in which David puts it in the fifty-first Psalm. David at last sees the truth. It was not that he had committed adultery and then murdered the husband of the woman with whom he had committed adultery. That is terrible, but that is not what breaks David's heart. It is, Why did he ever want to do that? What is it in him that made him do it, this desire, this lust, this passion?—What is the matter with him? He says, "Create in me a clean heart, O God" (v. 10). It is his heart that is wrong! It is not his mind, not his will; it is the heart that drives him, the passion, the lust, the evil, the desire, the love of the thing. "Purge me with hyssop, and I shall be clean: wash me, and I shall be whiter than snow" (v. 7).

That is where we must start. We must realize that the essence of our trouble, all of us, is that we love darkness. You say, "I wish that I could receive his fullness. If only . . ." My dear friend, the question is, do you really want it? The main reason why you do not have it is that you are loving something else instead of it. "And this is the condemnation . . ."

But secondly, it leads to self-protection. "This is the condemnation, that light is come into the world, and men loved darkness rather than light, because their deeds were evil" (John 3:19). Then comes the exposition: "For every one that doeth evil hateth the light, neither cometh to the light, [why?] lest his deeds should be reproved" (John 3:20). You see, he loves evil, and because he loves evil he does not want to come to the light. He knows that light exposes evil. It always does so.

But here is a man who does not want that because his deeds are evil, because he loves them; he now protects himself. He does not come to the light. He talks about it. He gives the impression, and he convinces himself as well as others that he really does want it, but he proves that he does not want it because he does not come to the light. And that is just another way of indicating self-protection. What experts we all are at this, what utter frauds we are, what hypocrites we are! We can even fool ourselves in this way. We say, "Now I really want to know the truth. I read these books, but I don't get this fullness. Why not?" Well, the real trouble is that you are not truly exposing yourself to the light. You are defending yourself; you are shielding yourself the whole time. God knows we must all plead guilty to this.

How do we do it? One method is what we call rationalizing our sins. That means that we can always explain them away. Of course, if we see somebody else doing the same thing it is wrong, and we see it at once, and we denounce it. But when it comes to our own wrongs, "Well, there were special circumstances. . . ." There was always some reason for it, and we can always explain it away in our own particular case. Again, consult the second chapter of the epistle to the Romans where Paul describes this: "Accusing or else excusing one another" (v. 15). That is part of this process. "I need not go to the light over that because, well, because it is not sin; it is this-that-or-the-other that I can explain."

There is another way in which this is done often, and this is, I suppose, one of the main reasons why many Christian people know so little about God's fullness. They are resting on a decision that they once made, perhaps early in their lives, and that they feel has made them Christians, and therefore they always fall back on that. Conscience accuses them, the Law of God accuses them, a sermon may accuse them, and they are in trouble. "But," they say, "I am all right—I have been born again. I made my decision when I was such and such an age and in such and such a meeting." And they use this "decision" to argue against their punishment; they put themselves right much too easily.

I remember, if I may illustrate this hurriedly, a man once coming to me to confess a sin he had committed, and I felt when I looked at the man that there was something wrong. He looked a little bit too happy for a man who was coming to confess a sin. Then he began telling me the story, and he said, "Of course, I know the blood of Jesus Christ covers this." I said, "If you say it like that, I am not sure that you do know it." That is healing "the hurt of the daughter . . . slightly, saying, Peace, peace; when there is no peace" (Jer. 6:14). So many do that; they fall back on something that has once happened.

But a decision is of no value unless it leads to a life of holiness. There is a kind of mechanics that has come into this whole realm that is holding people back from God's great blessing. A decision has done it! You have done it, you have taken it, you have said it! These are the very verses that are used: "God sent not his Son into the world to condemn the world; but that the world through him might be saved. He that believeth on him is not condemned: but he that believeth not is condemned already" (John 3:17–18). "Do you believe it?" "I do believe." "Very well, you are not condemned, you are all right." And they go on living on like that for the rest of their lives.

But that can be used by the Devil. An intellectual belief does not save. "Faith, if it hath not works, is dead" (James 2:17). But many people are shielding their consciences, hiding themselves against the light that has come in Christ and through his Word by always falling back upon something that once happened. That is a most dangerous thing to do.

Another way in which we can do this, of course, is to avoid anything that makes us feel uncomfortable. Oh, the tragedy of that! There are people talking with righteous indignation about things that are happening in the world. That is their way of shielding themselves against the accusations of their own conscience. It is an old form of doing it, and it is a very subtle one. But that is not coming into the light. You do not allow yourself to come to the light yourself because you are always doing it in terms of somebody else.

This can be done even in wrong ways of Bible study. This is almost incredible, but it is quite true. You can even use the Bible to shield yourself. How? Well, you only read certain favorite passages of yours. Perhaps you like devotional reading; you like reading about the love of God. So you do not really read the Bible—you only take out of the Bible that which you know is going to soothe you and make you feel happy. You are using the Bible to prevent the light from coming into you. That is a terrible thing, but it shows us something of the subtlety of Satan.

Or perhaps you read your Bible as a matter of duty. If you do not realize it is a living Word, if you do not pray for the Spirit to use it to open your understanding and to open your heart and to reveal your conscience, if you do not prepare yourself, if you just read your portion and rush off to catch your train, it is no use, my friend. You are just priding yourself because you are reading so much of the Bible every day. But you are preventing the light of the Bible from searching your heart. This is what is done by large numbers of people, and they never grow, they know nothing about this fullness. But they are very dutiful; they are very religious; they are very regular in these exercises. These are some of the ways we think put us right as it were, and thus we answer the accusations of the light of God through our conscience.

Another way we do this is by balancing our good works against our bad works. We say, "As long as I feel generous and as long as I give a good donation to a worthy cause, I cannot be all wrong, surely." And so we are answering the accusation of the light. We are trying to soothe our own consciences; we are trying to silence the light by painting our darkness and trying to make it like light.

We all, unfortunately, know far too much about these things. I am simply giving you some of them that I have done so often myself, and I know that what I have done, you have done. I am no worse than you, and you are no worse than I am. We are all equally bad. We are all by nature lovers of darkness, and we are hypocrites. We say we want the light, but do we?

What must we do about this? Our Lord makes it quite plain. The first thing is we must be honest in our intention. It is no use saying we want the light unless we really do, and we know perfectly well whether we do or not. Our intention must first be clear and right and honest and good; then the actions must follow. I say again, do you really want to receive "his fullness"? That is the fundamental question. If you are not clear about that, there is no need to go any further. You are all wrong; you will get nothing. "Thou desirest truth in the inward parts"—Psalm 51 again (v. 6). God knows everything; you cannot fool him. It is no use playing with God.

Then having done that, you must be absolutely open about this: not only do you desire this fullness, but you desire it at once. Remember the famous quote of Saint Augustine in his *Confessions*: "Lord, make me good; but not yet." That is no good at all. How often have we done this? "Make me good—oh, but not yet. I am too fond of this, I love this, I like it." He would not give up his mistress. He was disturbed, of course, he was under conviction, but as long as he remained like that, it was no good. He had to get over that. You do not set time limits. If you really want it, want it at once, immediately. And then be wholehearted about it; allow God to control the whole of your life. The light will search every part of it. That is why people hate the light; that is why we all hate it by nature. It exposes everything; it brings all the hidden things of darkness to light. So we must allow him to search and to control the whole of our life. Remember, he sees everything. "All things are naked and opened unto the eyes of him with whom we have to do" (Heb. 4:13). He will see every lurking thing that is trying to sneak under a stone, like those little crawling things on the ground; when the light comes he will bring them out. So we must be ready for him to do this. And *everything* must be brought into the light; there must be no reservation.

There is a great illustration of this in the story of John the Baptist and King Herod. Herod had taken his brother Philip's wife, but for some extraordinary reason King Herod liked John the Baptist. So when John was arrested, Herod protected him and used to go and listen to him preach and enjoyed doing so. But this is how we are told that—it is put in a most extraordinary way: Herod heard John, "and observed him; and . . . did many things, and heard him gladly" (Mark 6:20). Did you notice? Herod "did many things" when he heard John. He felt convicted, and he put them right. He did many things, but he did not do the one thing that John was pressing for, and that was that he should give up Herodias. It is no use giving up many things if you reserve the one thing. That is the thing he loved; that is the thing he held on to. And this is what vitiates the lives of so many of us as Christians. It is surrender up to a point, but then we reserve the peculiar object of our life, that "darling sin." That is no good. We must be whole; we must be entire. So we must examine ourselves and expose ourselves to this blessed light. The light has come! All the fullness is in him.

Why are you so poor spiritually? It is because you are shielding yourself, you are not honest; there is something that you prefer to that. And while you are in that condition it is no good; you must let it go. You must submit yourself to the light; you must come to him and stand before him and let him do as he will with you.

Why should you do this? Let me end with a word of exhortation. Christian people, cannot you see the folly of not coming to the light? Here it is: it is "condemnation." The light has come, but "Men loved darkness rather than light, because their deeds were evil" (John 3:19). Do you not see what that means—and this is the most terrible thing for a Christian? It is bad enough for a man or woman who is not a Christian, but it is ten times worse when it is true of a Christian. Look at the things that they hold on to; look at the things we all tend to hold on to.

What are they? "Darkness"! "Men loved darkness." That is what we are loving—ugliness, something shameful. That is why it is in the dark; it is ashamed of the light. People do things in the dark they would never dream of doing in the light, and if they thought that anybody had seen them, they would not do it. "Darkness"! "The hidden things of darkness" (1 Cor. 4:5). The dishonest things of darkness. Those are the things that people are holding on to! Examine yourself! Look at the thing you are holding on to! Really expose it! Look at it, and you will find that it belongs to the realm of "darkness." It is dying, it is putrefying even now, and it will soon be gone altogether. It belongs to the realm of evil and vice and foulness. Fancy holding on to that!

Or take it the other way round. Look at the glory of what you are missing. The light of God—the light of Jesus Christ—the kind of life that he lived and makes possible for us—that is what you are not receiving because you love this hidden, foul thing of darkness. The light makes you face these things. It says: Look at the darkness, look at the light, look at the possibility, look at the glory, look at the wonder, being "filled with all the fullness of God" (Eph. 3:19), being increasingly "conformed to the image" of Christ (Rom. 8:29)—being not only like the saints but becoming more and more as he was—and the glory of heaven that lies ahead.

And then, finally, remember this: "Every one that doeth evil hateth the light, neither cometh to the light, lest his deeds should be reproved"

(John 3:20). He thinks he is clever. He does not want to go to the light; he does not want to be made uncomfortable; he does not want to be made unhappy. He does not like anything that disturbs his conscience. So he does not go to the light. Oh, the fool! He has forgotten that a day is coming when he will have to stand in the light, and he cannot evade it. Life is short and fleeting and passing. We must all die, and after death the judgment. "We must all appear before the judgment seat of Christ; that every one may receive [be judged for] the things done in his body" (2 Cor. 5:10). You can stay away from the light while you are alive in this world, but you will stand in the light on that morning, and all that has been true of you while you were in this world will be revealed. "The day shall declare it" (1 Cor. 3:13). The hidden things of darkness you held on to in preference to receiving his fullness will all be exposed; it will all be brought to the surface; it will all be revealed. You will perhaps be saved, "so as by fire" (v. 15), but all you have done will be burned up. That is the language of the Apostle Paul in 1 Corinthians 3. You will have nothing left. You will be saved "so as by fire"—barely saved, scarcely saved. And you will be ashamed.

Those, then, are the considerations—the character of the darkness to which we hold on and the glory of the Light to which we are not turning and the certainty of the judgment throne of Christ and our all appearing before him. Beloved people, listen to this exhortation: "And this is the condemnation . . ." (John 3:19). Do not talk anymore about your intellectual problems and difficulties, your peculiar problems. It is nonsense; it is rubbish. We are all in the same boat; we are all in exactly the same position. It is the love of darkness that leads us to hate the light and not come to it. Let us see it, and let us here and now and as long as we live determine to keep ourselves in "the light," that our deeds "may be made manifest, that they are wrought in God" (John 3:21).

# 17

# The Friend of the Bridegroom

JOHN 3:30

Sunday morning sermon preached in
Westminster Chapel, May 22, 1966.

He must increase, but I must decrease. (John 3:30)

I take that particular statement out of this section because, as I will try
to show you, it sums up what is the essential teaching of this incident.

We are working our way through this great Gospel according to St.
John in order that we may concentrate our attention not so much upon
the detailed history but upon the great theme of the whole Gospel, which
is that what is offered us in our Lord and Savior Jesus Christ is eternal
life. The Gospels each give an account of our Lord, but it is generally
agreed that each has a kind of leading theme. While the facts are common to them all in general, it is clear that each was led by the Spirit to
emphasize a particular aspect of the life and work and ministry of our
blessed Lord, and there can be no doubt whatsoever that eternal life in
Christ is the great and leading theme in the Gospel according to St. John.

Now that is not merely my opinion—we have John's own statement
to that effect. He says in the last verse of the twentieth chapter, "But
these are written, that ye might believe that Jesus is the Christ, the Son
of God; and that believing ye might have life through his name." And as

we have been seeing, he states it very plainly in the sixteenth verse of the first chapter where he says, "And of his fullness have all we received, and grace for grace."

Here is this amazing offer: the Son of God came into the world and did all he did. He rose again, he ascended through the heavens, and he is seated at the right hand of God in glory everlasting. And this is what is offered us in him: we can "receive . . . of his fullness" (John 1:16). That is what it really means to be a Christian. It is not just living a good life; that is morality. It is not merely believing certain things about him; that can be a kind of dead orthodoxy. But this is true Christianity: we have received *life* from him, "life . . . more abundantly," the fullness that resides in him.

This is, as we have been seeing, the real theme of the whole of this Gospel, as it is indeed the theme of the whole of the New Testament. The picture of the church as the body of Christ conveys this so perfectly. All comes from the Head; the fullness is there. That is the nerve center, and every part and portion, every individual item, every member derives its life and being and sustenance from the Head. This is Christianity.

So we are examining ourselves in the light of this. Is that our idea of being Christian? Still more important, is that the impression we are giving to others of what Christianity is? We live in a world that is weary and tired, a world that is merely existing; it would not have to multiply its pleasures and be dependent upon them if it really had life. People who live on stimulants are confessing that they are lacking vital energy, and the world today is living on stimulants—it does not have life. Here is the greatest need, and here is the only source of life. But the great question is, do we who claim to be Christians have this? Have we received something of this fullness, and are we receiving more and more of it?

And now we are considering some of the hindrances to this. There is obviously something wrong. The Christian church would not be as she is if we were all receiving of this fullness. The church is weak; she is despised; she is dismissed; she is rejected. The world feels that the church has nothing at all, that she is just an anachronism in the modern world. But every time there is a true revival or reformation in the church, things are entirely changed, and the world begins to look to the church again. And that is the supreme need at this hour.

So the question is, what is robbing us of this fullness? Why do we not know more about it? Why is it that we are not filled with a spirit of rejoicing and praise and thanksgiving as the early Christians were and as Christian people always should be? There are many hindrances and obstacles, but it is ultimately because of our adversary, the Devil. He causes confusion in various ways, but, thank God, we are not ignorant of his devices. The Word of God teaches us concerning them. It exposes them to us; it makes them plain. So listening to its teaching we should all be able to see the very thing that is hindering us and get rid of it in order that we may receive God's fullness.

Let us look now at another of these hindrances that is indeed a very common one, and fortunately for us, it is put in the form of what was done by certain people. We have already seen the hindrances as they are represented in a man like Nicodemus. There was a man who was full of difficulties, problems, and hindrances that had to be overcome. He wanted the right thing, but he was so wrong in many respects; all these had to be put right.

Now here is a different picture but an equally important one. It is represented by the friends and followers, the disciples, of John the Baptist and what they said to John and what they tried to persuade John to do. But, thank God, the teaching that we stand in need of is found in the reaction of John the Baptist to these people and what he said to them so plainly and so clearly.

What is the problem? It is the problem of pride, and here is something that is taught universally in the whole Bible. The greatest hindrance and obstacle of all, perhaps, is pride. It takes many forms—pride of intellect, pride of achievement, pride of understanding. However, the form does not matter so much. It is pride in its essence that constitutes one of the greatest hindrances to our receiving "his fullness . . . and grace for grace" (John 1:16).

We are all proud—every one of us. There is no person who is not proud. This is universal, and it is, of course, the result of sin. The original sin was the sin of pride. The Devil in effect said to Eve, "Has God said that you should not eat of that fruit? He has said so because he wants to keep you down. He knows that if you eat of it you yourselves will become as gods." And that appealed to the woman and to the man. That is pride, and it was the original source of trouble. You can trace most of the manifestations of sin ultimately back to pride—the desire to be great and important, this belief in ourselves. This incident in John shows us so plainly and so clearly, and we must pay great attention to this, that this is not only in us all by nature, but it is often encouraged in us by our friends, by our well-wishers.

This is a most extraordinary fact that is illustrated here so perfectly. How often has this been seen in the long history of the church and God's people, in its outstanding leaders as well as in its most ordinary members. Nothing has so frequently crippled God's saints and leaders as this very sin of pride. You see it in many instances in the Old Testament. David was humbled several times because of his pride, which had lifted him up in a wrong and in a sinful manner.

These disciples of John had been helping him, and the crowds had been surrounding them. John was a remarkable man. After a period of roughly four hundred years from the days of Malachi, the last of the Old Testament prophets, the Word of God had not been given in this particular way. But suddenly it had come to John, the son of Zacharias, in the wilderness. He had become a great phenomenon, and people had crowded out from everywhere, Jerusalem included, in order to see this strange man and to hear his extraordinary message and to submit to his baptism. John had gathered a number of disciples who were helping him, and here they were, full of activity.

But suddenly there comes this other person, Jesus of Nazareth, and after a while it is clear that more people are attending the ministry of the Lord Jesus Christ than are attending the ministry of John, and his followers and disciples become concerned about this. They are concerned about his reputation, concerned about his greatness. They want to defend his position, and they want him to do something about it. And this leads them to dislike and to criticize the ministry of our Lord and Savior.

This suggestion that there could be anything beyond what John has is to them intolerable, it is insulting, and they are filled with what they regard as a sense of righteous indignation. "Is there anything beyond John's teaching? Who is this other teacher? Shouldn't John stop him?" Filled with a sense of pride themselves, they try their utmost to feed and to stimulate pride in John the Baptist. So they go to him and say to him, "Rabbi, he that was with thee beyond Jordan, to whom thou barest witness, behold, the same baptizeth, and all men come to him" (John 3:26). They are on the verge of saying the kind of things I have been suggesting to you when "John answered and said . . ." (John 3:27). John interrupts them and answers them and silences them completely.

Now there is the picture, but, of course, it is not only true history, it is also a parable. Here is something that is true of each of us, and what a terrible thing it is. This thing that is in these men drives them to resent and to resist the teaching of the Lord Jesus Christ and all that he has to offer. That is the terrible problem by which we are confronted.

So how does this work itself out in us? Why have we not received "of his fullness . . . and grace for grace" (John 1:16)? The first answer is, because we feel we do not need it—we are doing very well as we are. Was not John doing well preaching, baptizing, attracting the crowds? And we have exactly the same feelings. We are all right; we are doing well.

This is, as I have often pointed out, the particular danger of religious people. I say religious as distinct from Christian. It is possible to be religious without being Christian. It is possible to be religious within the realm of the Christian church without being Christian. This is the great trouble. We have seen it in the case of Nicodemus, and we are looking at the same thing from another aspect in these disciples of John the Baptist—feeling that all is well. There is no greater hindrance to receiving his fullness than that. There are those who feel like this. They have understood all the doctrine, and they rest upon this knowledge and criticize everything else; they are in a state of self-satisfaction.

Others are thoroughly satisfied with themselves because of the life they live and the good they do. They, like the Pharisees, thank God that they are not as other people are. They see people on the streets in London and read about them in the newspapers, and they thank God they are not like that. They are not living in the resorts of vice and of evil; they are not stooping to foul and flagrant sins. They are good people, and they have never done things like that; they are horrified at them, and they would not dream of doing such things. But in addition to that they are doing good, they are concerned, and they are out to help people. Have they not done this-that-and-the-other? Our Lord has pictured this once and forever in the person of the Pharisee who goes up to the temple, right to the front, and thanks God that he is not as other people are, extortioners and so on. He fasts twice in the week and gives a tenth of his goods to feed the poor. What more does he need? He needs nothing, and he does not ask for anything. He has everything; he is doing everything.

The religious man in contradistinction to the Christian is like the Pharisee in contradistinction to the publican. The religious man does not see any need of anything further—he is doing it all! He does not even see the need of forgiveness. What has he done to need forgiveness? He certainly does not need any further addition or any greater fullness. The pity is that everybody is not as he is—that is what troubles him.

That is the position of these disciples of John the Baptist, and this is something that many of us have known so well, especially those who have been brought up to be religious and have had every kind of sheltered life, always in the realm of the church, who have never been out in the world and in the gutters of life. What do we need? Surely we do not need anything further; our lives are all right—look at what we are doing.

This works itself out also in the realm of experience. There are people who say, "Well, I have had my experience. I made my decision. Surely I need nothing more. I am a Christian now; I have been ever since that day." They are always talking about this. It may have happened years ago, but they rest on it, and there they remain. We dealt with that in the previous chapter, so I will not elaborate on it again. But it is astonishing again to remind ourselves how easily one can be relying upon something that has once happened. "We have it all, and therefore we need no more." There is no possible growth; you received it all at your regeneration, at your conversion.

So here is one of the ways in which this manifests and demonstrates itself. And, of course, because of this feeling that we are doing well and of self-satisfaction, we automatically dislike any new emphasis, anything that comes to us that we have not heard before. That was the trouble with these men. John's teaching—that was it! But this other teaching—what is this? It is slightly different, and they dislike this new emphasis. If what we have is everything, then what is this suggestion that there is something else?

You will find as you read the history of the church and every great movement of reformation and of revival that all new emphases of the ancient gospel have always had to face grievous opposition. There has always been an opposition to what people have regarded as a novelty, something new. This happened, of course, at the time of the Protestant Reformation. The Roman Catholic Church with its mixture of Aristotelian philosophy, bits of the New Testament, and much of the Old Testament had elaborated a teaching and a system. Thomas Aquinas had elaborated it in his great *Summa*. Here was the teaching, and they were teaching and preaching that; they had lost contact with the New Testament almost entirely. They still used it mechanically, but really they were teaching this dogma, this body of teaching. Suddenly Martin Luther was illuminated and began to preach justification by faith, which he had discovered in the Scriptures, and they resented this. They said, "This is a new teaching," and they objected to it.

In other words, the church can reach a state in which the old teaching becomes a new teaching. And in the eighteenth century when George Whitefield under the power of the Spirit began preaching regeneration and the absolute necessity of the rebirth in London and in other places in the country, he was regarded as an innovator; this was a new doctrine. Religion consisted of a bit of morality—that was people's idea of religion. For the deists and others who had excluded the supernatural, it was no longer even personal, it was just a matter of duties, a dull and an arid kind of morality. They had preached it with much literary flourish and quotations, but that was it, and when George Whitefield began to preach a doctrine of regeneration and rebirth they said, "What is this new teaching?" The old teaching had become something new and strange. We have arrived at that position today. If you want to be odd in the Christian church today, preach the New Testament gospel. It is regarded almost as something new and something strange. This is the extraordinary thing that can happen to good religious people in the realm of the church. They can get so far away that when the true message is presented, it is resented because it seems to be a novelty, something different and strange.

That is coupled with something else, and that is our dislike of being disturbed. We all like to manage our own lives, even our religion; we like to have it under our control. And this is all because of the fall and because of sin. It is the manifestation of sin in us that we dislike anything that examines us and disturbs us, anything that causes us to face the truth, anything that suggests that we are not as we ought to be.

Again I could illustrate that so easily to you in the long history of the church, and we all surely know something about this by experience. I have often quoted the statement that puts it so perfectly. Lord Melbourne, Queen Victoria's first prime minister, a worldly-wise man, said, "Things are coming to a pretty pass if religion is going to start being personal." Religion is something that you bring in on a state occasion, something general and vague, with marvelous pomp and ceremony. But it is not meant to make you feel uncomfortable or to disturb you or to make you feel that there is some inadequacy in you. This is resented, and that is why the Pharisees hated our Lord, and that is what caused these disciples of John to be annoyed and to speak in the way and manner in which they did.

My dear friend, let us be honest in the sight of God. Do we resent teaching and preaching that examines us and disturbs us? If we do, we are in the very position of these people, and that is one of the greatest hindrances to receiving his fullness and grace upon grace. Always in the spiritual realm there is a sifting; there is an excluding before the great blessing comes. There is always a going down before you go up; there is always repentance before there is release. But these are the ways in which this self-satisfaction shows itself as it did with these people, and ultimately it comes to disliking the idea that there is something more that we can have, the very idea that what we are doing is not enough. This is, I think, a great curse at the present time. Experience number one, go on to experience number two, now you have it all. So you are no longer open, and if there is a suggestion that there is any defect in what you have, it is resented. Evangelical people are not to be disturbed; they have everything; they look down on others. Is there anything that they need? Is there a lack among evangelicals? You will find that if you present this other aspect of the truth, the greatest opposition may well come through evangelical people because they have this circumscribed idea of religion. It is all so simple, and it is all so neat and tidy. There is never any disturbance; there must never be anything explosive and dynamic. They do not like this; it seems to be wrong.

We must each examine ourselves, because the outcome of all this kind of feeling is that instead of seeking the fullness, we spend our time defending ourselves and showing that we do not need anything, we are all right. It is possible for us even to resent the teaching of the Lord Jesus Christ. It is possible for us to resent his offer of this "fullness," because it carries the implication that we are not complete as we are and that we need something further.

So there is nothing more vital for us to consider than the way in which we react to these glorious offers of the blessed gospel. "Of his fullness have all we received"—"that ye might be filled with all the fullness of God" (John 1:16; Eph. 3:19). Do we know anything about that? Have we received it?

Now we know, do we not, that the natural man or woman reacts in a wrong way to the preaching of the cross, and especially to the teaching of regeneration. They never object to the teaching of the ethics and the morality of the Bible. They believe in that because they believe they can do it. But what they do always resent is the preaching of the cross. "The preaching of the cross is to them that perish foolishness" (1 Cor. 1:18). The preaching of the cross was "unto the Jews a stumblingblock, and unto the Greeks foolishness" (v. 23).

I read a statement made by a man this last week, which said, "The cross appeals always to the natural man"—imagine a man saying that in the name of Christianity—because here "was Someone who was ready to die for the truth." Yes, they will accept it if it is put like that; but Christ did not die for the truth, he died for *us*. He died for sinners; he died in our stead. If you put it like that, they will resent it; they always have. They resent the preaching of the cross; they resent the doctrine of regeneration. Why? Because they both suggest that we are hopeless and that we are helpless. "If Christ had to die for me, then I must be in a desperate condition. If I must be born again, then the implication is that I am so rotten that I cannot be improved—I must be made anew from the very foundation." The natural man hates that, though it is offered to him by the Son of God. I am suggesting that this kind of spirit persists even in the Christian life and that we are always ready to say that we have arrived and need nothing further.

What is the answer to this? Here is the trouble as depicted by the disciples and friends of John the Baptist, wanting to bolster up his pride, wanting to feed his self-satisfaction. You know this in yourself, and others will say this to you. If you begin to be dissatisfied and you want to get more and more of God's fullness, your friends, or perhaps your relatives, will say to you, "Look here now, religion is all right in moderation, but be careful, you must not take this thing too seriously. You will be fanatical if you are not careful; you will go to excess." Have you not known something like this? They think they are helping you, as these men were trying to bolster up John the Baptist and defending his name and reputation and praising him. But thank God, John the Baptist sees through it all, and you and I need to listen to his teaching.

First of all let us observe his reaction. John reacts in such a glorious manner. Some of his disciples come and say, "Rabbi, he that was with thee beyond Jordan, to whom thou barest witness, behold, the same baptizeth, and all men come to him." John answered and said, "A man can receive nothing, except it be given him from heaven. Ye yourselves bear me witness, that I said, I am not the Christ, but that I am sent before him. He that hath the bride is the bridegroom: but the friend of the bridegroom, which standeth and heareth him, rejoiceth greatly because of the bridegroom's voice: this my joy therefore is fulfilled. He must increase, but I must decrease" (John 3:27–30).

What is the teaching here? John, far from resenting our Lord and his teaching and his popularity, rejoices in it; he is open to it. His disciples are disturbed; they dislike this. Not John! I will tell you why in a moment. But first, let me make a point because this immediate general reaction is so important. Lest anybody may think I am just drawing on my imagination, I would assure you that I am not doing that. I am drawing on my own experience, and I want to support it with that of others. If you have read the story of D. L. Moody, the great evangelist, you know that Moody was a converted man; not only that, he felt a call to enter the ministry. He had given up his work as a salesman of boots and shoes and had become a full-time minister in charge of a mission hall in the city of Chicago. He was getting results; he was doing good work. But the story goes that one afternoon, at the end of a service, two ladies came up to him and said, "Mr. Moody, we are praying for you. We are praying that you may have the fullness of the Holy Spirit, that you may have more power in your ministry." And Moody was honest enough to report afterward that he resented this, he did not like it.

Why not? Because he had the same spirit in him as the friends of John the Baptist. Was he not a successful preacher? Was he not doing well? Weren't people being converted? The idea that he needed to be prayed for—absurd! What a terrible thing sin is, that you can even be annoyed when people tell you they are praying for you. But he saw the implication; he saw that these two ladies felt that there was something lacking in him. We never like to be told that, do we? We never like to be told that we are lacking in any respect at all, and Moody was man enough to admit he did not like it, he resented it. He felt like telling them that they had better be praying for others, that he did not need it. There were other ministers in Chicago who greatly needed their prayers, but not D. L. Moody. However, he came to see how right they were.

Now let me give you the opposite to that; let me give you somebody who reacted as John the Baptist did, and it is another John, as it happens, John Wesley. Here is the difference. Here again was a good man, a godly, religious man. Here was a man who took his religion so seriously that he resigned the Fellowship of his college at Oxford and all his glittering prospects and decided to cross the Atlantic—this was over two hundred years ago—to preach to the poor pagans in Georgia. You could not wish, in many ways, for a better man, but go on with the story. There was a storm at sea, and it looked as if they were going to be shipwrecked, and all would be drowned. And John Wesley was afraid to die! But he noticed some Moravian brethren on the same boat who were perfectly calm, quite happy. They went on praying and singing exactly as they had been doing when there was calm before the storm, and John Wesley saw in a flash that those Moravians had something he did not have. And far from resenting it, he coveted it, he desired it. That is the right reaction; that was the reaction of John the Baptist. That was John Wesley's reaction, and it led ultimately to his receiving a blessing that made him the man he became. And this has been true of all God's saints throughout the centuries.

So I ask this first question: What is your reaction to a teaching that tells you, "You can be filled with all the fullness of God; you can receive his fullness and grace piled up upon grace"? How do you react to that? Does it disturb you? Do you say, "What is this? I thought that as long as I am a member of a church and attend every Sunday that is more than sufficient. I live a good and moral life. What is this?" How do you react to such teaching? Is there resentment, or is there a longing for it?

Let us, then, discover why John the Baptist reacted in this most excellent way and why we must react in the same way if we are to have this fullness increasingly. The first answer of course is this: John recognized the Lord. He had borne witness to him, and the Lord had called two of John's disciples. In the first chapter he pointed to Jesus and said, "Behold the Lamb of God, which taketh away the sin of the world" (John 1:29), and on this current occasion "He that cometh from above is above all: he that is of the earth is earthly, and speaketh of the earth: he that cometh from heaven is above all. And what he hath seen and heard, that he testifieth; and no man receiveth his testimony. He that hath received his testimony hath set to his seal that God is true. For he whom God hath sent speaketh the words of God: for God giveth not the Spirit by measure unto him" (John 3:31–34). John recognizes the Lord. "He must increase"

(v. 30). Why? Because of who and what he is. "I am only a man—he is the Son of God. I am of the earth—he is from heaven. He is the Son of God!"

Parts of the church celebrate Ascension Day. We must never lose sight of the ascension. We worship the One who has conquered all enemies—death, the Devil, and hell. And he has risen; he has passed through the heavens. There he is in glorious power; there is nothing he cannot do for you. You must start with that. If you think of your Christianity in terms of your little life, you will have nothing. But if you look at him and realize who he is, that there is literally no limit and that there are endless possibilities, then you will begin to receive his fullness. The Christian church is as she is because she has become uncertain about her Lord. There are men in Christian pulpits, in prominent positions, who deny his deity, deny his miracles, deny his sacrificial atoning death, deny the literal, physical resurrection, deny the fact of the ascension, which happened visibly, when he went up into the heavens and out of sight. There is no hope for such people. If you are not clear about the doctrine concerning the Lord, you will never receive his fullness. It is an utter impossibility. That is basic; that is fundamental.

The next thing is that John the Baptist had a true estimate of himself. John was not ambitious; John did not desire great things for himself. He was a humble man. Ambition is always a curse; ambition is always ugly. I have always felt that ambition is the ugliest of all the sins. There is nothing worse than a proud, ambitious person. But in this realm it is completely fatal. The glory of John the Baptist is his humility. He does not want to set himself up in competition. He knows himself, he knows his own size; he knows what he is. And this is one of the things our Lord himself laid down in the Sermon on the Mount as being the key to entry into this fullness. He said, "Blessed are the poor in spirit" (Matt. 5:3). A man who is not poor in spirit will never receive that fullness. You cannot put anything into a jug that is already full. Only into an empty jug can you pour the fullness. "Blessed are the poor in spirit" (v. 3); "Blessed are the meek" (v. 5); "Blessed are they which do hunger and thirst after righteousness" (v. 6). Why? Because they know they do not have it. They are aware of their need. Oh, look at this man John the Baptist—let us learn a lesson from him. If you are ignorant of this fullness, it is probably because of your pride, because of your false estimate of yourself. What do you know of God? What do you know of the Lord Jesus Christ? What do you know of the love of God shed abroad in your heart? What do you know of a power greater than yourself? John was aware of his own position and of his own size.

Then he says this next thing, which to me is such a great and glorious one; it was his first reply to them. "John answered and said, A man can receive nothing, except it be given him from heaven" (John 3:27). This means that we never have anything to be proud of, because we have always received whatever we have. John says in essence, "You are proud of me and my position, but who put me into that position? I did not put myself there. I have been put there. It is God who put me there. All I have I received. My position, my baptizing and teaching have all been given to me. Do not make me proud—I have nothing to be proud of. I am but the instrument, the vehicle, the channel."

The apostle Paul says the same thing to the members of the church at Corinth. They were not only proud themselves, but they were taking pride in the various teachers. One said, "I am of Paul." Another said, "I am of Apollos." "I am of Cephas," said a third. "I am of Christ," said the fourth. They were proud of themselves and of their favorite teachers, and they were quarreling over this. And Paul's answer is, "Who maketh thee to differ from another? and what hast thou that thou didst not receive? now if thou didst receive it, why dost thou glory, as if thou hadst not received it?" (1 Cor. 4:7). We have nothing to be proud of at any time. We have not created what we have; we have not produced it. And the moment you realize that, you cease to be proud, you become humble, and you are ready to listen and receive.

The other thing I notice about John is this—he is interested in the truth, in the propagation of the truth, in the coming of the truth. He is not interested in himself. John is not worried about how the truth affects him. That is what his disciples were trying to urge him to do. They were saying, "Look here, you must stop this because it is going to replace you." That is what we often do when the truth comes to us. "How does it affect me? What is it going to do to me? What is it saying to me?" Forget yourself; look at it objectively as John does. John is only interested in the truth itself and its success, and not in its effect upon him or its consequences for him. John knows that the Lord has the truth. He is the Bridegroom who can handle and deal with and bless the bride. John is only "the friend of the bridegroom," and he is concerned about the well-being of the bride, the truth, and all that the Lord can do for his people.

In the next step that leads him, as we are told in the twenty-ninth verse, to be perfectly content with his position. "He that hath the bride is the bridegroom: but the friend of the bridegroom, which standeth and heareth him, rejoiceth greatly because of the bridegroom's voice: this my joy therefore is fulfilled" (John 3:29). In Eastern weddings, up to a certain stage the friend of the bridegroom was the man in charge, as it were; he was preparing everything. Suddenly the voice of the bridegroom is heard. So John says, "Do you really think that I, as the friend of the bridegroom, ought to resent the coming of the bridegroom and that I ought to say, 'I am remaining at center stage. Who is he to replace me?' That is what you are saying to me. But you are mad," says John. "The business of the friend of the bridegroom is only to prepare. He, of all men, ought to be rejoicing when he hears the voice of the bridegroom. He stands back, he is the preparer, he is the forerunner, and the bridegroom follows. That is my position, and I rejoice in it. You know," says John, "far from resenting his coming I am very proud of what is happening. I cannot imagine a greater honor than to be the friend of the bridegroom. What a wonderful thing to have any place at all in his kingdom and in his coming, and what a wonderful thing to be even a forerunner who disappears off the scene. 'He must increase, but I must decrease.' Of course. But what a wonderful thing to have my name associated with him."

That is the spirit. You cease to be concerned about yourself or particular gifts or being greater than somebody else; self has gone out of it. People who are always talking about themselves and their gifts are people who had better examine themselves as to whether what they have is psychological rather than spiritual. The effect on the spiritual is always to humble us and to make us interested in the truth itself and the glory of the Lord, not in what *we* have. Looking at it from the standpoint of self always leads to trouble. The Holy Spirit is sent to glorify the Lord Jesus Christ, and he always does. And people who are filled with the Spirit talk more about the Lord Jesus Christ than about themselves or their particular gifts. That was the whole error in Corinth, was it not? They were talking about the gifts and comparing them and contrasting them, and the place was in confusion. The Lord had been forgotten.

John the Baptist is content to fill any little place; it does not matter how small it is. It is not *he* that matters—it is the Lord—and he only desires the fullness that the Lord can give, so that it may enable him to function more truly and thoroughly in the particular place in which the Lord has set him. The less "comely parts" (1 Cor. 12:24), says Paul, using the analogy of the body, are as important as the comely parts. It does not matter what part you are in the body of Christ as long as you are in it and as long as you are functioning and as long as life and nutriment and power is passing through you. That is the thing to concentrate on, remaining content with being associated with him. It is all in this one question—the relative prominence of "he" and "I" in your life and in mine. In other words, keep your eye always on him and on his glory. "He must increase, but I must decrease" (John 3:30). God gives us grace to be honest with ourselves and open in the presence of God.

# 18

# The Baptism with the Holy Spirit

## JOHN 3:30

Sunday morning sermon preached in
Westminster Chapel, May 29, 1966, Whitsunday morning.

He must increase, but I must decrease. (John 3:30)

Let me start by reminding you of the context of these words.

John also was baptizing in Aenon near to Salim, because there was much water there: and they came, and were baptized. For John was not yet cast into prison. Then there arose a question between some of John's disciples and the Jews about purifying. And they came unto John, and said unto him, Rabbi, he that was with thee beyond Jordan, to whom thou barest witness, behold, the same baptizeth, and all men come to him. John answered and said, A man can receive nothing, except it be given him from heaven. Ye yourselves bear me witness, that I said, I am not the Christ, but that I am sent before him. He that hath the bride is the bridegroom: but the friend of the bridegroom, which standeth and heareth him, rejoiceth greatly because of the bridegroom's voice: this my joy therefore is fulfilled. He must increase, but I must decrease. He that cometh

from above is above all: he that is of the earth is earthly, and speaketh of the earth: he that cometh from heaven is above all. And
what he hath seen and heard, that he testifieth; and no man receiveth his testimony. He that hath received his testimony hath set
to his seal that God is true. For he whom God hath sent speaketh
the words of God: for God giveth not the Spirit by measure unto
him. The Father loveth the Son, and hath given all things into his
hand. (John 3:23–35)

I am anxious to consider this portion of Scripture in the light of what
Whitsunday (Pentecost) reminds us of and what it commemorates. It is
good that we should remind ourselves constantly of the great historical
events on which our faith is based. This is not mere philosophy here;
this is not just a teaching. This is a record of history, and a record of the
meaning of that history. When the people on the day of Pentecost heard
Peter preaching, and earlier the other apostles who also spoke in tongues,
they heard them all dealing with "the wonderful works of God," and it is
vital that we should always bear that in mind.

What, then, is the message of that day to us? It is first and foremost a
reminder of that great historical fact, that great event. There were these
people, 120 of them, gathered together in the upper room, and suddenly
the Holy Spirit came down upon them, as described in the second chapter of the book of Acts.

Now without believing that and knowing something of what that
means, we cannot be Christians at all. There never would have been a
Christian church but for that. Every Christian, in some shape or form, is
related to that great and fundamental experience, the baptism with the
Holy Spirit.

So the question is, what is its relevance to us? What does it have to say
to us? Is this just something that is true as an event in the history of the
past, or does it speak to us in a living manner today? What is the meaning of this baptism with the Holy Spirit? Our Lord, after his resurrection
and just before the ascension, had told his assembled apostles that they
would be baptized not many days hence with the Holy Spirit, and what

happened on the day of Pentecost was the fulfillment of that promise and of that prophecy. So what does this mean to us? What is its message?

I want to suggest that one of the best ways of considering that is to consider the contrast between the baptism that was administered by John the Baptist and the baptism with the Holy Spirit. That is what is dealt with in the portion of the third chapter of John's Gospel that we are considering. We read how the disciples of John the Baptist came to him and were very annoyed and jealous of the fact that this other teacher, Jesus of Nazareth, was baptizing people and that great crowds were gathering around him. Indeed, the crowds seem to have been leaving John and were attending the ministry of our Lord. John's disciples were troubled by this, and they felt that it was all wrong. But John himself dealt with them and answered the question in the way that is recorded here. And it is here that we find the difference between the baptism of John the Baptist and the baptism administered by the Lord Jesus Christ himself, which is known as the baptism with the Holy Spirit. John says in essence, "You are all wrong. You must not take this attitude. You must not think there is any rivalry involved. You particularly must not think that I am greater than he. You must not be jealous on my behalf." "He must increase, but I must decrease" (John 3:30).

There are many reasons why John said that. Several of them are given here, and it is very important that we should bear them in mind. John says that he is just the friend of the Bridegroom, but that Jesus of Nazareth is the Bridegroom himself. The bride is the church, and there is this special relationship between the bride and the Bridegroom, between the church and the Lord Jesus Christ. John is a friend of the Bridegroom; he has his part to play. He is the forerunner, the herald, but he is no more than that. And now, he says, his work is coming to an end as Christ's work is beginning, and is beginning to succeed. "The friend of the bridegroom, which standeth and heareth him, rejoiceth greatly because of the bridegroom's voice: this my joy therefore is fulfilled" (John 3:29). But then John goes on to give certain other reasons, and these are what we are concerned about now. "He must increase, but I must decrease" (v. 30). Why? Because "he that cometh from above is above all" (v. 31). John says in effect, "I am only a man. He is more than a man. He has come from above. I am a man born like all other men, but he is not. He 'cometh from above [and] is above all.'" In other words, John here, once more, gives this testimony to our Lord and his person, which is described to us in the prologue, in the first chapter of this great Gospel. John sums it up in those words "from above." "He that is of the earth is earthly, and speaketh of the earth" (v. 31). "At my best," says John, "I am only a human, a human servant. I have a message, and it is a message that has been given to me by God. But I am only a man. I have this treasure, as it were, in an earthen vessel, but he is entirely different 'He that cometh from heaven is above all.'" He constantly, you notice, repeats that. "And what he hath seen and heard, that he testifieth" (v. 32). Then he goes on to say that this testimony is not being received. But he adds, "He whom God hath sent speaketh the words of God" (v. 34).

Now you see the difference. John, in a sense, had been speaking the words of God also, but only at special times, only when he was under special inspiration. At other times he spoke as a natural man. Not all of the words of John were the words of God; the words of John were imperfect. But there is a contrast here: "He whom God hath sent speaketh the words of God" (v. 34). All of Jesus's words were the words of God—all his words without any exception whatsoever. And then John added to it this tremendous statement: "For God giveth not the Spirit by measure unto him" (v. 34). The Spirit is given by measure to me. The Spirit was upon John the Baptist by measure. Here is One, said John, who has received the Spirit in his fullness, not by measure, not in a partial manner but in all his fullness.

This is the key to understanding what happened on the day of Pentecost. "The Father loveth the Son, and hath given all things into his hand" (v. 35). And one of the things he gave to him was the Holy Spirit, in order that he might give him to the church. And that is what happened on the day of Pentecost. So the baptism with the Spirit is a baptism that is administered by the Lord Jesus Christ himself. He has been given the Spirit by the Father in all his fullness, not only for himself while he was here in this world, but also in order that he might give the Spirit to those who believe in him and who become the children of the Father.

There, then, are the reasons given by John for why his foolish disciples should not feel jealous on his behalf. He says in effect, "My baptism is in a sense nothing but a preparatory one. His will be the real baptism." That is all implicit in what we have here.

But remember that John had already stated this in another form even more clearly and explicitly. It is recorded in Luke 3 and in its parallels. John was preaching and baptizing, and people came crowding out to listen to him. Then we are told,

> And as the people were in expectation, and all men mused in their hearts of John, whether he was the Christ, nor not; John answered, saying unto them all, I indeed baptize you with water; but one mightier than I cometh, the latchet of whose shoes I am not worthy to unloose: he shall baptize you with the Holy Ghost and with fire: whose fan is in his hand, and he will thoroughly purge his floor, and will gather the wheat into his garner; but the chaff he will burn with fire unquenchable. (vv. 15–17)

John later said, "He must increase, but I must decrease" (John 3:30). The water baptism was only preparatory; here was the baptism, "He will baptize you with the Holy Ghost and with fire.

Now there is the same contrast as is brought out in the third chapter of John. Let me give you one other Scripture that helps us understand exactly what John is saying at this point. Later on John the Baptist was languishing in prison. It was a terrible thing to be in prison in those days; they did not treat prisoners then as they do now. Now they almost tend to treat them with luxury, and we feel sorry for the poor prisoner. But in those days they threw them into dank, unhealthy dungeons and gave them little food. And John had been there for some time. Poor John had become depressed and uncertain, so he sent two of his disciples to our Lord asking, "Art thou he that should come or do we look for another?" (Matt. 11:3), and our Lord sent back an answer.

But having done that, our Lord then addressed the multitude around him and said—he pays a great tribute to John here—

> What went ye out into the wilderness to see? A reed shaken with the wind? But what went ye out for to see? A man clothed in soft raiment? behold, they that wear soft clothing are in kings' houses. But what went ye out for to see? A prophet? yea, I say unto you, and more than a prophet. For this is he, of whom it is written, Behold, I send my messenger before thy face, which shall prepare thy way before thee. Verily I say unto you, Among them that are born of women there hath not risen a greater than John the Baptist: notwithstanding he that is least in the kingdom of heaven is greater than he. (Matt. 11:7–11)

That throws great light upon the whole situation. John says, "He must increase, but I must decrease" (John 3:30). John says, "Mine is a water baptism; he will baptize with the Holy Ghost and with fire. Do not compare me with him. I am not in the same field; I am not in the same realm. I am a man, earthy; he is above all. He is the Lord who has come from heaven."

But notice that our Lord takes this even a step further. He says, "Among them that are born of women there hath not risen a greater than John the Baptist," and yet "he that is least in the kingdom of heaven is greater than he" (Matt. 11:11). What does this mean? Here again I want to show you how this throws great light upon the whole question of the baptism with the Holy Spirit. Does this mean that John the Baptist is not a saved man? Does it mean that John the Baptist is not in the kingdom of heaven at all? It clearly cannot mean that because the tribute that is paid to him proves this is not the case. Indeed our Lord goes on to say, "And from the days of John the Baptist until now the kingdom of heaven suffereth violence, and the violent take it by force" (Matt. 11:12). John is a child of God—there is no question about that.

All the Old Testament saints were children of God. The apostle Paul teaches the Galatians that all of us who are Christians are in a sense the children of Abraham. "Know ye therefore that they which are of faith, the same are the children of Abraham" (Gal. 3:7). Abraham was a child of God, and he is in the kingdom. Our Lord himself said that on another occasion. He told the Jews they would see people from all parts of the world sitting in the kingdom with Abraham and Isaac and Jacob, and they themselves shut out. The Old Testament saints and all the children of faith are all in the kingdom of God, and they are all children of God.

So what is the meaning of the statement, "Notwithstanding he that is least in the kingdom of heaven is greater than he" (Matt. 11:11)? Surely there is only one adequate explanation: John the Baptist was not baptized with the Holy Spirit. John is in a preliminary stage, water baptism.

We are told this same thing in another passage, and these distinctions are important for us to observe. In the seventh chapter of John's Gospel we read of the incident that took place on the last day of a feast. "In the last day, that great day of the feast, Jesus stood and cried, saying, If any man thirst, let him come unto me, and drink. He that believeth on me, as the scripture hath said, out of his belly shall flow rivers of living water. (But this spake he of the Spirit, which they that believe on him should receive: for the Holy Ghost was not yet given; because that Jesus was not yet glorified)" (John 7:37–39). John the Baptist lived in that phase and in that stage—the Spirit was not yet given in that way. John belonged to a preliminary stage.

What is the difference between John the Baptist and one who is baptized with the Holy Spirit? It is the difference between a child and an adult. A child is as much a child of the family when he is but a day old as he will be when he is twenty or thirty years of age. He is not more a son of his parents when he reaches maturity; the moment he is born he is their child. So the question of relationship is not the vital one in that case. The difference is that of maturity, the difference between a child and an adult. And I suggest to you that that is the essential difference between this baptism of John and the baptism with the Holy Spirit. And therefore I would take these words that John used of himself and apply them to us: "He must increase, but I must decrease" (John 3:30).

In other words, it is possible for us to be Christians and yet only children. It is possible for us to be truly saved and in the kingdom but still remain only children. The baptism with the Holy Spirit lifts us from that kind of childhood condition into this adult condition.

Now let us work out this a little because it helps illustrate the whole meaning. John had understood it; it was given to John to see this. "I indeed baptize you with water. . . . He shall baptize you" (Luke 3:16). That is, "Do not look to me—look to him. I am simply here to point you to him, to the glorious thing that he has come to do and that he alone can do." "God giveth not the Spirit by measure unto him" (John 3:34). The Father has given the Son all things, and it is in his power, and in his power alone, to give us this baptism with the Holy Spirit. Here it seems to me is the great message that should come to us. The question we should ask ourselves is this: Have we been baptized with the Holy Spirit? I am not asking whether you are a Christian—I am assuming that. I am saying that you can be a Christian, born again, with the Spirit of God in you, and yet still be in the child condition, not knowing the baptism with the Holy Spirit.

What, then, is the difference between this childhood condition and the mature condition that is here described? Let us work it out in this way, using John the Baptist in particular as our example and our illustration. The first big difference, of course, is in understanding. That is the difference between the child and the adult. The child is the child of the parents; he has life from the parents in him, but he does not understand, he does not know, and as he grows and develops he will learn and understand things about the family and about the possibilities of life. But as he develops and matures he is amazed at the things he discovers and learns. No more a son, remember, in the real ultimate sense in those later years than at the beginning, but in understanding and in apprehension, oh, what a difference, what a contrast! Paul illustrates it all in 1 Corinthians 13:11: "When I was a child, I spake as a child, I understood as a child, I thought as a child [everything was as a child]: but when I became a man, I put away childish things." There is a great increase in understanding.

This is the essential difference between the Old Testament saints and the saints described in the New Testament. The Old Testament saints knew something about these things. Our Lord said, "Abraham rejoiced to see my day: and he saw it" (John 8:56). You read the account of that in the book of Genesis. Abraham did not understand it clearly, but he saw something. He did not understand it fully, but he knew that God was going to do something amazing for his seed. There is the child condition. You see something, but it is indistinct. It is not clear; you cannot follow it. It is enough to give you rejoicing and happiness, but there is no real grasp and understanding.

The same thing is true of the prophets and the psalmists. They were given glimpses of this. You find this in the Psalms; you find it still more clearly in the writings of the prophets. But listen to what Peter says about them in 1 Peter 1:10–12:

> Of which salvation the prophets have enquired and searched diligently, who prophesied of the grace that should come unto you: searching what, or what manner of time the Spirit of Christ which was in them did signify, when it testified beforehand the sufferings of Christ, and the glory that should follow. Unto whom it was revealed, that not unto themselves, but unto us they did minister the things, which are now reported unto you by them that have preached the gospel unto you with the Holy Ghost sent down from heaven; which things the angels desire to look into.

That is very clear and explicit, is it not? In other words, when you read the prophecies, you will find that they have a glimpse of this, they have the essence of it, but it is very indistinct, very unclear. Sometimes it is put in materialistic imagery, sometimes it is put in a historical mold, and you are in danger of materializing the truth as so many have done. The Jews themselves fell into that trap. But the spiritual message was what mattered; it really was about the coming of the Messiah. But the point is that they were not clear in their understanding. The author of the epistle to the Hebrews says, "God, who at sundry times and in divers manners . . ." (Heb. 1:1). In parts and portions, bits and pieces, a little here a little there. Each one saw something, but there was not full understanding or comprehension. They have the essential thing, they are the children of God, they are the children of faith, they are the seed of

Abraham, but they are only children. And indeed the apostle Paul, in the epistle to the Galatians, at the beginning of chapter 4, works it out quite definitely and says that they were children under a pedagogue, that the Law was a kind of schoolmaster to lead us to Christ.

You can be a child deficient and defective in understanding. Let us take what is perhaps the clearest illustration of all this, and that is the apostles themselves. Look at these men, read of them in the Gospels, and compare and contrast them then with what they became on the day of Pentecost and what they were afterward. It is quite clear in the Gospels that these men were already Christian men; they were born again. Our Lord in his High Priestly Prayer, for instance, draws a distinction between them and those who are in the world. He says, "I pray for them: I pray not for the world" (John 17:9). He says that these men have believed on him:

> They have kept thy word. Now they have known that all things whatsoever thou hast given me are of thee. For I have given unto them the words which thou gavest me; and they have received them, and have known surely that I came out from thee, and they have believed that thou didst send me. I pray for them: I pray not for the world, but for them which thou hast given me; for they are thine. (John 17:6–9)

Now these men were already Christians, they were regenerate, and yet you see how muddled they were in their minds and in their understanding and in their comprehension. Even when our Lord was crucified they were entirely confused. They were cast down and dejected. It took the resurrection to convince them as to his person. And then he instructed them in the Scriptures, and they were beginning to have understanding, but even then they did not have it. It was only on the day of Pentecost with the baptism with the Spirit that they really received this in its fullness. He had already "breathed" the Spirit upon them in the upper room, constituted them as the church, and given them the commission, and yet he told them to stay where they were in Jerusalem until they should be endued with this power from on high.

My contention is that there are many Christians like that. You cannot say they are not Christians. They are aware of their sin; they are aware of their helplessness to make atonement and to put themselves right with God. They are trusting only in the Lord Jesus Christ and his perfect work, and yet they are not clear about it. There is a kind of muddle that remains; they are "bound in shallows and in miseries," as Shakespeare put it. They are not enjoying the Christian life as they should. There is that state and condition in which one is in the kingdom but only a child, fumbling. With very little understanding you can become a Christian and a child of God. But the tragedy is that many remain on that level and have not realized the fuller possibilities in Christ. "He must increase, but I must decrease" (John 3:30). "He shall baptize you with the Holy Ghost and with fire" (Luke 3:16). So there is this difference in understanding.

Another difference, the second one, is the difference in certainty or in assurance. This is where John the Baptist is a particularly helpful illustration. I am giving you the facts about John, and I have reminded you of what we find at the beginning of Matthew 11 about poor John who had borne his witness and his testimony to the Lord Jesus Christ. He had done it at the Jordan. He had earlier said in essence, "I am not the Christ. I am unworthy to undo the latchet of his shoes. I indeed baptize with water—he shall baptize with the Holy Ghost, and with fire." Then on another day he had stood with two of his disciples when our Lord passed by and John said, "Behold the Lamb of God, which taketh away the sin of the world" (John 1:29). He had borne testimony to him, and he knew these things. He tells us that God had told him he would see the Spirit descending from heaven like a dove (v. 33) as he baptized Jesus, and that One would baptize with the Holy Ghost.

John knew all this, and he believed it all, and yet in prison, in adverse circumstances, with everything as it were against him, poor John became filled with doubts. Though he had seen this central truth, he was still held down by his own Jewish prejudices. The Jews were all wrong in their ideas about the Messiah. Their idea of the Messiah was of a great military, dignified personage who would come and gather an army, destroy the Romans and other enemies, set up his kingdom in Jerusalem, and elevate the Jews to the supreme position that they occupied in the time of David and Saul. But Jesus seemed to be spending his time with common, ordinary people away up there in Galilee, and John began to think about these things and said in effect, "Was I wrong after all? Is he the Christ?" So he sent two messengers to ask, "Art thou he that should come, or do we look for another?" (Matt. 11:3). In other words, "Are you the Messiah or are you not?"

Now there is this whole condition of belief and yet uncertainty, a belief that can be tested and even shaken, a belief that can be surrounded and almost overwhelmed by doubts at times. John, remember, is in the kingdom, he is a child of God, and yet here he is beset round and about by doubts. He is lacking in certainty; he is lacking in assurance. He has faith, but it is a troubled faith. That is the clear position of John the Baptist, and the apostles are exactly the same before the day of Pentecost. They believe, and yet they are not clear, they are not certain. At the beginning of the book of Acts, in chapter 1, verses 6–7, they ask that foolish question of theirs: "Wilt thou at this time restore again the kingdom to Israel?" and our Lord, in a sense, dismisses it and says in essence, "It is not for you to bother about things like that. You shall receive power. That is what you must lay hold of. Get rid of these Jewish notions; they must decrease. That kind of outlook and teaching is muddling and confusing you." This always, I say, leads to a condition of uncertainty.

What, then, of the baptism with the Spirit? The baptism with the Spirit is that which gives absolute certainty, full assurance of salvation. Look at it in the case of these apostles. What a transformation! This is particularly true of Peter—doubting, denying Peter, the man who denied his Lord to save his life—look at his boldness on the day of Pentecost. What is this? This is nothing but absolute certainty, full assurance. And this is the supreme object of the baptism with the Holy Spirit.

That is made clear in the book of Acts as it is everywhere else. Take the way in which the Apostle Paul puts it in Romans 8:15: "Ye have not received the spirit of bondage again to fear; but ye have received the Spirit of adoption, whereby we cry, Abba, Father." And he adds, "The Spirit itself [himself] beareth witness with our spirit [alongside of, in confirmation of], that we are the children of God: and if children, then heirs; heirs of God, and joint-heirs with Christ" (vv. 16–17). Then Paul goes on to those mighty affirmations, those incontrovertible certainties that are the glory of the eighth chapter of Romans:

> And we know that all things work together for good to them that love God. . . . I am persuaded, that neither death, nor life, nor angels, nor principalities, nor powers, nor things present, nor things to come, nor height, not depth, nor any other creature, shall be able to separate us from the love of God, which is in Christ Jesus our Lord. (vv. 28, 38–39)

"We *know*"! Oh, the great affirmations, the great certainty. "I know whom I have believed, and am persuaded that he is able to keep that which I have committed unto him against that day" (2 Tim. 1:12). This is absolute certainty. Sometimes this is described as being sealed with the Spirit. "In whom also after that ye believed, ye were sealed with that holy Spirit of promise, which is the earnest of our inheritance until the redemption of the purchased possession" (Eph. 1:13–14). That is the supreme purpose of the baptism with the Holy Ghost, to give us an absolute certainty that we are the children of God.

This again is the difference between the child and the adult. The child is the child but does not know it, is not certain of it in the way that the grown-up person is. He cannot investigate the title deeds; he does not have this assurance. But the adult condition includes this.

I could go on for hours illustrating this from the history of the church. There is nothing more glorious in church history than the way in which men and women who were Christians but who were filled with doubts and uncertainty suddenly came into this great and blessed assurance as the result of a baptism with the Spirit. The great revivals of history are all examples of this. That is what always happens in a revival. It generally starts in one man. Suddenly he is taken through a process that brings him into this great and glorious certainty. Everybody knows the story of what happened to John Wesley, but he is only one of many of whom the same thing is true. This has been the secret and the real explanation of all the great evangelists of history. They could point to a time when they were in this preliminary condition, and then God baptized them with his Spirit and made them the men they were.

This has also happened to many individuals who are quite unknown. Have you ever met people who have passed through a revival? I have known many such people. They had been Christians for years. They did believe, but they were unhappy—sometimes up, sometimes down—painfully, wearily trudging along as it were in the Christian life. Then revival came, and suddenly they were filled with this absolute certainty and assurance that nothing could shake—this immediate, direct witness and testimony of the Spirit. "He must increase, but I must decrease" (John 3:30). John the Baptist could not give anybody that. John was incapable of that, and he knew it. "He shall baptize you with the Holy Ghost, and with fire" (Matt. 3:11).

Another way in which this works out is this: the baptism with the Holy Spirit gives great and glorious satisfaction. You can be a Christian, and yet your Christianity can be almost a task. Do you not know something about that condition? God knows I have known it! Christian? Yes. Believing, saved, in the kingdom, and yet the whole thing was a task; there was a great deal of legalism still. The Devil could shake one when one fell into sin and make that believer doubt his salvation. There are many Christians to whom their Christianity seems to be a burden and a load and a task. That is why Paul says in Romans 8:15, "Ye have not received the spirit of bondage again." Do not go back to that, he says; you are misunderstanding what you have. But there are many like that. And there are many others who, while Christian, are still seeking and hoping for something more. But there is no rest, there is no quiet, there is no satisfaction in their soul. But the moment such a person is baptized with the Holy Spirit, there is a complete sense of satisfaction.

What does the Holy Spirit do? Well, as our Lord said, the Holy Spirit has been sent in order to "glorify" the Lord Jesus Christ. That is his primary function, his first object. That is what he always does, and the great test of whether a man or woman has been baptized with the Holy Spirit or not is that they know the Lord Jesus Christ and glorify him in a way that they have never done before and find complete satisfaction in him. This has often been expressed by hymn writers who had experienced this.

> Just as I am, poor, wretched, blind;
> Sight, riches, healing of the mind,
> *Yea, all I need in Thee to find,*
> O Lamb of God, I come, I come.[1]

Listen to Charles Wesley:

> Thou, O Christ, art all I want,
> More than all in Thee I find.[2]

Can you say that? Does he satisfy you completely? Listen to Paul again in Philippians 4. He is in prison, and he has been suffering a great deal, and he hears from the good people at Philippi. But he tells them that it is all right. "I rejoiced in the Lord greatly, that now at the last your care of me hath flourished again; wherein ye were also careful [anxious], but ye lacked opportunity. Not that I speak in respect of want: for I have learned, in whatsoever state I am, therewith to be content. I know both how to be abased, and I know how to abound: every where and in all things I am instructed both to be full and to be hungry, both to abound and to suffer need. I can do all things through Christ which strengtheneth me" (Phil. 4:10–13). There is a man who is fully satisfied. Our Lord himself had said this on that great day of the feast, that festival at Jerusalem when he cried out saying, "If any man thirst, let him come unto me, and drink. He that believeth on me, as the scripture hath said, out of his belly shall flow rivers of living water" (John 7:37–38).

Now he had already said that to the woman of Samaria. The account is given in John 4: "Jesus answered and said unto her, Whosoever drinketh of this water shall thirst again" (v. 13). Many Christians are living that sort of life—back and forth, back and forth; temporary satisfaction, then it is gone. But "Whosoever drinketh of the water that I shall give him shall never thirst [never!]; but the water that I shall give him shall be in him a well of water springing up into everlasting life" (v. 14). Complete satisfaction. The baptism with the Holy Spirit gives that, and he does it by revealing the Lord to us in all the fullness of his divine Saviorhood. You can believe in Christ as the Son of God and as the Savior of your soul, you can be clear about the atonement and so on, but I am asking this: do you know him as the full, final, complete, utter satisfaction of your every need and of every need that can ever arise in your life and experience? The baptism with the Holy Spirit does that. The New Testament is full of that kind of teaching. That is what made those people the people they were.

Which brings me to my next point: the baptism with the Holy Spirit always brings joy and gladness. Unfortunately, there is such a thing as a miserable Christian. It is almost a contradiction in terms but not quite. But when people are baptized with the Holy Spirit, they are filled with joy. Listen to the lyrical account we are given of these people in the early days of the church, at the end of the second chapter of the book of Acts: "And they, continuing daily with one accord in the temple, and breaking bread from house to house, did eat their meat with gladness and singleness of heart, praising God, and having favour with all the people" (vv. 46–47).

The apostle Peter talks about ordinary Christian people scattered throughout various parts of the world. He does not know them; he has never met them. But Peter, because he knows they are what they are in Christ, is able to say about them, in reference to Jesus Christ, "Whom having not seen, ye love; in whom, though now ye see him not, yet believing, ye rejoice with joy unspeakable [beyond expression] and full of glory" (1 Pet. 1:8). Do you have that? You can be a Christian without it. But once you have been baptized with the Holy Spirit, that is your condition. You "rejoice with joy unspeakable and full of glory," a gladness that is a kind of a foretaste of the final glory itself. The whole book of Acts is the most lyrical book in the world because it is a description and an account of men and women baptized with the Holy Spirit.

And lastly, not only does this baptism give us satisfaction and joy and gladness, as our Lord had promised there on that great day of the feast, it makes us become very fruitful persons: "Out of his belly [out of his innermost parts] shall flow rivers of living water" (John 7:38). This is a most vital point. At the present time there is nothing I know of that is more important. The masses of the people are outside the Christian church. What is needed above everything at the present time is men and women, Christian people, out of whose innermost parts shall flow rivers of living water. That is how Christianity conquered the ancient world; it was done through those Christian people. Other people could not understand them. Already on the day of Pentecost the crowd came and said, "What is this?" Some people thought the Christians were drunk. Why? Because they were so happy, because of the ecstasy, because of "joy unspeakable and full of glory." They could not understand them.

And this continued wherever they went. People were amazed at them. Looking at them they said, "What is this?" So they began to be concerned about their own souls. They said, "Is it possible for a human being to be like that?" They saw that when these people were arrested and even thrown to the lions in the arena, they thanked God they had been counted worthy to suffer for Jesus's name. And the onlookers said, "What is this?" "Out of his belly [innermost parts] shall flow rivers of living water" (John 7:38). Once men and women are baptized with the Holy Spirit, they are so transformed that they become a kind of magnet. They attract people and are anxious to help them. They have the knowledge that can enable them to do so. They can give the others a reason for the hope that is in them. They can show them the way of salvation; they have power to witness. "Ye shall receive power, after that the Holy Ghost is come upon you: and ye shall be witnesses unto me" (Acts 1:8). The baptism with the Holy Spirit makes people living witnesses to Christ. They are such transformed characters that people can see the difference. They are attracted and amazed by it, and they come in order to try to discover the reason and the explanation of it.

"He must increase, but I must decrease." Are you proud of your religion? Are you proud of the good life you are living? Believe me, once you know something about this you will hate all that; it will have to go, decrease, disappear. This is what he gives, and what he alone can give you.

It is not about John the Baptist but the Lord Jesus Christ. He himself has received the Spirit in all his fullness. He showed that while he was here on earth. When he ascended to heaven God gave him the gift of the Spirit again, that he might give it to us—not to make us Christians, but to make us happy Christians, to make us rejoicing Christians, to make us fruitful Christians, to make us such people that we shall be a benediction to all who are around us, for out of us shall flow rivers of living water to the dry, parched, thirsty, arid land that surrounds us all.

My dear friends, do you know this baptism? Are you in the position now to say, "Let him increase! And for myself I desire nothing but him and his glory and all that he has to give"?

# 19

# None of Self and All of Thee

JOHN 3:30

Sunday morning sermon preached in
Westminster Chapel, June 5, 1966.

He must increase, but I must decrease. (John 3:30)

In the last sermon we considered something of the results that come
to all who have received the baptism with the Holy Spirit—assurance,
certainty, understanding, contentment, power. So now we come again
to this great statement because apart from its own worth and value in
helping us understand the history concerning John the Baptist and the
immediate occasion that made him utter these words, there is here en-
shrined a principle that is true of the whole Christian life. We are going
through this great Gospel in order that we may discover the way to arrive
at what we are told in the sixteenth verse of the first chapter: "And of his
fullness have all we received, and grace for [upon] grace." Now that is
Christianity. Christianity is not only believing on the Lord Jesus Christ,
not only knowing your sins are forgiven. That is the beginning, but that
is only the beginning. Christianity is receiving "his fullness"—the life of
God in the souls of men; something of the eternal; being made "partakers
of the divine nature" (2 Pet. 1:4).

That is the great theme of the Gospel of John, which puts its emphasis on *life*, and I am trying to show that the most important thing in the world for every one of us is just this. Are we able to say, "I have received his fullness, and I am receiving grace upon grace"? That is what is offered, that is what it means to be a Christian, and therefore, this is the great question that should concern us all. How much do we know of this fullness, and if it is but little, why? There are many hindrances and obstacles to our receiving this. The Devil, the adversary of our souls, will do anything he can to keep us as "babes in Christ." We have been looking at some of these difficulties, and here I feel attention is concentrated on a very important aspect of this whole matter: "He must increase, but I must decrease" (John 3:30).

We are reminded here of one of the greatest hindrances, one of the greatest obstacles, this confusion that was in the mind of the followers of John the Baptist. It persists with us as Christian people, and the whole situation is put before us here in a succinct and pithy manner.

So let us look at this statement once more: "He must increase, but I must decrease" (v. 30). Let me make some general remarks about it. The first is that the measure of our spiritual state and condition is the relative positions of the "he" and the "I" in our experience. That is the best of all tests—"He . . . I." Where do they come in your life and in your experience? What are the relative positions? What are their relative proportions? Everything depends upon this personal relationship to Jesus Christ. Our danger ever is to put our faith in propositions, faith in our own actions, rather than in him. But this living communion, this life in Christ, life in the Spirit, is the true Christian position. Therefore, I repeat, this is the most perfect test of all. Do not ask yourself how much good you have done, do not ask yourself how busy you are and how active you are—that is not the test. We can do all that in the flesh. Here is the test: "he . . . I."

We move now to the second proposition, which is intimately related to the first. They are vitally connected and can never be separated. It is difficult to know how to put this exactly, but there is no question but that these two things always react together and at the same time. I have often thought that a good way of representing this, though it may sound trivial and almost childish, is what you can see in one of those little barometers that used to be sold—perhaps they still are. It was a little house with a man and a woman fixed upon a lever, and they had been so made that when the weather was fine and going to be finer the woman came out, and when the weather was going to be bad or was bad, the man came out. The point was that the man and the woman were on the same lever, the same bit of wood; one could not move without the other moving, and they always moved at the same time. If one was out, the other was in; then the other came out, and the first one went in. That is the kind of relationship, it seems to me, that is indicated here between "he" and "I." If he is out and prominent, I am out of sight; whereas if I am prominent, it is very difficult to see him. They are intimately related and bound together, and they cannot be separated. This is one of those fundamental laws of the spiritual life with which you cannot argue and that you cannot debate; it is an absolute rule.

The next point I would therefore make is to emphasize this word "must." "He *must* increase, but I *must* decrease." In saying that, John the Baptist was uttering one of his prophecies concerning our Lord. He had already referred to him as "The Lamb of God, which taketh away the sin of the world" (John 1:29). And having had the glimpse of who he was, and having remembered what God had told him about the One on whom he would see the Holy Spirit descending as a dove when he baptized him, John knew that he must increase because of who and what he is. And he knew, therefore, that his own work was coming to an end. That is the primary meaning.

But there is again a further and a deeper spiritual meaning in this, a meaning that relates to all of us. If we are to receive his fullness and grace upon grace, then he must increase, and equally certain we must decrease. There are certain musts, certain rules in this spiritual life. Have you noticed how, in this one chapter, John 3, this is the third of these *musts* that we have encountered? The first was the one uttered by our Lord to Nicodemus: "Ye must be born again." There is the first, and it is an absolute. "Marvel not that I said unto thee, Ye must be born again" (v. 7).

This is where the Christian message is different from everything else in the world that is being offered to mankind today. You cannot argue with this. You can suggest difficulties and oppositions, but they will not help you at all. Our Lord does not have a discussion with Nicodemus about this. He keeps on stopping him, he silences him. As Nicodemus is going to ask questions and say this and that, he is stopped: "You *must* . . ." "Verily, verily, I say unto thee, Except a man be born again, he cannot see the kingdom of God" (v. 3). "Except a man be born of water and of the Spirit, he cannot enter into the kingdom of God" (v. 5). "Ye must be born again." "The natural man receiveth not the things of the Spirit of God: for they are foolishness unto him: neither can he know them, because they are spiritually discerned" (1 Cor. 2:14). This is a great absolute at the very beginning of the Christian life. We cannot exercise faith by nature; it is impossible. Faith is the gift of God. "The natural man" has no faith; he cannot. All these things are foolishness to him. "Ye must be born again"— there it is at the very entry into life.

And there is another *must* that we have seen, and that is the must about our Lord's death. "And as Moses lifted up the serpent in the wilderness, even so *must* the Son of man be lifted up: that whosoever believeth in him should not perish, but have eternal life" (John 3:14–15). He came to die. If he had not died, there would be no salvation. His death was not an accident; it was "foreordained before the foundation of the world" (1 Pet. 1:20)—"the determinate counsel and foreknowledge of God" (Acts 2:23). The death of our Lord was no accident, not something done by men. "God was in Christ, reconciling the world unto himself, not imputing their trespasses unto them" (2 Cor. 5:19). "He hath made him to be sin for us, who knew no sin; that we might be made the righteousness of God in him" (v. 21). He *must* be lifted up. These are all fundamental laws, axioms of the spiritual life about which there can be no discussion whatsoever.

And the same is true of this one that we are looking at now. If we want to receive "his fullness . . . and grace for grace" (John 1:16), if we want to know that life and life more abundant, if we want to know "with all saints what is the breadth, and length, and depth, and height; and to know the love of Christ, which passeth knowledge, that ye might be filled with all the fullness of God," (Eph. 3:18–19) he must increase, and you and I must decrease. This is one of those absolutes. You can argue, and you can struggle against it, but you are just preventing yourself from receiving this great life and fullness.

My last general proposition about this is that this is a process that goes on. It is not something that happens once and forever. It is a continuous process. As you receive his fullness and grace upon grace, he goes on increasing and you go on decreasing in your life and in your experience.

There, then, are the fundamental postulates that are the basis of everything that is taught in the whole of this Gospel of John and in the whole of the New Testament teaching. I want now to concentrate on the negative side: "I must decrease." The greatest enemy in the Christian life is self. By that I mean the greatest enemy within us. The greatest enemy of all, of course, is the Devil, Satan, "the god of this world," but he works, above everything else, through self. What was the original temptation? "Has God said you must not eat of this fruit? Why did he say that? Ah, he knows that if you do eat it, you will be like gods and will know everything." The serpent appealed to pride; he appealed to self. That was the original sin, and it has continued to be our greatest hindrance and greatest obstacle in the whole of our Christian life.

And, therefore, what John is really saying here is this—and this is the point we must deal with: we cannot receive his fullness until this self of ours has decreased and has been dealt with. This is a familiar point. As has often been pointed out, if you have some wonderful liquid in a vessel, you cannot put it into another vessel if that other vessel is already full. If you are to fill the second vessel with the contents of the first, you must empty the contents of the second one. You can only fill an empty vessel with that wonderful liquid. Unless I decrease he cannot increase.

Therefore I would suggest that the best way whereby we can test ourselves is this: what are the signs and evidences of decreasing self—that life of "self-renouncing love" as the hymn puts it? This is a very good way of discovering exactly where we stand, and as I am giving you these tests, we shall incidentally be discovering the way in which we can cause self to decrease. These, then, are some of the tests. Do we have a true view of ourselves? The Greeks in their wisdom had a great statement that said the first law in a successful life is, "Know thyself." This is the first great principle in the Bible also. Nothing is more important than that we should know the exact truth about ourselves.

This is taught us repeatedly in the New Testament Scriptures. Here is a very good statement of it by the Apostle Paul in Romans 12:3: "I say, through the grace given unto me, to every man that is among you, not to think of himself more highly than he ought to think; but to think soberly [this is written, remember, to Christian people, not to unbelievers] according as God hath dealt to every man the measure of faith." We all get inflated notions; we are intoxicated with ourselves. Think soberly, think accurately, face the facts.

Or you have it again in Galatians 6:3: "For if a man think himself to be something, when he is nothing, he deceiveth himself." What wonderful statements, and how vitally important they are for us! Self-conceit robs us of God's fullness. So the first thing we must have is a true and accurate view of ourselves, and the great way of getting that is to indulge in what the Fathers, the old Puritans particularly, used to call "a law-work." The Law has been given very definitely in order to show us exactly what we are. "The law . . . was added," says Paul to the Galatians, "because of transgressions" (Gal. 3:19). It came to pinpoint sin, to convict us, to show us the truth about ourselves. Paul (he tells us himself) was very pleased with himself until "the commandment came, sin revived, and I died" (Rom. 7:9). That is the way to kill the self. The law showed him, through its emphasis on coveting, the exact condition that he was really in. He says the same thing in that bit of autobiography in Philippians 3. He thought he was so right, but then the law came, and he saw it all as dung and refuse and loss, useless, hopeless, and of no value.

All this "law-work" is essential in the introduction to the Christian life. That is why repentance comes first. We must see ourselves before we ever see our real and true need of the Lord Jesus Christ. Those who have come under the operation of the law are those who know the truth about themselves. They realize they have nothing of which to boast. That is the great and most wonderful characteristic of this mighty apostle Paul. With all his genius and all his astounding ability, the humility of the man is staggering. It is all of grace, always. It is not about him. He is amazed at himself; he is amazed that he is in the ministry at all. He says in his first epistle to Timothy,

> According to the glorious gospel of the blessed God, which was committed to my trust. And I thank Christ Jesus our Lord, who hath enabled me, for that he counted me faithful, putting me into the ministry; who was before a blasphemer, and a persecutor, and injurious: but I obtained mercy, because I did it ignorantly in unbelief. (1 Tim. 1:11–13)

Paul is amazed at himself. He knows the truth about himself. He reminds us, in writing to Titus, that this is the truth about every one of us by nature, "hateful, and hating one another" (Titus 3:3). That is what we were, he says, and we must realize this about ourselves. This is vital as we enter into the Christian life. It is all of grace, it is not of man, and there is nothing whereof we can boast. Justification is by faith only; that means it is all his and is entirely given.

And the more we realize that, the less we will think of ourselves. There is nothing more humbling than the law, for it shows us exactly where we are. But the point I am making is that this does not stop once you become a Christian; it must continue. We must be aware of our weakness; we must be aware of the poorness of our best acts. Again Paul is very clear about this. Here is a man thrilling with assurance of salvation, but let us never forget that the same man says things like,

> Not as though I had already attained, either were already perfect: but I follow after, if that I may apprehend that for which also I am apprehended of Christ Jesus. Brethren, I count not myself to have apprehended: but this one thing I do, forgetting those things which are behind, and reaching forth unto those things which are before, I press toward the mark. (Phil. 3:12–14)

So he had this same view of himself running right through his Christian life. He did not merely start like that; he continued like that. This is the principle that I am emphasizing: we must go on decreasing in this way, seeing ourselves as we are more and more and the blackness of our hearts and the unworthiness that is in us. We must say, "In me (that is, in my flesh,) dwelleth no good thing" (Rom. 7:18), and those who see that have decreased; they have this right and true view of themselves.

So let us take that for granted in order that we can go on to other aspects of this matter, because this is a very subtle point. We might say, "Right! I accept that. Justification by faith only, all of grace. Quite right." But then the Devil in his subtlety comes and suggests things to us, and above all he makes us self-centered. So the second good way whereby you can test whether self is decreasing is this: Are you less self-centered than you used to be, and increasingly so? Self-centeredness is the bane of the Christian life, the curse, the main relic of sin and of the fall in every one of us, even as Christians. This idea that this is all finished when you believe in Christ or "make your decision" is entirely false to the whole of the New Testament teaching. Your battle with self is really just beginning when you are converted. You did not know the truth about it before; you did not understand it; you could not possibly have done so. The Devil tempted our Lord along this line—"*If* thou be the Son of God, do this," appealing to self. It did not work.

So we must be rid of this self-centeredness. How does it show itself? These are some of the practical, simple tests that we must apply to ourselves. Is your self growing less and less, are you becoming smaller and smaller? You must lessen that unhealthy concern about yourself that you used to have. Some Christian people are always talking about themselves and their problems. Whenever you meet them it is always that—what they have said, what they have been doing, what they are hoping to do, what has happened to them, this difficulty or problem they are facing— always talking about themselves. What a terrible thing that is! It just shows that self is in the forefront, and Jesus is somewhere hidden in the back. Self has not been decreasing; it is still there, evidenced by all this self-concern. Charles Lamb talked about "the mumps and measles of the soul," and some people are always feeling their pulse and always wanting you to take it for them. It is all centered around self, this morbid self-concern, this unhealthy self-interest. As I decrease there is less of that.

Another way in which this shows itself is the terrible danger of thinking even of salvation in terms of the benefits that it brings to me. Now do not misunderstand what I am saying. There is a sense in which our first concern is about our soul's salvation, and that is right. When we come under the condemnation of the Law and see ourselves as hell-bound sinners, of course we are alarmed and concerned. We say, "What must I do to be saved?" All I am saying is that you must not continue like that. This is one of the differences that we saw earlier between the child and the adult. The child cannot help being self-centered. There is nothing wrong in that; it is natural to childhood. The child does not think of anybody; he wants something, and it does not matter whether anybody else has anything or not. The child is selfish and self-centered. But you must not go on like that. You do not remain as a child; you get older, and you stop that, you curb it and get rid of it.

But there is the danger of our doing this even with regard to this great salvation. We think of it in terms of what it is giving to us, the benefits that we are going to get. People talk about this, and they talk about these benefits, and you would think that this great salvation in our Lord is nothing but some kind of agency from which you can receive blessings almost automatically. You, with all your needs, start with yourself and what you need and what you want, and there is salvation, and then there is the supply. You say, "I have this and that; I am this and that." All self! Salvation is just for me!

Thank God, I say again, for the blessings salvation does give us personally, but the test of whether we are growing or not, whether he is increasing and we are decreasing, is that we talk less and less about it in terms of "*I*" and what *I* have, what *I* have received, what *I* am going to get, and what *I* am going to be and instead more and more in terms of the grand objectivity. You look at it as it was in the mind of God before the foundation of the world—the plan and the scheme of salvation, the glory of God. It is "Christ the power of God, and the wisdom of God"—not Christ who does this-that-and-the-other to me or for me (1 Cor. 1:24). You see the mind of the eternal pondering over the human state and situation before the foundation of the world, this great plan that no one but God could have conceived, and the working out of it and all that is involved. Oh, this is the characteristic of a decreasing self and an increasing Lord, that we are more and more concerned about the greatness of this salvation into which he has brought us and of which we are partakers. The thing that now thrills us is the thing to which he has brought us and not so much that we have been brought into it.

Perhaps this can be best illustrated by an ordinary human illustration. The man who really loves that girl he is going to marry or the girl he has married is a man who is more interested in her and in her excellencies than in what he is getting. That is what he sees. He is not talking about himself; he is talking about her. His friends have to endure it! He is describing her, praising her for all the wonderful things that are true of her. He does not say, "I am looking forward to having a good cook or someone to keep my house clean." Of course not! It is the person who is interesting to him.

My friends, examine yourselves in the light of that. How do you talk about this great salvation? What do you say about it? How do you describe it? How do you think of it? Here is the test. God forbid that we should reduce this glorious gospel of the blessed God to something that is merely an agency to provide particular blessings for us.

But let us go on to some other tests. Your prayer life is a very good test on this particular point. "He must increase, but I must decrease" (John 3:30). If that is happening, you will find that in your praying there are fewer and fewer petitions and demands, and there is more and more praise and thanksgiving and adoration. This is elementary, is it not? Demands, desires, petitions—that is the child again. That is all right; we are to make our requests known unto God. I am not saying we must not do these things. I am simply talking about the relative proportions. And this is something we all must know full well. The danger even for Christians is just to drop on their knees and say the Lord's Prayer, then put up two or three petitions; they may have a little list of people they pray for—petitions, demands, requests. But as self decreases and he increases, there is more expression of gratitude, praise, thanksgiving, wonder, adoration. You say to him:

> And can it be that I should gain
> An interest in the Savior's blood?
> Died He for me, who caused His pain—
> For me, who Him to death pursued?
> Amazing love! How can it be,
> That Thou, my God, shouldst die for me?[1]

Or with Isaac Watts, you "survey the wondrous cross" and are lost in wonder, love, and praise.

> When I survey the wondrous cross
> On which the Prince of glory died,
> My richest gain I count but loss,
> And pour contempt on all my pride.[2]

That is the way to get rid of this self and allow him to increase.

Are you unhappy in your Christian life? Do you feel that you do not know much about this fullness, and do you say, "I have been trying to get this—I have been praying—I have been seeking and searching, reading books, going to meetings"? Stop all that for the time being and just examine yourself and listen to yourself praying, and you will find self at the center. You want this and that; you start and end with yourself. But when Jesus begins to increase, there will be less and less of that, and there will be more of this abandon in praise and thanksgiving and adoration.

Or let me suggest another test. One of the best signs of all that self is decreasing is that we are less self-protective and less self-defensive. This is one of the commonest manifestations of self, is it not? Self is always sensitive; self is always looking for insults and injuries and attacks and suggestions. Self is a miserable thing, and it is always afraid; it is always having to watch and guard and safeguard itself. That is its great characteristic. So it spends the whole of its life doing this, and then if things go wrong it is always complaining about other people and even about God. "God has not been fair to me. I deserve better than this. Why should I be taken ill? Why should things go wrong with me? Why shouldn't I have success?" That is self, is it not, speaking in the way that we are all so familiar with, and we are ready to be hurt by others. This is just a sign that self is at the very center, holding the most prominent position, and Jesus scarcely seems to be there at all.

How different we are from the apostle Paul! Listen to this great man. He had been insulted by those foolish Corinthians who did not recognize his abilities and preferred Apollos or Peter. The apostle replies in 1 Corinthians 4 saying, "Let a man so account of us, as of the ministers of Christ, and stewards of the mysteries of God. Moreover it is required in stewards, that a man be found faithful" (vv. 1–2). Then listen to this: "But with me it is a very small thing that I should be judged of you, or of man's judgment: yea, I judge not mine own self. For I know nothing by myself; yet am I not hereby justified: but he that judgeth me is the Lord" (vv. 3–4). What enables a man to say a thing like that? There is only one answer—"I am crucified with Christ." That is the only answer. "Ye are dead," says Paul to the Colossians, "and your life is hid with Christ in God" (Col. 3:3).

It is the failure to realize that we are "dead" that accounts for this persisting self and this self-sensitiveness, self-protectiveness, and self-defensiveness. Do you remember that great statement made by George Müller in his autobiography? He says that the great turning point in his life and the most wonderful thing that ever happened to him was this: "There was a day when I died completely to George Müller or George Müller died completely to me." That was the blessed release that he discovered. He had finished with himself; he was not worth bothering about. All his pride in himself had been so wrong, so blind and ridiculous. In other words, he had obtained what the hymn reminds us of—"a heart at leisure from itself." That is the secret! The quiet heart, the peaceful heart, the heart that is no longer revolving perpetually around this miserable self. John Bunyan puts this so well:

He that is down needs fear no fall,
He that is low no pride;
He that is humble ever shall
Have God to be his guide.[3]

What profound philosophy! If you are already lying on the ground you cannot fall, can you? He is humbled in the presence of his God, his Maker and Creator and blessed Redeemer. Nothing can hurt him. He is down; he is humbled.

So it is not surprising that we can pray, in the words of John Greenleaf Whittier:

Take from our souls the strain and stress,
And let our ordered lives confess
The beauty of Thy peace.[4]

There, then, is the second great test: we are less self-centered.

Let me say just a word about the third test: it is that we become less self-reliant. Here is another valuable test for us to apply. Self, of course, is always confident; it has an inflated notion of itself and therefore of its abilities and all that it can do, and it naturally tends to rely upon this. We forget what our Lord said: "Without me ye can do nothing" (John 15:5). We think we can do it; so we make our plans, we draw out our programs, we rely upon our energies. We even say we must have what we call "prayer backing." I have often felt that is the most terrible phrase I have ever heard in my life. We make our plans and proposals; our arrangements are drawn up. We are going to do most of it, but we commit it to God to get God's blessing on it.

That is self in the forefront. Jesus is in the background somewhere giving us a bit of help and aid. Oh, what a tragic condition this is! It is all wrong, and it is all due to utter ignorance—ignorance of ourselves and ignorance of the nature of our task. What is the task confronting the church? Is it merely to get a number of converts? Of course not. "We wrestle not against flesh and blood, but against principalities, against powers, against the rulers of the darkness of this world, against spiritual wickedness in high places" (Eph. 6:12). Are you putting yourself up against that? With all that you can bring together of man and his ability and his organizing power and everything else you can think of, can man stand against this power, "spiritual wickedness in high places," "the god of this world"? "If our gospel be hid," says Paul, "it is hid to them that are lost: in whom the god of this world hath blinded the minds of them which believe not" (2 Cor. 4:3–4), lest they believe. They cannot; it is impossible. "The prince of the power of the air [is] the spirit that now worketh in the children of disobedience" (Eph. 2:2). The world is under the governance and dominion of the Devil, Satan; they cannot believe, and no man, nor any powers in man, nor the whole of the human race combined can ever stand up against this power. It is impossible. There is only One who can do so. And when you remember that we have indwelling sin in us, when you remember that the old nature is still here, you see it is ridiculous to trust in ourselves and to rely upon ourselves.

The apostle Paul, as usual, puts this perfectly for us in 2 Corinthians 10: "Though we walk in the flesh, we do not war after the flesh" (v. 3). I am a man, but I do not do my work in a human, earthly, carnal fashion, says Paul. "(For the weapons of our warfare are not carnal, but mighty through God to the pulling down of strongholds;) casting down imaginations, and every high thing that exalteth itself against the knowledge of God, and bringing into captivity every thought to the obedience of Christ" (vv. 3–5). That is the only way, and there is no other. That is why the apostle, with all the brilliance of his great mind, his logical ability, all his knowledge and erudition, tells the Corinthians that when he went to them, "I was with you in weakness, and in fear, and in much trembling" (1 Cor. 2:3). That is Paul the mighty colossus, this outstanding genius, this man of God who had been lifted up to the third heaven. "And my speech and my preaching was not with enticing words of man's wisdom, but in demonstration of the Spirit and of power: that your faith should not stand in the wisdom of men, but in the power of God" (2 Cor. 2:4–5).

Or take it as he puts it again—he constantly says this—in the second chapter of the Second Epistle to the Corinthians, describing his ministry:

> Now thanks be unto God, which always causeth us to triumph in Christ, and maketh manifest the savour of his knowledge by us in every place. For we are unto God a sweet savour of Christ, in them that are saved, and in them that perish: to the one we are the savour

of death unto death; to the other the savour of life unto life. And who is sufficient for these things? (vv. 14–16)

If ever a man had a right to feel that he was sufficient, it was the apostle Paul. He had everything that a man can need, surely, from every standpoint. But he looks at the task, he sees the responsibility, he sees the glory of God in the souls of men, and he says, "Who is sufficient for these things?" The self had decreased until it was virtually out of sight.

Paul says again in the fifth verse of the third chapter, "Not that we are sufficient of ourselves to think any thing as of ourselves; but our sufficiency is of God" (3:5). I think one of the greatest statements of all is at the end of the first chapter of the epistle to the Colossians: "Whom we preach, warning every man, and teaching every man in all wisdom; that we may present every man perfect in Christ Jesus: whereunto I also labour, striving [How does he strive?] according to his working, which worketh in me mightily" (vv. 28–29). No self-reliance here; it has gone. He relies on nothing in himself or in man; his reliance is entirely in God. So when he writes to the Philippians he winds up his letter by saying, "I can do all things through Christ which strengtheneth me" (Phil. 4:13).

"He must increase, but I must decrease" (John 3:30). Let me just close by reading to you a hymn that puts it all so well, the well-known hymn of Theodore Monod:

O the bitter shame and sorrow,
That a time could ever be,
When I let the Savior's pity
Plead in vain, and proudly answered,
"All of self, and none of Thee!"

Yet he found me; I beheld Him
Bleeding on the accursed tree;
Heard Him pray, "Forgive them, Father!"
And my wistful heart said faintly,
"Some of self, and some of Thee!"

Day by day, His tender mercy,
Healing, helping, full and free,
Sweet and strong, and ah! so patient,
Brought me lower, while I whispered,
"Less of self, and more of Thee!"

Higher than the highest heavens,
Deeper than the deepest sea,
Lord, Thy love at last hath conquered:
Grant me now my supplication,
"None of self, and all of Thee!"[5]

Is that your experience?

20

# Make the Poor Self
# Grow Less and Less

JOHN 3:30

Sunday morning sermon preached in
Westminster Chapel, June 12, 1966.

He must increase, but I must decrease. (John 3:30)

We have already explained the exact context of these words that were
spoken by John the Baptist when his foolish followers were feeling jealous on his behalf because of the preaching and the success of our Lord
and Savior. John corrects them and rebukes them and sums it all up
in this great statement: "He must increase, but I must decrease" (John
3:30).

Now we have been trying to show that the statement is important in
its own historical setting and, as a matter of a fact, of history. But we are
also showing that it contains within itself one of these great principles
that are of central importance in the whole matter of the culture of our
souls and the nurture of our spiritual life. Indeed we are looking at it in
this way: What is Christianity? What does it mean to be a Christian? And
we have been suggesting that the answer is really found in the sixteenth
verse of the first chapter of this Gospel, where we read, "And of his full-

ness have all we received, and grace for [upon] grace" (John 1:16). That is what it means to be a Christian. Not to live a good life, not even to believe only in the Lord Jesus Christ; it is to be united to him so that you receive his fullness—not in one act, for you go on receiving, "grace for grace." It is life in the Spirit, life in the Lord. "Christ in [us], the hope of glory" (Col. 1:27), and we in Christ.

This is essential Christianity, and this is how we are all meant to be. We are all meant to be men and women who show and demonstrate that we have received and are receiving increasingly this great and glorious fullness.

If only that were true of all of us, the whole situation would be entirely different and transformed. The church would not be as she is. She would not be weak; she would not be languishing; she would not be ineffective. The church would be filled with power and with vigor, and the world looking at her would be attracted, as the world is always attracted in times of reformation and of revival. The world is as it is and the masses of the people are outside the Christian church for one main reason—and that is that you and I who claim to be Christians are as we are. We so often give the impression that to become a Christian is something that deprives one of something; that it is the world that has life and that we are just negative with prohibitions and vetoes and restraints, that we give up things and that it is a hard task, and that we sometimes even wish we had never heard of it in order that we might enjoy ourselves and live a full life. That is why people are outside; they say Christianity is "narrow," "small," and "cramping."

Of course, that viewpoint is completely and entirely wrong, but we must not blame the world so much for thinking like that. You and I, my friends, have led them to think in that way. We have failed to show them the glory of this life, and that is because we have not received God's fullness and grace upon grace as we should have done. Therefore, we are studying all this in order to discover what it is that constitutes some of the main hindrances to our receiving this fullness. It is all there in the Lord Jesus Christ. "It pleased the Father that in him should all fullness dwell" (Col. 1:19). He is the Head out of which everything comes, and in him there is eternal abundance, "the unsearchable riches of Christ" (Eph. 3:8). And yet we are living as paupers; we are undernourished. What is the matter with us? What is the cause of our failure to receive this fullness?

We have considered many of the causes as they are put before us in the Gospel of John, and the one we are now looking at is one of the most important of all. Indeed I venture to say once more that nothing so frequently robs us as Christian people of this fullness as our *self*. Self is the enemy from the beginning to the very end, and so the Scripture is full of warnings against it. Self must go down before Jesus will go up: "I must decrease." There is no hope of his increasing in my life and my receiving his fullness unless I decrease.

Now the Scripture, I repeat, enforces this great principle everywhere. Let me remind you of another example. In Revelation 3:17 we read what the Spirit said—and indeed it is the Lord himself speaking through the Spirit—to the church of the Laodiceans: "Because thou sayest, I am rich, and increased with goods, and have need of nothing; and knowest not that thou art wretched, and miserable, and poor, and blind, and naked." Why were they like this? The answer is, because they had such a good opinion of themselves. People who think they have need of nothing will never receive God's fullness. People who think they already have it are not open to anything further. And this is the tragedy with so many modern Christians, even evangelical Christians, perhaps particularly so. They think they received everything at the moment of regeneration; there is nothing further to be had, so they just abide on that. That is the condition of the Laodiceans always—"have need of nothing." It is because they do not know that they are "wretched, and miserable, and poor, and blind, and naked."

Or take the statement of the Apostle Paul to the Corinthians. They were proud, puffed up with their knowledge and understanding and gifts and so on. Paul says, "Let him that thinketh he standeth take heed lest he fall" (1 Cor. 10:12).

So there is only one thing for us to do, and that is to heed this exhortation: self must decrease. I gave you some evidence in the previous sermon of how we may know for certain that self is decreasing in us. One is that we have a truer understanding of ourselves. Another is that we are less interested in self, less self-centered, talking less about ourselves and our problems and experiences and so on; everything is not revolving around us. If there is less and less of that, it means that we are decreasing. And the last point I made was, there is less self-reliance, less self-sufficiency, less self-confidence, and I gave you Scriptures to illustrate all that.

Before we proceed there is one further test that I would like to suggest to you. It is a very valuable, very delicate one, and it is this: it is a very good sign that self is decreasing when we live less and less on feelings and more and more by faith. Now we must be careful about this. Thank God for all feelings and experiences in the Christian life; without feeling there is no such thing as Christianity. The gospel takes up the entire person, not just one part of us, not merely our head or our will or our heart. The gospel takes up the whole, the mind and heart and will. And therefore it is an essential part of this Christian life that we have feelings of which we are conscious.

But there is a danger in connection with that, as there is, of course, a danger in connection with everything in this life, and that is all due to the fact that the Devil, the accuser of the brethren, our adversary, will always try to get us sidetracked. He will take a good thing and will make us so concentrate on it that it becomes a bad one, as he did with the brazen serpent with the children of Israel in the Old Testament, and as he has done throughout the centuries with some of the greatest things in the Christian life.

The danger is that of *living* on these things because they have a tendency in and of themselves to inflate self, to give us self-satisfaction, and to make us boastful. Second Corinthians 12 is such a great exposition of this very danger. Paul had had some amazing experiences. He had been lifted up into the third heaven, and he had heard things that are unspeakable and that cannot be repeated. Oh, what an experience, what a wonderful thing!

But then something happened to him—he was given "a thorn in the flesh," and he tells us why: "Lest I should be exalted above measure through the abundance of the revelations, there was given to me a thorn in the flesh, the messenger of Satan to buffet me" (2 Cor. 12:7). So he realizes this danger of being "exalted above measure" because of experiences (2 Cor. 12:7).

The first thing we must learn about the Christian life is that it is constantly a battle, always a calling for watchfullness and care. The Devil is subtle. Paul has been explaining in the previous chapter that the Devil can even transform himself into "an angel of light" (2 Cor. 11:14) and quote Scripture, and he will press us along the line of something that is essentially good to such an extent that it becomes bad and we become lopsided Christians. We lack balance, and eventually we fall to this terrible sin of pride and conceit.

Now the apostle was in that danger. So he had this affliction, and he thanks God for it. He said that God taught him that "My grace is sufficient for thee: for my strength is made perfect in weakness" (2 Cor. 12:9). He increases only as we decrease. It is always the same ruling. "Most gladly therefore will I rather glory in my infirmities, that the power of Christ may rest upon me. Therefore I take pleasure in infirmities, in reproaches, in necessities, in persecutions, in distresses for Christ's sake" (2 Cor. 12:9–10). Here it is again: "For when I am weak, then am I strong" (v. 10). When self has decreased, Christ has increased. This theme runs right through the whole of the New Testament teaching. I therefore put it in the form of a principle in this way: God in his kindness and in his compassion is pleased to give us experiences, conscious feelings, and enjoyment. The danger is, of course, that we live on those and desire to remain like that. It is this great analogy again that runs through the New Testament of being born as a babe and growing, being a child, then becoming a young man, then to middle age, old age, and so on.

Now God does with us in the infancy and the childhood of our spiritual life what parents do with their children. We shower gifts and so on upon them and give them things we know they enjoy. That is the way to handle a child. And the child, of course, wants to go on like that the rest of his life. It is exactly the same in the spiritual realm. We want to go on living on experiential feelings, and that is very bad for us, because feelings come and go; they are very treacherous. "I dare not trust the sweetest frame," says the writer of the hymn.[1] There is nothing stable about feelings. And so one who lives on feelings is doomed eventually to trouble and to disappointment and perhaps to failure. So I say it is a sign of the fact that we are growing and that self is decreasing when we live less and less on what we feel and more and more on our knowledge of Jesus Christ and our faith in him. Again, as the apostle has put it, "We walk by faith, not by sight" (2 Cor. 5:7). And, remember, the "sight" there includes this whole matter of feelings.

Or let me put this to you in another way. It is a sign of our decreasing and his increasing when we have an increasingly greater appreciation of the *graces* produced by the Spirit rather than the *gifts* given by the Spirit. Now these things, of course, should really not be compared, but we are driven to do so because of our tendency to go to extremes with regard to gifts. Was not that the whole essential trouble in the church at Corinth? Is not that the great message, really, of 1 Corinthians 12, 13, and 14? The Spirit gives gifts, thank God for that. But the trouble in Corinth was that they were living on gifts and always talking about them and vying with one another and comparing and contrasting with one another, being jealous of one another or despising one another and so on. And what the Apostle really tells them in effect is: "Yes, these gifts are excellent, they are God-given, they are given by the Spirit. But do not make too much of them. There is something still more important, and that is the graces, 'the fruit of the Spirit'" (Gal. 5:22; Eph. 5:9).

Now this is not to desire the gifts, nor to say that we should not be interested in them. We should. Paul has this perfect balance always. "Follow after charity, and desire spiritual gifts, but rather that ye may prophesy" (1 Cor. 14:1). He is not despising gifts; that would be so wrong. We must not despise any gift; all the gifts are given by the Spirit. But what Paul says is wrong is to lose your balance and to put the gifts before the grace. He puts it like this: "When I was a child, I spake as a child, I understood as a child, I thought as a child: but when I became a man, I put away childish things. For now we see through a glass, darkly; but then face to face: now I know in part; but then shall I know even as also

I am known. And now abideth faith, hope, charity, these three; but the greatest of these is charity" (1 Cor. 13:11–13).

When Paul says, "The greatest of these is charity," he is not depreciating faith and hope. He is saying that charity or love—the love of God shed abroad in our hearts and our love to God—is the profound, the fundamental grace. Why? Because God himself is love, and the measure and the extent to which we are filled with this love and are manifesting it and are concerned about it is the measure of the decreasing of self and the increasing of the Lord in our lives.

Indeed Paul says his argument can be put like this: "Though I speak with the tongues of men and of angels, and have not charity, I am become as sounding brass, or a tinkling cymbal" (1 Cor. 13:1). The Corinthians were talking about these gifts, certain ones in particular, and they were losing balance, going to excesses. Paul says in essence, "The gifts are all right, and you must desire them; but the thing for you to follow after with all the keenness that you are capable of is that you be filled with this love and that your life be governed by it. The fruit of the Spirit after all is greater than the gifts of the Spirit, but naturally we all by nature, with this childlike element in us, follow after the gifts that are spectacular. Gifts are exciting, and we all like excitement, and the less spectacular gifts seem so calm and quiet. It is the difference between a rushing, turbulent mountain stream and a great river flowing deeply, solidly through the plain. So it is a sign of decreasing self when we are more and more concerned about the growth of the graces within us rather than the manifestation of the gifts. There, then, is an additional test for us to bear in mind.

But now I want to go on to something very practical. Self must decrease. This is an absolute; there is no exception to this at all. As I say, the New Testament is full of this teaching; it presses it upon us everywhere. The greatest enemy to my knowledge of Christ and receiving his fullness is this wretched, poor self. Lavater, the hymn writer, said, "Make this poor self grow less and less," and that should be the ambition and the desire of every one of us.

How is that to be done? Is there anything we can do about it? There is a great deal, and the danger is, again, to think that self can be taken out of us in one experience. It cannot. There are experiences, thank God for them again, that take us upon this road a tremendous distance and enable us to run where formerly we were trudging, but still you and I must do many things. There are things prescribed for us that will teach us what to do in order that self may become less and less and continue to decrease until it has gone altogether as it were! No, not in this life, but we must get as near to that as we can.

So what are we to do? These things sound elementary, and yet these are the real answers to this problem. The first is the reading of the Scriptures. Why do I put this first? It is for this reason: ignorance is always the greatest cause of self-conceit and esteem—always. It is the man and woman who know a little who always think they know everything. It is said, "A little learning is a dangerous thing." The more you know, the more you realize what you do not know. So we need knowledge, we need instruction, and this has been provided for us by God in order to instruct us. "All scripture is given by inspiration of God." What for? "For reproof, for correction, for instruction in righteousness," as the apostle Paul tells us in 2 Timothy 3:16.

So if you want to get rid of self, the first rule is, read the Word of God. Read it constantly. I want to emphasize this. There are many ways of reading, not only the Scripture but any book you like. But with Scripture there is nothing more important and more vital than that we should know how to read it. It is the simplest thing in the world to say to people, "Read the Bible," and, of course, they can. I have advocated many methods of reading through the Bible in a given amount of time. I think every Christian should try to read through the Bible once a year at least. But there are dangers even there, and the danger is this: you have your system of Bible reading; you read so many chapters or so many verses each day; you get out your little guide and you say, "Ah, I am going to read this," and you rush through it. Right! Tick it off. Read the Scripture portion for today, and all is well. Or sometimes it is more than that with a little commentary, and you think you have read your Bible and that you know it. But you may be completely ignorant at the end.

We must read the Bible in the Spirit. We need to be prepared to read the Bible; we must pray before we read the Bible; we must pray for the Spirit of God to come upon us. We must "Take time to be holy,"[2] as the hymn says, but we must also take time to read the Bible. I suppose modern men and women need this exhortation more than they need anything else. Why are you reading the Bible? Have you ever asked yourself that question? Are you only reading it because you have been told by somebody to do it, somebody who instructed you? They say, "Every Christian should read the Bible." I agree, but is that your only reason for reading it? Are you reading it merely to say that you have read your daily portion and so you will have completed the Bible in a year?

Indeed let me go further. Are you reading the Bible only so you may have a knowledge of the contents of the Bible so that if somebody says to you, "Well now, what does Genesis teach? What is the teaching of Matthew? Mark? John?" you can give an account of the content? Is that the way in which you read the Bible? My dear friend, that is merely to read the letter, and if you put the letter before the spirit you are missing the whole value of Bible reading. The whole object of reading the Bible is so we may get at the spirit of the teaching and so the spirit of the teaching may get hold of us. And that is why I say it is essential that we should take our time in reading the Bible.

Far too often many of us read our Bible in much the same manner as James tells us that many people look into the perfect law of liberty. You remember how he puts its:

> For if any be a hearer of the word, and not a doer, he is like unto a man beholding his natural face in a glass: for he beholdeth himself, and goeth his way, and straightway forgetteth what manner of man he was. But whoso looketh into the perfect law of liberty, and continueth therein, he being not a forgetful hearer, but a doer of the work, this man shall be blessed in his deed. If any man among you seem to be religious, and bridleth not his tongue, but deceiveth his own heart, this man's religion is vain." (James 1:23–26)

So you can read your Bible and say, "I am a religious man—look at the amount of the Bible I read." But the question is, What does it do to you?

Do you remember in five minutes what you have read? Has the Bible *done* something to you? That is the test of the value of our Bible reading. You see, your mind is on the train you must catch, but you are reading the Bible. But you have not actually read your Scripture at all. You have almost been guilty of blasphemy for approaching it in that way. Take time to look quietly, calmly, persistently into "the perfect law of liberty" (v. 25), and let it examine you and search you. This is the way to get rid of self.

Now if you read the Bible truly, this is what you will discover. You will start by discovering something about the holiness of God. We all think we believe in God, do we not? Many in the world say, "I have always believed in God." But they know nothing about him. They do not believe in him. Stop and examine yourself for a moment. When you say, "I believe in God," what are you saying, what do you mean? This is the thing we say so glibly, but if you read your Bible, you will begin to know something about God—the holiness of God, the greatness and the glory of God.

> Immortal, invisible, God only wise,
> In light inaccessible hid from our eyes,
> Most blessed, most glorious, the Ancient of Days,
> Almighty, victorious, Thy great name we praise.[3]

If you and I knew something about God, we would not behave as we do in his presence, we would not speak about him as we do, we would not indulge in our antics as we do, using his name. If only we grasped the glory of God! "The house was filled with smoke" (Isa. 6:4). Wherever God is, that is what happens. The glory and holiness of God descend upon us.

Now the Bible alone can tell us that. As Paul argues in writing to the Romans, we should be able to deduce all this even from nature. Look at the flowers, or think of the mountains and the valleys, the rivers and the sea, the glory of the sun and the moon and the stars. We ought to be able to deduce the glory of God from them, but we do not. Instead we "worshipped and served the creature more than the Creator, who is blessed for ever" (Rom. 1:25). So it comes to this: it is only this Word that really teaches us about the glory of God, and the more we know about it, the less we will see of ourselves.

And then you go on and read about the Law of God. God has been pleased to reveal it in the Ten Commandments, in his moral law, and in various other forms, and it is only as you familiarize yourself with the teaching of the Bible that you will see it. You have been interested in your experiences and in your gifts and so on, and you are rushing here and there; self has been at the center. But then you read this, and you remember that the God whom you are talking about so glibly and who comes so easily off your lips is this everlasting and eternal Being. And as you read your Bible you hear a voice coming out of it saying to you what was said to Moses at the burning bush: "Draw not nigh hither: put off thy shoes from off thy feet, for the place whereon thou standest is holy ground" (Ex. 3:5). You do not rush in here. God is here—stand back!

Now this is only derived from the teaching of the Bible. It is an increasing knowledge of God in his holiness, in his law, in his justice, and in his righteousness. And then you come across an astonishing statement one day as you are reading your Bible carefully and slowly. David has fallen into sin, and at first, of course, he thinks he can put everything right. But then he realizes who God is and he says, "Thou desirest truth in the inward parts" (Ps. 51:6). That is what God demands, not superficial, glib knowledge. "All things are naked and opened unto the eyes of him with whom we have to do" (Heb. 4:13).

And then you read about the judgment to come—the judgment that God, "the Judge of all the earth" (Gen. 18:25), has appointed—and you realize that you will have to stand before God. This is the thing that humbles us. This is the way to get rid of self. The Apostle Paul says (and he included himself), "We must all appear before the judgment seat of Christ" and give an account of "the things done in his body . . . whether it be good or bad. Knowing therefore the terror of the Lord, we persuade men" (2 Cor. 5:10–11). You see the seriousness, the solemnity, the awe with which Paul presents this. It is because of his knowledge of what is coming.

Now the effect of reading your Bible in that way is—and I am merely giving you this as illustration—that in some shape or form we shall all have the experience that is described in the sixth chapter of the book of the prophet Isaiah. He says, "I saw also the LORD sitting upon a throne, high and lifted up, and his train filled the temple. Above it stood the seraphims: each one had six wings" and so on (Isa. 6:1–2). "And one cried unto another, and said, Holy, holy, holy, is the LORD of hosts: the whole earth is full of his glory. And the posts of the door moved at the voice of him that cried, and the house was filled with smoke" (vv. 3–4). Then there is the reaction. "Then said I [remember this is Isaiah speaking, a priest, a godly religious man], Woe is me! for I am undone; because I am a man of unclean lips, and I dwell in the midst of a people of unclean lips: for mine eyes have seen the King, the LORD of hosts" (v. 5). Once a man or woman gets a glimpse of him, they "decrease"; they are nothing, they are nobody. "Woe is me!" They feel unclean; they feel foul. The Apostle John tells us this at the beginning of his book of Revelation. He has a great vision, and this is the result: "I fell at his feet as dead" (Rev. 1:17). John, the aged apostle! The man of the great experiences! The favorite disciple of the Lord Jesus Christ, the one whom he loved in a special manner! Even John when he sees this says, "I fell at his feet as dead." This is the way to get rid of self, and it is indeed the most direct way to do that.

And then as you read your Bible you read about the saints, you read about the children of Israel, God's chosen people, the people who saw the miracles and wonderful signs in Egypt, the people who were led in a miraculous manner through the Red Sea, the people who were fed with the manna—people with great experiences. At first as you read about them you think these people can never go wrong again. After all, they have seen Pharaoh and his hosts discomfited and the chariots covered by the Red Sea and destroyed. They have had such exhibitions of the greatness and the glory of God that they will never forget it; they will sure be a marvelous people for the rest of their lives.

But are they? As you read the story you see them grumbling and complaining, falling into sin, turning to idolatry, bringing the name of their God into disgrace. And then you turn to the New Testament and you say, "Why was all this written? Why is it important for a Christian to read the Old Testament now that I am in Christ?" "All these things happened unto them for examples" (1 Cor. 10:11). You find the apostles in their epistles to Christian churches quoting what happened to the children of Israel under certain individual men. "All these things happened unto them for examples . . . upon whom the ends of the world are come" (v. 11). And you find that great list of saints in the eleventh chapter of the epistle to the Hebrews and so on. You read your Bible, and you see this revelation of God in his being, in his glory. You find his Law; you get these accounts of his people, and you have these warnings, these examples. You see the saints in their heights and in their depths, and you begin to understand that you are nothing. So your self is rapidly decreasing solely as the result of reading the Scriptures.

What do I put next to reading the Scriptures? Well, next to reading the Scriptures—and remember I have included there that you pray before and after you do so—I would put the lives of the saints. There is no question about this; the lives of the saints are of inestimable value. Nothing has been of such help to me in my little life next to the Bible as to read biographies of the saints of God. Preachers, if you think that you have preached a magnificent sermon, go home and pick up a volume of *George Whitefield's Journals*. You will soon feel, if you are spiritual at all, that you have never preached in your life, that you are nothing, that you do not know what preaching is, that you are almost like "sounding brass, or a tinkling cymbal" (1 Cor. 13:1).

Oh, my dear friends, what fools we are! Read, I say, the lives of God's saints and people throughout the centuries, and then you will see what God can do with a man or woman, what God can make of them. What pygmies we are! There is nothing that is so helpful and valuable in the decreasing of self as to read about these people. You will read about them in the height of their achievements, you will read about them also in their failures, and you will say to yourself, "Who am I? If people like that could fall into error or fall into sin, if men and women like that are fallible, if people like that could be deceived by the Devil, who am I?" You not only read about the saints in the Bible, you read about the saints who have served in the church since then. You see these giants, and you feel you are nothing. You see their failure, and you fly to Christ. "He must increase, but I must decrease" (John 3:30). Who am I? I am nothing and less than nothing. This is the way you do it.

And then another very good thing, I find, is—and it has been advocated so often—meditation on the fleeting character of life and meditation on death and on eternity. Of course, I know that when I say that, I am saying something that is utterly unpopular at the present time. This is something that is practically never indulged in. But there was a time when God's people used to spend a lot of their time meditating on the fleeting nature and character of this life. "The world is too much with us," says Wordsworth.[4] And if this has always been true it is particularly true today. One of the most difficult things in the modern world is to meditate. The world makes us so busy, our agendas are so crowded—newspapers, journals, books, television, radio, meetings, and all this and that. We are here, there, and everywhere, and we never stop and think. Remember how the poet W. H. Davies put it:

What is this life if, full of care,
We have no time to stand and stare?[5]

When did you last "stand and stare" in a spiritual sense? The world keeps us on the rush, and we forget the things that finally matter and finally count. We get excited, we get inflated, our values go all wrong, we do not stop and think. The old hymn is right—we must "Take time to be holy."[6] You will never be holy if you do not take time. It cannot be done. The saints have always been people who have taken time to be holy. And, of course, one of the best ways, I say, of doing this is just to stop and remind yourself of the fleeting nature and character of your life. Edmund Burke, that great English statesman of the eighteenth century, was once campaigning for a special election in Bristol. He had just ascended the platform to deliver an oration when a man handed him a message on a piece of paper. The message was that his opponent had suddenly dropped dead. And Edmund Burke, the great political theorist, the man who wrote so wonderfully on the French Revolution and on the American War of Independence and so on, one of the great political thinkers of all time, this man with his great ideas who had so much to say, when he received that message, did not deliver his great oration. He just said to the crowd, "What phantoms we are, and what phantoms we pursue." We get excited about these things, and eternity is forgotten.

Let old John Bunyan have the final word about this. Bunyan gives us this advice: "If a man would live well let him fetch his last day to him and make it always his company keeper"[7] In the midst of your busyness and your excitement and your feelings, which we all tend to get, believing that the world could not go on without us and that everything would collapse if we were not here to keep it going and to sustain it, remind yourself that you must die and that you must go out of this world, that you will go on into eternity. "Let him fetch his last day to him and make it always his company keeper." Nothing is more calculated to humble us to the very dust and to make us nothing than to realize that we are here today and gone tomorrow. We are not as important as we think. We all need to be told that. And there is nothing that so certainly tells us that and keeps us in the consciousness of that as meditating upon our last day and upon eternity that lies beyond it. I may be wonderful in this world, but what shall I be there? Am I as big as I think I am? When I stand there in that glory, where will I be?

My friends, the world does everything it can to puff up this self of ours. It makes self bigger and bigger and bigger—the modern man and his importance and what he is doing. The antidote to that, in order to get rid of this self, is to meditate upon eternity, to meditate upon the fleeting character of life. "Change and decay in all around I see," as the hymn says.[8] Where are the fathers? They are gone, and you and I are going too. You will see your size when you meditate upon that. In the midst of all your activity always remind yourself of this, and you will get a true sense of proportion, and you will be able to live your life in a better way than you have ever done before.

Then add to this self-examination. "Examine yourselves, whether ye be in the faith" (2 Cor. 13:5). Paul is writing to Christians. He says in essence, "You think you are Christians; you believe you are; you are boasting about your gifts. But examine yourselves—are you really Christians?"

You test that by your graces, by the extent to which you have received God's fullness, not by what you are doing. Examine yourself! Take time!

And then realize the truth that is taught us in the sixth verse of the sixth chapter of the epistle to the Romans: "Our old man is [was] crucified with him." Realize that the only man you are responsible for is the "old man," and he was so bad and so rotten he could not be improved; he had to die. So you have nothing to boast of, do you? All you are now is the "new man" in Christ Jesus. We must learn to say with Paul, "I am crucified with Christ: nevertheless I live; yet not I, but Christ liveth in me: and the life which I now live in the flesh I live by the faith of the Son of God, who loved me, and gave himself for me" (Gal. 2:20). He is saying, "I was that old man. I was a proud Pharisee, and I did things, but I am dead. I have died with Christ." The old man is gone; he is finished with. And anything that you are now or that is in you is entirely the result of the fact that Christ is living in you. So the glory is his and not yours.

So I come to my last word, and this is it: "Let this mind be in you, which was also in Christ Jesus" (Phil. 2:5). That is it. "Look not every man on his own things, but every man also on the things of others" (v. 4), says Paul to the Philippians.

> Let this mind be in you, which was also in Christ Jesus: who, being in the form of God, thought it not robbery to be equal with God [he did not regard that as a prize to be clutched at and to be held on to and to say, "This is mine; I am holding on to it"]: but made himself of no reputation, and took upon him the form of a servant, and was made in the likeness of men: and being found in fashion as a man, he humbled himself, and became obedient unto death, even the death of the cross." (vv. 5–8)

He "made himself of no reputation" (v. 7). How did he do it? Why did he do it? The answers have already been given. He did it by not looking on himself and his own things but on the things of others. He saw us and our need, and for our sakes he "made himself of no reputation."

My dear friends, look to Jesus. "Let this mind be in you, which was also in Christ Jesus" (v. 5). And as that becomes true of us, self will decrease. May the Spirit give us the understanding and the ability to implement these apparently simple things and yet all of which are vital. Oh, let us do these things so that our poor self may become less and less, and so he may increase and we may "receive . . . of his fullness . . . and grace for grace" (John 1:16).

# 21

# He Must Increase

JOHN 3:30

Sunday morning sermon preached in
Westminster Chapel, June 19, 1966.

He must increase, but I must decrease. (John 3:30)

We come back once more to this statement that expresses the very essence of our whole life and position as Christian people, and we are looking at it because it is a principle that runs through the whole Christian life. It is even important at the very beginning of the Christian life. The most difficult thing that every one of us has ever had to do is to realize that we can do nothing. We are anxious to save ourselves—justification by works. We will do anything rather than admit we can do nothing. So at the very entry into the Christian life this is the rule: he is everything, and I become nothing.

But this persists as a principle running through the whole Christian life. After all, Christianity, as we are trying to show, is really what is described in 1:16 of John's Gospel: "And of his fullness have all we received, and grace for [upon] grace." That is what it means to be a Christian—not merely to believe on the Lord Jesus Christ, but to receive of his fullness, to be a part of him, to receive his life ("Christ in you, the hope of glory" [Col. 1:27]), and we are in him.

That is essential Christianity, and the New Testament lays it open before us in all its richness and its greatness, its wonder and its glory. It is to receive of "the unsearchable riches of Christ" (Eph. 3:8). The greatest thing in the universe is the Christian life, Christian salvation. Nothing is so staggering, as one reads the New Testament, as this constant emphasis upon the majesty of it all. Oh, how it dwarfs everything else into insignificance.

But the point we are now making is that the reason why so many of us know so little of this fullness is that we are so full of ourselves. Self, as we have been seeing, is the biggest hindrance to growth in the Christian life and to experiencing the fullness of the Lord Jesus Christ. Self is the first and the last enemy in this respect. It is always there, and this is the very thing, therefore, that is emphasized in this great statement of John the Baptist: "I must decrease" (John 3:30). So we must implement what we are told here by John the Baptist, and so far we have been dealing with the evidences of a decreasing self. We have given the tests that can be applied in order to make sure of that. And in the previous sermon we dealt with some of the things we can do in a very practical way in order to promote the decrease of self.

But now we turn to the other side. The best way, finally, of getting rid of self is allowing Christ to increase. "He must increase, but I must decrease" (v. 30). As I have pointed out, these two things are bound together. So as they are so intimately related to one another, the ultimate way of getting rid of self is to make sure that he is increasing in our lives—in our esteem, in our experience, and in every respect.

Now this does not mean that the negative is not important, for it is—that is why I began with it. We must positively take measures that will lead to the decreasing of self. I am not detracting from that in any way; the negative is essential. But it is not enough. The final way to get rid of self is to see Christ. As he increases, self must and inevitably will decrease.

Thomas Chalmers, one of the great Scottish theologians and church leaders of the early part of the nineteenth century, had a great phrase and a very vital one; he talked about "the expulsive power of a new affection." He meant by this that ultimately the way to get rid of bad affections is to get a good affection; then the good affection pushes out the bad. You can see this as it happens in nature. Ultimately what gets rid of the dead leaves on the trees in the spring is the coming of the new leaves; they finally push off the old dead ones. But, remember, before the new leaf has come, before the bud and the sprouting of anything has happened, there has been a process already loosening the old, dead leaves. And then the new leaf just gives the final push, and off goes the dead one. It is something like that in the spiritual realm.

This negative process is important, and we must never forget it. There is a danger that people think all they need is one positive experience. That is a fallacy. The Bible is full of the negative as well as the positive. It has its precise instructions, and we ignore them at our peril. This negative work of loosening the whole of self must be carried out, as we have seen. But the thing that really brings new life is his increasing.

There are many illustrations of this in the Scriptures, how the sight of him and of something of his glory humbled and humiliated men and really brought them to a true knowledge of themselves, that "poor self" that does us so much harm in our Christian life. We saw how Isaiah had his great vision, and the moment he saw that, he said, "Woe is me! . . . I am a man of unclean lips" (Isa. 6:5). But this is not confined to Isaiah. We see exactly the same thing, and perhaps in an even more dramatic manner, happening to the bold, impulsive Apostle Peter. Peter was always a self-assured, confident man, but one night he and some of his fellow disciples had been out fishing and had caught nothing. So back they came in the morning, most disconsolate, and then our Lord told them what to do. He said,

> "Launch out into the deep, and let down your nets for a draught." And Simon answering said unto him, "Master, we have toiled all the night, and have taken nothing: nevertheless at thy word I will let down the net." And when he had this done, they inclosed a great multitude of fishes: and their net brake. (Luke 5:4–6)

They brought the fish to the land, and then this follows: "When Simon Peter saw it, he fell down at Jesus' knees, saying, Depart from me; for I am a sinful man, O Lord" (v. 8).

Why did he feel that way? Our Lord had not rebuked him for any particular sin; he had not chastened him in any way. What had happened was this: our Lord manifested something of his eternal power and Godhead; he gave just a touch of it. And Peter, realizing Jesus's glory and greatness, felt immediately that he was a sinful man unworthy to even be near such a glorious and great person.

That is the kind of thing that we are looking at together now. One of the most important and greatest things of all in the Christian life is to realize our Lord's greatness. If we are right at this point, we will be right everywhere; if we are wrong here, we shall be constantly in trouble.

Now this was the great ambition of the Apostle Paul—"That I may know him" (Phil. 3:10). In all his work and labors, in his successes, in everything, this is what kept him humble. "Not as though I had already attained" (v. 12)—oh, how much we need it! "That I may know him"— that is the supreme thing in the Christian life, the thing that will keep us right. Putting it negatively, the failure to realize his greatness and the truth concerning him tends to be the greatest cause of trouble in our Christian experience.

Again there are endless examples of this. Take Paul's epistle to the Colossians. Why did he ever write that letter, and why did he write in the way that he did? The answer is that the Colossians were beginning to go astray through philosophy. He puts that quite specifically to them in verse 8 of the second chapter: "Beware lest any man spoil you through philosophy and vain deceit, after the tradition of men, after the rudiments of the world, and not after Christ." A heresy was creeping into the churches, particularly in that part of the world. It was a heresy that consisted of a kind of jumble of philosophy and a bit of the old Jewish law, a teaching of what were called mystery religions. And the effect of this teaching was to make less and less of the Lord Jesus Christ. He was seen as merely one of a great hierarchy of intermediaries between man and God. That is why Paul wrote that letter; they were in trouble about the person of Christ.

Another great letter in the New Testament was written for exactly the same reason, and that is the great epistle to the Hebrews. Here were people again in grievous trouble, depressed, unhappy, discouraged, some of them looking back at their old religion and proposing to go back to it. Why? There is only one answer. They were failing to realize as they should the preeminence of Christ. That was the trouble, and the whole object of the epistle to the Hebrews is really just to show us his preeminence. The writer keeps on saying something like this: "If you only realized the truth about him, you would not only not be in trouble, you would never even dream of looking back. You are looking back because you do not realize who he is and what he is and what he has done. He is not increasing enough in you. You are allowing other things to increase and are allowing him to decrease." That is the whole message of the epistle to the Hebrews.

Here, therefore, is something that is really of the most crucial importance to all of us. Look at the New Testament—our Lord dominates it. Look at the Gospels—they are all about him; he is the center. Look at the epistles—they are all doing the same thing. They are all designed in some way or another to bring out this great truth concerning Jesus Christ. Paul speaks about "the unsearchable riches of Christ" (Eph. 3:8). He wants the Ephesians to know "what is the breadth, and length, and depth, and height; and to know the love of Christ, which passeth knowledge" (Eph. 3:18–19).

As Christian people, are we concerned about that? Is that the thing that is interesting us today? Is this foremost in our thinking and in all our speaking? Are we consumed with a passion to know him in this way, that he might ever have the preeminence over everything and everybody, that he will become the sole object of our desire? This is the thing, I repeat, that leads to receiving his fullness and grace for grace.

Let us look at it positively: "He must increase" (John 3:30). Remember that it is our Lord himself who must increase—he himself. Is he increasing in our lives? Is he dwelling in our hearts richly by faith? And is he continuing to do so more and more, with self decreasing and vanishing? Is this true? What can we do about it?

Let me again start with a negative, and we ignore these negatives, I say once more, at our peril. This, I know, is not liked today. The great slogan today is "We must be positive!" But the Bible is full of negatives, and the creeds are full of negatives. Man will ever go wrong, and he has to be told what is wrong. It must be emphasized. We must grasp the negatives as well as the positives, and there are certain vital negatives here. Let me sum them up in a principle by putting it like this: we must avoid at all costs everything that tends to detract from Christ's greatness—I do not care what it is. Anything that detracts from his greatness and preeminence must be avoided.

What am I talking about? Well, here is an example, and it is very common at the present time. Nothing so detracts from our Lord's greatness, his glory, and his preeminence more than to regard him as just "one among many." A recent service was held in St. Martin's-in-the-Fields [a famous church in London at that time], with Christians (so-called), Muslems, Buddhists, Hindus, Confucianists, and so on all joining together in one service. Not Jesus only. Oh no, we must have Confucius, Buddha, and Mohammed, too.

But, my friends, that detracts from the greatness and glory of Jesus Christ; that causes him to decrease. He is not merely one of the great religious leaders, one of the great teachers. To claim that he is is a lie, and it detracts from his glory. He is alone, and he will not share his glory with any other. But that is a way in which men and women are causing him to decrease in their own estimate, in their own understanding. This idea that you must not be exclusive, that you must not be arrogant in your claims, that you must recognize the good in everything (who are we to say that we alone are right!)—this is modern looseness!

Of course, we are so utterly inconsistent. We are surprised at the immorality of our country; we are surprised at the problems in our country, the lack of discipline that is so evident in industry, politics, and everywhere else. That is because we do not understand. Once you derogate from his supremacy, his preeminence, his supreme glory over all, you must expect what you are getting. If that which calls itself the Christian church mixes with others and joins in Congresses of World Faiths or whatever, if it so pleases them, it is denying the central tenet of the Christian faith. It is causing Christ to decrease. If you put anybody by his side as his equal, you have detracted from him. He is alone.

Another way in which this is done is to supplement him. This is just an extension, of course, of the first one, but sometimes this happens even when there is no mixture of different teachings. Very often there is teaching that supplements what he has done or is doing.

Again you say, "This is all negative." It is negative, but since foolish people look at a man on television and say, "He seems to be a very nice and charming man, and therefore everything he says must be right," I must remind you of negatives. This has been the great sin of the Roman Catholic Church. They supplement Jesus with his own mother. They say we need Mary, that it is only through her that we can get to him. I once entered a Roman Catholic Church, and facing me as I went through the door was Mary. I had to look behind Mary to see the Lord Jesus Christ. That is causing him to decrease; it is even hiding him.

Further, if the priesthood becomes necessary, if the church is essential, if the sacraments are essential in the way that the Roman Catholic Church teaches, if these are essential to salvation, then Jesus is not enough. You must add to him, you must supplement him, as the Galatian heresy was doing by saying that circumcision was essential. If you say that anything is essential apart from Jesus Christ and his work, you are taking away from his greatness and his glory and his preeminence.

These are ways in which that is done. We must be clear in our thinking. That is why Paul writes that majestic first chapter of Colossians. Somebody once wrote a book on it, and this is the title he gave it, very rightly: *Paul amongst the Intellectuals*. The Colossians claim they are intellectuals, but they have gone astray with their great intellects, and Paul puts the truth before them. There is nothing more profound perhaps than that chapter and the parallel chapters and statements in the epistle to the Ephesians. Paul is correcting these errors of adding to Christ, making him one of the intermediaries. Even though you put him on the top, if you add anybody to him you are detracting from him. He is complete in and of himself. He is the Alpha and Omega, the first and the last, the beginning and the end. All is in him; we are complete in him. That is New Testament teaching. If you say that you must have a church or a priesthood or sacraments or anything, you are taking away from his supreme, glorious preeminence.

Another way in which we tend to do this, of course, is to be more interested in what he gives rather than in our Lord himself. Now we must be careful here. Thank God for what he gives. We would all be undone were it not for the gifts he gives us, the gift of salvation—everything. Even faith is a gift. "By grace are ye saved through faith; and that not of yourselves: it is the gift of God" (Eph. 2:8). Oh, the glory, the wonder of God's gifts! But what I am trying to emphasize now is this: it is a terrible thing to be more interested in his gifts than to be interested in him. You know what you feel about the kind of person who, while pretending to be interested in you, at the same time makes it perfectly clear that his sole interest in you is what he can get from you or get out of you. There is nothing more insulting to a person than to be more interested in what the person gives than in the person himself or herself. That is using people to get something we want from them, and we are all very guilty of this.

I remember a statement made by our friend William Nagenda from Africa. On his first visit to this country he had gone around telling something of the story of the revival that they had experienced in his part of Africa. Then a year or two passed, and he came back on a second visit, and he told me, "I had a very strong conviction that this time I should not go around the country just telling people about the revival. I felt I must preach the Lord Jesus Christ to them. But," he said, "do you know what is happening as a result? People come to me at the end of a meeting and say, 'Thank you for your message, but we had hoped and thought that you were going to tell us a bit more about the revival.' You see, they do not want to hear about Jesus—they want to be entertained by stories about the revival."

So you see that even that detracts from Jesus. If ever you and I get into a state or condition in which we are more interested in the thrilling and exciting stories about conversions than in our Lord who produces them, we have already detracted from his glory; we are causing him to decrease. We are saying, "Yes, we know about Jesus, but we want to hear about the revival." My dear friend, may God save every one of us from pushing aside Jesus because of our interest in the gifts that he gives us and the things that he does.

There is another way in which we are often guilty of causing him to decrease, as it were, in his influence in our lives and in our experience. We become more interested in our knowledge of the truths concerning him than we are in him. This is the besetting sin of theologians. This is always the trouble with more intellectual Christians. They are all about him, explaining him and his person, the teaching about him. You can grapple with the profundities of the epistles to the Ephesians and the Colossians—there is nothing more profound in the whole of literature than those two epistles—and you study them and you discover the meaning of each term and word. You read books about them, and you have great knowledge, but you have forgotten all about Jesus. You may have been so busy reading that you have even stopped praying to him. You are not interested in him as a person. He becomes just an idea, a center of a great group of thoughts and concepts, but you have lost him—the living person!

But the experience of knowing him is *living*, it is real. It is his *fullness*—not a knowledge about him, but he himself. Here is this terrible danger that he may decrease in us and that we increase in our pride of knowledge and of understanding and of ability to handle these great and wonderful doctrines. May God preserve us from these subtle errors and temptations! What is better than knowledge? If our knowledge of theology does not lead us to know more of him personally, may God have mercy upon us and all our theology! It can be our greatest curse. The Devil is always there to lead us astray.

Finally, I would say that another way in which we are often guilty of decreasing him is to be overconcerned even about activities in his name. We should test ourselves day by day. What matters is not what have I done but what has he been to me. Our Lord himself gives us a tremendous warning about this, one of the most solemn things he ever said. It is at the end of the Sermon on the Mount in Matthew 7:

> Not every one that saith unto me, Lord, Lord, shall enter into the
> kingdom of heaven; but he that doeth the will of my Father which
> is in heaven. Many will say to me in that day, Lord, Lord, have we

not prophesied in thy name? and in thy name have cast out devils? and in thy name done many wonderful works? And then will I profess unto them, I never knew you: depart from me, ye that work iniquity." (vv. 21–23)

They thought they were doing things in his name, but they were so interested in their own activities that he was not there. They had not known him, and he had not known them. This is a terrible thing, but these are the warnings of Scripture to us, these negative warnings that stand before us all. So the question is: Where does he come in—he himself, this blessed person? Anything that obtrudes itself between you and him causes him to decrease and causes you therefore to increase.

There, then, are the negatives; let us hurry on to the positives.

Having avoided these things that tend in that way to detract from his supreme preeminence—I do not care what they are, they have no right to stand between me and him and must be brushed aside so that I may see him and know him—what am I to do positively? I do not know of a better method than the method adopted by the author of the epistle to the Hebrews. As I have said, the man's whole object in writing was to bring out the preeminence of Christ and to show these foolish people, who were toying with the thought of going back to the temple and the old Jewish rituals and ceremonies, that all their troubles were due to the fact that they had forgotten the things they had been taught. He tells them, "Therefore we ought to give the more earnest heed to the things which we have heard, lest at any time we should let them slip," or "we should slip away from them" (Heb. 2:1). That is what they were doing.

So what the writer has to say to them in effect is: "Take all that you are proposing to go back to and then put them side by side with Christ, and you will find that they will vanish as nothing and he will go on increasing, He will stand out in all his unique glory." This is his method. He compares the Lord Jesus Christ with prophets, with angels, with Moses, with Aaron and all the priests, and he shows that the moment you do that you see how foolish you have been and you see how he stands alone.

The author of Hebrews is so full of this that he bursts out at the very beginning of his epistle. There is no preliminary salutation, nothing like that at all. He just bursts out, "God, who at sundry times and in divers manners spake in time past unto the fathers by the prophets, hath in these last days spoken unto us by his Son" (1:1). That is it. He has thrown down the gauntlet. He says, "It is the Son that you have forgotten." He proceeds then to hold up the Son of God and to contrast all these others with him—the prophets, angels, Moses, Aaron, and so on—to show who he is and what he is.

And that is the way that you and I must follow if we want to be sure that Christ is increasing in us and that we go on to receive his fullness and grace upon grace. This is what the writer of Hebrews says. He says in summary, "He alone is great if you look at him in his person. He is essentially great." You and I are so interested in ourselves and in our little aches and pains and always talking about them because we do not know him. We are instructed that we are to help one another, to bear one another's burdens. But if a church does only that, it is missing the great and glorious truth that it is to declare Christ, to look at him, to bring people to knowledge of him. This is the supreme thing we can say, "That I may know him," and we start by looking at his person and looking at him as he is essentially.

Then the writer of Hebrews continues, "Hath in these last days spoken unto us by his Son, whom he hath appointed heir of all things, by whom also he made the worlds; who being the brightness of his glory, and the express image of his person, and upholding all things by the word of his power . . ." (vv. 1–3). Here is the essential description of him. These people want to go back to the prophets; they want to go back and talk about angels; they want to discuss Moses. Moses is wonderful. Moses's teaching, Aaron, the priesthood, the sacrifices, the ceremonies, the rituals—these are the things they want. "Stop and look at him again," says this man, "the Son of God!" He goes on to put this in specific language. "Being made so much better than the angels, as he hath by inheritance obtained a more excellent name than they. For unto which of the angels said he at any time, Thou art my Son, this day have I begotten thee? And again, I will be to him a Father, and he shall be to be a Son?" (vv. 4–5).

Have we had a glimpse of this person? He is the very effulgence of the glory of God, the express image of his person. He is full of the glory of God. John has already reminded us of that: "We beheld his glory, the glory as of the only begotten of the Father, full of grace and truth" (John 1:14). My dear friends, this is our supreme need, to know him, this blessed person, to have just a glimpse of this glory that is described there. "Thou art my Son" (Acts 13:33). Again John has spoken of this: "In the beginning was the Word, and the Word was with God, and the Word was God" (John 1:1). Think of his eternality! "In the beginning"—which means there was no beginning for him; when the beginning of creation happened, he already was. He was always there. He is coequal, coeternal with the Father. He was always "with God." Or as one of those verses can be translated, "He was looking eternally into the face of the Father" because he and the Father are one.

Then think of his eternal holiness. All the attributes of God are in him. He is the second person in the blessed holy Trinity. So he is eternally holy. That is why the archangel in announcing his birth to Mary, his physical mother, said, "That holy thing which shall be born of thee" (Luke 1:35). "That holy thing"! You cannot speak of men like this. What is the use of talking to me about Moses and Aaron or about the prophets or about anybody? Only Jesus can be called "that holy thing"! "Such an high priest became us," says this man later on, "who is holy, harmless, undefiled, separate from sinners" (Heb. 7:26).

My friends, am I boring you? Perhaps you object, "We are living in a difficult world, you know. There is a strike on, and the whole country might be in jeopardy. I want a bit of comfort." Is that your feeling? Am I boring you by describing this blessed person? If I am, I venture to suggest to you that you have never been a Christian at all. If you do not like to hear about him, if you are not more thrilled by hearing about this person, "the brightness of [God's] glory," than in anything else in the universe, I say you had better examine your foundations again. If this does not move you and excite you with a holy excitement and thrill you with rapture and a sense of glory, I say again, go on your knees and ask Jesus Christ to manifest himself to you, ask God to give you the unction and the anointing of the Spirit.

Christians are those who delight to think of Jesus and to mediate concerning him, and the more they hear about him and his glory and his greatness, the happier they are. That is the whole endeavor of these New Testament writers. This is Paul's supreme ambition: "That I may know him" (Phil. 3:10). Paul was saying, "I know so much, but oh, the depths that I do not know!" This is what is moving him and thrilling his mighty being. Is this true of us? That is how Jesus Christ increases. We need to be clear as to his essential being: "I and my Father are one" (John 10:30). "He that hath seen me hath seen the Father" (John 14:9). We see his blessed person, our Savior, the One in whom we claim to believe. It is because we know so little about his essential greatness that we are interested in getting this-that-and-the-other from him. Stop for a moment; forget everything and just desire to look at him and to see something of him as he is in his everlasting glory.

And then think of his great work in creation. Notice how the writer of Hebrews slips this in at once: "Hath in these last days spoken unto us by his Son, whom he hath appointed heir of all things, by whom also he made the worlds" (Heb. 1:2). Paul in writing to the Colossians says exactly the same thing. John in the prologue to his Gospel says, "All things were made by him; and without him was not any thing made that was made" (John 1:3). "All things"! The author of Hebrews says in effect, "You want to talk about angels? Jesus made the angels!" "And of the angels he saith, Who maketh his angels spirits, and his ministers a flame of fire" (Heb. 1:7). He made the angels; he made everything. Going back to John, "Without him was not any thing made that was made" (John 1:3)—angels included and all the heavenly beings. He is the author of them all.

Not only that, Paul reminds the Colossians that all things were made for him. The universe was made for the Lord Jesus Christ, "whom he hath appointed heir of all things" (Heb. 1:2). Yes, God made the world for him, and he will inherit the world. It is all "for him" (Col. 1:16). The Father gives it as his love gift to his Son. That is why Jesus Christ is the Mediator. And that is why Paul tells the Ephesians, in perhaps the greatest statement of all, in the tenth verse of the first chapter, "that in the dispensation of the fullness of times he might gather together in one all things in Christ, both which are in heaven, and which are on earth; even in him."

Oh, that we had some conception of all this! Not only were all things made by him and for him, but by him all things consist; all things are held together by him. Were it not for our blessed Lord the universe would collapse; it would disintegrate. He upholds "all things by the word of his power" (Heb. 1:3). He is the Master of the house, says the Word. The author of Hebrews says in effect, "You are talking about Moses, you Hebrew Christians, you Jews. You are ridiculous." Hebrews 3 tells us, "Wherefore, holy brethren, partakers of the heavenly calling, consider the Apostle and High Priest of our profession, Christ Jesus; who was faithful to him that appointed him, as also Moses was faithful in all his house" (vv. 1–2). Listen now!

> For this man was counted worthy of more glory than Moses, inasmuch as he who hath builded the house hath more honour than the house. For every house is builded by some man; but he that built all things is God. And Moses verily was faithful in all his house, as a servant, for a testimony of those things which were to be spoken after; but Christ as a son over his own house; whose house are we, if we hold fast the confidence and the rejoicing of the hope firm unto the end. (vv. 3–6)

Do you see what he is doing? He is writing to Hebrew Christians who were depressed and unhappy and disconsolate because they were being persecuted and were being tried. They were having a hard time, and they felt they needed sympathy and a little bit of help and this and that. "No, no," says this man. "All your troubles are due to the fact that you have taken your eyes off him. He has decreased in your estimate and in your experience, and you are looking back to angels and to Moses and to Aaron. He is the Son over all. Moses was a good servant but nothing but a servant. The builder of the house is greater than the house. So let us remind ourselves of this."

Think, too, of his eternal knowledge. "God, who at sundry times and in divers manners spake in time past unto the fathers by the prophets . . ."

(Heb. 1:1). The prophets are the people they wanted to go back to, to the Old Testament; they wanted to go back to the Jewish teaching. They said that was marvelous and wonderful, and it spoke to their condition; they wanted to go back to that. Listen, says this man, that was only parts and portions, that was bits and pieces. They were all given by God, but add them all together and you have only bits and pieces, parts and portions. But the God who did that in the past "hath in these last days spoken unto us by his Son" (v. 2). He has spoken the last word; there is nothing more. "In him dwelleth all the fullness of the Godhead bodily," says Paul (Col. 2:9). And the Son says, "I am the light of the world" (John 8:12). "He that hath seen me hath seen the Father" (John 14:9). He is the One "in whom are hid all the treasures of wisdom and knowledge" (Col. 2:3). "It pleased the Father that in him should all fullness dwell" (Col. 1:19).

Is this what you are after, to know this blessed person? When you think of him as your Savior, do you think of him or just the fact that your sins have been forgiven? That is the way we test ourselves. If you are more interested in the forgiveness of your sins than in him, I will grant that you are a Christian, but you are a very poor one, and you know nothing about his fullness. Oh, that we might realize who this blessed, glorious person is, this One whom we call Savior and Redeemer because he is!

It is only as you start by realizing who he is that you begin to understand what he has done. You know nothing about his love until you know who he is, what he is, his essential being—"The brightness of [God's] glory, and the express image of his person" (Heb. 1:3). Oh, the glory of the Lord Jesus Christ, his supreme preeminence. "Light of the world! forever, ever shining," as the hymn says.[1] "Jesus Christ, the same yesterday, and today, and for ever" (13:8). Is he increasing in your sight, in your estimate, in your affections, in the whole of your being? If he is, you are blessed of God. If he is not, humble yourself at his feet and ask the blessed Spirit of God who has been sent, yes, to give us gifts, but preeminently and above all else to glorify Jesus, to reveal him to you and your wondering gaze.

# 22

# Is He Everything?

JOHN 3:30

Sunday morning sermon preached in
Westminster Chapel, June 26, 1966.

The words to which I would like to call your attention are found in the Gospel according to St. John in the third chapter and the thirtieth verse: "He must increase, but I must decrease."

We come back to this great statement of John the Baptist once more because it enshrines within itself the great and most important principle in connection with the Christian life that you and I can ever learn. John speaks it in the particular historical setting that is described in this chapter. John's disciples had lost their heads a bit and had become jealous of the Lord Jesus Christ and wanted John to assert himself, and this is how John answered them. They were just showing their ignorance, their lack of spiritual understanding. "He must increase, but I must decrease."

We have been considering together this principle that governs the whole Christian life. If you have any confidence whatsoever in yourself or in the flesh, you are not a Christian, you are outside. Paul says to the Philippians, "We are the circumcision" (Phil. 3:3). What are the characteristics of such people? They "worship God in the spirit, and rejoice in Christ Jesus, and have no confidence in the flesh" (Phil. 3:3). So that is the way in which you enter into this life. You see that you are nothing.

You see the uselessness of all your good deeds; they are all dung and loss and refuse, filthy rags, with no value at all. You become nothing; he is everything.

But you not only start in the Christian life like that, you must continue like that. The Devil appeals to self, and self is the greatest curse in our lives. The most devastating thing that sin and the fall have done to us all was introducing this element of self—self-centeredness, self-righteousness, self-protection, and self-concern. Self can become so important and so inflated as even to hide the Lord himself. So this principle governs the whole of our lives. It was the cause of trouble in the church at Philippi. That was obviously a good church, a church that the Apostle loved, and yet there was trouble there because of this. So he exhorted them "Look not every man on his own things, but every man also on the things of others" (2:4). They were self-centered, self-concerned, and two women, Euodias and Syntyche, had quarreled and formed parties in the church. The answer to all that kind of problem is given us in this great statement: "He must increase, but I must decrease" (John 3:30).

Christianity, as we have been seeing, means receiving his blessed fullness, and more and more of it as you go on. Is this true of us? If it is not, probably the main explanation is that self is standing in the way. We have been considering what we can do about this, and we have started with the negative that self must "decrease." We have shown the indications of a decreasing self, and we have considered some of the practical measures we can take in order to hasten the death and the end of this poor self.

Then we began last time to look at the positive because the two things are interrelated. As he increases, we inevitably decrease. So we must look at the two sides, and looking at the positive we have seen that we must gaze at him. This is the ultimate secret of it all. This is the way in which we can make sure that he does and will increase in our minds, in our thoughts, in our estimate, in our hearts, in our love, and in the whole of our being, until we are finally lost in him and self has vanished altogether.

How can we so look at him that he may "increase" in every way in our lives and experiences? We began by seeing the preeminence of Christ, by looking at him in his essential being as the eternal and everlasting Son of God, coequal and coeternal with the Father, the One in whom all the fullness dwells and who has all knowledge, who is the light and the life of men and of the world.

But we cannot leave it at that. We want to go a step further now. So let us try to look at his greatness as it has been revealed to us in what he has done. This is in many ways the leading theme of the New Testament. The four Gospels were written in order to show men and women and to establish and fix once and forever our Lord's true greatness and glory. Take the Gospel of John. Why was he led by the Spirit to write it? He tells us himself at the end of chapter 20: "And many other signs truly did Jesus in the presence of his disciples, which are not written in this book: but these are written, that ye might believe that Jesus is the Christ, the Son of God; and that believing ye might have life through his name" (vv. 30–31).

Now it is generally agreed that the motive behind this Gospel is in contradistinction to that of John's first epistle, which was probably written in order to establish the fact that the eternal Son of God had truly been "made flesh" (John 1:14). There has been heresy, false teaching, in the church from the very beginning. There is nothing new about false teaching. The idea that notorious gentlemen today with their "new theology" are saying something new is just childish. It had all been said in the first century. And John wrote his first epistle in order to establish the fact that Jesus Christ had come "in the flesh," that he was not a phantom or a mere appearance, that the incarnation was indeed a fact.

But the motive behind the Gospel of John is a different one; it is almost the exact opposite. These heresies always go together. Some say that our Lord is God and that he merely took the "appearance" of man. But the greater, more common heresy is that he is nothing but a man, that Jesus of Nazareth was only a man like other men—a great man, a great religious genius, even a political genius, some would say. John wrote his Gospel specifically for this reason, to show that Jesus of Nazareth is the eternal Son of God. So he bursts upon us at the very beginning, "In the beginning was the Word . . ." (John 1:1). Oh, the glory of Christ! That is the whole object of this Gospel, as it is, indeed, the object of all the other Gospels.

We must remember that the church had been in existence before the Gospels were written. There were many years when the church did not have them. So why were they written? They were written, first, because it was essential to establish the facts concerning our Lord lest Christianity become nothing but a philosophy. But, second, they were written in order to bring out the glory of his person and his being and the glory of what he had done, to show the greatness of this "so great salvation" (Heb. 2:3). That is the object of the Gospels, and this has always been the leading theme in all times of reformation and revival as well. The emphasis has always been upon Christ and upon his greatness and his glory. What happens in a revival, always, is that he "increases."

This is a very wonderful thing. As you read your New Testament, you find that the four Gospels are devoted entirely to him. Then you read the book of Acts and the epistles and even the book of Revelation. And what do you find? You will find (if one may use such terms) that all the great and astounding passages are always those in which he is mentioned and in which his glory shines forth. Watch the Apostle Paul in particular. Paul has a great pastoral heart. He writes most of his letters in order to deal with difficulties and with problems, but he can never do that without mentioning this person. And the moment he does that, he takes wings as it were, and all the brilliance and the glory and the splendor of his writing and his language burst upon us. That is so typical of the writing of the great apostle. "Whatever the problems, whatever the difficulties," he seems to say, "the answer is to get to know him, to look away from yourselves, to look at him." "Looking unto Jesus"—that is the great theme always.

That is what you find when you read the New Testament. And as you note the subsequent history of the church, you will always find the same thing. Read the hymns in a hymnbook, and you will find they can be classified in several ways. But there is one very important classification, and it is this one: hymns that deal with the greatness and the glory of God (the Father, the Son, and the Holy Spirit) and hymns that look into us and our moods and feelings and states. What a contrast! The great hymns are always the objective hymns, the hymns about God. Some of the greatest hymns in the hymnbook are those of Isaac Watts, Charles Wesley, Robert Robinson, and many others. Keep your eye on them. For example, Robert Robinson writes:

> Mighty God, while angels bless Thee,
> May a mortal sing Thy name?

Then he goes on to describe him in all the fullness and the splendor of his glory.

> Through Thine empire's wide domain,
> Wings an angel, guides a sparrow,
> Blessed be Thy gentle reign. . . .
> From the highest throne of glory
> To the cross of deepest woe.[1]

What is Robinson doing? He is expressing in that wonderful poetry something of the greatness, the majesty, the glory of the Son of God. "He must increase . . ." and that is the way in which he does increase. You look at him, and you consider the truth concerning him.

So let us also do this in the way it is done in the New Testament. Perhaps you are facing some great problem, some grievous difficulty, and you prefer that I would deal with that particular problem or a particular sin that gets you down, that anxiety, that worry, or that neighbor, husband, wife, or child. Perhaps you want help for that, and you are thinking, "I hope he is not going to just preach on the Lord Jesus Christ. I hope he is going to deal with my problem. I hope he will be practical." My dear friend, what a fallacy! If you but know him, your problems will not long be problems for you. He is the solution to every problem, and our fundamental need always is to know him. Problems are dealt with in the Scripture, but the great emphasis of the Scripture is the person of our Lord and what he has done. Is he big, is he great, is he glorious in your esteem?

Let me put it like this: Do you think and feel you know all about the Lord Jesus Christ? You say, "I know all about that. I don't want you to go over all that again. I have known that since I was a child." That is a fallacy! You have to meditate upon these things; you have to measure them, "the breadth, and length, and depth, and height" (Eph. 3:18). There is no end to it. You go on looking at him and contemplating him and considering him, and he grows and increases. Oh, the trouble with all of us is that we do not know him. It is our ignorance of him that accounts for most of our problems and all our failures.

I am taking you over facts that appear to be well-known, but let us pray that God the Spirit will give us eyes and understanding, that we may truly realize them and know that he has done all these things for us and for our salvation. That is what we need to know. "That I may know him, and the power of his resurrection" (Phil. 3:10). So let us continue to look at him. We have considered him in his essential greatness and glory, but if you really want to try to measure these, if you want him to increase in your whole outlook, look at what he has done, look at his self-abasement, his self-humbling.

There are many statements of this in the Scriptures. I do not want to stay with any one of them. I just want now to put these great salient facts before you. We have already emphasized the first fact: "Who, being in the form of God, thought it not robbery to be equal with God" (Phil. 2:6). He is God. He always has been God. He is God the eternal Son, coequal and coeternal with the Father.

Do you want to know what true greatness is? Do you want to see something of the majesty and the glory of the person of our Lord? Here it is: "Who, being in the form of God, thought it not robbery to be equal with God" (Phil. 2:6). That is an unfortunate translation. It means, "He regarded not his equality with God as a prize to be held on to and to be clutched at all costs." Rather, he "made himself of no reputation." Words are utterly, ridiculously inadequate! There was an attempt at the turn of the century to change that translation into "He emptied himself." That is wrong! He could not empty himself of the Godhead. That is a contradiction in terms; it is a sheer impossibility. He did not empty himself. What he did—and it is much more marvelous, much more glorious—was to divest himself of the signs, the insignia, the manifestations of that eternal glory that he had shared from eternity with the Father.

You read at times of a king traveling incognito or of some great person traveling as a private individual, calling himself Mr. Smith or something like that. That is what our Lord did. He is the eternal Son of God, the effulgence of the glory of God, always a part of his being. He somehow— I say somehow because it was a miracle—stripped himself of that. He remains the eternal Son of God everlastingly. He cannot change himself. God cannot deny himself. God cannot empty himself of deity. The glory, the marvel, the mystery of the incarnation is that, remaining God in all the fullness of the term, he "made himself of no reputation." He was born as a baby "and took upon him the form of a servant, and was made in the likeness of men" (Phil. 2:7). That is it. He was in the likeness of God, but he came into the world in the likeness of men.

Now here is the measure of the glory of our Lord's person. He did all this so that you and I might be redeemed, that we might be delivered from hell and the punishment we so richly deserve, that we might be made the children of God and heirs of eternal bliss. From the highest courts of glory, from the equality, from looking into the face of God, the Son humbled himself from the glory everlasting to the virgin's womb. Not to a palace, not to a mansion, not to wealth and riches and the world at its best, but to abject poverty, born in a stable with cattle and straw, a helpless baby, in utter weakness.

Now this, remember, is the One by whom "all things were made . . . and without him was not any thing made that was made" (John 1:3). That is what we are told in all those statements about him and his part in the original creation. We are told that he upholds "all things by the word of his power" (Heb. 1:3). But there he is, a helpless baby, being handled by human hands. He can do nothing for himself. I repeat, words are useless, and imagination is equally useless. We need the Spirit of God to give us a mind and an understanding to contemplate such a thing. This is how Jesus increases when we see something of who he is and what he has done. He was made "in the likeness of men" (Phil. 2:7). Indeed the apostle Paul, in writing to the Romans says he was made "in the likeness of sinful flesh" (8:3). That does not mean that he was a sinner—he was not. His human nature was not sinful; he was made in the *likeness* of sinful flesh.

But the great fact we must grasp is that because of his greatness and his glory, he humbled himself even to that. The greater the man, the more humble he is. But here is the acme of it all; here is One who is in a class of his own. There is nothing comparable to this—from the highest courts of heaven to the stable in Bethlehem. He came into the world as a man, and he lived as a man while still God. This is the marvel; this is the mystery. This is the truth that should ravish our hearts and move us to the depth of our being, that he actually has done all this.

The purpose of the four Gospels is to bring home to us that though he was still God in the fullest sense of the word, he did not use and employ the attributes of the Godhead. He lived as a man. That is why he found it essential to pray; that is why he needed to be baptized with the Spirit when he began his public ministry. When he was baptized by John in the Jordan, the Spirit came upon him, and he said later when speaking in the synagogue in Nazareth, "The Spirit of the Lord is upon me, because he hath anointed me" (Luke 4:18). That was necessary because though he is God eternal, the Son of God, he chose to live as a man. He has "made himself of no reputation" (Phil. 2:7). He has assumed the form of a man, the "likeness" of a man, and even "the form of a servant" (v. 7). He says again, "I speak not of myself, but the Father who sent me has given me these words. The works that I do, I do not myself, but the Father who sent me has given me these works to do." Toward the beginning of his great High Priestly Prayer he tells the Father, "I have finished the work which thou gavest me to do" (John 17:4). He has become a man. He has made himself of no reputation. He has come into the world to live as a man among men and so is utterly dependent upon his Father and upon the Spirit. This is a marvelous, wonderful truth, and it was all done so that you and I might be the children of God.

His baptism is also significant. Why was he baptized? From the human standpoint and from the lack of understanding that is characteristic of all of us, John the Baptist rightly objected to this. Our Lord came to John to be baptized, as so many were at that time, and John demurred and said, "I have need to be baptized of thee" (Matt. 3:14). That is, "I cannot baptize you; you ought to be baptizing me." And our

Lord's reply to John was, "Suffer it to be so now: for thus it becometh us to fulfill all righteousness" (v. 15).

What does this mean? Have you analyzed that story, have you considered it, have you realized exactly what it is conveying to us? Why did Jesus insist on being baptized, as all these others were being baptized, by John the Baptist? This is an amazing thing—it is here that he identifies himself not only with us but with our sins. We are always in a hurry and so busy these days. We have so much to do; we have no time to think and to meditate. We rush from meeting to meeting, and we think we know all about Christian truth. But we do not know as we should the very elements of the Christian faith, and here is one of them.

Why was Jesus baptized? The apostle Paul answers the question by putting it like this: "When the fullness of the time was come, God sent forth his Son, made of a woman, [yes, but also] made under the law, to redeem them that were under the law" (Gal. 4:4–5). "Under the law." He is the Lawgiver! He is the One who gives the Law. He gave it to Moses through the mediation of angels, and yet he is born "under the law." Cannot you see what is happening? He is identifying himself with us; he is taking his stand with us. And he is doing so in a literal manner. He is standing shoulder to shoulder with sinners. He has put himself into a position where our burden becomes his burden. He is "under the law." The Law makes demands on him as a man. He is subject to it as we are. And that is the essential meaning of his baptism by John the Baptist.

But oh, let us remember who it is who is being baptized. He is the Son of God, "holy, harmless, undefiled, separate from sinners" (Heb. 7:26). He is the Holy One, and yet he submits to baptism and is under the law. He is in the position of transgressors, and he does it deliberately.

These are the facts on which you and I need to concentrate and meditate. Forget yourself and your problem, decrease, get out of sight. Look at him! This is Christianity, this is Christian salvation—this person and what he has done. His baptism gives us an insight into that.

But there is something even more extraordinary. He was subject to temptation. Why is that surprising? James reminds us, rightly, in chapter 1 of his epistle, verse 13, "God cannot be tempted with evil." It is impossible. "God cannot be tempted with evil, neither tempteth he any man." He is eternally the opposite of evil; evil is abhorrent to him. He hates it with all the intensity of his divine nature. "God cannot be tempted with evil." The Son of God is coequal and coeternal with the Father, and yet we read in the epistle to the Hebrews what we have already read in detail in the Gospels: "In that he himself hath suffered being tempted, he is able to succour them that are tempted" (Heb. 2:18). "We have not an high priest which cannot be touched with the feeling of our infirmities; but was in all points tempted like as we are, yet without sin" (4:15).

My dear friend, are you having a hard time? Are things going against you? Are people unkind to you? Are they cruel to you? Are they hindering you? Are they molesting you? Are they persecuting you? Are you in difficulties? Are you in trouble? Here is the answer: look at the Son of God, the everlasting God, who was "in all points tempted like as we are" (v. 15). He knows all about it. The author of Hebrews expands that thought in the fifth chapter of his great epistle. He says it is essential that the one who should help us and be our great High Priest should be one who can sympathize with our infirmities, and our blessed Lord can do that! He knows what it is to be tried and tested by men and troubled. We are told in the epistle to the Hebrews that he "endured such contradiction of sinners against himself" (12:3).

We know something about the contradiction of sinners against us, do we not? But when we consider him, we know nothing at all. Listen to the way the author of Hebrews puts it again in the fifth chapter:

> Who in the days of his flesh, when he had offered up prayers and supplications with strong crying and tears unto him that was able to save him from death, and was heard in that he feared; though he were a Son, yet learned he obedience by the things which he suffered; and being made perfect [in that respect], he became the author of eternal salvation unto all them that obey him. (5:7–9)

Now I hope that if I am doing nothing else I am introducing you to a great principle, and the principle, I repeat again, is this: the author wrote the letter to these Hebrew Christians because they were having practical difficulties and problems. They were being persecuted, they had been robbed of their goods, they had been molested, and some of them had even been put to death. So they were cast down. So what does the writer do, how does he help them? Does he just pat them on the back and say, "Cheer up, things are going to be better" or just make them forget their troubles for the moment by singing and singing until they all feel wonderful? No! He hurls at them this mighty theology, this great discourse upon the Lord Jesus Christ as "priest for ever after the order of Melchisedec" (v. 6).

That is the answer! Look unto Jesus, he says. Do not look at yourselves or these other people or your problems or your difficulties. Get right about him. If he increases in your estimate, these other things will be nothing to you. And that is still the answer. So if he is to increase, we must consider these things in detail. He was "in all points tempted like as we are, yet without sin" (Heb. 4:15). He was "touched with the feeling of our infirmities" (v. 15).

In every pang that rends the heart,
The Man of Sorrows had a part.[2]

He has taken our human nature up into the heavens. It is in him there, and he knows all about us. What we need is that he should increase, and this is the way in which he does so. As you look at what he has done, you go through all these things and try to enter into the depth of their meaning and their teaching.

So let me take you a step further. Look at our Lord's amazing obedience and submission to the Father. Though they are coequal and though they are coeternal, "being found in fashion as a man, he humbled himself, and became obedient unto death, even the death of the cross" (Phil. 2:8). There is nothing more marvelous than the subordination of the Son to the Father and the subordination of the Holy Spirit to the Father and the Son. But look at the supreme example of this in the garden of Gethsemane. He has chosen three of his disciples to be with him, Peter and James and John. They always constituted a kind of inner circle, and at moments of crisis or of unusual importance they were the men who were always singled out, and there they are with him in the garden. He says to them in essence, "Stay here for a moment and pray while I go on." He is facing the ultimate crisis. But they sleep. "The spirit . . . is willing, but the flesh is weak" (Matt. 26:41). There he is alone, and he is in agony, and he is sweating great drops of blood. Can we conceive of such an agony? The Son of God, the Creator of the universe, the spotless One, the Holy One, the One who owns all things and for whom the whole creation was made is sweating great drops of blood in an agony of soul.

Why is this? We are given the answer. He is praying, "O my Father, if it be possible, let this cup pass from me." Then he hastens to add, "Nevertheless not as I will, but as thou wilt" (Matt. 26:39). He knows what salvation for men is going to cost him; it will cost him separation from the face of God. He was not shrinking from physical death; that is a foolish, monstrous suggestion. The martyrs have not done that, and he is greater than all martyrs. He who had from eternity enjoyed perfect fellowship with the Father saw that man's sin was coming between them and that there would be a terrible moment when he would not be able to look into the face of God. He said in effect, "Is there no other way? Cannot men and women be saved by some other method? Must it come to this? 'If it be possible, let this cup pass from me.' But if there is no other way, I will go on with it: 'nevertheless not as I will, but as thou wilt.'" This was utter obedience to the Father. "Being found in fashion as a man, he humbled himself, and became obedient unto death, even the death of the cross" (Phil. 2:8).

Watch him a little later with a heavy cross on his shoulder. He is trying to carry it, and he cannot. The physical agony and the suffering in the garden plus the weight of the cross is too much for him, and he is staggering under its weight as he climbs up Golgotha. He is the Son of God, Creator of the universe, the Holy One of God, and yet here he is with the crowd jeering and mocking. Then go to the cross, look at him there! "Even the death of the cross" (Phil. 2:8)! He is the author of life, but he is dying! In his sermon, recorded in Acts 3, Peter says in essence, "You have put to death the author of life." What a paradox!

The thing that you and I will have to answer for at the bar of judgment is this: we have reduced this glorious gospel of the blessed God to something cheap and ordinary and sentimental instead of being amazed at the glory of it all. Look at that paradox: "[You] killed the prince of life," says Peter—which means "the author of life," "the Creator of life." Death! Life! The Creator dying! The thing is monstrous, but it is also part of the glory of this person and his divine saviorhood. There he is upon the cross. He came into the world in order to die. That is the teaching of the New Testament. "He was made a little lower than the angels," says Hebrews 2:9, "for the suffering of death . . . that he by the grace of God should taste death for every man." He came to die. His death was not an accident. His death was not produced by men. It was the Father's purpose. God sent him as his Lamb. God had been telling the people that he was coming, picturing a lamb to be slain. Jesus Christ is the Lamb of God, "made a little lower than the angels for the suffering of death" (Heb. 2:9).

Is he growing in your esteem? Is he becoming greater and greater? Is he "increasing"? Are you beginning to see and to feel that nothing matters except that you should know this blessed person and enter more and more into the realization of what he has done for you and for your sins? Do you feel that everything else has become trivial, that you just want to know and understand more of him? There he is suffering on the cross. They are mocking him, they are jeering at him, they are laughing at him. "He is despised and rejected of men" (Isa. 53:3). He is in an agony; he is in a shameful position. "Cursed is every one that hangeth on a tree" (Gal. 3:13 from Deut. 21:23).

What is most amazing of all is this: he is doing it all himself. We are told in the Gospels that at this moment of supreme crisis, "They all forsook him, and fled" (Mark 14:50). Peter denied him with curses and oaths. There is an old prophecy that said it was going to be like that: "I have trodden the winepress alone" (Isa. 63:3). The innocent, the pure, the guiltless has come from the glory, but having identified himself with the sins of man, he has to tread the winepress alone. The author of the epistle to the Hebrews catches this well in 1:3: "Who being the brightness of his glory, and the express image of his person, and upholding all things by the word of his power, when he had by himself purged our sins."

He did it "by himself." He was alone. And indeed this loneliness involved the cry of dereliction: "My God, my God, why hast thou forsaken me?" (Matt. 27:46). "We did esteem him stricken, smitten of God" (Isa. 53:4), forsaken of men. He trod the winepress alone. "He had by himself purged our sins" when he died (Heb. 1:3). The author of life, the sustainer of all being, died! They took down his body and buried it in a grave.

But remember the glory of the resurrection. He came out of the grave. He burst asunder the bands of death, he rises triumphant over the grave, and death cannot hold him. Why? Because he is the author of life; he is the everlasting God. So out he comes, conquering death and the grave and all things that are set against us. And he manifested himself to chosen witnesses for forty days. And then, in the presence of some of them on a mount called Olivet, he literally, physically ascended into the heavens before their very eyes. He passed through the heavens and "sat down on the right hand of the Majesty on high" (Heb. 1:3). Consider again that glorious third verse of Hebrews 1: "Who being the brightness of his glory, and the express image of his person, and upholding all things by the word of his power, when he had by himself purged our sins, sat down on the right hand of the Majesty on high." And there he sits, and there he reigns. He has been exalted because he became so low. It is expressed again by Paul in the second chapter of Philippians:

> Being found in fashion as a man, he humbled himself, and became obedient unto death, even the death of the cross. *Wherefore* [because of that] God also hath highly exalted him, and given him a name which is above every name: that at the name of Jesus every knee should bow, of things in heaven, and things in earth, and things under the earth; and that every tongue should confess that Jesus Christ is Lord, to the glory of God the Father." (Phil. 2:8–11)

> O for a thousand tongues to sing
> My great Redeemer's praise,
> The glories of my God and King,
> The triumphs of His grace![3]

All I wanted to do was thus to hold before you the panorama of redemption. The Son went from the highest courts of heaven to the cross of deepest woe—to death, to the grave, to Hades. But he did not stop there. He went back again to the highest courts of heaven. He is the Son of God, the unique One, the Lord of everything.

But I want to ask you a question: As you have considered him with me, has he been increasing? Have you forgotten the things that were on your mind and on your heart earlier? That is the test. If you have not, then you do not know him, and whether you think you are a Christian or not, I tell you you are not. If the thought of him does not relieve you and deliver you, if you cannot say, "With him I am ready to face anything and everything, hell included," then you do not know him, and you need to spend your time not looking at yourself and your problems but at him. "Looking unto Jesus the author and finisher of our faith" (Heb. 12:2).

A hymn sums up everything I have been trying to say.

Who is this, so weak and helpless,
Child of lowly Hebrew maid,
Rudely in a stable sheltered,
Coldly in a manger laid?
'Tis the Lord of all creation,
Who this wondrous path hath trod;
He is God from everlasting,
And to everlasting God.

Who is this, a Man of sorrows,
Walking sadly life's hard way,
Homeless, weary, sighing, weeping,
Over sin and Satan's sway?
'Tis our God, our glorious Savior,
Who above the starry sky
Now for us a place prepareth,
Where no tear can dim the eye.

Who is this? behold Him shedding
Drops of blood upon the ground!
Who is this, despised, rejected,
Mocked, insulted, beaten, bound?
'Tis our God, who gifts and graces
On His church now poureth down;
Who shall smite in righteous judgment
All His foes beneath His throne.

Who is this that hangeth dying
While the rude world scoffs and scorns,
Numbered with the malefactors,
Torn with nails, and crowned with thorns?
'Tis the God who ever liveth
'Mid the shining ones on high,
In the glorious golden city,
Reigning everlastingly.[4]

My dear friends, nothing matters except that we know him and his glory and his greatness and his majesty. He is our Savior if we believe in him. He is our "all, and in all" (Col. 3:11). "But of him are ye in Christ Jesus, who of God is made unto us wisdom, and righteousness, and sanctification, and redemption" (1 Cor. 1:30). He is everything! Look unto Jesus!

Go, return immortal Saviour,
Leave Thy footstool, take Thy throne.[5]

Let us look to him and say to him, "Even so, come, Lord Jesus." He must increase, and he will, and it is my privilege to tell you why and how he must increase, but we must decrease.

Be Thou alone my soul's delight,
My passion and my love.[6]

# 23

# Prophet, Priest, and King

JOHN 3:30

Sunday morning sermon preached in
Westminster Chapel, July 3, 1966.

He must increase, but I must decrease. (John 3:30)

We come back once more to these great words, and as I have been trying to show, there is in many ways no more important statement from
the standpoint of our growth and development in the Christian life. We
have looked at its actual context, and we have considered it negatively,
but now we are looking at the positive, "He must increase," and we have
seen that the essence of the Christian life is that our whole thinking, our
feelings, our everything is dominated by him, that we see his greatness,
his glory, his wonder.

But how does that come about? We are taught in the Scriptures that
you and I can do a great deal about this, and fortunately we are also
told exactly what we must do. So I have suggested that a very good way
of doing this—namely, that he may increase in us in every respect—is
to adopt the expedient method adopted by the author of the epistle to
the Hebrews. So we are doing this very thing. We have tried to look at
Jesus, at his essence, as he is, "the brightness of [God's] glory, and the
express image of his person" (Heb. 1:3). Then in the previous sermon we

went on to consider how we see his greatness and his glory in what he did in the whole grand movement in connection with the working out of our salvation. And as you do that, as you meditate upon these great historical events on which our whole position is based, he will increase. He will increase in your mind, in your understanding, in your heart and affections. He will move your will. This is the whole secret of Christian living, to look at him and to consider him. That is the word used by the author of Hebrews, "Consider him," he says; "looking unto Jesus" (12:2). That is his great exhortation.

So we are going on with this, and I want now to try to look at him, as we are enabled by the Spirit of God who alone can enable us in these matters, to look at him in his offices, because there was a purpose to all he did. If we really look at the great movement from eternity into time and back again, it will fill us with a sense of wonder, but we must realize that there was a purpose to all this. This is not merely a tableau, a kind of spectacle; it is not merely some kind of manifestation to fill us with a sense of wonder. Something was being achieved, something was being done. And the best way of considering that, in many ways, is to consider it in terms of his offices, and the customary way of looking at him in his offices is to look at him as prophet, priest, and king.

In the Old Testament God dealt with his people through men occupying those three offices. You read of the kings, you read of the priests, and you read of the prophets. God was dealing with a people, giving the revelation of himself through the children of Israel, and he did it in that way, and each one of them had a special function. So as we come to look at our blessed Lord in his offices, we look at him in terms of these three, and at once we see his preeminence in that he is all three in one.

This was the message to people like those who received the epistle to the Hebrews, and it is an equally good message for us today, tempted as we are to look at other teachings and to wonder whether or not they could help us. We hear the cults and other people reporting that they have found great happiness, and so we say, "This is what we want"; so we turn to this and that. But all we need is in him. He is the Prophet, he is the Priest, he is the King. There has never been anybody else like this. In the Old Testament you find particular men, wonderful men—prophets. Yes, but they were only prophets in respect to him. It is a great thing to be called a prophet and to be endued and endowed with the propensities that constitute a prophet. What a privilege! But the prophets were prophets and nothing more. Others were priests, another great and exalted office, but they were only priests. And others were kings. Each man was allotted a particular task. But the moment you look at our Lord, you see that he is alone. He is the Prophet and the Priest and the King. He is everything. He combines everything in himself.

Now the New Testament is constantly praising him in this way. He is the Alpha, but he is the Omega as well. He is the beginning, of course, but he is also the end. He is "the author and finisher of our faith" (Heb. 12:2), "who of God," says Paul to the Corinthians, "is made unto us wisdom, and righteousness, and sanctification, and redemption" (1 Cor. 1:30). He is everything; there is nothing that he is not. Christ is "all, and in all" (Col. 3:11). He is everything that you need.

Now here is a way of contemplating his greatness and his glory, and as you do so, he increases and becomes greater and greater, and you marvel and are filled with amazement at him. You say with Paul, "Great is the mystery of godliness" (1 Tim. 3:16), and you work it out in all its details. So remember that Jesus combines all offices in himself. He needs no help, he needs no assistant, he needs no supplement. You do not have to add another to him to carry out some other function. He does not need it, and if you feel he does, you are detracting from his glory, and he is decreasing instead of increasing in your estimate and in your sight. That is why any teaching, whether in the name of a church or not, that adds anybody to him takes away from his glory, his completeness, his fullness, his absolute perfection. All the offices are filled to overflowing by him who is indeed the Son of God.

The Apostle Paul had to deal with this kind of modern problem in his own day and time. The Colossians rather fancied themselves as intellectuals. They were dabbling in philosophy, in mystery religions and things of that type, and the Apostle turns on them and says, "In him dwelleth all the fullness of the Godhead bodily. And ye are complete in him" (Col.

2:9–10). He is Prophet, Priest, and King. Do not add to him; do not say you need any help or aid from anybody else. We are complete in him because everything is complete in him. He is "all, and in all."

All that strikes us at once, but we must work this out a little, and as we do so, we shall find him constantly increasing. Look at him for a moment as prophet. There were great prophets in the Old Testament, and in many ways the first of them was none other than Moses himself. He was the teacher of the people, and he was their guide and instructor and leader. But Moses was the meekest of men, and he realized he was merely foreshadowing one that was to come. So he said, "The LORD thy God will raise up unto thee a Prophet from the midst of thee, of thy brethren, like unto me; unto him ye shall hearken" (Deut. 18:15).

So there is this great prophecy, and from that point forward the children of Israel were always waiting for the coming of this great Prophet predicted and prophesied by Moses. In the great scene that took place at Caesarea Philippi when our Lord turned to the disciples and said, "Whom do men say that I am?" the answer given was, "John the Baptist; but some say, Elias; and others, One of the prophets," or the Prophet that was to come (Mark 8:27–28). They were waiting for the coming of this final instructor, this teacher, one who was to appear from among themselves, but was to be *the* Prophet, *the* Teacher. And it is only in Jesus of Nazareth that he has come. That is why he did not hesitate to stand up and say, "I am the light of the world: he that followeth me shall not walk in darkness, but shall have the light of life" (John 8:12). Or again, "I am the way, the truth, and the life: no man cometh unto the Father, but by me" (14:6). And here, of course, is something that we can go on meditating on forever.

What has he done? He has given us knowledge of God that no one else could give. There are particular aspects of knowledge concerning God that we can obtain. We can obtain them from nature, for example. "The invisible things of him from the creation of the world are clearly seen . . . his eternal power and Godhead" (Rom. 1:20). You see it in flowers, you see it in the whole of nature, in the sun shining in the heavens. "The heavens declare the glory of God"—the sun and the moon and the stars and all these other things (Psalm 19). Ah, but they are only partial, they are incomplete. So we find John saying in the prologue to his Gospel, "No man hath seen God at any time, the only begotten Son, which is in the bosom of the Father, he hath declared him" (John 1:18).

Now the prophets in the Old Testament had made many declarations concerning him, and they are marvelous and wonderful; it is glorious to read them. But they are partial. As the author of the epistle to the Hebrews puts it, God spoke "at sundry times and in divers manners" (Heb. 1:1). But these parts and portions were imperfect because they were not full. They were perfect in and of themselves but imperfect in the sense that they were partial. There is only One who has "*declared*" God, who has really revealed and manifested him. "No man hath see God at any time." No man can, for God dwells "in the light which no man can approach unto; whom no man hath seen, nor can see" (1 Tim. 6:16). But here is One who has come out of eternity into time. Our Lord has already said it all to Nicodemus: "No man hath ascended up to heaven, but he that came down from heaven, even the Son of man which is in heaven" (John 3:13). Here is One who has looked into the face of the Father from all eternity, and he has come, and he reports to us that he is the perfect Prophet.

He does this not only in his teaching but in the whole of his life. So he was able to say later on to the disciples when they were in trouble and Philip had said to him, "Lord, show us the Father, and it sufficeth us," and Jesus answered "Have I been so long time with you, and yet hast thou not known me, Philip? He that hath seen me hath seen the Father; and how sayest thou then, Show us the Father? Believest thou not that I am in the Father, and the Father in me?" (14:8–10).

That is something that no one else has ever been able to claim. No one else could claim, "He who hath seen me hath seen the Father." He is, therefore, the supreme Prophet. He reveals, he manifests God. He teaches us about him. He shows us God in his eternal glory.

But not only does he teach us like that and act as Prophet with regard to God, he does the same with regard to the Law of God. This is the particular theme of the Sermon on the Mount. God had given his Law, and there had been able expositors of it. The prophets had expounded it, and so had others, and in the time of our Lord the Pharisees and scribes in particular were doing this. But the whole point of the Sermon on the Mount is that there was a misunderstanding of it, and there is only One who really teaches us concerning the true spiritual meaning of the Law of God, and it is this same blessed person. You must listen to him. He will say to you, "Ye have heard that it hath been said by them of old time . . . but I say unto you . . ." (Matt. 5:33–34). He is the final authority. "He taught them as one having authority, and not as the scribes" (7:29), and he alone can deliver us from the thralldom of the legalism that is so often produced by a misunderstanding of the Law. He shows us the spiritual nature and character of the Law, and he employs various illustrations. Many a man says, "I am not guilty of murder" because he is externalizing it and taking it merely in a literal manner—he has never actually killed a man! "But wait a minute," says our Lord in essence. "Whosoever says to his brother 'Thou fool' is a murderer" (5:22). It is the essence of murder to hate your brother and to say, "Thou fool."

And likewise the teaching concerning adultery. It is not merely the act, it is the desire, coveting. This is what our Lord brings out in his teaching, the thing that the Apostle Paul as Saul of Tarsus, though he was an expert in the Law, had never really understood. He later said in essence, "When I was caught by the command, 'Thou shalt not covet,' I was undone." He was finished—"sin revived, and I died" (Rom. 7:9). So it is the Lord alone who can teach us this, and this is where we are brought to the very essence of an understanding of our relationship with God. The Pharisees and scribes were very good people, very godly, and when the Pharisee says, "I fast twice in the week, and I give a tenth of my goods to feed the poor," he is not exaggerating. He is stating a literal fact; he is describing what he actually does. The Pharisees and scribes were in that sense very religious, moral individuals, and they were looked up to by all the people as being paragons of what a man should be in a religious and in a moral sense. But our Lord shatters the whole conception by saying, "Except your righteousness shall exceed the righteousness of the scribes and Pharisees, ye shall in no case enter into the kingdom of heaven" (Matt. 5:20).

Here is the Teacher. They could not understand him; they said, "How knoweth this man letters, never having learned?" (John 7:15). And yet he spoke "as one having authority" (Matt. 7:29). He is the Lawgiver. He is the exponent of it and the giver of it. He is the supreme Prophet.

And it is exactly the same with regard to the love of God and the whole way of redemption. You read about this in the Gospels, and you see that the disciples stumble at it; they cannot understand it. When our Lord announces his coming death to them Peter objects, "Be it far from thee, Lord" (Matt. 16:22). Peter does not understand. But Jesus himself said, "The Son of man is not come to be ministered unto, but to minister, and to give his life a ransom for many" (Matt. 20:28). Later on the apostles understand it, but only as the result of the enlightenment and the unction of the Holy Spirit. Again Jesus taught, "The Son of man is come to seek and to save that which was lost" (Matt. 18:11; Luke 19:10). He insisted upon being baptized, and he set his face steadfastly to go to Jerusalem. All this concerns the way of salvation, and the love of God is stated incomparably in parables like the parable of the prodigal son and so on. Here is the supreme Prophet. You do not need any other teaching, you do not need to look to anybody else—it is all in him.

But then at the end Jesus says, "I will pray the Father, and he shall give you another Comforter . . . he will guide you into all truth" (John 14:16, 13). He prophesies that the Holy Spirit will bring to our mind and to our remembrance all the things that Jesus has said and "will shew you things to come" (John 16:13). So he sent the Spirit, and he continues to teach through the Spirit. "He shall glorify me," he says. "He shall not speak of himself" in the sense of his own ideas, but he would pass on what Jesus had given to him. As our Lord had done that himself, so the Spirit will do that. But it is all to teach us further about Jesus. If you claim to have received the Spirit in some special sense, here is the way you test it—your knowledge of Jesus, your increasing sense of his glory and his wonder: "He shall glorify me" (Heb. 16:14). He shall increase, and I will decrease as the result of this teaching.

There, then, is just a glimpse of him as *the* Prophet, but let us turn to this second aspect, Jesus Christ as the Priest. That is especially the theme of the epistle to the Hebrews—Jesus Christ our "great high priest" (Heb. 4:14). Oh, how wonderful! I hesitate as I turn to this because any man who attempts to handle such a theme must be acutely conscious of his inability and unworthiness, the theme is so exalted. I also hesitate for a second reason. The author of the epistle to the Hebrews says he wanted to tell his readers that our Lord was

> called of God an high priest after the order of Melchisedec. Of whom we have many things to say, and hard to be uttered, seeing ye are dull of hearing. For when for the time ye ought to be teachers, ye have need that one teach you again which be the first principles of the oracles of God; and are become such as have need of milk, and not of strong meat. For every one that useth milk is unskilful in the word of righteousness: for he is a babe. But strong meat belongeth to them that are of full age, even those who by reason of use have their senses exercised to discern both good and evil. (Heb. 5:10–14)

This is a great and exalted, a deep, a profound subject, and it is particularly difficult in days and times like these when people say they do not have time to read or to meditate and just want to be entertained. But here is a theme that can occupy you for the rest of your time on earth and throughout eternity—Jesus Christ, the great High Priest.

What are you doing, says the writer to the Hebrew Christians, why are you looking back at the temple, what are you going to find there? Yes, you will find priests, the greatest of them, the first of them, the great high priest Aaron. Wonderful, you are right in boasting in him. But, listen, when you put Aaron by the side of this One, he is nothing; he is just a shadow and not the substance. Aaron and all his successors in the high priesthood and as priests become nothing when you put them by the side of this "great high priest." "Seeing then that we have a great high priest, that is passed into [or through] the heavens, Jesus the Son of God, let us hold fast our profession" (Heb. 4:14).

Not only that, let us try to look at him, this One who is so different, who stands alone as our great High Priest. In what ways is he preeminent over Aaron and over everybody else? According to this teaching, he is supreme even in the matter of his calling: "called of God an high priest after the order of Melchisedec" (5:10). Consider the exposition of that in the seventh chapter of the epistle to the Hebrews.

> For this Melchisedec, king of Salem, priest of the most high God, who met Abraham returning from the slaughter of the kings, and blessed him; to whom also Abraham gave a tenth part of all; first being by interpretation King of righteousness, and after that also King of Salem, which is, King of peace; [Now notice] without father, without mother, without descent, having neither beginning of days, nor end of life; but made like unto the Son of God; [he] abideth a priest continually. (Heb. 7:1–3)

Then the writer goes on to expound this. He points out that if our Lord was not a man, he never would have been a priest or a high priest at all. He did not come from the tribe of Levi, but the priests did come from the tribe of Levi. But here is One who is not of the tribe of Levi. Why not? Because he is above and beyond all those rules. He is the great High Priest himself; he is the Son of God. So he says things like this about him: "And it is yet far more evident: for after that the similitude of Melchisedec there ariseth another priest, who is made, not after the law of a carnal commandment, but after the power of an endless life. For he testifieth, Thou art a priest for ever after the order of Melchisedec." His calling, therefore, is quite different and unique. He does not come as one of a series. He does not come by lineal descent. Everything about him is unique—no earthly father, born of a virgin, conceived by the Holy Spirit. He is the Son of God. He is called and set in his position because he is who and what he is.

Then consider his offering. The high priests would place their hands on the head of an animal, perhaps a bull, metaphorically transferring the sins of the people to that animal. Then the animal would be killed, and his blood would be collected. Also the high priest had the great privilege of going, once a year, into the Most Holy Place to make atonement for the sins of the people, and he did so by carrying in this blood. There he presented it before the altar, where God came down to meet the people on the mercy seat with the Law underneath it. And thus the sins of the people were covered over. The blood of bulls and of goats, sacrificial animals, was presented.

But then turn to the ninth chapter of Hebrews. This is where you see Jesus's glory and uniqueness.

> Christ being come an high priest of good things to come, by a greater and more perfect tabernacle, not made with hands, that is to say, not of this building; neither by the blood of goats and calves, but by his own blood he entered in once into the holy place, having obtained eternal redemption for us. For if the blood of bulls and of goats, and the ashes of an heifer sprinkling the unclean, sanctifieth to the purifying of the flesh: how much more shall the blood of Christ, who through the eternal Spirit offered himself without spot to God, purge your conscience from dead works to serve the living God? (Heb. 9:11–14)

What more can we say? He offered his own blood! What a sacrifice! He is the victim and the Priest, the Offerer and the thing offered. He offered himself. He carried in and presented his own blood.

Where did he do this? The writer again makes a great contrast.

> Almost all things are by the law purged with blood; and without shedding of blood is no remission. It was therefore necessary that the patterns of things in the heavens should be purified with these; but the heavenly things themselves with better sacrifices than these. For Christ is not entered into the holy places made with hands. (Heb. 9:22–24)

These people were looking back at the temple in Jerusalem, as people look at cathedrals today and at ceremonies and rituals and a priesthood; they are going back. But "Christ is not entered into the holy places made with hands, which are the figures of the true; but into heaven itself, now to appear in the presence of God for us" (v. 24). He has purified a heavenly sanctuary, not an earthly sanctuary.

And then the writer makes another great and wonderful point. I am just testing you as I go along like this. Are you enjoying this? Is this moving you? Is this thrilling you? Do you feel that it is more wonderful to be a Christian than you have ever realized before? It is not just something in you and your own feeling or some little experience you have had—it is seeing him and all that he has done for you. Is this almost bringing you to your feet with a desire to praise him and to magnify his great and wonderful name?

But even further, he has done it once forever! The writer keeps on making this point. He says in the ninth chapter,

> Nor yet that he should offer himself often, as the high priest entereth into the holy place every year with blood of others; for then must he often have suffered since the foundation of the world: but now once in the end of the world hath he appeared to put away sin by the sacrifice of himself. And as it is appointed unto men once to die, but after this the judgment: so *Christ was once offered to* bear the sins of many; and unto them that look for him shall he appear the second time without sin unto salvation. (Heb. 9:25–28)

This man is so thrilled by this that he goes on repeating it. And preachers should repeat themselves. Why? Because they are talking about the most glorious theme on earth. Have you noticed that musicians get a good theme, and they repeat it, they play variations of it. Quite right! So listen to this, from the tenth chapter:

> By the which will we are sanctified through the offering of the body of Jesus Christ once for all. And every priest standeth daily ministering and offering oftentimes the same sacrifices, which can never take away sins: but this man, after he had offered one sacrifice for sins for ever, sat down on the right hand of God; from henceforth expecting till his enemies be made his footstool. For by one offering he hath perfected for ever them that are sanctified. (Heb. 10:10–14)

Once and forever! You cannot repeat this sacrifice, and no priest or authority should ever have the impertinence to claim that he can do so. Once and forever! Never to be repeated! I do not want to have a dialogue with people who say that this offering is repeated. That is a denial of the thing that has happened once and forever. "It is finished." He had completed the work.

Add to all this the fact that our great High Priest "ever liveth to make intercession for [us]" (Heb. 7:25).

> They truly were many priests, because they were not suffered to continue by reason of death: but this man, because he continueth ever, hath an unchangeable priesthood. Wherefore he is able also to save them to the uttermost [to the very end] that come unto God by him, seeing he ever liveth to make intercession for them. (Heb. 7:23–25)

What a High Priest! You cannot rely on earthly priests. They may be ill, or they may be late, and there is constant change, new appointments, much coming and going. But, my dear friend, it does not matter where you are, it does not matter what is happening to you, when you are in need and in trouble and you want to pray to God, go in confidence, for your High Priest is always there, He will never be absent; he "shall neither slumber nor sleep" (Ps. 121:4). "He ever liveth to make intercession for [us]" (Heb. 7:25). He is seated "on the right hand of God" (10:12), and there he is always and ever will be making intercession for the saints. He is our "great high priest" (4:14), and we need no other priests, whether past, present, or future. He is our all in all.

Jesus Christ is also the King. The promise made to Mary by the archangel Gabriel before Jesus's birth was that Jesus would occupy the throne of his father David. "He shall be great, and shall be called the Son of the Highest: and the Lord God shall give unto him the throne of his father David: and he shall reign over the house of Jacob for ever; and of his kingdom there shall be no end" (Luke 1:32–33). Here is the King, "the seed of David" (John 7:42), promised throughout the centuries. And at last he comes—in the typical divine manner—not into a king's palace but into a stable. He is the everlasting King, and he manifests the power of his kingship and rule and reign.

He manifests his power through his miracles. He says, "If I with the finger of God cast out devils, no doubt the kingdom of God is come upon you" (Luke 11:20). This is the touch of the King. The people ask, "Who is this who commands the raging of the sea and the blowing of the winds?" That is the most appropriate question to ask. Who is he? He is the King. He commands everything because he owns everything. He is the King of the universe. He has all power, and he manifests it not only in his life and in his miracles but still more in his death. Peter preaching on the day of Pentecost says, "It was not possible that he should be holden of [death]" (Acts 2:24). Why not? Because he is the King! Death is nothing to him. He rules over everything; he has command over everything.

Then he rises from the dead, but just before he goes to heaven he turns to his poor disciples, whom he is leaving in this world, and says to them, "All power is given unto me in heaven and in earth" (Matt. 28:18). "All power"! He means what he says, and this power has been "given" to him. He is Jesus! The Lord! The Christ! He is seated at the right hand of God, and all power is in his hand. Christian people, why are we in the spiritual doldrums? Why are we unhappy and complaining? Why are we weak and failing? Why is the church as she is? There is only one answer. We have forgotten that he is the King, and all power is in his hands. "Go ye therefore, and teach all nations, baptizing them in the name of the Father, and of the Son, and of the Holy Ghost: teaching them to observe all things whatsoever I have commanded you: and lo, I am with you always, even unto the end of the world" (v. 19–20).

And we are told in Hebrews 10 that he is "expecting [sitting and waiting] till his enemies be made his footstool" (Heb. 10:13). The apostle Paul delights to describe him from this kingly aspect. He tells us in the first chapter of the epistle to the Ephesians that we really need to know

> What is the exceeding greatness of [God's] power to us-ward who believe, according to the working of his mighty power, which he wrought in Christ, when he raised him from the dead, and set him at his own right hand in the heavenly places, far above all principality, and power, and might, and dominion, and every name that is named, not only in this world, but also in that which is to come: and hath put all things under his feet. (Eph. 1:19–22)

That is his position.

The apostle never tires of speaking of this. So having reminded the Philippians of how the Son "became obedient unto death, even the death of the cross," he goes on to say, "Wherefore God also hath highly exalted him, and given him a name which is above every other name: that at the name of Jesus every knee should bow" (Phil. 2:9–10). All should be decreased; all should be flattened on their faces! "Every knee should bow, of things in heaven, and things in earth, and things under the earth; and that every tongue should confess that Jesus Christ is Lord, to the glory of God the Father" (vv. 10–11). That is his position now. And this glorious King is also to be revealed, for he will come again, riding the clouds of heaven, surrounded by the holy angels. He will come to conquer and to judge all his enemies and send them to everlasting judgment away from the presence of the Lord. He will come to set up his great and eternal kingdom of glory.

Let me give it to you again in the words of the author of the epistle to the Hebrews: "See that ye refuse not him that speaketh. For if they escaped not who refused him that spake on earth, much more shall not we escape, if we turn away from him that speaketh from heaven: whose voice then shook the earth: but now he hath promised, saying, Yet once more I shake not the earth only, but also heaven" (Heb. 12:25–26). He is the only one who can shake England. Nobody else can do that. In fact here is One who can not only shake England but will shake the whole earth and also heaven. "And this word, Yet once more, signifieth the removing of those things that are shaken, as of things that are made, that those things which cannot be shaken may remain. Wherefore we receiving a kingdom which cannot be moved, let us have grace, whereby we may serve God acceptably with reverence and godly fear: for our God is a consuming fire" (Heb. 12:27–29).

How impossible it is to describe him in his three great and glorious offices!

> His kingdom cannot fail,
> He rules o'er earth and heaven,

> The keys of death and hell
> Are to our Jesus given.
> Lift up your heart, lift up your voice;
> Rejoice, again I say, rejoice![1]

Christian people, is he increasing? Is he getting bigger and bigger in your sight? Have you lost your morbidity and introspection, your self-concern? Have you seen him, and has he so increased that you have forgotten yourself? "He must increase, but I must decrease" (John 3:30).

# 24

# Lost in Wonder, Love, and Praise

## JOHN 3:30

Sunday morning sermon preached in
Westminster Chapel, July 10, 1966.

He must increase, but I must decrease. (John 3:30)

In the previous studies we have seen that if we are to grow and to develop in the Christian life and receive increasingly of God's fullness, then we must decrease, and he must increase. His increasing is the key to the other. What really gets rid of self is that he increases and that we realize the truth about him as we are meant to do.

Fortunately, in the New Testament there is a wealth of teaching that enables us to do this, and we are more or less following the method adopted by the author of the epistle to the Hebrews, in order that we may see the preeminence of our Lord. This has always been necessary for Christian people. All our troubles ultimately stem from the fact that we do not realize who Jesus Christ is and what he is, what he can do for us and our position in him. That is the source of all our troubles. It was the source of the troubles of the early Christians, and that is equally true of us. So we must look at him and consider his preeminence. "Looking unto Jesus, the author and finisher of our faith" (Heb. 12:2). That is still the main thing that we must all do, and we have been trying to do this. We have been looking at him in his essential glory: "The brightness of [God's] glory, and the express image of his person" (1:3). We looked at him in his eternal creatorship, we have looked at him also in the great acts of redemption, how he left the courts of glory and came on earth, humbled himself, even to the death of the cross, died and was buried, rose again, and went back once more to the glory—that great sweep, that movement in connection with our redemption.

And then in the last sermon we were looking at him as he is described to us in the New Testament in terms of his offices—Prophet, Priest, King! He is the great prophet of our God and also our "great high priest" who "passed into [through] the heavens" (4;14) and who "ever liveth to make intercession for [us]" (7:25). He is the King seated "on the right hand of God" (10:12). He said, "All power is given unto me in heaven and in earth" (Matt. 28:18). And he is coming again to destroy his enemies and set up his eternal kingdom. There is no one like him. We must not put him in any class or category; we must not put any name on the same level as his. He is the One and Only.

That is the way the New Testament puts the teaching concerning him, and as we look at it he increases in our sight. We see him more and more as he is, the eternal Son of God who came so low in order that we might live.

This is the theme that could occupy us for the rest of our lives on earth and will be the theme that will occupy us in the glory when we get there. Those in heaven sing the praises of God and of the Lamb. "Blessing, and honour, and glory, and power, be unto him that sitteth upon the throne, and unto the Lamb for ever and ever" (Rev. 5:13). "They sing the song of Moses . . . and the song of the Lamb" (15:13). As we grasp this teaching and comprehend it in a measure, he increases in our sight more and more.

Here is again something that shows us his greatness and his glory and that he is the Head of a new humanity. We do not grasp this New Testament teaching as we ought. The idea that we need any help or additional aid or anyone to supplement what Jesus has done for us and can do for us becomes utterly ridiculous when we realize exactly what God has appointed him to do, and this is a subject that is well worthy of our consideration and deep meditation. He is the Head of a new humanity, and that is, again, another evidence of his uniqueness and why it was essential that the Son of God should come into the world and why he alone can save us and redeem us. God made a man—Adam. He was perfect; he was made in the image and the likeness of God. But he fell into temptation; he could not resist the subtlety and the power of the Devil.

How can mankind that has fallen in Adam be redeemed and restored and saved? It is clear that to make another man, even though he may be made perfect, will not solve the problem. Perfect man has already proved to be inadequate; he has fallen. So you begin to see the absolute necessity of the incarnation and the coming of the Son of God into this world. The teaching that we are given concerning him is this: he is the Head of a new humanity.

This teaching is found mainly in two places in the New Testament—the fifth chapter of Paul's epistle to the Romans and the fifteenth chapter of his first epistle to the Corinthians. The apostle makes a great contrast between the first man and the second man, and this is, indeed, one of the most glorious aspects of the whole doctrine of salvation and redemption. "Wherefore, as by one man sin entered into the world, and death by sin; and so death passed upon all men, for that all have sinned" (Rom. 5:12). That is one side, but then he continues, "For if by one man's offence death reigned by one; much more they which receive abundance of grace and of the gift of righteousness shall reign in life by one, Jesus Christ" (Rom. 5:17). So there is this contrast between the one man and this other man—Adam and the Lord Jesus Christ. And in 1 Corinthians 15 this contrast between the first and the second man is put still more plainly and explicitly. "The first man Adam was made a living soul; the last Adam was made a quickening spirit" (1 Cor. 15:45). "The first man is of the earth, earthy; the second man is the Lord from heaven. As is the earthy, such are they also that are earthy: and as is the heavenly, such are they also that are heavenly. And as we have borne

the image of the earthy, we shall also bear the image of the heavenly"
(vv. 47–49).

Now this is a most thrilling concept, and it is only as we grasp something of the meaning of this that we shall see how Jesus must inevitably
increase. This is the only way whereby any single one of us could be
saved. God is forming a new humanity, and the Head of this new humanity is none other than the Lord Jesus Christ. John the Baptist cannot be
the head of a new humanity. John is a man, a fallen man. He is one of the
children of Adam; he is one of this fallen race. He cannot be the Savior.
That is what John is saying: "He must increase, but I must decrease"
(John 3:30). He can teach, he can baptize, but he cannot be the head of a
new humanity; he cannot be the Redeemer. But here is One who is great
enough to be our Savior. He is the Son of God. He has taken unto himself
human nature, purified by the operation of the Holy Spirit in the womb
of Mary. So he is the Head of this new humanity. Here, and here alone,
is there a true and a real and a secure hope of our salvation.

I leave that thought with you. Meditate upon it. You cannot say that
about anybody else. And that is why those who put his name among the
prophets and the philosophers and others are guilty of such indescribable folly. We needed a new man, and here he is, "the last Adam," and he
is none other than this blessed Son of God. He came in the likeness of
sinful flesh, but he was not a sinner. Here is something absolutely new,
the beginning of a new race of redeemed people.

And following from that, of course, is the second truth that he is the
Head of the church. We have seen him as the Prophet and the Priest and
the King; we have seen him as the great Creator. But here is something
that is special and unique and that the New Testament emphasizes in its
teaching. Let me show it to you, for instance, at the end of the first chapter of Paul's epistle to the Ephesians—Christ's kingly glory. The apostle
is praying that these Ephesians might understand the greatness of God's
power toward them. He says it is the same power

> Which he wrought [exercised] in Christ, when he raised him from
> the dead, and set him at his own right hand in the heavenly places,

far above all principality, and power, and might, and dominion, and every name that is named, not only in this world, but also in that which is to come: and hath put all things under his feet. (Eph. 1:20–22)

Then he goes on, "and gave him to be the head over all things to the church, which is his body, the fullness of him that filleth all in all" (vv. 22–23).

Paul comes back to that in the fourth chapter of Ephesians:

But speaking the truth in love, may grow up into him in all things, which is the head, even Christ: from whom the whole body fitly joined together and compacted by that which every joint supplieth, according to the effectual working in the measure of every part, maketh increase of the body unto the edifying of itself in love. (vv. 15–16)

What a statement! All we are concerned about is this: the church is the body of Christ, and he is the Head.

Here is the great central doctrine of the New Testament. The redeemed for the time being are in the church. The form that the kingdom of God is taking now is the Christian church, and through the church God is going to make and establish his great kingdom that will cover the whole universe. So the church is of vital significance and importance for us, and in that connection, it is very important that we should realize that all the church has comes from Jesus Christ. He is "the head over all things to the church" (Eph. 1:22). Every blessing that we have and derive comes from him. Our life comes from him, our substance, our everything.

Paul prays for the Colossians "that their hearts might be comforted, being knit together in love, and unto all riches of the full assurance of understanding, to the acknowledgement of the mystery of God, and of the Father, and of Christ; in whom are hid all the treasures of wisdom and knowledge" (Col. 2:2–3). Or again take the phrase at the end of the first chapter of the first epistle to the Corinthians: "Who of God is made unto us wisdom, and righteousness, and sanctification, and redemption"

(1 Cor. 1:30). It is all in him, and we derive everything that we have from our contact with him. Think of it in terms of the analogy of the body. All is concentrated in the head. The brain is the seat of light and activity and power. The body cannot function without it. There is the central control, and it all comes out of that, and this is the teaching we are given about Christ.

Here once more you see how utterly unique he is. Men can help us in part; they can teach us a bit here and a bit there. I am not disparaging what men can do for us, but to put any man anywhere near Jesus or to say that anybody can add to what he has given is simply ridiculous. It is a failure to see his greatness, his glory, his preeminence. He must increase, and everybody else and everything else must decrease. This is the teaching. If you and I are lethargic and lifeless and weak and are failing as Christian people, then shame on us; we have no right to be like that! The energy, the power, the life, the vitality, everything we need is all in him. If we are as described above, it is because we do not realize that truth and are either looking at ourselves and commiserating with ourself or trying foolishly to do things in our own energy and strength and power. That is the cause of failure. All we need is found in him. He has been made Head over all things unto the church.

This is the truth that is contained in embryo in the statement of John the Baptist in John 3:30. How utterly ridiculous and monstrous it is in any way to put anybody or anything on the same level as Jesus. He is all. He is everything. He is the beginning and end. He is the all and in all.

There, then, is the essence of this great doctrinal teaching concerning him. But now let me move onward and become a little more practical, and I do this not merely that we may understand the doctrine, but that we may test ourselves and examine ourselves in the light of it and in order that we may derive the benefit that we are meant to derive from it. "Of his fullness have all we received, and grace for [upon] grace" (John 1:16). Have we? What can we receive? What has he made possible for us? What is there in him for us? This is another excellent way for him to increase in our understanding and in our affections and in our whole outlook. What has he made possible for us? This, again, is a theme that is developed and worked out by the author of the epistle to the Hebrews. He starts by pointing out the essential preeminence of our Lord over prophets and angels and Moses and Aaron. Jesus is beyond everybody as Prophet, Priest, and King. And because of that he is "the mediator of the new covenant" (Heb. 12:24).

Here again is a great biblical principle—the covenants between God and men. All our blessings arise from the fact that we have a covenant-making and covenant-keeping God. God does not merely bless us. He tells us what he is doing, and he tells us why he does it. He makes a covenant, an agreement. A covenant is a legal deed, a covenant, a testament. God has always dealt with mankind in that way. The author was writing to Hebrew Christians, and of course, they were well aware of this teaching. It was their proud boast as Jews that God had made a covenant with their father Abraham. Then he had renewed it, as it were, with Moses, the great lawgiver, and had defined it further in that enactment. So they knew all about the covenant. The Old Testament is the account of the old covenant. The New Testament is the new covenant that God has made with mankind.

The author of Hebrews takes up all this, and it is very important that we should understand something about it. He argues that there is a kind of correspondence between the mediator of the covenant and the nature of the covenant, and that, of course, is what we would expect. The covenant that the Jews were most concerned about was the covenant made through Moses—the Ten Commandments, the moral law and all that was involved in that. They were proud of this; they said, "God has given us his oracles." The other nations did not have "the oracles of God" (Rom. 3:2). They were pagans, outsiders. As Paul reminds the Ephesians, they were "strangers": "At that time ye were without Christ, being aliens from the commonwealth of Israel, and strangers from the covenants of promise, having no hope, and without God in the world" (Eph. 2:12).

The Jews were very proud of all this, and these Hebrew Christians, because of the persecutions they were enduring and various other problems and difficulties, were beginning to look back to the old dispensation, looking back with longing eyes to the temple, threatening to go back to the Jewish religion. So the writer says in essence, "You do not realize what you are doing, you do not realize who you are turning from, and you do not realize the covenant you are turning from. Are you going back to the old covenant? Do you not realize the character and the nature of the new covenant? Do you not realize what has been made possible for you in and through the Lord Jesus Christ? You must not go back to that!" The author of Hebrews reminds them,

> We have such an high priest, who is set on the right hand of the throne of the Majesty in the heavens; a minister of the sanctuary, and of the true tabernacle, which the Lord pitched, and not man. For every high priest is ordained to offer gifts and sacrifices: wherefore it is of necessity that this man have somewhat also to offer" (Heb. 8:1–3)

And he goes on with his great argument. "But now," he says, "hath he obtained a more excellent ministry, by how much more also he is the mediator of a better covenant, which is established upon better promises" (v. 6).

Here is the comparison. God is going to deliver the children of Israel from the bondage and the captivity of Egypt and take them into Canaan. So he comes down and makes a covenant with them through the mediation of his servant Moses. It was a wonderful covenant, but it was nothing when you put it beside the new covenant. To start with, it was only temporary; its main blessings were temporal. When you put it beside the new covenant you see how lacking it was. That is why a man was good enough to be the mediator of that, but a man is not good enough to be a mediator of this. This is "a better covenant . . . established upon better promises." So the author opens our understanding to the better things that come to us through the Lord Jesus Christ. That is what makes it so tragic, even pathetic, that people should turn back in any sense to an old ceremonial type of religion instead of realizing the spirituality of this covenant and all the fullness that it contains.

Now what does he mean, what is he talking about? Again we are looking into and glimpsing the essential glory of this Christian salvation, and, my dear friends, it is something that so transforms human ability and understanding that nothing but the enlightenment of the Holy Spirit can enable us even to glimpse it. That is why Paul prays for the Ephesians, "I . . . cease not to give thanks for you, making mention of you in my prayers; that the God of our Lord Jesus Christ, the Father of glory, may give unto you the spirit of wisdom and revelation in the knowledge of him" (Eph. 1:16–17). Do you pray that prayer for yourselves? Or do you think you received the whole of Christianity when you made your decision for Christ? Do you pray that you may have this "spirit of wisdom and revelation in the knowledge of him" (v. 17)? Do you spend any time looking into this mystery? Paul is praying that "the eyes of your understanding [may be] enlightened" (v. 18). Remember, he is writing to Christian people. Here are people who have believed the gospel, they have been "sealed with that holy Spirit" (v. 13), he reminds them, and yet he prays for them "that ye may know what is the hope of his calling, and what the riches of the glory of his inheritance in the saints, and what is the exceeding greatness of his power to us-ward who believe." Why are we failing, faltering, stumbling? It is because we do not know "the exceeding greatness of his power to us-ward who believe" (vv. 18–19).

Paul goes on in the third chapter of that same epistle to say that he is praying this for them:

> I desire that ye faint not at my tribulations for you, which is your glory. For this cause I bow my knees unto the Father of our Lord Jesus Christ . . . that he would grant you, according to the riches of his glory, to be strengthened with might by his Spirit in the inner man; that Christ may dwell in your hearts by faith; that ye, being rooted and grounded in love, may be able to comprehend with all saints what is the breadth, and length, and depth, and height; and to know the love of Christ, which passeth knowledge, that ye might be filled with all the fullness of God. (Eph. 3:13–14, 16–19)

That is it.

He had earlier said about his calling as an apostle,

> Whereof I was made a minister, according to the gift of the grace
> of God given unto me by the effectual working of his power. Unto
> me, who am less than the least of all saints, is this grace given, that
> I should preach among the Gentiles the unsearchable riches of
> Christ. (Eph. 3:7–8)

That is the content of the better covenant, the new covenant—"the unsearchable riches of Christ."

Yet here are Hebrew Christians turning back to the temple, wanting
to go back to the Jews' religion. "Ah," they say, "ever since I have followed
Christ I have only had persecution and suffering, I don't seem to be getting much out of it." And there are Christian people who talk like that
now. They say, "What is in this Christianity for me? Hadn't we better
follow the crowd that has already turned its back upon it?" What is the
matter with them? They have never heard of or know nothing about "the
unsearchable riches of Christ," the new covenant, this new arrangement
that God has made, the new pledge, the new promise, a better covenant,
better promises. My friends, it is only as you begin to understand these
things that you see him growing and becoming yet more glorious in your
sight. He increases, and you feel that you are nothing.

Consider the communion table and the words that the Apostle wrote
to the Corinthians in the first epistle:

> I have received of the Lord that which also I delivered unto you, that
> the Lord Jesus the same night in which he was betrayed took bread:
> and when he had given thanks, he brake it, and said, Take, eat:
> this is my body, which is broken for you: this do in remembrance
> of me. After the same manner also he took the cup, when he had
> supped, saying, This cup is the new testament [the new covenant]
> in my blood: this do ye, as oft as ye drink it, in remembrance of me.
> (1 Cor. 11:23–25)

That is the meaning of the Lord's Supper. What we really do when we
eat the bread and drink the wine is to remind ourselves of the terms of
the new covenant. It reminds us of all that he has made possible for us
by his life, death, resurrection, and intercession.

Read the second half of the ninth chapter of the epistle to the Hebrews and you will find that a testament is of no value until the death of the testator. He makes his will, but he must die before you get the benefits. That is what we are doing in the Lord's Supper. We are reading the title deed, the will, reminding ourselves of all the promises of the new covenant. If you and I are unhappy Christians, it is because we do not know the will, we do not know the terms of this new, better covenant. God puts aside the first that he may establish the second, this better covenant, this greater covenant that he has made with mankind through his own Son.

What does this mean? Let me just mention some of the items in the will for you—this is what is made possible. The old covenant told us how to live, but it did not give us the power to do so. The high priest went in once a year into the Most Holy Place, taking the blood of a bull or of goats that he had shed. He presented it, but what did that do? Did it get rid of sins? No. It just covered them. It was a temporary covering; it made people ceremonially clean. The writer argues that all that sacrifice was able to do had regard to the body—"carnal ordinances" he calls them, "imposed on them until the time of reformation" (Heb. 9:10). "The blood of goats and calves" is all right, he says, for "sprinkling the unclean [and] sanctifieth to the purifying of the flesh" (v. 13). But it cannot do any more. He argued earlier, again in great detail, in the seventh chapter, "The law made nothing perfect, but the bringing in of a better hope did; by the which we draw nigh unto God" (Heb. 7:19).

That is the way in which this great argument must be worked out. So what we remind ourselves of is this—in the Lord Jesus Christ we are forgiven freely, perfectly, completely. "The blood of Jesus Christ his Son cleanseth us from all sin" (1 John 1:7). "How much more shall the blood of Christ, who through the eternal Spirit offered himself without spot to God, purge your conscience from dead works to serve the living God?" (Heb. 9:14).

And it does more than that. It means that we have died with him. The law is ever against us, but in Christ, according to this teaching, we are dead to the law because we have died with him. "Christ is the end of the law for righteousness to every one that believeth" (Rom. 10:4). If you are a believer in the Lord Jesus Christ, if you are a regenerate person, you have died with him. The argument of Romans 5 is this: when Adam sinned we all sinned in him. He was the first man, the representative. He fell, and we all fell with him. "Death passed upon all men, for that all have sinned" with Adam (Rom. 5:12). But correspondingly, when Christ died we died. He died for us, yes, but we died with him also.

This is where we see the excellence of this new covenant. We are not merely forgiven, we are "dead to the law" (Rom. 7:4; Gal. 2:19). That which held us in bondage is dead, Paul argues in Romans 7. Or let me put it like this: we are all born into this world and are children of Adam. There is no choice about that; we cannot help it. We are inevitably the children of Adam. We inherit his nature; we inherit everything that was true of him. The most important thing is that we are "in Adam." But the moment we are regenerate and believe in the Lord Jesus Christ, we are no longer in Adam but are "in Christ." "Knowing this," says Paul in Romans 6, "that our old man is crucified with him" (v. 6). "The old man" is gone; he is dead; he is finished. We are no longer in Adam. We are in Christ.

This is the most amazing, liberating thought anyone can ever come across. This has been the single most liberating thing I have ever discovered in the New Testament—the death of "the old man." This is not something I must do; it happened on the cross. As I sinned in Adam, so I died in Christ to the law and to the old Adamic nature. Not only are we dead with Christ to the law and to the Adamic nature, we have also risen with him "in newness of life" (Rom. 6:4). All these great affirmations are made by the great Apostle Paul. "If we have been planted together in the likeness of his death, we shall be also in the likeness of his resurrection: knowing this, that our old man is crucified with him, that the body of sin might be destroyed" (vv. 5–6). "Now if we be dead with Christ, we believe that we shall also live with him" (v. 8). "In that he died, he died unto sin once: but in that he liveth, he liveth unto God. Likewise reckon ye also yourselves to be dead indeed unto sin, but alive unto God through Jesus Christ our Lord" (vv. 10–11). Nobody else can do this to you. No man can help you; one cannot do this for himself. We are "dead indeed unto sin, but alive unto God." We thus begin to live for the first time, and we live to God, we share the life of God. This is all open to us by the blessed Savior.

So Paul appeals to us, "Let not sin therefore reign in your mortal body. . . . Neither yield ye your members as instruments of unrighteousness unto sin: but yield yourselves unto God, as those that are alive from the dead" (vv. 12–13). Do you realize that? You are "alive from the dead." You are living; you have been raised with Christ because you are in him. That is the teaching—"alive in Him, my living Head," as the Wesley hymn[1] says, "alive unto God" (v. 11). "Sin shall not have dominion over you: for ye are not under the law, but under grace" (v. 14).

We could go on forever on such a theme. But we have reviewed the elements of this glorious position in which we are. And in addition to this, we are being formed anew after Christ's image, we are partakers of this new humanity. As we had descended formerly from the first Adam, we now descend from the second Adam. We are the new humanity, a new race of people, God's children gathered out of every tribe and nation under heaven, redeemed by the gospel. Not merely forgiven, but born again, made "partakers of the divine nature" (2 Pet. 1:4), the new humanity, put into the new kingdom, put into the body of Christ, the church. And in this position we become partakers of "the unsearchable riches of Christ" (Eph. 3:8).

What are they? Let the writer put it to us again in that eighth chapter of the epistle to the Hebrews: "This is the covenant that I will make with the house of Israel after those days, saith the Lord; I will put my laws into their mind" (Heb. 8:10). God gave the children of Israel laws through Moses. Where did he put them? On tables of stone, outside them. There they were—"Do this, don't do that." The Law was written on stone, it was external, and that is why nobody can keep it. But here is a better covenant, and it takes the Law of God and puts it into our mind. "I will put my laws into their mind, and write them in their hearts" (v. 10). What a wonderful redemption! What a Savior!

The whole trouble about keeping a law is that your heart is against it. You do not like it, you prefer the evil, you prefer the sin, and you are always fighting with your heart and trying to exert your willpower against your mind and against your heart in particular. But here is a new covenant. The law is in your mind and is written in your heart, engraved there. The commandments are no longer grievous. "I delight to do thy will, O my God" (Ps. 40:8). Not only that: "And I will be to them a God, and they shall be to me a people: and they shall not teach every man his neighbour, and every man his brother, saying, Know the Lord" (Heb. 8:10–11). It is not to be a matter of external instruction and classes and memorizing. "For all shall know me, from the least to the greatest" (v. 11). It is internal; it is the operation of God. God manifests himself within us; he reveals himself in us. "I will be merciful to their unrighteousness, and their sins and their iniquities will I remember no more" (v. 12).

Here, then, are of the terms of the new covenant. The Holy Spirit is put within us, and he works in us "both to will and to do of his [God's] good pleasure" (Phil. 2:13). He strengthens us; he gives us ability; he creates within us a great desire to live to the glory of God. Let me sum it up in the words of Paul. "There is therefore now no condemnation to them which are in Christ Jesus. . . . For the law of the Spirit of life in Christ Jesus hath made me free from the law of sin and death" (Rom. 8:1–2). I am delivered; I am emancipated. There is a grand redemption, my soul is free, and I even have the promise of the redemption of the very body in which I still live. "If Christ be in you," says Paul to the Romans, "the body is dead because of sin; but the Spirit is life because of righteousness. But if the Spirit of him that raised up Jesus from the dead dwell in you, he that raised up Christ from the dead shall also quicken your mortal bodies by his Spirit that dwelleth in you" (Rom. 8:10–11). The redemption of the body is a final and an ultimate glorification.

All that is offered to us, "the unsearchable riches of Christ" (Eph. 3:8), all the fullness of the Godhead, is all in Christ. He alone can mediate such a covenant, and he has done so. "He must increase" (John 3:30). Of course! He is the one and only. He is the second Adam.

To bring this to a practical conclusion, I want to ask some questions. I have been holding the doctrine concerning Jesus Christ before you, and I trust that as I have been doing so, he has been increasing in your mind and in your heart and in the whole of your life, but let me test it. Do you find complete satisfaction in him?

> Object of my first desire,
> Jesus, crucified for me.[2]

Can you say honestly:

> Thou, O Christ, art all I want,
> More than all in Thee I find.[3]

Do you? You should. "In him dwelleth all the fullness of the Godhead bodily" (Col. 2:9). It is all in him, everything. Do you find in him all you need, and infinitely more?

> Jesus, Thou joy of loving hearts,
> Thou fount of life, Thou light of men,
> From the best bliss that earth imparts,
> We turn unfilled to Thee again.[4]

Can you say so?

> Thou hidden source of calm repose,
> Thou all-sufficient love divine.[5]

Is he that to you?

> Plenteous grace with Thee is found,
> Grace to cover all my sin;
> Let the healing streams abound;
> Make and keep me pure within.

> Thou of life the fountain art,
> Freely let me drink of Thee;
> Spring Thou up within my heart;
> Rise to all eternity.[6]

Is that true, my dear friend, of you? Have you found final, complete satisfaction in him? Have you ever gone to him in vain? Has he ever failed you in any respect? If he has, it is because you do not know him. All is in him, the fountainhead, and he gives complete and final satisfaction.

Or let me try a second question. Are you desiring to know him more and more? If you see his glory, his preeminence, his greatness, if he is increasing in your sight, then you will say with the apostle Paul, "That I may know him, and the power of his resurrection, and the fellowship of his sufferings, being made conformable unto his death; if by any means I might attain unto the resurrection of the dead. Not as though I had already attained . . ." (Phil. 3:10–12). Are you self-satisfied? If you are, my dear friends, it is because you do not know him.

Let me try another question: Do you have an increasing concern for Christ's glory and the extension of his kingdom? John the Baptist did. "He must increase, but I must decrease" (John 3:30). "He . . . is the Bridegroom." I am only the friend of the Bridegroom (John 3:29). Have you seen Jesus Christ in his glory? Do you long to see his kingdom extended? Do you long to see people bowing the knee to him? Do you want him to be made greater and greater? Do you want to magnify him in the sight of all? That is a sure sign of having seen his greatness and his glory.

And finally, do you long for his appearance? Do you look upon this sinful, war-ridden world and see its hopelessness and its despair? You have long since seen through the folly of trusting to any action on the part of man, and you have come to the conclusion that Paul presses upon Titus: "The grace of God that bringeth salvation hath appeared to all men, teaching us that, denying ungodliness and worldly lusts, we should live soberly, righteously, and godly, in this present world; looking for that blessed hope, and the glorious appearing of the great God and our Saviour Jesus Christ" (Titus 2:11–13). The whole of the New Testament is looking forward to this. Paul says to the Philippians,

> Our conversation [citizenship] is in heaven; from whence also we look for the Saviour, the Lord Jesus Christ: who shall change our vile body [the body of our humiliation], that it may be fashioned like unto his glorious body [the body of his glorification], according

to the working whereby he is able even to subdue all things unto himself. (Phil. 3:20–21)

Are you looking forward to that? Do you realize you are in a passing world? "Here have we no continuing city, but we seek one to come" (Heb. 13:14). Are you looking for "a city which hath foundations, whose builder and maker is God"? (11:10). Are you looking for the crowning day that is coming, when the Son of God will return, conquering all his enemies and setting up his kingdom, in which we shall be glorified and spend our eternity with him? These are the questions. As he increases in our sight, these are the inevitable reactions.

What can we do about this? The instruction is quite simple. The first is to count your blessings.

Count your blessings, name them one by one,
Count your blessings, see what God hath done!
Count your blessings, name them one by one,
And it will surprise you what the Lord hath done.[7]

When you feel tempted to grumble and to complain and to ask "Why this and that?" count your blessings, and realize that every one of them has come to you because "God so loved the world, that he gave his only begotten Son" (John 3:16). Count your blessings.

What else? "Rejoice in the Lord always; and again I say, Rejoice" (Phil. 4:4). In other words, when you look at the world and you are depressed, when you look at yourself and you are depressed, when things happen to depress you, don't look at them, look at him. Realize the truth about him, realize that you are in him, realize that though the world, the flesh, the Devil, and all hell fight against you, you are safe, you are secure, and your destiny is secure, and your glorification is to come. "Rejoice in the Lord always; and again I say, Rejoice."

What else? The apostle in his second epistle to the Corinthians, at the end of the third chapter, says, "We all, with open face beholding as in a glass the glory of the Lord, are changed into the same image from glory to glory, even as by the Spirit of the Lord" (2 Cor. 3:18).

Changed from glory into glory,
Till in heaven we take our place,
Till we cast our crowns before Thee,
Lost in wonder, love, and praise.[8]

Look at him. The veil has been taken away. "We all, with open face [without a veil] beholding [gazing intently upon] . . . the glory of the Lord" (2 Cor. 3:18). As you spend time gazing upon him in all his glory—his essential glory, the glory of his offices, the glory of his work, the glory of all he has made possible—as you look at it all and dwell upon it and meditate upon it, he will increase, and you will decrease. You will lose yourself in him and will be lost in wonder, love, and praise.

# Notes

*Chapter 1: Nicodemus*

1. Edward Mote, "My Hope Is Built" (1834).

*Chapter 4: The Sign of the New Birth*

1. Charles Wesley, "And Can It Be That I Should Gain?" (1738).
2. Ibid.

*Chapter 5: Marks of the Spiritual Life*

1. Horatius Bonar, "Go, Labor On: Spend, and Be Spent," (1843).
2. Karl Johann Philipp Spitta, "We Praise and Bless Thee, Gracious Lord," trans. Jane Borthwick (1855).

*Chapter 6: The Christian and the World*

1. Henry F. Lyte, "Abide with Me," (1847).
2. William Cowper, "O for a Closer Walk with God," (1772).
3. Edward Mote, "My Hope is Built," (1834).
4. Johann C. Lavater, "O Jesus Christ, Grow Thou in Me," trans. Elizabeth L. Smith (1860).

*Chapter 8: Loving the Brethren*

1. Bernard of Clairvaux, "Jesus, the Very Thought of Thee," trans. Edward Caswall (1849).

*Chapter 9: Knowing God*

1. Sarah F. Adams, "Nearer, My God , to Thee," (1841).

*Chapter 10: A Personal Knowledge of God*

1. Oliver W. Holmes, Sr., "Lord of All Being," (1848).
2. Charles Wesley, "O Love Divine, How Sweet Thou Art," (1749).
3. Ray Palmer, "Jesus, These Eyes Have Never Seen," (1858).
4. Isaac Watts, "When I Survey the Wondrous Cross," (1707).
5. John Newton, "How Sweet the Name of Jesus Sounds," (1774).

6. Bernard of Clairvaux, "Jesus, the Very Thought of Thee," trans. Edward Caswall (1849).
7. Charles Wesley, "Jesus, Lover of My Soul," (1740).
8. William Ralph Featherstone, "My Jesus, I Love Thee," (1864).
9. Wesley, "O Love Divine."
10. "The God of Abraham Praise," paraphrased by Thomas Olivers (c. 1770).
11. Robert Grant, "O Worship the King All Glorious Above," (1833).

### Chapter 11: The Fellowship of the Holy Spirit

1. William Cowper, "O for a Closer Walk with God," (1772).
2. William Cowper, "God Moves in a Mysterious Way," (1774).
3. Joseph Hart, "Come, Holy Spirit, Come," (1759).
4. Edwin Hatch, "Breathe on Me, Breath of God," (1878).
5. Ibid.

### Chapter 12: Heavenly Things

1. Charles Wesley, "And Can It Be That I Should Gain?" (1738).
2. Isaac Watts, "We Give Immortal Praise," (1709).

### Chapter 13: Assurance

1. Horatio G. Spafford, "It Is Well with My Soul," (1873).
2. Anna L. Waring, "My Heart Is Resting, O My God," (1854).

### Chapter 14: Alive in Christ

1. Isaac Watts, "When I Survey the Wondrous Cross," (1707).

### Chapter 15: The Love of God in the Salvation of Men and Women

1. Henry Wadsworth Longfellow, "A Psalm of Life."
2. Augustus M. Toplady, "Rock of Ages," (1776).
3. Oswald Allen, "Today Thy Mercy Calls Me," (1861).

### Chapter 16: Darkness and Light

1. Charles Wesley, "Jesus, Lover of My Soul," (1740).

### Chapter 18: The Baptism with the Holy Spirit

1. Charlotte Elliott, "Just as I Am," (1835).
2. Charles Wesley, "Jesus, Lover of My Soul," (1740).

### Chapter 19: None of Self and All of Thee

1. Charles Wesley, "And Can It Be That I Should Gain," (1738).
2. Issac Watts, "When I Survey the Wondrous Cross," (1707).
3. John Bunyan, "He That Is Down Needs Fear No Fall," from *The Pilgrim's Progress,* part 2 (1684).

4. John Greenleaf Whittier, "Dear Lord and Father of Mankind," from "The Brewing of Soma,"(1872).
5. Theodore Monod, "None of Self and All of Thee," (1874).

*Chapter 20: Make the Poor Self Grow Less and Less*

1. Edward Mote, "My Hope Is Built," (1834).
2. William D. Longstaff, "Take Time to Be Holy," (1882).
3. Walter C. Smith, "Immortal, Invisible, God Only Wise," (1876).
4. William Wordsworth, "The World Is Too Much with Us."
5. W. H. Davies, "Leisure."
6. Longstaff, "Take Time to Be Holy."
7. John Bunyan, *The Pilgrim's Progress*, part 2.
8. Henry Francis Lyte, "Abide with Me," (1847).

*Chapter 21: He Must Increase*

1. Horatius Bonar, "Light of the World! Forever, Ever Shining."

*Chapter 22: Is He Everything?*

1. Robert Robinson, "Mighty God, While Angels Bless Thee," (1774).
2. Michael Bruce, "Where High the Heavenly Temple Stands," (1764).
3. Charles Wesley, "O for a Thousand Tongues to Sing," (1739).
4. William W. How, "Who Is This So Weak and Helpless," (1867).
5. Robert Robinson, "Mighty God, While Angels Bless Thee," (1774).
6. Johann C. Lavater, "O Jesus Christ, Grow Thou in Me," trans. Elizabeth L. Smith (1860).

*Chapter 23: Prophet, Priest, and King*

1. Charles Wesley, "Rejoice the Lord Is King," (1744).

*Chapter 24: Lost in Wonder, Love, and Praise*

1. Charles Wesley, "And Can It Be That I Should Gain?" (1738).
2. Augustus Toplady, "Object of My First Desire."
3. Charles Wesley, "Jesus, Lover of My Soul," (1740).
4. Bernard of Clairvaux, "Jesus, Thou Joy of Loving Hearts," trans. Ray Palmer (1858).
5. Charles Wesley, "Thou Hidden Source of Calm Repose," (1749).
6. Wesley, "Jesus, Lover of My Soul."
7. Johnson Oatman, Jr., "Count Your Blessings," (1897).
8. Charles Wesley, "Love Divine, All Loves Excelling," (1747).

# Also Available from Martyn Lloyd-Jones

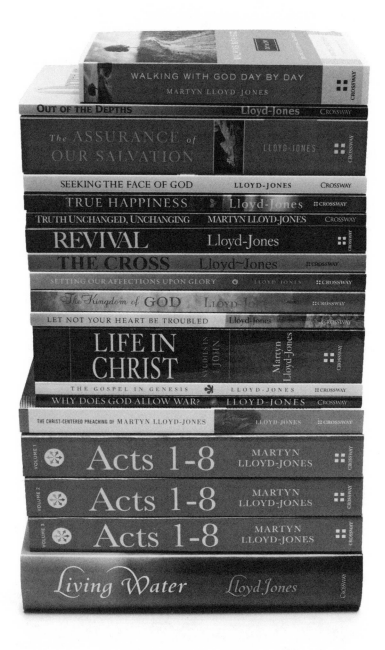